Fantasy For Children

Fantasy For Children

AN ANNOTATED CHECKLIST

by

Ruth Nadelman Lynn

R. R. BOWKER COMPANY
New York & London, 1979

To Bruce,
and to the memory of my parents,
Hilde M. and Alfred H. Nadelman

Published by R. R. Bowker Company
1180 Avenue of the Americas, New York, N.Y. 10036
Copyright © 1979 by Xerox Corporation
All rights reserved
Printed and bound in the United States of America

Library of Congress Cataloging in Publication Data
Lynn, Ruth Nadelman, 1948–
   Fantasy for children, an annotated checklist.

   Includes indexes.
   1. Children's stories—Bibliography. 2. Tales—
Bibliography. 3. Fairy tales—Bibliography.
4. Fantastic fiction—Bibliography. I. Title.
Z1037.9.L96   [PN1009.A1]   028.52   79-21401
ISBN 0-8352-1232-7

Contents

Preface

In fantasy, the impossible takes place; animals talk, magical events occur, the barriers of time dissolve, mythical creatures exist, and inanimate objects come to life. The imaginative appeal of children's fantasy has long been recognized by librarians, writers, publishers, psychologists, and, above all, children themselves. Today, the abiding interest in modern fantasy that has established it as one of the most popular genres in children's literature continues to flourish as new books are published and rediscovered titles come back into print.

Fantasy for Children, a comprehensive bibliographic guide to more than 1,650 recommended fantasies for children in grades three through eight, is intended for use by librarians, teachers, and parents. Approximately 1,200 titles are main entries; the remainder are sequels or related works that are mentioned in the annotations and are useful with the main entry. All titles were published in English in the United States (including translations into English) between 1900 and 1978, although a number of earlier classics, such as *Alice in Wonderland*, have also been included.

To facilitate reference, and because children often ask for another book "just like" their favorite, titles have been arranged in 13 chapters by type of fantasy, such as alternative worlds and imaginary lands, magical toys, mythical beings and creatures, and time travel. In general, science fiction, particularly books about space travel, technology, or scientific phenomena, is outside the scope of this book and has been omitted. Because many subject areas overlap and some books do not fall exclusively into one category, numerous cross-references are provided.

Despite the recent rise of interest in children's fantasy, a number of notable titles are currently out of print. To assist librarians whose collections include such books, and to encourage publishers to reissue outstanding titles, an unannotated list of out-of-print works is provided at the end of each chapter. If the hardcover edition of a book is out of print but a paperback edition is available, publication information for the paperback edition has been included in the in-print section. Both the in-print and out-of-print listings are arranged alphabetically by author.

Entries contain the following bibliographic information: author's name or pseudonym (the real names of pseudonymous authors are included in parentheses), title, alternate or British title, original publication date, publisher and date of publication for edition cited, translator, illustrator, pagination, and suggested grade level. Annotations provide a brief description of the book (for in-print works), and a list of sequels or related works by the same author, including publisher and date. (If the publisher of a series title or related work is the same as that for the title that begins the entry, only the date of publication is given.) A notation of major awards won and a list of review citations from 14 book review journals and children's literature texts completes the entry. To be considered for inclusion, each title must have been recommended by at least one of the review sources.

Entries for in-print titles also contain one of four recommendation symbols, which were assigned by considering both the number of favorable reviews cited for each title and the degree of recommendation expressed in the reviews. Recommendation symbols have been adapted from the coding system used in the *Bulletin* of the Center for Children's Books. Books of outstanding quality are indicated by an asterisk (*) at the beginning of the entry; other symbols—R, A, and M—appear in brackets at the end of the bibliographic information, following the suggested grade level. R (recommended) designates titles that received four or more recommendations; A (acceptable) indicates books that received two to three recommendations; and M (marginal) denotes books that, despite recommendation by one of the review sources, are of marginal value for most collections. A list of review sources with abbreviations used in the entries appears on page ix.

Publication information for fantasies available in the United Kingdom has been provided in a separate section, beginning on page 197. The directory of publishers, which precedes the index, lists both United States and British publishers. There are two indexes: an author and illustrator index, and a title index, which include sequels and related works. Primary sources used to verify publication information include, in addition to the 14 review journals and texts, *American Book Publishing Record*, *Books in Print 1978-79*, *British Books in Print 1978*, *Cumulative Book Index*, and *National Union Catalog*.

While *Fantasy for Children* will be extremely useful in building collections, compiling bibliographies, and advising readers, this author also hopes it will broaden the horizons of fantasy aficionados and tempt uninitiated readers into the extraordinary world of children's fantasy.

Abbreviations of Books
and Review Journals Cited

Journal reviews are cited by volume and page number, except for reviews from *School Library Journal*, which are indicated by month, year, and page number. Citations from the *Times Literary Supplement* prior to 1962, when the journal began consecutive paging with each annual volume, also include full date (month, day, year) and page number.

Adv   *Adventuring with Books*, rev. ed. National Council of Teachers of English, 1977.

Arb   Arbuthnot, May, and Sutherland, Zena. *Children and Books*, 5th ed. Scott Foresman, 1977.

BL   *Booklist*. American Library Association.

CC   *Children's Catalog*, 13th ed. H. W. Wilson Co., 1976; Supplements, 1977, 1978, 1979.

CCBB   *Center for Children's Books Bulletin*. Univ. of Chicago Press.

Eakin   Eakin, Mary. *Good Books for Children, 1950–1965*, 3rd ed. Univ. of Chicago Press, 1966.

HB   *Horn Book Magazine*. Horn Book, Inc.

JHC   *Junior High School Library Catalog*, 3rd ed. H. W. Wilson, Co., 1975; Supplements, 1976, 1977, 1978.

KR   *Kirkus Reviews*. Kirkus Service, Inc.

LJ   *Library Journal*. R. R. Bowker Co.

SLJ   *School Library Journal*. R. R. Bowker Co.

Suth   Sutherland, Zena. *The Best in Children's Books, 1966–1972*. Univ. of Chicago Press, 1973.

TLS   *Times Literary Supplement*. Times Newspapers, Ltd.

TN   *Top of the News*. American Library Association.

1
Allegory and Fable

The books in this chapter are tales with both simple and abstract levels of meaning. Unlike traditional fables, modern allegorical fantasies often concern characters other than animals, and the full significance of the stories may not be obvious.

ADAMS, Richard. *Shardik*. Simon, 1975. 525 pp. Gr. 8 up. [A]
In Ortelga, a giant bear found by a young hunter is proclaimed Lord Shardik, the sacred messenger of God. (BL 71: 892 and 905; KR 43: 251 and 322; LJ 100: 688)

* ADAMS, Richard. *Watership Down*. Macmillan, 1974. 429 pp. Gr. 6 up.
Premonitions of destruction drive a small band of rabbits from their peaceful hillside warren into the wilderness. Carnegie Medal. (Arb: 221; BL 70: 852; CC: 476; CCBB 27: 121; HB 50: 365 and 405; JHC: 378; LJ 99: 1148 and 1235; TN 30: 433)

ALLEN, Judy. *The Lord of the Dance*. See Chapter 12, Travel to Another World.

ALLEN, Judy. *The Spring on the Mountain*. See Chapter 6, Magic Adventure.

ANDERSEN, Hans Christian. *The Emperor's New Clothes*. (Orig. pub. 1948) Houghton, 1949. Illus. by Virginia Burton. 44 pp. Gr. K–4. [R]

Thieves who pretend to create a magnificent new suit for the vain emperor fool everyone in the kingdom except one small boy. (BL 46: 51 and 70: 336; CC: 479; HB 25: 523 and 524; KR 41: 961; LJ 74: 1533 and 1612, 99: 197; TLS 1973 p. 384 and 1121)

ANDERSEN, Hans Christian. *The Fir Tree.* (Orig. pub. 1938) Harper, 1970. Illus. by Nancy Ekholm Burkert. 34 pp. Gr. 3–6. [R]
A little fir tree glories in being a Christmas tree, and then mourns the fate that awaits him. (Arb: 202; BL 67: 375; CC: 479; CCBB 24: 53; HB 47: 66; KR 38: 1142; LJ 96: 3487; Suth: 13; TLS 1971 p. 1343)

ANDERSEN, Hans Christian. *The Little Match Girl.* (Orig. pub. 1944) Houghton, 1968. Illus. by Blair Lent. 43 pp. Gr. 2–5. [R]
One cold winter night, a little match seller is forced to use up all of her matches just to keep warm, but the visions she sees in the flames make her happy. (Arb: 202; CC: 479; CCBB 22: 121; KR 36: 1039; LJ 93: 3953; Suth: 13)

ANDERSEN, Hans Christian. *The Nightingale.* (Orig. pub. 1896) Harper, 1965. Tr. by Eva Le Gallienne. Illus. by Nancy Eckholm Burkert. 32 pp. Gr. 2–5. [R]
The emperor's beautiful nightingale, banished and replaced by an artificial bird, is the only one able to save the emperor's life. (Arb: 202; BL 34: 78, 61: 995; CC: 480; CCBB 18: 157; Eakin: 6; HB 41: 389; KR 33: 373; LJ 90: 2393; SLJ May'75 p. 45; TLS 1967 p. 1143, 1972: 1332)

ANDERSEN, Hans Christian. *The Snow Queen.* (Orig. pub. 1929) Atheneum, 1968.
Tr. by R. P. Keigwin. Illus. by June Corwin. 94 pp; Viking, 1979. Adapt. by Naomi Lewis. Illus. by Errol Le Cain. 32 pp. Gr. 3–5. [R]
Little Gerda faces many perils as she tries to save her friend, Kay, who has been imprisoned in the Snow Queen's ice palace. (BL 39: 37, 65: 650, 69: 531, 75: 1627; CC: 480; CCBB 22: 21 and 73; HB 49: 141; KR 36: 820, 40: 1307; LJ 67: 884 and 910, 93: 3753 and 3964, 98: 999; TLS 1968 p. 586; TN 25: 309)

ARKIN, Alan. *The Lemming Condition.* See Chapter 9, Talking Animals.

BABBITT, Natalie. *Kneeknock Rise.* Farrar, 1970. Illus. by the author. 117 pp. Gr. 3–5. [R]
The people living closest to the hill called Kneeknock Rise are both proud and fearful of the noisy monster said to live there, until a boy named Egan discovers the real cause of the terrible noise. (Adv: 234; Arb: 216; BL 67: 99 and 659; CC: 482; CCBB 24: 53; HB 46: 295; KR 38: 551; LJ 95: 2306; Suth: 24)

BABBITT, Natalie. *The Search for Delicious.* See Chapter 5B, Imaginary Lands.

* BABBITT, Natalie. *Tuck Everlasting.* Farrar, 1975. 139 pp. Gr. 4–6.
The Tucks discover the fountain of youth, but an evil stranger wants it all
to himself. (Adv: 234; BL 72: 510; CC 1977 Suppl. p. 59; HB 52: 47; KR 43:
1181; SLJ Dec'75 p. 50)

BACON, Martha. *Moth Manor: A Gothic Tale.* See Chapter 7, Magical
Toys.

BAKER, Betty. *Dupper.* See Chapter 9, Talking Animals.

BATO, Joseph. *The Sorcerer.* See Chapter 13, Witches, Wizards, Sorcerers,
and Magicians.

BENARY-ISBERT, Margot. *The Wicked Enchantment.* Harcourt, 1955. Tr.
by Richard and Clara Winston. Illus. by Enrico Arno. 181 pp. Gr. 5–8.
[R]
Anemone and her dog, Winnie, are forced to run away from home when an
evil spell is cast over their town. (BL 52: 18; CC: 487; Eakin: 29; HB 31:
374; KR 23: 538; LJ 80: 2644)

BENCHLEY, Nathaniel. *Feldman Fieldmouse: A Fable.* See Chapter 9,
Talking Animals.

BRADBURY, Ray. *Something Wicked This Way Comes.* See Chapter 13,
Witches, Wizards, Sorcerers, and Magicians.

BURNFORD, Sheila. *Mr. Noah and the Second Flood.* Washington Square,
1974 (pap.). Illus. by Michael Foreman. 64 pp. Gr. 6 up. [A]
When a pollution-caused flood inspires Mr. Noah and his family to rebuild
the ark, they discover the number of animals humanity has made extinct.
(CCBB 27: 59; KR 41: 753; LJ 98: 3474; TLS 1973 p. 386)

CARROLL, Lewis. *Alice's Adventures in Wonderland.* See Chapter 12,
Travel to Another World.

CERVANTES SAAVEDRA, Miguel de. *Don Quixote.* (Orig. pub. 1605)
Dodd, 1954. Illus. by Walter Crane. 245 pp.; Knopf, 1960. Illus. by Warren
Chappell. 307 pp.; Walck, 1960. Illus. by Edward Ardizzone. 219 pp. Gr.
5 up. [R]
Don Quixote and Sancho Panza, knight and page, ride off to defend the
poor and rescue ladies in distress. (BL 46: 47, 57: 130; HB 36: 308; KR 28: 621;
LJ 85: 3869; TLS Dec 4, 1959 p. xii)

COATSWORTH, Elizabeth. *The Cat Who Went to Heaven.* (Orig. pub.
1930) Macmillan, 1967. Illus. by Lynd Ward. 62 pp. Gr. 4–7. [R]
When a poor Japanese artist paints his little white cat into a picture of
the dying Buddha, he lets his pet into heaven. Newbery Medal. (BL 27: 107,
55: 191; CC: 503; HB 35: 146)

COLLODI, Carlo. *The Adventures of Pinocchio*. See Chapter 7, Magical Toys.

CRESSWELL, Helen. *The Winter of the Birds*. Macmillan, 1976. 243 pp. Gr. 6–8. [R]
Neighbors unite when old Mr. Rudge foretells the coming of "terrible steel birds" that kill live birds and bring evil to the town. (BL 72: 1404; CC 1977 Suppl: 62; CCBB 30: 80; HB 52: 404; KR 44: 482; SLJ Sept'76 p. 130; TLS 1975 p. 1457)

CUNNINGHAM, Julia. *Come to the Edge*. Pantheon, 1977. 79 pp. Gr. 5–7. [R]
Unable to trust adults after his father's betrayal and the loss of his friend, Gravel Winter continually runs away from foster homes. (CC 1978 Suppl. p. 49; BL 74: 37; CCBB 31: 11; HB 53: 449; KR 45: 4; SLJ May'77 p. 60)

CUNNINGHAM, Julia. *Dorp Dead*. Pantheon, 1965. Illus. by James Spanfeller. 88 pp. Gr. 6 up. [R]
Gilly is taken from an unhappy life in an orphanage to an even more miserable foster home, from which he escapes to avoid being kept in a cage. (Arb: 234; CCBB 19: 30; Eakin: 87; JHC: 395; LJ 90: 2018)

CUNNINGHAM, Julia. *Tuppenny*. Dutton, 1978. 96 pp. Gr. 7–10. [R]
The appearance of a young girl named Tuppenny changes the lives of three families: one whose daughter ran away from home, one whose retarded daughter is institutionalized, and one whose daughter was murdered. (BL 75: 371; CCBB 32: 112; HB 55: 639; KR 46: 1309; SLJ Nov'78 p. 72)

DE REGNIERS, Beatrice. *The Boy, the Rat, and the Butterfly*. See Chapter 6, Magic Adventure.

DICKENS, Charles. *A Christmas Carol*. (Orig. pub. 1843) Lippincott, 1952. Illus. by Arthur Rackham. 147 pp.; Macmillan, 1963. Illus. by John Groth. 128 pp. Gr. 5 up. [R]
Mean old Ebenezer Scrooge is cured of his miserliness when he is visited by the ghosts of Christmases Past, Present, and Yet to Come. (BL 49: 147, 58: 194; CC: 510; JHC: 396; KR 29: 564; LJ 86: 4046)

DICKINSON, Peter. *The Blue Hawk*. See Chapter 5A, Alternative Worlds.

DICKINSON, Peter. *The Weathermonger*. See Chapter 5A, Alternative Worlds.

DOBBS, Rose. *No Room: An Old Story Retold*. McKay. 1944. Illus. by Fritz Eichenberg. 44 pp. Gr. 3–5. [R]
Not wishing to share his tiny home with his daughter and her family, an old man consults a wise man and gets some unexpected advice. (BL 41: 61; HB 20: 375; KR 12: 429; LJ 69: 763 and 865)

DONOVAN, John. *Family: A Novel.* Harper, 1976. 148 pp. Gr. 6–9. [R]
Four apes escape from a scientific laboratory only to find that survival in the wild is impossible for them. (BL 72: 112; CCBB 29: 173; HB 52: 404; KR 44: 405; SLJ Sept.'76 p. 131)

EDMONDS, Walter. *Beaver Valley.* See Chapter 9, Talking Animals.

ENRIGHT, Elizabeth. *Tatsinda.* See Chapter 5B, Imaginary Lands.

FARMER, Penelope. *A Castle of Bone.* Atheneum, 1972. 151 pp. Gr. 5–8. [R]
Hugh panics when his friend Penn enters a magic cupboard and is changed into a baby. (Arb: 214; BL 69: 572; CCBB 26: 153; HB 49: 52; KR 40: 1201; LJ 98: 652; TLS 1972 p. 802; TN 29: 356)

FOX, Paula. *The Little Swineherd and Other Tales.* See Chapter 2, Collected Tales.

FRANKO, Ivan, and MELNYK, Bohdan. *Fox Mykyta.* See Chapter 9, Talking Animals.

GODDEN, Rumer. *The Mousewife.* (Orig. pub. 1951) Penguin, 1971 (pap.). Illus. by William Pène Du Bois. 48 pp. Gr. 1–4. [R]
In return for wonderful descriptions of the world outside, a little mouse sets a caged dove free. (Arb: 239; BL 47: 297; Eakin: 143; HB 27: 93 and 102; KR 19: 61; LJ 76: 781; TLS 1951 p. 9)

GRAHAME, Kenneth. *The Wind in the Willows.* See Chapter 9, Talking Animals.

GRIPE, Maria. *In the Time of the Bells.* Delacorte, 1976. Tr. by Sheila La Farge. Illus. by Harald Gripe. 208 pp. Gr. 6–9. [R]
Young Prince Arvid's disregard for his royal duties bodes ill for the kingdom, until the astrologers discover that his "whipping boy" is his brother and true heir to the throne. (BL 73: 600 and 606; CC 1977 Suppl. p. 64; CCBB 30: 76; HB 53: 51; KR 44: 982; SLJ Jan'77 p. 92; TLS 1978 p. 767)

GRIPE, Maria. *The Land Beyond.* Delacorte, 1974. Tr. by Sheila La Farge. Illus. by Harald Gripe. 214 pp. Gr. 5–7. [A]
A world not found on any map is discovered by an explorer, a young king, and a misfit princess. (HB 51: 152; KR 42: 949; LJ 99: 3045; TLS 1975 p. 1457)

HAYWOOD, Carolyn. *A Valentine Fantasy.* Morrow, 1976. Illus. by Glenys and Victor Ambrus. unp. Gr. 2–4. [A]
Valentine's refusal to shoot the golden-hearted bluebird causes the king to imprison him, but the bird itself saves him. (BL 72: 1113; KR 44: 316; SLJ Apr.'76 p. 60)

HEARNE, Betsy. *South Star.* See Chapter 8J, Giants.

* HOBAN, Russell, *The Mouse and His Child*. Harper, 1967. Illus. by Lillian Hoban, 181 pp. Gr. 4 up.
A broken windup mouse and his son set out to find happiness and are pursued by an evil rat intent on enslaving them. (Adv: 188; Arb: 226; BL 64: 593; CCBB 21: 143; KR 35: 1134; LJ 92: 4612; Suth: 185; TLS 1969 p. 357)

ISH-KISHOR, Sulamith. *The Master of Miracle: A New Novel of the Golem*. Harper, 1971. Illus. by Arnold Lobel. 108 pp. Gr. 5–8. [R]
A huge clay being, created by the Rabbi of Prague to protect the Jews from anti-Semitic attacks, goes on a rampage when its creators try to destroy it. (BL 68: 394 and 669; CC: 535; HB 47: 611; KR 39: 1120; LJ 96: 3902; TN 28: 310)

JARRELL, Randall. *The Animal Family*. Pantheon, 1965. Illus. by Maurice Sendak. 179 pp. Gr. 4–6. [R]
A lonely hunter and a mermaid fall in love and acquire a family consisting of a bear cub, a lynx kitten, and a shipwrecked boy. (Arb: 216; BL 62: 487; CC: 536; CCBB 19: 100; Eakin: 171; HB 42: 45; LJ 90: 5516; TLS 1976 p. 392)

JONES, Diana Wynne. *Cart and Cwidder*. See Chapter 5A, Alternative Worlds.

JUSTER, Norton. *The Phantom Tollbooth*. See Chapter 12, Travel to Another World.

KENDALL, Carol. *The Gammage Cup*. See Chapter 8Q, Miniature People.

KENNEDY, Richard. *Come Again in the Spring*. Harper, 1976. Illus. by Marcia Sewall. 47 pp. Gr. 3–4. [R]
Old Hank is afraid to die and leave his birds to fend for themselves in midwinter, so he strikes a bargain with Death: if Hank can answer three questions, Death will wait until spring to take him. (BL 73: 253; CC 1978 Suppl. p. 51; HB 53: 154; KR 44: 904; SLJ Feb'77 p. 56)

KENNEDY, Richard. *The Dark Princess*. Holiday, 1978. Illus. by Donna Diamond. 32 pp. Gr. 5–7. [A]
A princess's blinding beauty serves as a test for prospective suitors and prevents her from finding love, until the court fool risks blindness to declare his love. (HB 55: 641; KR 46: 1137; SLJ Dec'78 p. 53)

KINGSLEY, Charles. *The Water Babies*. See Chapter 8H, Fairies.

KIPLING, Rudyard. *Just So Stories*. See Chapter 2, Collected Tales.

KRENSKY, Stephen. *Woodland Crossings*. See Chapter 2, Collected Tales.

LAMORISSE, Albert. *The Red Balloon*. Doubleday, 1957. Illus. with photographs from the movie. 45 pp. Gr. 1 up. [R]
A young French boy has trouble keeping his magical balloon safe from a gang of older boys. (BL 54: 82; CC: 540; KR 25: 581; LJ 82: 2187; TLS Nov 15, 1957 p. xix)

LA MOTTE FOUQUÉ, Friedrich de. *Undine.* (Orig. pub. 1908; written in 1811) Hyperion, 1978. Tr. by Edmund Gosse. Illus. by Arthur Rackham. 136 pp. Gr. 5 up. [A]
Huldbrand, a knight married to the water nymph Undine, is threatened with death if he should ever betray her. (BL 5: 195; CCBB 25: 5; KR 39: 236; TLS 1929 p. 180)

* LAWSON, John S. *You Better Come Home with Me.* Crowell, 1966. Illus. by Arnold Spilka. 125 pp. Gr. 5 up.
An Appalachian scarecrow adopts a wandering boy and introduces him to a witch, a fox, and a snowman. (Arb: 240; BL 63: 419; CCBB 20: 92; HB 42: 711; LJ 91: 5232; Suth: 241)

LE GUIN, Ursula. *A Wizard of Earthsea.* See Chapter 4, Good versus Evil.

LEWIS, C. S. *The Lion, the Witch and the Wardrobe.* See Chapter 12, Travel to Another World.

LINDGREN, Astrid. *The Brothers Lionheart.* Viking, 1975. Tr. by Joan Tate. Illus. by J. K. Lambert. 183 pp. Gr. 6–8. [A]
Two brothers, Jonathan and Karl, are reunited after death in a land called Nangiyala, where they fight a vicious tyrant and his dragon to liberate the other inhabitants. (HB 51: 594; KR 43: 777; SLJ Oct'75 p. 100)

MACDONALD, George. *At the Back of the North Wind.* (Orig. pub. 1871) Macmillan, 1964. Illus. by George and Doris Hauman. 402 pp. Gr. 6 up. [R]
A beautiful lady takes a boy named Diamond on fabulous journeys. The final journey is to the land at the back of the North Wind. (Arb: 210; BL 6: 146, 47: 162; CC: 547; HB 26: 490, 34: 122)

MACDONALD, George. *The Golden Key.* (Orig. pub. 1906) Farrar, 1976. Illus. by Maurice Sendak. 85 pp. Gr. 4 up. [R]
After Tangle discovers the key to the door at the end of the rainbow, he and his sister search for the mystical land beyond the door. (HB 43: 464; KR 35: 609; LJ 92: 3187)

MACDONALD, George. *The Light Princess* (Orig. title: *Dealing with Fairies,* 1867). Crowell, 1962. Illus. by William Pène du Bois. 48 pp.; Farrar, 1977. Illus. by Maurice Sendak. 110 pp. Gr. 3–6. [R]
Angry Aunt Makemnort's curse removes all of the princess's gravity, leaving the girl to laugh but never cry and float but never walk on the ground. (Arb: 210; BL 59: 499, 66: 623; CC: 547; CCBB 23: 162; HB 28: 422, 38: 605, 46: 41; KR 37: 1257; LJ 87: 427, 95: 1640; Suth: 262)

McGINLEY, Phyllis. *The Plain Princess.* Lippincott, 1945. Illus. by Helen Stone. 64 pp. Gr. 2–4. [A]
A selfish little princess learns kindness and helpfulness from Dame Goodwit and is suddenly thought to be pretty. (Arb: 240; BL 42: 133; CC: 547; HB 21: 454 and 447; KR 13: 297; LJ 70: 950 and 1138)

McKILLIP, Patricia. *The Forgotten Beasts of Eld.* See Chapter 5A, Alternative Worlds.

McKINLEY, Robin. *Beauty: A Retelling of the Story of Beauty and the Beast.* See Chapter 5B, Imaginary Lands.

MAYNE, William. *A Year and a Day.* See Chapter 8H, Fairies.

MERRILL, Jean. *The Black Sheep.* See Chapter 9, Talking Animals.

MERRILL, Jean. *The Pushcart War.* See Chapter 10, Tall Tales.

MILES, Patricia. *The Gods in Winter.* Dutton, 1978. 140 pp. Gr. 6–8. [R] Strange things begin happening after Mrs. Korngold moves in as the Brambles' housekeeper. She changes cousin Crispin into a lizard, saves Lottie's life, and seems to be the cause of an extremely severe winter. (BL 75: 51; CC: 1979 Suppl. p. 51; CCBB 32: 48; HB 55: 518; KR 46: 750; SLJ Oct'78 p. 147; TLS 1978 p. 764)

NICKL, Peter. *Crocodile, Crocodile.* See Chapter 9, Talking Animals.

O'BRIEN, Robert C. *Mrs. Frisby and the Rats of NIMH.* See Chapter 9, Talking Animals.

RUSKIN, John. *The King of the Golden River, or the Black Brothers.* (Orig. pub. 1841) Greenwillow, 1978. Illus. by Krystyna Turska. 40 pp. Gr. 2–5. [A]
Little Gluck's cruel older brothers torment him until the King of the Golden River and the South-West Wind come to his aid. (Arb: 202; BL 42: 304; HB 22: 213, 28: 422, 55: 520; KR 46: 1017; SLJ Oct'78 p. 138)

* SAINT-EXUPÉRY, Antoine de. *The Little Prince.* Harcourt, 1943. Tr. by Katherine Woods. Illus. by the author. 91 pp. Gr. 5 up.
A pilot stranded in the Sahara meets a strange boy who tells him of his travels through the universe. (Arb: 215; BL 39: 354; CC: 562; JHC: 426; LJ 68: 248)

SCHWARZ, Eugene. *Two Brothers.* Harper, 1973. Tr. by Elizabeth Hapgood. Illus. by Gabriel Lisowski. 44 pp. Gr. 1–4. [A]
Impatient with his younger brother, Big Brother locks him out in the cold. But when Little Brother is captured and frozen by Great-grandfather Frost, Big Brother sets out to save him. (Adv: 199; KR 41: 559; LJ 98: 2644)

SINGER, Isaac Bashevis. *A Tale of Three Wishes.* Farrar, 1976. Illus. by Irene Lieblich. 30 pp. Gr. 2–4. [A]
Three children make wishes that cause unexpected problems on the night of Hoshanah Rabbah. (Adv: 101; BL 72: 1118; CCBB 30: 18; KR 44: 201; SLJ Apr'76 p. 65)

SINGER, Isaac Bashevis. *Zlateh the Goat and Other Stories.* See Chapter 2, Collected Tales.

SMITH, Agnes. *An Edge of the Forest.* McClain, 1974 (Repr. of Viking, 1959 ed.). Illus. by Roberta Moynihan. 192 pp. Gr. 6-9. [R]
An orphaned lamb who accidentally wanders into the forest is saved from death and adopted by a black leopardess. (Arb: 242; BL 55: 578; Eakin: 301; HB 35: 10; KR 27: 91; LJ 84: 1700)

SNYDER, Zilpha. *Below the Root.* See Chapter 5A, Alternative Worlds.

STEELE, Mary Q. *The Journey Outside.* See Chapter 5A, Alternative Worlds.

STEELE, Mary Q. *The Owl's Kiss: Three Stories.* See Chapter 2, Collected Tales.

STEELE, Mary Q. *The True Men.* Greenwillow/ Morrow, 1976. 144 pp. Gr. 5-7. [A]
Driven from his home with the True Men because his skin has begun to glow in the dark, Ree is taken in by two weavers. (CCBB 30: 82; HB 53: 55; KR 44: 1045; SLJ Jan'77 p. 97)

STEVENSON, Robert Louis. *The Touchstone.* Morrow, 1976. Illus. by Uri Shulevitz. 47 pp. Gr. 5-7. [A]
Two rival princes searching for the "touchstone of truth" to exchange for the hand of a princess find very different solutions to their quest. (Adv: 101; KR 44: 844; SLJ Nov'76 p. 63)

STEWART, Mary. *Ludo and the Star Horse.* Morrow, 1975. Illus. by Gino D'Achille. 191 pp. Gr. 4-8. [A]
Ludo and his old horse fall into a hidden pit and journey through the twelve houses of the zodiac. (BL 71: 967; KR 43: 376; SLJ Sept'75 p. 112: TLS 1974 p. 1380)

STOCKTON, Frank R. *The Bee-Man of Orn.* Holt, 1964. Illus. by Maurice Sendak. 44 pp. Gr. 4-6. [R]
An old beekeeper, told by a sorcerer that he was transformed from another sort of being, decides to find out what he originally was. (Arb: 242; BL 61: 528; CC: 570; Eakin: 312; HB 40: 611; LJ 89: 4643; TLS 1976 p. 376)

STRANGER, Joyce. *The Fox at Drummer's Darkness.* Farrar, 1977. Illus. by William Geldart. 108 pp. Gr. 6-9. [A]
A drought on the moors drives a fox, a huntsman, and a night watchman to search for water. When toxic chemicals poison them, the ghost of the watchman rises up to warn the town. (BL 73: 1731; HB 53: 534; KR 45: 540; SLJ May'77 p. 72)

TAZEWELL, Charles. *The Littlest Angel.* (Orig. pub. 1946) Childrens, 1966. Illus. by Sergio Leone. 21 pp. Gr. 3 up. [A]
The newest angel in Paradise is lonely among the well-behaved adult angels, until he is befriended by the Understanding Angel. (KR 14: 592; LJ 71: 1810)

TERLOUW, Jan. *How to Become King.* See Chapter 5B, Imaginary Lands.

THEROUX, Paul. *A Christmas Card.* Houghton, 1978. Illus. by John Lawrence. 96 pp. Gr. 5 up. [R]
Lost in a blizzard on Christmas Eve, Marcel and his family are welcomed into the house of a man called Pappy, whose magic helps them find their way home. (BL 75: 227; CC: 1979 Suppl. p. 55; KR 46: 1358; SLJ Oct'78 p. 113)

THURBER, James. *The 13 Clocks.* Simon, 1950. Illus. by Mark Simont. 124 pp. Gr. 5 up. [R]
To marry the princess, Prince Zorn must find a thousand jewels to start all of the stilled clocks in the land. (Arb: 242; BL 47: 174; CC: 575)

THURBER, James. *The White Deer.* (Orig. pub. 1945) Harcourt, 1968 (pap.). Illus. by the author and Don Freeman. 115 pp. Gr. 5 up. [R]
Since he once married a princess who appeared from the enchanted forest in the guise of a white deer, King Clode and his three sons are tempted to hunt in the forest when another white deer is sighted. (BL 42: 57; CC: 575; HB 21: 447; KR 13: 43)

THURBER, James. *The Wonderful O.* Simon, 1957. Illus. by Marc Simont. 72 pp. Gr. 6 up. [R]
Wicked Black and his pirate crew decide to destroy everything spelled with the letter "O." (Arb: 242; BL 53: 559; KR 25: 308; LJ 82: 1780)

TOLKIEN, J. R. R. *The Hobbit; or There and Back Again.* See Chapter 4, Good versus Evil.

TOLKIEN, J. R. R. *Smith of Wootton Major.* See Chapter 6, Magic Adventure.

WAHL, Jan. *How the Children Stopped the Wars.* (Orig. pub. 1969) Avon, 1972 (pap.). Illus. by Mitchell Miller. 95 pp. Gr. 4–6. [A]
A shepherd boy envisions terrible wars, gathers children from all the surrounding villages and marches them to the battlefield to stop the fighting. (CCBB 23: 136; HB 46: 164; KR 37: 1260; LJ 95: 782 and 3610)

WANGERIN, Walter, Jr. *The Book of the Dun Cow.* Harper, 1978. 241 pp. Gr. 8 up. [R]
In this complex Christian allegory, Chaunticleer the rooster and Mundo Cani Dog save the world from the evils of the giant, Wyrm, and his "minion," Cockatrice. (BL 75: 927; CCBB 32: 92; KR 46: 1255; SLJ Oct'78 p. 160)

WARBURG, Sandol. *On the Way Home.* Houghton, 1973. Illus. by Dan Stolpe. 137 pp. Gr. 6–9. [R]
Alexi, his friend Bear, and Alexi's double, Twain, rescue a fair maiden, kill an ice-worm monster, and escape from the Monkey King. (BL 70: 546; CC: 577; KR 41: 1202 and 1351; LJ 99: 578)

WERSBA, Barbara. *Amanda, Dreaming.* Atheneum, 1973. Illus. by Mercer Mayer. Unp. Gr. 1–4. [A]
Amanda dreams of flowers, carousel horses, dragons, and "mice dressed in lace." (Adv: 202; KR 41: 881; LJ 99: 567)

WERSBA, Barbara. *Let Me Fall before I Fly.* Atheneum, 1971. Illus. by Mercer Mayer. 31 pp. Gr. 3–5. [A]
A two-inch-high circus performs daily in a young boy's garden, but when he leaves for a week, the circus disappears, and reappears only in his dreams. (Adv: 203; CCBB 26: 66; HB 47: 616; KR 39: 1124; LJ 97: 1611)

WESTON, John. *The Boy Who Sang the Birds.* Scribner, 1976. Illus. by Donna Diamond. 106 pp. Gr. 4–6. [A]
Two boys try to stop a flock of strange birds that seems to have caused a catastrophic winter in their village. (BL 72: 1272; KR 44: 257; SLJ: Apr'76 p. 79)

WHITE, E. B. *Charlotte's Web.* See Chapter 9, Talking Animals.

WIGGIN, Kate. *The Birds' Christmas Carol.* (Orig. pub. 1888) Houghton, 1941. Illus. by Jessie Gillespie. 84 pp. Gr. 3–5. [A]
Carol Bird saves the Ruggles's Christmas. *Polly Oliver's Problem* (1896) is the sequel. (BL 38: 137; CC: 578)

WILDE, Oscar. *The Happy Prince.* (Orig. pub. 1888) Methuen, 1977. Illus. by Kaj Beckman. Unp. Gr. 3 up. [A]
A bejeweled statue of a prince, unhappy at the misery of the people around him, persuades a swallow to carry his jewels and gold to the needy. (Arb: 202; HB 41: 630; KR 45: 1320; LJ 91: 430; SLJ Jan'78 p. 92)

WILDE, Oscar. *The Selfish Giant.* (Orig. pub. 1888) Harvey, 1967. Illus by Gertrude and Walter Reiner. Unp. Gr. 3–6; Methuen, 1978. Illus. by Michael Foreman and Freire Wright. 30 pp. Gr. 1–4. [A]
A giant has a change of heart about allowing children to play in his garden, and assures himself a place in heaven. (Arb: 202; BL 75: 551; KR 46: 1242; LJ 93: 2117; SLJ Jan'79 p. 49; TLS 1967 p. 1137)

WILLARD, Nancy. *Sailing to Cythera, and Other Anatole Stories.* See Chapter 12, Travel to Another World.

WRIGGINS, Sally, ed. *The White Monkey King: A Chinese Fable.* Pantheon, 1977. Illus. by Ronni Solbert. 113 pp. Gr. 4–6. [R]
In ancient China, a monkey prankster with magical powers meets his match when he challenges the Buddha. (CCBB 31: 104; HB 53: 529; KR 45: 487; SLJ Mar'78 p. 135)

YOLEN, Jane. *The Boy Who Had Wings.* Crowell, 1974. Illus. by Helga Aichinger. 25 pp. Gr. K–4. [R]

Aetos must use his wings to rescue his father from a mountain blizzard, although he has been forbidden to use them. (BL 71: 296; CC: 581; HB 50: 687; LJ 99: 3270)

YOLEN, Jane. *The Girl Who Loved the Wind.* Crowell, 1972. Illus. by Ed Young. 31 pp. Gr. 1–4. [R]
A wealthy merchant tries to protect his beautiful daughter from unhappiness by keeping her a prisoner in their palace, but a whispering wind makes the girl discontented with her life. (Adv: 134; BL 69: 575; CCBB 26: 100; HB 48: 585; KR 40: 1353; LJ 98: 998; TLS 1973 p. 1431)

YOLEN, Jane. *The Transfigured Hart.* Crowell, 1975. Illus. by Donna Diamond. 86 pp. Gr. 4–6. [M]
Richard and Heather's discovery of an albino hart, or deer, completely changes their lives. (KR 43: 662; SLJ Sept'75 p. 115)

ZIMNIK, Reiner. *The Bear and the People.* Harper, 1971. Tr. by Nina Ignatowicz. Illus. by the author. 78 pp. Gr. 3–7. [R]
Bearman and his talking bear, Brown One, entertain throughout the countryside, until jealous villagers attack them. (BL 68: 670; CC: 582; KR 39: 436; LJ 96: 2367 and 4160; TLS 1972 p. 1328)

Allegory and Fable: Out-of-Print Works

ANDERSEN, Hans Christian. *The Ugly Duckling.* Scribner, 1965. Tr. by R. P. Keigwin. Illus. by Adrienne Adams. 45 pp. Gr. 1–4. (Arb: 203; BL 62: 270; CC: 480; CCBB 19: 141; HB 41: 627; KR 33: 899; LJ 90: 4602)

BANKS, Richard. *The Mysterious Leaf.* Harcourt, 1954. Illus. by Irene Haas. 53 pp. Gr. 2–5. (BL 51: 251; HB 31: 111; KR 22: 633; LJ 79: 2253)

BOYLE, Kay. *The Youngest Camel.* (Orig. pub. 1939) Harper, 1959. Illus. by Ronni Solbert. 96 pp. Gr. 3–4. (HB 15: 295 and 380, 35: 387; LJ 64: 870)

BRYHER, Winifred. *A Visa for Avalon.* See Chapter 12, Travel to Another World: Out-of-Print Works.

BULLA, Clyde. *The Moon Singer.* Crowell, 1969. Illus. by Trina Schart Hyman. 48 pp. Gr. 3–6. (HB 45: 671; KR 37: 1111; LJ 95: 2307)

COATSWORTH, Elizabeth. *They Walk in the Night.* Norton, 1969. Illus. by Stefan Martin. 64 pp. Gr. 5–7. (CCBB 23: 94; HB 45: 402; KR 37: 236; LJ 94: 3818)

CRAIG, M. Jean. *Pomando: The Story of a Royal Artist.* Norton, 1969. Illus. by Enrico Arno. 90 pp. Gr. 4–5. (HB 45: 403; KR 37: 559; LJ 94: 4602)

DOLBIER, Maurice. *A Lion in the Woods.* See Chapter 10, Tall Tales: Out-of-Print Works.

DRUON, Maurice. *Tistou of the Green Thumbs* (British title: *Tistou of the Green Fingers*). Scribner, 1958. Tr. by Humphrey Hare. 178 pp. Gr. 4–6. (Arb: 238; BL 55: 221; HB 34: 382; KR 26: 659; LJ 83: 3006; TLS Nov 21, 1958 p. x)

ELIOT, Ethel. *The Wind Boy*. (Orig. pub. 1923) Viking, 1945. Illus. by Robert Hallock. 244 pp. Gr. 5–7. (BL 42: 61; KR 13: 370; LJ 70: 980)

FENTON, Edward. *The Nine Questions*. See Chapter 5B, Imaginary Lands: Out-of-Print Works.

FOLLETT, Barbara. *The House without Windows and Eepersip's Life There.* Knopf, 1927. 166 pp. Gr: 4–6. (BL 23: 347)

GOODWIN, Harold. *The Magic Number*. See Chapter 9, Talking Animals: Out-of-Print Works.

GOUDGE, Elizabeth. *The Valley of Song*. Coward, 1952. Illus. by Richard Floethe. 281 pp. Gr. 5–8. (BL 49: 92; HB 28: 395 and 405; KR 20: 552; LJ 77: 1822; TLS 1951 p. 15)

HARTWICK, Harry. *Farewell to the Farivox*. Four Winds, 1972. Illus. by Ib Spang Ohlsson. 46 pp. Gr. 3–5. (LJ 98: 994; KR 40: 401)

HAUFF, Wilhelm. *The Heart of Stone: A Fairy Tale*. See Chapter 6, Magic Adventure: Out-of-Print Works.

HUGHES, Ted. *How the Whale Became*. See Chapter 2, Collected Tales: Out-of-Print Works.

KÄSTNER, Erich. *The Animal's Conference*. (Orig. pub. 1949) McKay, 1953. Illus. by Walter Trier. Tr. by Zita de Schauensee. 62 pp. Gr. 4 up. (BL 49: 380; HB 29: 271; KR 21: 333)

KING, Alexander. *Memoirs of a Certain Mouse*. See Chapter 9, Talking Animals: Out-of-Print Works.

LAURENCE, Margaret. *Jason's Quest*. See Chapter 9, Talking Animals: Out-of-Print Works.

LEICHMAN, Seymour. *The Boy Who Could Sing Pictures*. Doubleday, 1968. Illus. by the author. 59 pp. Gr. 2–4. (CCBB 22: 160)

LESKOV, Nikolai. *The Steel Flea, a Story*. (Orig. pub. 1943) Harper, 1964. Adapt. by Babette Deutsch and Avrahm Yarmolinsky. Illus. by Janina Domanska. 56 pp. Gr. 3–5. (BL 40: 167, 60: 1004; CCBB 19: 65; HB 40: 178; LJ 89: 1452)

LEZRA, Giggy. *The Cat, the Horse, and the Miracle*. See Chapter 9, Talking Animals: Out-of-Print Works.

LIFTON, Betty. *The Dwarf Pine Tree*. Atheneum, 1963. Illus. by Fuku Akino. 37 pp. Gr. 3–6. (BL 60: 262; CC: 544; Eakin: 210; HB 39: 499)

LIVELY, Penelope. *Astercote*. Dutton, 1971. 154 pp. Gr. 7–9. (HB 47: 172; TLS 1970 p. 421)

LONGMAN, Harold. *Andron and the Magician*. See Chapter 5B, Imaginary Lands: Out-of-Print Works.

MAETERLINCK, Maurice. *The Children's Blue Bird*. (Orig. pub. 1913) Dodd, 1962. Tr. by Alexander De Mattos. Adapt. by Georgette Leblanc. 182 pp. Gr. 3–5. (BL 10: 163)

MAUGHAM, W. Somerset. *Princess September*. Harcourt, 1969. Illus. by Jacqueline Ayer. Unp. Gr. 3–5. (CCBB 22: 131; HB 45: 308; LJ 94: 2104; TLS 1970 p. 420)

MERRILL, Jean. *The Superlative Horse: A Tale of Ancient China*. Addison-Wesley, 1961. Illus. by Ronni Solbert. 79 pp. Gr. 4–6. (BL 58: 287; CC: 550; Eakin: 234; HB 38: 48)

MOON, Sheila. *Kneedeep in Thunder*. See Chapter 12, Travel to Another World: Out-of-Print Works.

NESS, Evaline. *The Girl and the Goatherd, or This and That and Thus and So*. Dutton, 1970. 32 pp. Gr. 1–4. (BL 67: 270; HB 47: 159; KR 38: 944; LJ 95: 4038)

NORTH, Joan. *The Cloud Forest*. See Chapter 6, Magic Adventure: Out-of-Print Works.

NORTH, Joan. *The Whirling Shapes*. See Chapter 11, Time Travel: Out-of-Print Works.

ORMONDROYD, Edward. *The Tale of Alain*. Follett, 1960. Illus. by Robert Frankenberg. 94 pp. Gr. 4–6. (HB 36: 290; LJ 85: 2678)

OSBORNE, Maurice. *Ondine: The Story of a Bird Who Was Different*. See Chapter 9, Talking Animals: Out-of-Print Works.

PEARCE, (Ann) Philippa. *The Squirrel Wife*. Crowell, 1972. Illus. by Derek Collard. 61 pp. Gr. 2–4. (BL 68: 822; CC: 557; CCBB 26: 14; HB 48: 265; KR 40: 194 and 1412; LJ 97: 2479; Suth: 307)

ROCCA, Guido. *Gaetano the Pheasant: A Hunting Fable*. Harper, 1966. Illus. by Giulio Cingoli and Giancarlo Carloni. 60 pp. Gr. 3–5. (CCBB 20: 115; HB 42: 431; KR 34: 418; LJ 91: 3252; Suth: 335)

SANCHEZ-SILVA, José. *The Boy and the Whale*. (Orig. pub. 1962) McGraw, 1964. Tr. by Michael Heron. Illus. by Margery Gill. 80 pp. Gr. 3–5. (HB 40: 376; KR 32: 453)

SEREDY, Kate. *Lazy Tinka.* Viking, 1962. Illus. by the author. 56 pp. Gr. 3–4. (BL 59: 450; KR 62: 683; TLS 1964 p. 605)

WEISS, Renee K. *The Bird from the Sea.* Crowell, 1970. Illus. by Ed Young. Unp. Gr. 3–5. (LJ 95: 4039; TN 27: 432)

WERSBA, Barbara. *A Song for Clowns.* See Chapter 5B, Imaginary Lands: Out-of-Print Works.

YOLEN, Jane. *The Seventh Mandarin.* Seabury, 1970. Illus. by Ed Young. 36 pp. Gr. 1–4. (Adv: 134; BL 67: 343; CC: 581; CCBB 24: 84; KR 38: 1142; LJ 96: 1112; Suth: 432; TLS 1971 p. 388)

ZIMNIK, Reiner. *The Crane.* (Orig. pub. 1956) Harper, 1970. Illus. by the author. Tr. by Nina Ignatowicz and F. N. Monjo. 95 pp. Gr. 4–6. (Adv: 203; CC: 582; KR 38: 1039; LJ 95: 4049; TN 27: 209)

2

Collected Tales

Collections of fantastic tales in the form of short stories are listed in this chapter. These tales often resemble traditional folktales in style.

AIKEN, Joan. *The Faithless Lollybird.* Doubleday, 1978. Illus. by Eros Keith. 255 pp. Gr. 5–8. [R]
These thirteen modern fairy tales include stories about a witch, a haunted tower, and a mermaid. (BL 74: 1614; CC 1979 Suppl. p. 56; CCBB 31: 153; HB 54: 281; KR 46: 594; SLJ Apr'78 p. 90; TLS 1977 p. 863)

AIKEN, Joan. *The Green Flash and Other Tales of Horror, Suspense, and Fantasy.* Holt, 1971. 163 pp. Gr. 6–9. [R]
Fourteen frightening tales including "Marmalade Wine," "The Dreamers," "Dead Language Master," and "The Windshield Weepers." (BL 68: 428; HB 48: 54; JHC: 442; KR 39: 1131; LJ 96: 4200)

AIKEN, Joan. *A Necklace of Raindrops and Other Stories.* (Orig. pub. 1969) Dell, 1971 (pap.) Illus. by Jan Pienkowski. 96 pp. Gr. 3–5. [A]
Eight stories, including "There's Some Sky in This Pie," "The Elves in the Shelves," and "The Patchwork Quilt." (CCBB 23: 37; HB 45: 530; KR 37: 631; LJ 95: 238)

AIKEN, Joan. *Not What You Expected: A Collection of Short Stories* (These stories were published in Britain in three collections: *A Small Pinch*

of Weather, A Harp of Fishbones, and *All and More).* Doubleday, 1974.
320 pp. Gr. 6–9. [R]
Twenty-one tales, including "The Boy with a Wolf's Foot," "The Lost Five
Minutes," and "The Third Wish." (Arb: 236; BL 71: 377; CCBB 28: 73; HB 51:
151; JHC 1976 Suppl. p. 58; KR 42: 1258; SLJ Jan'75 p. 42)

AINSWORTH, Ruth. *The Bear Who Liked Hugging People and Other
Stories.* (Orig. pub. 1976) Crane Russak, 1978. Illus. by Antony Maitland.
102 pp. Gr. K–4. [A]
Especially well suited for reading aloud, these thirteen tales involve witches,
a mermaid, animals, and magic. (BL 74: 1487; SLJ Oct'78 p. 141)

AINSWORTH, Ruth. *The Phantom Carousel and Other Ghostly Tales.*
See Chapter 3, Ghosts.

ALDEN, Raymond. *Why the Chimes Rang and Other Stories.* (Orig. pub.
1908) Bobbs-Merrill, 1954. Illus. by Rafaello Busoni. 146 pp. Gr. 3–7. [A]
Eleven tales of kings, knights, giants, and magic. (BL 42: 170; CC: 582)

ALEXANDER, Lloyd. *The Foundling and Other Tales of Prydain.* Holt,
1973. Illus. by Margot Zemach. 87 pp. Gr. 4–5. [R]
Six tales of the land of Prydain before the birth of Taran, Assistant Pig
Keeper, who is the main character of The Book of Three (1964) and its
sequels. (Arb: 207; BL 70: 594 and 826; CC: 582; CCBB 27: 122; HB 50:
278; KR 41: 1308; LJ 98: 3688 and 3704)

ALEXANDER, Lloyd. *The Town Cats, and Other Tales.* Dutton, 1977. Illus.
by Laszlo Kubinyi. 144 pp. Gr. 4–5. [R]
Eight fairy tales about wise and heroic cats. (BL 74: 472; CC 1978 Suppl. p.
57; CCBB 31: 89; HB 54: 42; KR 45: 1096; SLJ Nov'77 p. 52)

ANDERSEN, Hans Christian. *Andersen's Fairy Tales.* Macmillan, 1963.
Illus. by Lawrence Smith. 542 pp. Gr. 3–6. [A]
Fifty-three of Andersen's fairy tales. (BL 58: 797, 60: 387; CC: 582)

ANDERSEN, Hans Christian. *The Complete Fairy Tales and Stories.*
Doubleday, 1974. Tr. by Erik Haugaard. 1101 pp. Gr. 4 up. [R]
All 156 of Hans Christian Andersen's stories in one volume. (Arb: 202 and
236; BL 70: 738; CC: 583; CCBB 27: 122; HB 50: 269; KR 42: 12; LJ 99: 568;
TLS 1974 p. 1377)

ANDERSEN, Hans Christian. *Dulac's The Snow Queen and Other Stories
from Hans Andersen.* (Orig. pub. 1911) Doubleday, 1976. Illus. by Edmund
Dulac. 143 pp. Gr. 3–5. [R]
A beautifully illustrated edition of five of Andersen's most familiar tales:
"The Snow Queen," "The Emperor's New Clothes," "The Wind's Tale,"

"The Nightingale," and "The Little Mermaid." (BL 73: 1159; CC 1977 Suppl. p. 72; SLJ Feb'77 p. 60)

* ANDERSEN, Hans Christian. *Hans Andersen: His Classic Fairy Tales.* Doubleday, 1978. New tr. by Erik Haugaard. Illus. by Michael Foreman. 185 pp. Gr. 3–5.
"The Snow Queen," "The Red Shoes," "The Little Match Girl," "The Steadfast Tin Soldier," "The Swineherd," "The Tinderbox," "The Nightingale," "The Ugly Duckling," "The Princess and the Pea," and nine other tales. (BL 74: 1730; CC 1979 Suppl. p. 56; KR 46: 879; SLJ Nov'78 p. 54)

ANDERSEN, Hans Christian. *It's Perfectly True, and Other Stories.* Harcourt, 1938. Tr. by Paul Leyssac. Illus. by Richard Bennett. 305 pp. Gr. 4–7. [R]
Twenty-eight stories. (Arb: 202 and 236; BL 34: 303; CC: 583; HB 14: 153)

ANDERSEN, Hans Christian. *Seven Tales.* Harper, 1959. Tr. by Eva Le Gallienne. Illus. by Maurice Sendak. 127 pp. Gr. 2–5. [R]
"The Fir Tree," "The Ugly Duckling," "The Princess and the Pea," "The Happy Family," "The Darning Needle," "It's Absolutely True," and "The Steadfast Tin Soldier." (Arb: 202 and 236; BL 55: 512; CC: 583; HB 35: 297; KR 27: 264; LJ 84: 1692)

ANNIXTER, Paul. *The Best Nature Stories of Paul Annixter.* See Chapter 9, Talking Animals.

AVERY, Gillian, ed. *Victorian Doll Stories, by Brenda, Mrs. Gatty and Frances Hodgson Burnett.* See Chapter 7, Magical Toys.

BABBITT, Natalie. *The Devil's Storybook.* See Chapter 8C, Demons, Devils, and Imps.

BOMANS, Godfried. *The Wily Witch and All the Other Fairy Tales and Fables.* Stemmer, 1977. Tr. by Patricia Crampton. Illus. by Wouter Googendijk. 205 pp. Gr. 3–5. [R]
Forty-five fairy tales, including "The Rich Blackberry Picker," "The Princess with Freckles," and "The Curse." Twenty-four of these tales were originally published in *The Wily Wizard and the Wicked Witch and Other Weird Stories* (Watts, 1969). (Arb: 236; BL 73: 1726; CC 1979 Suppl. p. 56; CCBB 23: 156, 31: 6; LJ 95: 777; SLJ Sept'77 p. 121; TLS 1969 p. 3521)

BRÖGER, Achim. *Bruno.* See Chapter 10, Tall Tales.

BURGESS, Thornton W. *Old Mother West Wind.* See Chapter 9, Talking Animals.

CHESNUTT, Charles. *Conjure Tales.* Retold by Ray Shepard. Dutton, 1973. Illus. by John Ross and Clare Romano. 99 pp. Gr. 4–7. [R]
Seven tales of magic and witchcraft set against a background of nineteenth-

century plantation life. (CC: 588; CCBB 27: 126; HB 50: 48; JHC: 452; KR 41: 1035 and 1152; LJ 98: 3689 and 3705)

CHRISMAN, Arthur. *Shen of the Sea: Chinese Stories for Children.* Dutton, 1926; redesigned, 1968. Illus. by Elsie Haselriis. 221 pp. Gr. 5–8. [R]
A collection of humorous Chinese fairy tales. Newbery Medal. (Arb: 237; BL 22: 167; CC: 584; TLS 1969 p. 1193)

COATSWORTH, Elizabeth. *The Snow Parlor and Other Bedtime Stories.* Grosset, 1972. Illus. by Charles Robinson. Unp. Gr. 3–4. [A]
Five tales about talking animals, toys that come to life, a pine tree that walks, and a boy who enters a mountain to find out where snow comes from. (CCBB 25: 137; LJ 97: 2476; KR 39: 1011)

DAVIS, Robert. *Padre Porko: The Gentlemanly Pig.* See Chapter 9, Talking Animals.

ESTES, Eleanor. *The Sleeping Giant and Other Stories.* Harcourt, 1948. Illus. by the author. 101 pp. Gr. 2–5. [R]
Three tales: "The Sleeping Giant," "The Lost Shadow," and "A Nice Room for Giraffes." (BL 45: 123; HB 25: 35; KR 16: 571; LJ 73: 1825)

FARBER, Norma. *Six Impossible Things before Breakfast.* Addison-Wesley, 1977. Illus. by Tomie De Paola, Trina Schart Hyman, Hilary Knight, Friso Henstra, Lydia Dabcovich, and Charles Mikolycak. 43 pp. Gr. 3–6. [A]
Four poems and two stories about magic, a unicorn, and a princess, each illustrated by a different artist. (CCBB 30: 123; HB 53: 307; SLJ Apr'77 p. 66)

FLEISCHMAN, Sid. *Jim Bridger's Alarm Clock, and Other Tall Tales.* See Chapter 10, Tall Tales.

FLORA, James. *Grandpa's Ghost Stories.* Atheneum, 1978. Illus. by the author. 32 pp. Gr. 2–4. [R]
Grandpa has scary tales to tell: about a screaming skeleton, a ghost, a witch, and a werewolf. (BL 75: 216; HB 55: 510; KR 46: 1066; SLJ Oct'78 p. 132)

FOX, Paula. *The Little Swineherd and Other Tales.* Dutton, 1978. Illus. by Leonard Lubin. 104 pp. Gr. 3–6. [R]
Five tales: four fables about a rooster, a pony, an alligator, and a raccoon, and one story about an abandoned swineherd. (BL 75: 292; CC 1979 Suppl. p. 57; CCBB 32: 43; HB 55: 516; KR 46: 1071; SLJ Oct'78 p. 144)

FRANKO, Ivan, and MELNYK, Bohdan. *Fox Mykyta.* See Chapter 9, Talking Animals.

GARDNER, John. *Dragon, Dragon, and Other Tales.* Knopf, 1975. Illus. by Charles Shields. 75 pp. Gr. 5 up. [R]
Four "fractured fairy tales" about dragons, giants, and magic. (BL 72: 684; CCBB 29: 109; HB 52: 154; KR 43: 1129)

GARDNER, John. *Gudgekin the Thistle Girl and Other Tales.* Knopf, 1976. Illus. by Michael Sporn. 59 pp. Gr. 5–6. [M]
Four sophisticated humorous tales including "The Shape-Shifters of Snorm" and a Cinderella story called "Gudgekin the Thistle Girl." (CCBB 30: 90; KR 44: 1093)

GARFIELD, Leon. *The Restless Ghost: Three Stories.* Pantheon, 1969. Illus. by Saul Lambert. 132 pp. Gr. 5–7. [R]
Only the title story concerns ghosts; the other two concern the sea and ships. (CCBB 23: 143; HB 46: 45; KR 37: 1122; LJ 94: 4295; Suth: 142)

HALE, Lucretia. *The Complete Peterkin Papers.* See Chapter 10, Tall Tales.

HARRIS, Rosemary. *Sea Magic and Other Stories of Enchantment* (British title: *The Lotus and the Grail*; includes eight additional stories). Macmillan, 1974. 178 pp. Gr. 6–8. [R]
Ten tales about magic, superstitions, monsters, and spirits, from ten different countries. (BL 70: 819; CCBB 28: 9; HB 50: 145; KR 42: 192; LJ 99: 2290)

HEWETT, Anita. *The Bull beneath the Walnut Tree and Other Stories.* McGraw-Hill, 1967. Illus. by Imero Gobbato. 155 pp. Gr. K–4. [R]
Eighteen short tales, including "The Singing Witch," "The Five Little Men," and "The Galloping Hedgehog." (BL 64: 501; HB 43: 588; KR 35: 804; LJ 92: 3178; TLS 1966 p. 1092)

HOKE, Helen, ed. *Devils, Devils, Devils.* See Chapter 8C, Demons, Devils, and Imps.

HOUSMAN, Laurence. *The Rat-Catcher's Daughter: A Collection of Stories.* Atheneum, 1974. Ed. by Ellin Greene. Illus. by Julia Noonan. 169 pp. Gr. 4–7. [R]
Twelve tales of princesses, magic, and little people, including "The White Doe" and "The Cloak of Friendship." (Adv: 189; BL 70: 874; CC: 586; HB 50: 379; KR 42: 244; LJ 99: 1451 and 1473)

HUNTER, Mollie. *A Furl of Fairy Wind: Four Stories.* See Chapter 8H, Fairies.

IRESON, Barbara, ed. *The April Witch and Other Strange Tales.* Scribner, 1978. Illus. by Richard Cuffari. 238 pp. Gr. 7–9. [A]
Fourteen eerie stories by such well-known authors as Ray Bradbury, H. G. Wells, and Nicholas Stuart Gray. (BL 74: 1676; KR 46: 599; SLJ Sept'78 p. 159)

JOHNSON, Sally, ed. *The Princesses: Sixteen Stories about Princesses.* See Chapter 5B, Imaginary Lands.

JONES, Louis. *Things That Go Bump in the Night.* Hill, 1959. Illus. by Erwin Austin. 208 pp. Gr. 5–8. [A]

Tales of ghosts, witches, and haunted houses, mainly from New York State. (BL 55: 559; KR 27: 205; LJ 84: 1275)

KIPLING, Rudyard. *The Jungle Book*. (Orig. pub. 1893) Grosset, 1950. Illus. by Fritz Eichenberg. 279 pp; Macmillan, 1964. Illus. by Robert Shore. 371 pp. Gr. 4–7. [R]
Tales of Mowgli, a boy adopted by wolves; Kotik the seal, Rikki-Tikki-Tavi, the mongoose; and other jungle animals. *The Second Jungle Book* (1895, 1923) is the sequel. (Arb: 240; BL 47: 162; CC: 586)

KIPLING, Rudyard. *Just So Stories* (Orig. pub. 1897–1902) Doubleday, 1972. Illus. by Etienne Delessert. 111 pp. Gr. 4–7. [R]
Twelve tales including "How the Camel Got His Hump," "How the Leopard Got His Spots," and "How the Rhinoceros Got His Skin." (Arb: 217; CC: 586; CCBB 26: 93; Eakin: 188; KR 40: 940 and 1413; LJ 98: 1682)

KRENSKY, Stephen. *Woodland Crossings*. Atheneum, 1978. Illus. by Jan Bowler. 43 pp. Gr. 3–5. [M]
Five tales of forest life involving a caterpillar, a weasel, a worm, an autumn leaf, and a flower king. (KR 46: 497; SLJ May'78 p. 69)

LEACH, Maria. *The Thing at the Foot of the Bed and Other Scary Tales*. World, 1959. Illus. by Kurt Werth. 126 pp. Gr. 5–8. [A]
A collection of ghost and witch tales including "The Thing at the Foot of the Bed," "Wait Til Martin Comes," and "The Golden Arm." (BL 55: 543; CC: 587; Eakin: 204; KR 27: 265; LJ 84: 1697)

LEE, Tanith. *Princess Hynchatti and Some Other Surprises*. Farrar, 1973. Illus. by Velma Ilsly. 183 pp. Gr. 4–5. [R]
A collection of humorous fairy tales including one in which a prince falls in love with a witch, and another about a prince who turns a beautiful swan into an awkward, yellow-eyed princess. (Adv: 192; BL 69: 1021; HB 69: 948; KR 41: 457; LJ 98: 2195; TLS 1972 p. 1332)

LE GUIN, Ursula. *The Wind's Twelve Quarters: Short Stories*. Harper, 1975. 303 pp. Gr. 8 up. [R]
Seventeen stories of fantasy and science fiction, including "Winter's King" and "The Day before the Revolution." (BL 72: 615; KR 43: 942; LJ 100: 1950; SLJ Mar'76 p. 120; TLS 1976 p. 950)

MENDOZA, George. *Gwot! Horribly Funny Hairticklers*. See Chapter 8R, Monsters and Sea Serpents.

NESBIT, E. *The Complete Book of Dragons*. See Chapter 8E, Dragons.

NESBIT, E. (pseud. of Edith Bland). *The Magic World*. British Book Center, 1974 (Repr. of 1912 ed.). Illus. by H. R. Millar and Spencer Pryse. 280 pp. Gr. 5–7. [A]

Twelve tales of magic, including "The Cat-Hood of Maurice," "Accidental Magic" and "The Magician's Heart." (BL 57: 32; HB 36: 309)

NYE, Robert. *The Mathematical Princess and Other Stories* (British title: *Poor Pumpkin,* 1971). Hill, 1972. Illus. by Paul Bruner. 125 pp. Gr. 4–6. [R]
Six stories, including the tale of a princess who puts all of her suitors to sleep with her lectures on Euclid. (Adv: 196; HB 48: 468; KR 40: 673; LJ 98: 646)

PICARD, Barbara. *The Faun and the Woodcutter's Daughter.* (Orig. pub. 1951) Abelard, 1964. Illus. by Charles Stewart. 255 pp. Gr. 4–7. [R]
This collection of fourteen fairy tales begins with the story of a woodcutter's daughter who meets a faun in the woods and cannot live without him. (Arb: 209; BL 61: 436; CC: 587; CCBB 18: 168; Eakin: 261; HB 41: 57; LJ 89: 5010)

PROYSEN, Alf. *Little Old Mrs. Pepperpot and Other Stories.* Astor-Honor, 1960. Illus. by Bjorn Berg. Tr. by Marianne Helwig. 95 pp. Gr. 3–5. [R]
Twelve stories, mostly about a woman who can shrink to the size of a pepper shaker. The sequels are *Mrs. Pepperpot Again* (1961), *Mrs. Pepperpot to the Rescue* (Pantheon, 1964), *Mrs. Pepperpot in the Magic Wood* (Pantheon, 1968), and *Mrs. Pepperpot's Outing* (Pantheon, 1971). Three British sequels are *Mrs. Pepperpot's Busy Day, Mrs. Pepperpot's Christmas,* and *Mrs. Pepperpot's Year.* (CC: 587; HB 36: 216; KR 28: 235; LJ 85: 2042; TLS May 29, 1959 p. xiii)

PYLE, Howard. *Pepper and Salt, or Seasoning for Young Folks.* (Orig. pub. 1885) Harper, 1923. Illus. by the author. 109 pp. Gr. 4–7. [R]
Eight tales, including "The Skillful Huntsman," "Clever Peter and the Two Bottles," and "The Apple of Contentment." (Arb: 202; BL 20: 384; HB 1: 29)

PYLE, Howard. *The Wonder Clock.* (Orig. pub. 1887) Harper, 1943. Verses by Katherine Pyle. Illus. by the author. 318 pp. Gr. 5–7. [R]
Twenty-four tales, including "One Good Turn Deserves Another," "The Princess Golden Hair and the Great Black Raven," and "King Stork." (Arb: 241; HB 1: 31, 19: 48)

SANDBURG, Carl. *Rootabaga Stories.* (Orig. pub. 1922) Harcourt, 1951. Illus. by Maud and Miska Petersham. 218 pp. Gr. 5–8. [R]
A collection of forty-nine tales. *Rootabaga Pigeons* (1923) is the sequel. An omnibus volume was published in 1936. (Arb: 241; BL 19: 92; CC: 587; HB 27: 129)

SILVERBERG, Barbara. *Phoenix Feathers: A Collection of Mythical Monsters.* Dutton, 1973. Illus. with old prints. 206 pp. Gr. 8–10. [R]
A collection of tales about dragons, griffins, unicorns, and the phoenix. (BL 70: 737; CC: 588; JHC: 452; KR 41: 820; LJ 98: 3457)

SINGER, Isaac Bashevis. *The Fools of Chelm and Their History.* See Chapter 10, Tall Tales.

SINGER, Isaac Bashevis. *Naftali the Storyteller and His Horse, Sus, and Other Stories.* Farrar, 1976. Tr. by Joseph Singer, Ruth Finkel and the author. Illus. by Margot Zemach. 129 pp. Gr. 4 up. [R]
Eight tales, including stories about the foolish people of Chelm, and an imp called the lantuch. (BL 73: 670; CC: 72; CCBB 30: 98; HB 53: 162; KR 44: 1139; SLJ Dec'76 p. 56)

SINGER, Isaac Bashevis. *Zlateh the Goat and Other Stories.* Harper, 1966. Illus. by Maurice Sendak. 90 pp. Gr. 4–7. [R]
Seven stories, including three tall tales about the foolish people of Chelm, two about the Devil, and an allegorical tale about a young boy and his goat who are lost in a blizzard. (BL 63: 378; CCBB 20: 79; HB 42: 712; KR 34: 1045; LJ 91: 6197; Suth: 368; TN 23: 196)

STEELE, Mary Q. *The Owl's Kiss: Three Stories.* Greenwillow/Morrow, 1978. 99 pp. Gr. 6–8. [A]
In these three tales, a little girl fears owls will kill her for stealing her grandmother's fruit, an older girl longs to become a witch, and a man is falsely accused of theft. (BL 75: 53; HB 55: 522; KR 46: 878; SLJ Dec'78 p. 57)

STOCKTON, Frank R. *The Storyteller's Pack, a Frank R. Stockton Reader.* (Orig. pub. 1897) Scribner, 1968. Illus. by Bernarda Bryson. 358 pp. Gr. 5 up. [A]
Seventeen stories including "The Bee-Man of Orn," "The Griffin and the Minor Canon," and "The Lady or the Tiger." (BL 65: 1019; HB 45: 60; LJ 94: 891)

WILDE, Oscar. *The Happy Prince and Other Stories.* Dent, 1977 (dist. Biblio). (Repr. of 1968 ed.) Illus. by Peggy Fortnum. 154 pp. Gr. 4–6. [R]
A collection of magical tales about kings, queens, witches, mermaids, dwarfs, and sorcerers, including "The Happy Prince" and "The Selfish Giant." (Arb: 202; CC: 588; KR 36: 826; TLS 1977 p. 352)

WILLARD, Nancy. *Sailing to Cythera, and Other Anatole Stories.* See Chapter 12, Travel to Another World.

WILLIAMS, Jay. *The Practical Princess and Other Liberating Fairy Tales.* Parents, 1978. Illus. by Rick Schreiter. 99 pp. Gr. 3–5. [R]
Six lively tales originally published separately: "The Practical Princess," "Stupid Marco," "The Silver Whistle," "Forgetful Fred," "Petronella," and "Philbert the Fearful." (BL 75: 937; CCBB 32: 166; KR 47: 7)

YOLEN, Jane. *The Girl Who Cried Flowers and Other Tales.* Crowell, 1974. Illus. by David Palladini. 55 pp. Gr. 3–5. [R]

Five tales, including one about a girl who cries flowers instead of tears. (Adv: 133; Arb: 243; BL 71: 48 and 768; CC: 588; CCBB 28: 88; KR 42: 741; LJ 99: 2744; SLJ Dec'78 p. 33)

YOLEN, Jane. *The Moon Ribbon and Other Tales.* Crowell, 1976. Illus. by David Palladini. 54 pp. Gr. 3–5. [A]
Six tales including "The Moon Child," "Somewhen," "Rosechild," and "Honey-Stick Boy." (BL 73: 328; KR 44: 792; SLJ Feb'77 p. 70)

YOLEN, Jane, ed. *Shape Shifters: Fantasy and Science Fiction Tales about Humans Who Can Change Their Shapes.* Seabury, 1978. 182 pp. Gr. 6–9. [A]
Twelve tales about people who change into animals, monsters, and machines, including "The Boy Who Would Be a Wolf," "The Enchanted Village," and "Judas Fish." (BL 74: 1259; CCBB 32: 40; KR 46: 552; SLJ Sept'78 p. 167)

YOLEN, Jane. *The Wizard Islands.* Crowell, 1973. Illus. by Robert Quackenbush. 115 pp. Gr. 4–7. [A]
A collection of legends about islands, including tales involving ghosts and pirate treasures. (CCBB 27: 167; HB 50: 162; KR 41: 1368; LJ 99: 1224)

Collected Tales: Out-of-Print Works

AIKEN, Joan. *Smoke from Cromwell's Time and Other Stories.* Doubleday, 1970. 163 pp. Gr. 4–7. (BL 67: 142; CCBB 24: 37; HB 46: 476; KR 38: 742; LJ 95: 3044)

ANDERSEN, Hans Christian. *Hans Andersen's Fairy Tales.* Walck, 1962. Tr. by L. W. Kingland. Illus. by Ernest Shepard. 327 pp. Gr. 3–6. (BL 58: 797; CC: 583; KR 30: 111; LJ 87: 2409; TLS Dec 1, 1961 p. xii)

BLAISDELL, Mary Frances. *Bunny Rabbit's Diary.* See Chapter 9, Talking Animals: Out-of-Print Works.

BOURLIAGUET, Léonce. *The Giant Who Drank from His Shoe and Other Stories.* Abelard-Schuman, 1966. Unp. Gr. 4–6. (KR 34: 179; LJ 91: 3531; TLS 1965 p. 1140)

BOWEN, William. *The Enchanted Forest.* (Orig. pub. 1920) Macmillan, 1926. Illus. by Maud and Miska Petersham. 197 pp. Gr. 3–5. *Solario the Tailor* (1922) is the sequel. (BL 17: 220)

COLUM, Padraic. *The Stone of Victory and Other Tales.* McGraw, 1966. Illus. by Judith Brown. 121 pp. Gr. 4–6. (BL 63: 794; HB 43: 200; KR 34: 980; LJ 91: 5746; Suth: 85)

CUNNINGHAM, Julia. *Candle Tales.* See Chapter 9, Talking Animals: Out-of-Print Works.

DE LA MARE, Walter. *Broomsticks and Other Tales.* (Orig. pub. 1925) Knopf, 1942. 334 pp. Gr. 5–7. (BL 22: 252; HB 18: 180)

DE LA MARE, Walter. *The Magic Jacket.* Knopf, 1962. Illus. by Paul Kennedy. 227 pp. Gr. 5–8. (BL 58: 689; CC: 584; Eakin: 97; HB 38: 276; KR 30: 180; LJ 87: 1316)

DE LA MARE, Walter. *A Penny a Day.* Knopf, 1960. Illus. by Paul Kennedy. 209 pp. Gr. 4–7. (Arb: 238; BL 57: 219; CC: 584; Eakin: 98; HB 36: 503; LJ 85: 4565)

DOLBIER, Maurice. *The Half-Pint Jinni, and Other Stories.* Random, 1948. Illus. by Allan Thomas. 242 pp. Gr. 4–7. (BL 45: 36; KR 16: 280; LJ 73: 1097)

FARJEON, Eleanor. *Italian Peepshow and Other Tales.* (Orig. pub. 1926) Walck, 1960. Illus. by Edward Ardizzone. 96 pp. Gr. 3–5. (BL 24: 125, 57: 274; HB 36: 406; KR 28: 904; LJ 85: 4566; TLS Nov 25, 1960 p. vii)

FARJEON, Eleanor. *The Little Bookroom: Eleanor Farjeon's Short Stories for Children Chosen by Herself.* Walck, 1956. Illus. by Edward Ardizzone. 302 pp. Gr. 3–7. Carnegie Medal. (BL 52: 415; CC: 585; HB 32: 179 and 270; LJ 81: 1719)

FARJEON, Eleanor. *Martin Pippin in the Apple Orchard.* See Chapter 5B, Imaginary Lands: Out-of-Print Works.

FARJEON, Eleanor. *The Old Nurse's Stocking Basket.* (Orig. pub. 1931) Walck, 1965. Illus. by Edward Ardizzone. 102 pp. Gr. 2–4. A companion to *Jim at the Corner* (1958; Orig. title: *Old Sailor's Yarn Box*, 1934). (HB 42: 193; LJ 91: 2209)

FLETCHER, David. *Mother O'Pearl: Three Tales.* Pantheon, 1970. Illus. by Susan Obrant. 101 pp. Gr. 4–6. (LJ 96: 267; KR 38: 1192)

GRAY, Nicholas. *Mainly in Moonlight: Ten Stories of Sorcery and the Supernatural.* Meredith, 1967. Illus. by Charles Keeping. 181 pp. Gr. 4–6. (HB 43: 462; KR 35: 207; LJ 92: 2449; TLS 1965 p. 1130)

GREEN, Kathleen. *Philip and the Pooka and Other Irish Fairy Tales.* Lippincott, 1966. Illus. by Victoria de Larrea. 93 pp. Gr. 4–6. (BL 62: 831; CCBB 20: 25; HB 42: 305; LJ 91: 2210)

GREEN, Roger. *A Cavalcade of Magicians.* See Chapter 13, Witches, Wizards, Sorcerers, and Magicians: Out-of-Print Works.

GREEN, Roger, ed. *Modern Fairy Stories.* Dutton, 1956. Illus. by Ernest Shepard. 270 pp. Gr. 5–7. (BL 52: 369; HB 30: 121)

GRIPARI, Pierre. *Tales of the Rue Broca.* Bobbs-Merrill, 1969. Tr. by Doriane Grutman. Illus. by Emily McCully. 111 pp. Gr. 5–7. (CCBB 23: 128; LJ 95: 1942; KR 37: 1112; Suth: 159)

HEWETT, Anita. *A Hat for Rhinoceros and Other Stories.* See Chapter 9, Talking Animals: Out-of-Print Works.

HOUGH, Charlotte. *Red Biddy and Other Stories.* Coward, 1967. Illus. by the author. 127 pp. Gr. 4–5. (CCBB 22: 8; HB 43: 463; KR 35: 413; LJ 92: 2450)

HUGHES, Richard. *The Spider's Palace.* (Orig. pub. 1932) Looking Glass, 1961. Illus. by George Charlton. 166 pp. Gr. 4–6. (HB 37: 53; TLS 1931 p. 957)

HUGHES, Ted. *How the Whale Became.* Atheneum, 1964. Illus. by Rick Schreiter. 100 pp. Gr. 2–6. (BL 61: 482; HB 40: 498; KR 32: 650; LJ 89: 4196)

JOHNSON, Crockett (pseud. of David Leisk). *Ellen's Lion: Twelve Stories.* Harper, 1959. 62 pp. Gr. 2–4. (HB 35: 379; KR 27: 370; LJ 84: 3625)

JUSTER, Norton. *Alberic the Wise and Other Journeys.* Pantheon, 1965. Illus. by Domenico Gnoli. 67 pp. Gr. 4–6. (CCBB 19: 150; HB 42: 54; LJ 49: 45)

KIPLING, Rudyard. *All the Mowgli Stories.* See Chapter 9, Talking Animals: Out-of-Print Works.

KIPLING, Rudyard. *Phantoms and Fantasies: Twenty Tales.* See Chapter 3, Ghosts: Out-of-Print Works.

KOTZWINKLE, William. *The Oldest Man and Other Timeless Stories.* Pantheon, 1971. Illus. by Joe Servello. 66 pp. Gr. 4–6. (CCBB 26: 27; KR 39: 1013; LJ 97: 1914)

McLAUGHLIN, Lorrie. *Shogomoc Sam.* See Chapter 10, Tall Tales: Out-of-Print Works.

MILNE, A. A. *Prince Rabbit and the Princess Who Could Not Laugh.* See Chapter 5B, Imaginary Lands: Out-of-Print Works.

MOLESWORTH, Mary. *Fairy Stories.* Roy, 1958. Ed. by Roger L. Green. 159 pp. Gr. 4–6. (HB 34: 478; KR 26: 659; LJ 83: 3002)

MONTROSE, Anne. *The Winter Flower and Other Fairy Stories.* Viking, 1964. Illus. by Mircea Vasiliu. 144 pp. Gr. 4–6. (HB 40: 611; LJ 89: 4642)

MÜNCHHAUSEN, Karl. *Baron Münchhausen, His Wonderful Travels and Adventures.* See Chapter 10, Tall Tales: Out-of-Print Works.

PICARD, Barbara. *The Goldfinch Garden: Seven Tales.* Criterion, 1963. Illus. by Anne Linton. 121 pp. Gr. 4–6. (Arb: 209; BL 62: 532; HB 42: 55; KR 33; 1042)

PICARD, Barbara. *The Lady of the Linden Tree.* (Orig. pub. 1954) Criterion, 1962. Illus. by Charles Stewart. 214 pp. Gr. 4–6. (Arb: 209; BL 58: 694; Eakin: 261; HB 38: 276; KR 30: 176; LJ 87: 2027)

PICARD, Barbara. *The Mermaid and the Simpleton*. (Orig. pub. 1949) Criterion, 1970. Illus. by Philip Gough. 253 pp. Gr. 4–6. (BL 47: 225, 67: 150; HB 26: 488; KR 18: 642, 38: 454; LJ 76: 55, 95: 2535 and 4326)

PREUSSLER, Otfried. *The Wise Men of Schilda*. See Chapter 10, Tall Tales: Out-of-Print Works.

PURSCELL, Phyllis. *Old Boy's Tree House and Other "Deep Forest" Tales*. See Chapter 9, Talking Animals: Out-of-Print Works.

REEVES, James. *Sailor Rumbelow and Other Stories*. Dutton, 1962. Illus. by Edward Ardizzone. 223 pp. Gr. 4–6. (BL 59: 498; HB 38: 605)

SLEIGH, Barbara. *Stirabout Stories, Brewed in Her Own Cauldron* (British title: *West of Widdershins*). Bobbs-Merrill, 1971. Illus. by Victor Ambrus. 143 pp. Gr. 5–7. (CCBB 26: 49; LJ 97: 3805; TLS 1971 p. 1321)

WEAVER, Jack. *Mr. O'Hara*. See Chapter 10, Tall Tales: Out-of-Print Works.

WILLIAMS, Jay. *The Magical Storybook*. American Heritage, 1972. Illus. by Edward Sorel. 43 pp. Gr. 3–5. (Adv: 203; CCBB 26: 115; LJ 98: 256)

3

Ghosts

Tales about ghosts fascinate both children and adults. Ghost fantasy, however, should not be confused with tales of horror and the occult, because it usually has humorous elements.

AIKEN, Joan. *The Green Flash and Other Tales of Horror, Suspense, and Fantasy.* See Chapter 2, Collected Tales.

AINSWORTH, Ruth. *The Phantom Carousel and Other Ghostly Tales* (British title: *The Phantom Roundabout and Other Ghostly Tales).* Follett, 1978. Illus. by Shirley Hughes. 176 pp. Gr. 4–5. [A]
Ten stories about children who meet ghosts: in an old cradle, in a garden next door, and in the form of a sailor returning for the bone of his amputated leg. (BL 74: 1489; KR 46: 176; SLJ Feb'78 p. 62; TLS 1977 p. 1414)

ANASTASIO, Dina. *A Question of Time.* Dutton, 1978. Illus. by Dale Payson. 90 pp. Gr. 4–6. [A]
After her unwanted move from Manhattan to Minnesota, Syd discovers a connection between her new friend, Laura, some antique dolls, and an all-but-forgotten town tragedy. (BL 75: 287; CCBB 32: 109; KR 46: 1246; SLJ Dec'78 p. 68)

ARTHUR, Ruth M. *The Whistling Boy.* Atheneum, 1969. Illus. by Margery Gill. 200 pp. Gr. 6–9. [A]

Deeply unhappy after her father's remarriage, Kristy meets and falls in love with a young man haunted by visions of a suicidal ancestor. (BL 65: 1173; HB 45: 310; KR 37: 244; LJ 94: 1789; TLS 1969 p. 1199)

BACON, Martha. *Moth Manor: A Gothic Tale.* See Chapter 7, Magical Toys.

BACON, Peggy. *The Ghost of Opalina, or Nine Lives.* Little, 1967. Illus. by the author. 243 pp. Gr. 4–7. [A]
Phillip, Ellen, and Jeb Finley's "new" house is haunted by the talkative ghost of a Persian cat who has lived nine lives. (BL 64: 866; KR 35: 648; LJ 92: 4608)

BARBER, Antonia. *The Ghosts.* See Chapter 11, Time Travel.

BELLAIRS, John. *The House with a Clock in Its Walls.* Dial, 1973. Illus. by Edward Gorey. 179 pp. Gr. 5–7. [R]
Lewis is impressed by his warlock uncle's magic abilities, but when he tries some magic himself, he unwittingly summons up a sinister ghost. *The Figure in the Shadows* (1975) and *The Letter, the Witch and the Ring* (1977) are the sequels. (Adv: 235; Arb: 236; BL 70: 227; CC: 486; CCBB 27: 37; KR 41: 514; LJ 98: 1701)

BOSTON, L. M. *The Children of Green Knowe.* See Chapter 6, Magic Adventure.

BROCK, Betty. *The Shades.* (Orig. pub. 1971) Avon, 1973. (pap.). Illus. by Victoria de Larrea. 128 pp. Gr. 3–5. [R]
Hollis enters an old walled garden and finds the Shade family, shadows of past visitors to the garden. (BL 68: 290; HB 48: 47; KR 39: 1069; LJ 96: 4198; TLS 1973 p. 386)

BYFIELD, Barbara. *The Haunted Ghost.* Doubleday, 1973. Illus. by the author. 38 pp. Gr. K–4. [A]
Master spy and ghost, Sir Roger de Rudisill is horrified to find that his castle is haunted. This is the sequel to *The Haunted Spy* (1969) and *The Haunted Churchbell* (1971), and is followed by *The Haunted Tower* (1976). (CCBB 27: 4; KR 41: 680; LJ 98: 3719)

* CAMERON, Eleanor. *The Court of the Stone Children.* Dutton, 1973. 191 pp. Gr. 5–8.
The ghost of a nineteenth-century French girl, whose father was executed for treason, begs Nina Harmsworth to help her prove her father's innocence. National Book Award. (Arb: 237; BL 70: 486 and 826; CC: 495; CCBB 27: 75; HB 50: 151; KR 41: 1159 and 1349; JHC: 389; LJ 98: 3718; TN 30: 205)

CHURCH, Richard. *The French Lieutenant: A Ghost Story.* Day, 1972. 153 pp. Gr. 5–7. [A]
Robert doesn't believe in the eighteenth-century ghost said to haunt the castle near his home, until he actually sees the ghost himself. (BL 69: 44; KR 40: 398; LJ 97: 1927; TLS 1971 p. 766)

CLAIRE, Keith. *The Otherwise Girl.* Holt, 1976. 130 pp. Gr. 8 up. [A]
Chloe, the ghost of a young girl who drowned, cannot leave the scene of her death until she is helped by Matt, a fifteen-year-old summer visitor. (BL 73: 121 and 132; KR 44: 339; LJ 101: 1445)

COBALT, Martin. *Pool of Swallows* (British title: *Swallows*). Nelson, 1974. 139 pp. Gr. 6–8. [R]
A family of ghosts causes the ponds on Martin's farm to become an ocean that swallows up a herd of cattle and Martin's father as well. (Arb: 237; BL 70: 999; CCBB 28: 26; LJ 99: 2286)

CORBETT, Scott. *Captain Butcher's Body.* Little, 1976. 168 pp. Gr. 4–6. [R]
The ghost of the legendary pirate, Captain Butcher, is due to make its once-every-hundred-years appearance—and George and Leo don't want to miss seeing it. (BL 73: 1010, 75: 305; CCBB 30: 139; KR 44: 973; SLJ Dec'76 p. 68)

CORBETT, Scott. *The Discontented Ghost.* Dutton, 1978. 180 pp. Gr. 5–7. [R]
The ghost of Sir Simon de Canterville retells the Oscar Wilde tale, *The Canterville Ghost,* and sets the record straight about his attempts to rid his home of its new American owners. (BL 75: 859 and 865; HB 55: 190; KR 46: 1307; SLJ Feb'79 p. 62)

CRESSWELL, Helen. *A Game of Catch.* Macmillan, 1977. Illus. by Ati Forberg. 48 pp. Gr. 4–6. [R]
Kate and Hugh's games of ice skating, tag, and catch near an old castle bring to life the children who played there long ago. (BL 73: 895; CC 1979 Suppl. p. 46; CCBB 30: 173; HB 53: 312; KR 45: 4; SLJ Feb'77 p. 62; TLS 1969 p. 1388)

CURRY, Jane. *The Bassumtyte Treasure.* See Chapter 11, Time Travel.

CURRY, Jane. *Poor Tom's Ghost.* See Chapter 11, Time Travel.

DICKENS, Charles. *A Christmas Carol.* See Chapter 1, Allegory and Fable.

ERWIN, Betty. *Who is Victoria?* Little, 1973. Illus. by Kathleen Anderson. 134 pp. Gr. 4–6. [R]
No one seems to know the elusive girl who keeps turning up around town, so Margaret, Polly, and Emilie resolve to find out who she is. (Arb: 238; BL 70: 385; KR 41: 1035; LJ 99: 208)

EZO. *Avril.* See Chapter 9, Talking Animals.

FISHER, Leonard E. *Sweeney's Ghost.* Doubleday, 1975. Illus. by the author. 133 pp. Gr. 4–6. [M]
The Framer family's plans for a quiet vacation are disrupted by the pirate's ghost who haunts their rented villa. (CCBB 29: 8; KR 43: 567; SLJ Sept'75 p. 102)

FLEISCHMAN, (Albert) Sid(ney). *The Ghost in the Noonday Sun.* Little, 1965. Illus. by Warren Chappell. 173 pp. Gr. 4–6. [R]
Pirates kidnap Oliver Finch in the hopes that he will be able to see the ghost of Gentleman Jim, guardian of buried treasure. (Arb: 229; BL 62: 54; CC: 519; CCBB 19: 43; Eakin: 121; HB 41: 490; KR 33: 245 and 472; LJ 90: 3790)

FLORA, James. *Grandpa's Ghost Stories.* See Chapter 2, Collected Tales.

FREEMAN, Barbara. *A Haunting Air.* Dutton, 1977. Illus. by the author. 158 pp. Gr. 5–7. [R]
When Melissa and her neighbor hear the ghostly singing of a Victorian child named Hanny, they search old letters and newspapers to discover why. (BL 74: 811; CC 1979 Suppl. p. 47; CCBB 31: 141; HB 54: 163; JHC 1978 Suppl. p. 48; KR 45: 1270; SLJ Feb'78 p. 57)

FREEMAN, Barbara. *A Pocket of Silence.* See Chapter 11, Time Travel.

GARFIELD, Leon. *Mister Corbett's Ghost.* Pantheon, 1968. 87 pp. Gr. 5–8. [R]
The ghost of his former master, Mr. Corbett, returns to haunt Benjamin after his idle wish for the man's death is fulfilled. (BL 65: 450; CC: 522; CCBB 22: 92; HB 44: 560; KR 36: 824; LJ 73: 8; Suth: 141; TLS 1969 p. 350)

GARFIELD, Leon. *The Restless Ghost: Three Stories.* See Chapter 2, Collected Tales.

GRAY, Genevieve. *Ghost Story.* Lothrop, 1975. Illus. by Greta Matus. 46 pp. Gr. 3–5. [A]
The Ghost family finds that they have a lot of haunting to do after vagrants move into their home. (Adv: 187; BL 71: 690; CCBB 28: 177; KR 43: 122; SLJ Apr'75 p. 52)

HARRIS, Rosemary. *Sea Magic and Other Stories of Enchantment.* See Chapter 2, Collected Tales.

HARRIS, Rosemary. *The Seal-Singing.* See Chapter 8T, Seal People.

HAYNES, Betsy. *The Ghost of the Gravestone Hearth.* Nelson, 1977. 160 pp. Gr. 4–6. [A]
Charlie spends the summer searching for buried treasure after the ghosts of a drowned boy and his pirate enemies appear. (BL 74: 41; CCBB 31: 60; KR 45: 351; SLJ May'77 p. 77)

HENDRICH, Paula. *Who Says So?* See Chapter 6, Magic Adventure.

IBBOTSON, Eva. *The Great Ghost Rescue.* Walck, 1975. Illus. by Giulio Maestro. 135 pp. Gr. 5–7. [A]

Upset at losing their traditional haunting grounds when England's great mansions are put to new uses, Humphrey the Horrible and family ask the Prime Minister for help. (HB 51: 593; KR 43: 605; SLJ May'75 p. 70)

JONES, Louis. *Things That Go Bump in the Night.* See Chapter 2. Collected Tales.

LAWRENCE, Louise. *Sing and Scatter Daisies.* Harper, 1977. 256 pp. Gr. 8-10. [R]
Seventeen-year-old Nicky Hennessy's jealousy of the love between his favorite aunt, Anna, and a ghost named John Hollis, nearly blinds him to the fact that Anna is dying. This is the sequel to *The Wyndcliffe* (1975). (BL 73: 1084 and 1092; CCBB 30: 162; HB 53: 450; KR 45: 358; SLJ Apr'77 p. 77)

LEACH, Christopher. *Rosalinda.* Warne, 1978. 124 pp. Gr. 7-9. [A]
Rosalinda died in the 1700s at age seventeen, but anguish over a thwarted romance causes her to reach into the twentieth century to control the life of Anne, daughter of the curator of the Warrender estate. (BL 74: 1552; CCBB 32: 12; SLJ Sept'78 p. 142; TLS 1978 p. 765)

LEACH, Maria. *The Thing at the Foot of the Bed and Other Scary Tales.* See Chapter 2, Collected Tales.

LIVELY, Penelope. *The Driftway.* See Chapter 11, Time Travel.

LIVELY, Penelope. *The Ghost of Thomas Kempe.* See Chapter 11, Time Travel.

LIVELY, Penelope. *A Stitch in Time.* Dutton, 1976. 140 pp. Gr. 4-7. [R]
Maria is convinced that the girl from the hundred-year-old photograph hanging in her summer house still lives in the house. (BL 73: 610; CCBB 30: 129; HB 53: 52; KR 44: 1169; SLJ Jan'77 p. 94; TLS 1976 p. 885)

LUNN, Janet. *Twin Spell.* See Chapter 11, Time Travel.

MacKELLAR, William. *Alfie and Me and the Ghost of Peter Stuyvesant.* Dodd, 1974. Illus. by David Stone. 150 pp. Gr. 5-7. [A]
Peter Stuyvesant returns to New York to give Billy and Alfie a map showing that treasure is buried beneath Times Square. (KR 42: 877; LJ 99: 3268)

MacKELLAR, William. *A Ghost around the House.* McKay, 1970. Illus. by Marilyn Miller. 117 pp. Gr. 4-6. [A]
Exploring dilapidated Strowan Castle on Halloween Eve, Jasper meets Malcolm MacDhu, a 250-year-old ghost who is under a curse. (KR 38: 876; LJ 95: 4352)

MacKELLAR, William. *The Witch of Glen Gowrie.* See Chapter 13, Witches, Wizards, Sorcerers, and Magicians.

McKILLIP, Patricia. *The House on Parchment Street.* (Orig. pub. 1973) Atheneum, 1978 (pap.). Illus. by Charles Robinson. 190 pp. Gr. 5-7. [A]

Carol's cousins can't believe that she has seen ghosts from the seventeenth century in their cellar. (BL 69: 1093; CC: 548; CCBB 26: 173; KR 41: 115; LJ 98: 1701)

MAYNE, William. *It.* Greenwillow, 1978. 189 pp. Gr. 6 up. [A]
The ghost of a witch's familiar alerts Alice to other supernatural occurrences. (CCBB 32: 84; HB 55: 646; KR 46: 1017; SLJ Dec'78 p. 62; TLS 1978 p. 376)

MIAN, Mary. *Take Three Witches.* See Chapter 13, Witches, Wizards, Sorcerers, and Magicians.

ORMONDROYD, Edward. *Castaways on Long Ago.* Parnassus, 1973. Illus. by Ruth Robbins. 182 pp. Gr. 5–7. [R]
Tantalized by the fifty-year-old ban on visiting Long Ago Island, Richard, Linda, and Dudley secretly explore it and meet its single, ghostly inhabitant. (Adv: 196; CCBB 27: 99; HB 50: 150; LJ 99: 575)

PAYNE, Joan. *The Leprechaun of Bayou Luce.* See Chapter 8N, Leprechauns.

* PECK, Richard. *The Ghost Belonged to Me: A Novel.* Viking, 1975. 184 pp. Gr. 5–8.
Encounters with the ghost of a girl named Inez Dumaine convince Alexander Armsworth that he has second sight. *Ghosts I Have Been* (1977) is the sequel. (Arb 241; BL 71: 1129; CC 1977 Suppl. p. 68; CCBB 28: 182; HB 51: 471; JHC 1976 Suppl. p. 56; KR 43: 456; SLJ Sept'75 p. 109, Dec'76 p. 32; TLS 1977 p. 348)

PECK, Robert. *The King of Kazoo.* See Chapter 10, Tall Tales.

PEYTON, K(atherine) M. *A Pattern of Roses.* Crowell, 1973. Illus. by the author. 186 pp. Gr. 7–9. [R]
The old drawings Tim finds signed with his own initials enable him to see a ghost whose mysterious death was never explained. (Arb: 241; BL 70: 124 and 827; CCBB 27: 49; HB 49: 473; JHC: 423; KR 41: 819; LJ 98: 2661 and 3691; TN 30: 82)

POPE, Elizabeth. *The Sherwood Ring.* See Chapter 11, Time Travel.

SEVERN, David (pseud. of David Unwin). *The Girl in the Grove.* Harper, 1974. 266 pp. Gr. 7–9. [R]
Jonquil becomes jealous when her friend Paul spends more and more time with a ghostly girl named Laura. (BL 71: 93 and 102; JHC 1976 Suppl. p. 56; KR 42: 1111; LJ 99: 3277; TLS 1974 p. 717)

SHECTER, Ben. *The Whistling Whirligig.* Harper, 1974. 143 pp. Gr. 4–6. [R]
While staying with his history teacher, Josh meets Matthew Hubbard, the hundred-year-old ghost of a runaway slave, who has been hiding since the Civil War. (BL 71: 463; CCBB 28: 138; HB 50: 693; KR 42: 1253; LJ 99: 2721)

SNYDER, Zilpha Keatley. *Eyes in the Fishbowl*. Atheneum, 1970. Illus. by Alton Raible. 168 pp. Gr. 6–9. [R]
Dion thinks the strange girl he meets in the Alcott-Simpson Department Store might be a ghost. (Arb: 242; BL 64: 1097; CCBB 21: 181; HB 44: 182; KR 36: 124; LJ 93: 1804)

SNYDER, Zilpha Keatley. *The Truth about Stone Hollow*. Atheneum, 1974. Illus. by Alton Raible. 211 pp. Gr. 6–8. [R]
Jason teaches Amy to see the ghosts at Stone Hollow. (BL 70: 825; CC: 568; CCBB 27: 164; HB 50: 380; JHC: 428; KR 42: 245; LJ 99: 576 and 1451; TN 30: 435)

SPEARING, Judith. *The Ghosts Who Went to School*. (Orig. pub. 1966) Scholastic, 1970 (pap.). Illus. by Marvin Glass. 186 pp. Gr. 5–7. [A]
Bored with haunting the house, Wilbur and Mortimer Temple decide to go to school. *The Museum House Ghosts* (1969) is the sequel. (BL 62: 920; HB 42: 308; LJ 91: 1710)

STAHL, Ben. *Blackbeard's Ghost*. Houghton, 1965. Illus. by the author. 184 pp. Gr. 5–8. [A]
J.D. and Hank accidentally summon up the ghost of Blackbeard the pirate, who discovers that the tavern he built three hundred years earlier is about to be torn down. *The Secret of Red Skull* (1971) is the sequel. (HB 41: 393; KR 33: 244; LJ 90: 2897)

STRANGER, Joyce. *The Fox at Drummer's Darkness*. See Chapter 1, Allegory and Fable.

SYKES, Pamela. *Mirror of Danger*. See Chapter 11, Time Travel.

TURKLE, Brinton. *Mooncoin Castle; or Skulduggery Rewarded*. Viking, 1970. 141 pp. Gr. 4–6. [A]
A ghost, a witch, and a jackdaw join forces to prevent their Irish castle from being torn down and replaced by a shopping center. (BL 67: 149; KR 38: 554; LJ 95: 3054)

WAHL, Jan. *The Screeching Door: Or, What Happened at the Elephant Hotel*. Four Winds, 1975. Illus. by J. W. Higginbottom. 76 pp. Gr. 3–5. [A]
Ephram and Myrtle Runkle meet a voraciously hungry ghost who demands to be fed. (BL 72: 858; KR 46: 920; SLJ Dec'75 p. 67)

WESTALL, Robert. *The Watch House*. See Chapter 11, Time Travel.

WILLIAMS, Ursula Moray. *Castle Merlin*. Nelson, 1972. 142 pp. Gr. 4–6. [R]
While vacationing at Castle Merlin, Susie and Bryan meet Dame Alys Hemingway and an imprisoned writer, both ghosts from the Middle Ages. (BL 69: 765; HB 48: 471; KR 40: 1029 and 1414; LJ 98: 265; TLS 1972 p. 474)·

WRIGHTSON, Patricia. *An Older Kind of Magic.* See Chapter 6, Magic Adventure.

YOLEN, Jane. *The Wizard Islands.* See Chapter 2, Collected Tales.

Ghosts: Out-of-Print Works

ARTHUR, Ruth. *The Autumn People.* See Chapter 11, Time Travel: Out-of-Print Works.

BENDICK, Jeanne. *The Goodknight Ghost.* Watts, 1956. Illus. by the author. 51 pp. Gr. 3–5. (HB 32: 446; KR 24: 432)

BRENNER, Anita. *The Timid Ghost: Or What Would You Do with a Sackful of Gold?* Addison-Wesley, 1966. Illus. by Jean Charlot. 48 pp. Gr. 3–5. (BL 62: 954; HB 42: 193; KR 34: 179; LJ 91: 2206)

BROWN, Bill and Rosalie. *The Department Store Ghost.* Coward, 1961. Illus. by Leonard Shortall. 38 pp. Gr. 3–5. (KR 28: 920; LJ 86: 874)

CHASE, Mary. *The Wicked Pigeon Ladies in the Garden.* See Chapter 11, Time Travel: Out-of-Print Works.

DU BOIS, William Pène. *Elizabeth the Cow Ghost.* (Orig. pub. 1936) Viking, 1964. Illus. by the author. 41 pp. Gr. 3–5. (HB 40: 120; LJ 89: 2208)

HOWARD, Joan. *The Witch of Scrapfaggot Green.* See Chapter 13, Witches, Wizards, Sorcerers, and Magicians: Out-of-Print Works.

KIPLING, Rudyard. *Phantoms and Fantasies: Twenty Tales.* Doubleday, 1965. Illus. by Burt Silverman. 302 pp. Gr. 5–8. (KR 33: 533; LJ 90: 3133)

LAMPMAN, Evelyn. *Captain Apple's Ghost.* Doubleday, 1952. Illus. by Ninon MacKnight. 249 pp. Gr. 5–7. (HB 28: 406; KR 20: 405; LJ 77: 1739, 78: 70)

LAWSON, John S. *The Spring Rider.* See Chapter 11, Time Travel: Out-of-Print Works.

LIFTON, Betty. *The Cock and the Ghost Cat.* Atheneum, 1965. Illus. by Fuku Akino. 32 pp. Gr. 1–4. (BL 62: 162; CC: 544; CCBB 19: 35; Eakin: 210; HB 41: 492; KR 33: 672; LJ 90: 4618)

LIVELY, Penelope. *The Wild Hunt of the Ghost Hounds.* See Chapter 4, Good versus Evil: Out-of-Print Works.

LOVE, Edmund. *An End to Bugling.* See Chapter 11, Time Travel: Out-of-Print Works.

McGOWEN, Tom. *Sir Machinery.* See Chapter 13, Witches, Wizards, Sorcerers, and Magicians: Out-of-Print Works.

MacKELLAR, William. *The Ghost in the Castle.* McKay, 1960. Illus. by Richard Bennett. 86 pp. Gr. 4–6. (BL 57: 500; HB 36: 396; KR 28: 624; LJ 85: 4568)

NETHERCLIFT, Beryl. *The Snowstorm.* Knopf, 1967. Illus. by Joseph Schindelman. 182 pp. Gr. 4–6. (KR 36: 1219; TLS 1967 p. 1140)

PREUSSLER, Otfried. *The Little Ghost.* Abelard-Schuman, 1967. 126 pp. Gr. 4–6. (KR 35: 1271; LJ 92: 4617; TLS 1967 p. 445)

SHURA, Mary. *Simple Spigott.* Knopf, 1960. Illus. by Jacqueline Tomes. 90 pp. Gr. 3–5. (BL 56: 609; Eakin: 299; HB 36: 291; LJ 85: 2043)

4

Good versus Evil

This type of fantasy is often referred to as mythic fantasy, and many, although not all, of these books have roots in Welsh folklore. Most of the stories listed here involve a struggle between good and evil forces that transcends their specific plots and characters. A few stories, including those by Julia Cunningham, describe children's efforts to overcome adult evil. The best of these books are among the finest that fantasy has to offer.

ALEXANDER, Lloyd. *The Book of Three*. See Chapter 5A, Alternative Worlds.

BABBITT, Natalie. *Tuck Everlasting*. See Chapter 1, Allegory and Fable.

BOND, Nancy. *A String in the Harp*. See Chapter 11, Time Travel.

CAMERON, Eleanor. *Time and Mr. Bass: A Mushroom Planet Book*. See Chapter 11, Time Travel.

CHANT, Joy. *Red Moon and Black Mountain: The End of the House of Kendreth*. See Chapter 12, Travel to Another World.

CLARKE, Pauline. *The Two Faces of Silenus*. See Chapter 6, Magic Adventure.

* COOPER, Susan. *Over Sea, under Stone*. Harcourt, 1966. Illus. by Margery Gill. 252 pp. Gr. 5–8.

Simon, Jane, and Barney Drew set out to find King Arthur's grail, and touch off the struggle between the Light and the Dark. In the second volume of this series, *The Dark Is Rising* (Atheneum, 1973), Will Stanton must travel into the past to search for six magic signs to give the forces of Light the power to hold back the rising Dark. In *Greenwitch* (Atheneum, 1974), it falls to Jane, Simon, and Barney to retrieve a manuscript needed to interpret the inscription on King Arthur's grail. In *The Grey King* (Atheneum, 1975; Newbery Medal), an albino boy named Bran Davies helps Will search for the golden harp that will awaken six sleeping knights for the last battle. In the fifth volume, *Silver on the Tree* (Atheneum, 1977), all five children are summoned to a Welsh mountainside. Will and Bran must find Eiras, the crystal sword, while the Drews meet King Arthur and prepare for the ultimate battle against the forces of Darkness. (Arb: 208; BL 63: 118; CC: 505; TLS 1965 p. 513)

CRESSWELL, Helen. *The Winter of the Birds*. See Chapter 1, Allegory and Fable.

CUNNINGHAM, Julia. *Come to the Edge*. See Chapter 1, Allegory and Fable.

CUNNINGHAM, Julia. *Dorp Dead*. See Chapter 1, Allegory and Fable.

CUNNINGHAM, Julia. *Tuppenny*. See Chapter 1, Allegory and Fable.

CURRY, Jane. *The Sleepers*. See Chapter 13, Witches, Wizards, Sorcerers, and Magicians.

GARNER, Alan. *Elidor*. See Chapter 12, Travel to Another World.

* GARNER, Alan. *The Owl Service*. Walck, 1968. 202 pp. Gr. 5 up.
A curse on the set of owl-decorated dishes found by Gwyn, Alison, and Roger turns the two boys against each other and threatens Alison's life. Carnegie Medal. (Arb: 209; BL 65: 310 and 900; HB 44: 563; JHC: 403; KR 36: 1058; LJ 93: 3980; Suth: 143; TLS 1967 p. 1134, 1969 p. 1384)

* GARNER, Alan. *The Weirdstone of Brisingamen*. (Orig. pub. 1961) Collins, 1979. 224 pp. Gr. 7 up.
Susan and her brother, Colin, learn that the stone on Susan's bracelet is the key to power over 140 knights who lie in an enchanted sleep within a nearby mountain. When this weirdstone is stolen, two dwarfs help the children on a torturous journey to recover the stone and return it to its rightful owner. *The Moon of Gomrath* (1967, 1979) is the sequel. (Arb: 209; HB 46: 45; KR 37: 940; LJ 95: 786)

GRIMSHAW, Nigel. *Bluntstone and the Wildkeepers*. See Chapter 8Q, Miniature People.

HOBAN, Russell. *The Mouse and His Child*. See Chapter 1, Allegory and Fable.

KENDALL, Carol. *The Gammage Cup.* See Chapter 8Q, Miniature People.

* LAWRENCE, Louise. *Star Lord.* Harper, 1978. 176 pp. Gr. 8–10.
A young Star Lord crashes into the Welsh mountains and is hidden from the British Security by Rhys Williams and his family. (BL 75: 369; CCBB 32: 65; HB 55: 525; KR 46: 1310; SLJ Oct'78 p. 156)

* LE GUIN, Ursula. *A Wizard of Earthsea.* Parnassus, 1968. Illus. by Ruth Robbins. 205 pp. Gr. 6–8.
While studying the art of wizardry, Ged accidentally conjures up a terrifying creature that threatens the existence of the entire land of Earthsea. *The Tombs of Atuan* (Atheneum, 1971) and *The Farthest Shore* (Atheneum, 1972) complete the trilogy. National Book Award. (Arb: 207; BL 65: 546 and 901; CC: 542; CCBB 22: 144; HB 45: 59; LJ 94: 2073, 2104 and 4582; TLS 1973 p. 379, 1977 p. 863)

L'ENGLE, Madeleine. *A Swiftly Tilting Planet.* See Chapter 11, Time Travel.

LEWIS, C. S. *The Lion, the Witch and the Wardrobe.* See Chapter 12, Travel to Another World.

McGOWEN, Tom. *The Spirit of the Wild.* See Chapter 8Q, Miniature People.

McKILLIP, Patricia. *The Forgotten Beasts of Eld.* See Chapter 5A, Alternative Worlds.

McKILLIP, Patricia. *The Riddle-Master of Hed.* See Chapter 5A, Alternative Worlds.

MAYNE, William. *Earthfasts.* See Chapter 11, Time Travel.

MURPHY, Shirley Rousseau. *The Ring of Fire.* See Chapter 5A, Alternative Worlds.

NEWMAN, Robert. *The Shattered Stone.* Atheneum, 1975. Illus. by John Gretzer. 231 pp. Gr. 6–8. [A]
In fulfillment of an ancient prophecy, two children without memories search for part of a stone inscription that will bring peace to their land. (BL 72: 305; HB 51: 465; KR 43: 1186; SLJ Nov'75 p. 81)

NORTON, André. *The Crystal Gryphon.* See Chapter 5A, Alternative Worlds.

NORTON, André (pseud. of Alice Mary Norton). *Quag Keep.* Atheneum, 1978. 224 pp. Gr. 7–12. [A]
With identical bracelets locked to their wrists, seven strangers journey to the lair of the powerful being who has enslaved them. (BL 74: 1176; HB 54: 285; SLJ Mar'78 p.139)

NORTON, André. *Steel Magic.* See Chapter 12, Travel to Another World.

PRICE, Susan. *The Devil's Piper.* Greenwillow/Morrow, 1976. 216 pp. Gr. 5–7. [R]
A town makes a pact with the Devil after a green-clad luchorpan kidnaps Mike Slater and his friends to avenge a 200-year-old murder. (Adv: 198; BL 72: 981; HB 52: 292; KR 44: 392; SLJ Apr'76 p. 92; TLS 1973 p. 1429)

STRANGER, Joyce. *The Fox at Drummer's Darkness.* See Chapter 1, Allegory and Fable.

* TOLKIEN, J(ohn) R(onald) R(euel). *The Hobbit; or There and Back Again.* (Orig. pub. 1937) Houghton, rev. ed. 1966. 317 pp. Gr. 6 up.
A wizard tricks Bilbo Baggins into going on a hazardous quest to recover stolen dwarf treasure from the dragon, Smaug. The Lord of the Rings trilogy consists of three sequels: In *The Fellowship of the Ring* (1967; orig. pub. 1954), Bilbo's ring turns out to be the magic one lost by Sauron, the Lord of Darkness, and it plunges Middle Earth into the War of the Ring. In *The Two Towers* (1967; orig. pub. 1955), Bilbo's nephew, Frodo, bears the ring to the borders of Mordor, the Dark Kingdom, while the members of the Company of the Ring battle the wizard Saruman and his army of goblins. And in *The Return of the King* (1966; orig. pub. 1956), Frodo and his servant Sam bring the ring to Mount Doom, and plunge it into the fire that created it. (Adv: 273; Arb: 205; BL 34: 304; CC: 575; HB 14: 92, 94, and 174; LJ 63: 385; TLS 1937 p.714)

WANGERIN, Walter, Jr. *The Book of the Dun Cow.* See Chapter 1, Allegory and Fable.

WHITE, T. H. *The Sword in the Stone.* See Chapter 5B, Imaginary Lands.

WRIGHTSON, Patricia. *The Nargun and the Stars.* Atheneum, 1974. 184 pp. Gr. 4–7. [R]
The lives of Simon Brent and his elderly cousins are threatened by the Nargun, a rocklike monster from the past. *The Ice Is Coming* (1977) and *The Dark Bright Water* (1979) are the sequels. (Arb: 243; BL 70: 1108, 71: 768; CCBB 28: 72; HB 50: 382; KR 42: 302; LJ 99: 2300; TLS 1973 p. 1434)

ZIMNIK, Reiner. *The Bear and the People.* See Chapter 1, Allegory and Fable.

Good versus Evil: Out-of-Print Works

CURRY, Jane. *Beneath the Hill.* See Chapter 6, Magic Adventure: Out-of-Print Works.

LIVELY, Penelope. *The Wild Hunt of the Ghost Hounds* (British title: *The Wild Hunt of Hagworthy*). Dutton, 1972. 141 pp. Gr. 5–8. (Adv: 242; BL 68: 1004; CCBB 26: 28; HB 48: 376; KR 40: 402; LJ 97: 2964)

5

Alternative Worlds and Imaginary Lands

The stories in this chapter are set in worlds or histories other than our own. There is no travel between our world and these imaginary worlds—such books are listed in Chapter 12, Travel to Another World. Two types of other-world settings will be noted here. Titles listed in part A, Alternative Worlds, take place in a serious world, modeled somewhat on our own, but with its own laws, customs, history, or topography. These tales are sometimes referred to as high fantasy. Stories listed in part B, Imaginary Lands, are set in a fairy-tale version of our own world and often involve kings, queens, princes, and princesses. Science fiction tales set in futuristic worlds have not been included.

A. ALTERNATIVE WORLDS

ADAMS, Richard. *Shardik*. See Chapter 1, Allegory and Fable.

AIKEN, Joan. *The Wolves of Willoughby Chase*. See Chapter 10, Tall Tales.

ALEXANDER, Lloyd. *The Book of Three*. Holt, 1964. 217 pp. Gr. 4–7. [R]
In this first book of the chronicles of Prydain, a pig-keeper named Taran and a warrior named Gwydion set out to battle the Horned King. The sequels are: *The Black Cauldron* (1965), *The Castle of Llyr* (1966), *Taran Wanderer* (1967), and *The High King* (1968), winner of the Newbery Medal. Other tales set in Prydain are *Coll and His White Pig* (1965) and *The Truthful Harp* (1967). (Arb: 207; BL 61: 344; CC: 477; CCBB 18: 157; Eakin: 4; HB 40: 496; LJ 89: 3465; TLS 1966 p. 1089)

CHRISTOPHER, John. *The Prince in Waiting*. Macmillan, 1970. 182 pp. Gr. 5–8. [R]
After our world is destroyed by earthquakes, Luke is rescued by a seer who draws him into a struggle for the medieval civilization that has arisen. The sequels are: *Beyond the Burning Lands* (1971) and *The Sword of the Spirits* (1972). (Arb: 231; BL 67: 306; CCBB 24: 154; HB 47: 54; Kr 38: 1160; LJ 95: 4051; TLS 1970 p. 1460; Suth: 72)

DE LARRABEITI, Michael. *The Borribles*. Macmillan, 1978. 239 pp. Gr. 6–9. [A]
After eight Borribles (violent street urchins who look like children) successfully raid a group of enemy creatures called Rumbles, they return home and find betrayal and disillusionment. (BL 74: 1420 and 1429; CCBB 31: 174; KR 46: 182; SLJ May'78 p. 76; TLS 1976 p. 1547)

* DICKINSON, Peter. *The Blue Hawk*. Atlantic-Little, 1976. 229 pp. Gr. 7–12.
In what could be Ancient Egypt, a boy named Tron defies the high priests by saving a sacrificial hawk, hides the dead king's coffin, and joins the new king's fight to rule his own land. (BL 72: 1584 and 1595; HB 52: 503; KR 44: 490 and 549; LJ 101: 1142; SLJ Nov'76 p. 74; TLS 1976 p. 375)

DICKINSON, Peter. *The Weathermonger*. Little, 1969. 216 pp. Gr. 5–9. [R]
Able to control the weather through magic, Geoffrey Tinker returns to an England that has reverted to the Middle Ages in hope of uncovering the cause of the enchantment. *Heartsease* (1969) and *The Devil's Children* (1970) are also set in England in the time of the "Changes." (Arb: 232; BL 65: 1075; CC: 511; CCBB 22: 156; KR 37: 501; LJ 94: 2499; Suth: 103)

ELDRIDGE, Roger. *The Shadow of the Gloom-World*. Dutton, 1978. 191 pp. Gr. 6 up. [A]
Exiled from his tunnel-filled world due to curiosity about other lands, Fernfeather meets an outcast girl named Harebell, and together they explore the deadly world above ground. (CC 1979 Suppl. p. 47; HB 54: 401; SLJ May'78 p. 76)

GRIPE, Maria. *In the Time of the Bells*. See Chapter 1, Allegory and Fable.

HARRIS, Rosemary. *The Shadow on the Sun*. Macmillan, 1970. 198 pp. Gr. 5–8. [R]
The young king of Egypt disguises himself while courting the chamberlain's daughter, Meri-Makhmet, and when she is kidnapped, he sends his friend, Reuben, to rescue her. This is the sequel to *The Moon in the Cloud* (1968; Carnegie Medal) and is followed by *The Bright and Morning Star* (1972). (BL 67: 307; CC: 528; CCBB 24: 157; HB 46: 481; KR 38: 886; LJ 95: 4044; Suth: 169; TLS 1970 p. 711)

HEARNE, Betsy. *South Star*. See Chapter 8J, Giants.

JONES, Diana Wynne. *Cart and Cwidder*. Atheneum, 1977. 193 pp. Gr. 6–9.
[R]
Moril inherits an ancient cwidder, a lutelike instrument, whose mystical
powers save Moril and his family from the murderous Southern warriors.
Drowned Ammet (1978) and *The Spellcoats* (1979) are also set in the land of
Dalemark. (BL 73: 1014; CCBB 30: 161; HB 53: 443; KR 45: 224; SLJ May'77
p. 70; TLS 1975 p. 764)

JONES, Diana Wynne. *The Power of Three*. Greenwillow, 1977. 250 pp. Gr.
6–8. [R]
An ancient curse is revived, and entangles three psychic children, a race of
giants, and a group of shape-shifting Dorig in a struggle for water. (BL 74:
298; CC 1978 Suppl. p. 51; HB 54: 47; KR 45: 790; SLJ Nov'77 p. 58; TLS 1976
p. 383)

JONES, McClure. *Cast Down the Stars*. Holt, 1978. 186 pp. Gr. 7–10. [A]
Glory and her friend, Honor, must repair a gap in the ancient serpent line to
keep out barbarian invaders. (BL 75: 178; CCBB 32: 100; HB 55: 68; SLJ
Dec'78 p. 53)

KENDALL, Carol. *The Gammage Cup*. See Chapter 8Q, Miniature People.

LE GUIN, Ursula. *A Wizard of Earthsea*. See Chapter 4, Good versus Evil.

LINDGREN, Astrid. *The Brothers Lionheart*. See Chapter 1, Allegory and
Fable.

McCAFFREY, Anne. *Dragonsong*. See Chapter 8E, Dragons.

MACE, Elisabeth. *Out There* (British title: *Ransome Revisited*). Greenwillow, 1978. 181 pp. Gr. 7–10. [A]
A fearsome journey in search of the legendary "Colony" where there is no
poverty, misery, hunger, or cold, seems the only way for the unnamed main
character to escape his unhappy life. (BL 74: 807; CCBB 31: 145; KR 46: 111;
SLJ Mar'78 p. 138)

* McKILLIP, Patricia. *The Forgotten Beasts of Eld*. Atheneum, 1974. 217
pp. Gr. 6–9.
Sybel, a sorceress, lovingly raises an abandoned baby named Tam, only
to discover that his real father is the greatest enemy of the man she loves. (Arb:
240; BL 71: 173 and 767; CCBB 28: 82; KR 42: 743; LJ 99: 2748)

* McKILLIP, Patricia. *The Riddle-Master of Hed*. (Orig. pub. 1976)
Ballantine, 1978 (pap.). 240 pp. Gr. 6–9.
Morgan, the peace-loving ruler of Hed, is driven to uncover the meaning of
the three stars on his forehead. The sequels are *Heir of Sea and Fire*
(Atheneum, 1977) and *Harpist in the Wind* (Atheneum, 1979). (Adv: 142; BL
73: 468 and 475; CC 1977 Suppl. p. 66; CCBB 30: 109; HB 52: 625; JHC 1978
Suppl. p. 52; KR 44: 1044; SLJ Oct'76 p. 119)

McKILLIP, Patricia. *The Throme of the Erril of Sherill.* Atheneum, 1973. Illus. by Julia Noonan. 68 pp. Gr. 4–6. [A]
Before permitting his daughter to wed Cnite Caerles, King Magnus orders the young man to bring him the Throme, an ancient magical document. (CCBB 27: 82; KR 41: 686; LJ 98: 2654)

MURPHY, Shirley R. *The Ring of Fire.* Atheneum, 1977. 232 pp. Gr. 7–9. [A]
Zephy and Thorn search for a lost jade runestone that will protect them from the tyrants of Kubal. *The Wolf Bell* (1979) is set in a previous time. (BL 74: 368 and 378; KR 45: 791; SLJ Oct'77 p. 116)

NEWMAN, Robert. *The Shattered Stone.* See Chapter 4, Good versus Evil.

NORTON, André (pseud. of Alice Mary Norton). *The Crystal Gryphon.* Atheneum, 1972. 243 pp. Gr. 6–9. [R]
Kerovan and his wife Joisan fight foreign invaders and the Dark Powers to regain the throne of Ulm. *The Jargoon Pard* (1974) is a companion volume. (Arb: 241; BL 69: 192 and 204; JHC: 420; KR 40: 948; LJ 97: 4080; TLS 1973 p. 1114)

NORTON, André. *Quag Keep.* See Chapter 4, Good versus Evil.

SNYDER, Zilpha Keatley. *Below the Root.* Atheneum, 1975. Illus. by Alton Raible. 231 pp. Gr. 7–9. [R]
Raamo D'ok's curiosity about the dreaded land beneath his treetop world of Greensky leads him to rescue a girl named Terra and uncover the secret of the world below. The sequels are *And All Between* (1976) and *Until the Celebration* (1977). (Arb: 242; BL 71: 764; CC 1977 Suppl. p. 69; CCBB 28: 186; JHC 1977 Suppl. p. 47; KR 43: 239; SLJ Sept'75 p. 112)

STEELE, Mary Q. *The Journey Outside.* Viking, 1969. Illus. by Rocco Negri. 143 pp. Gr. 5–8. [R[
Dilar escapes the subterranean life of the Raft People and finds his way up to an unfamiliar sunlit world. (Arb: 242; BL 65: 1276; CC: 569; CCBB 23: 119; HB 45: 309; KR 37: 506; LJ 94: 3227; TLS 1970 p. 1264; TN 26: 208)

STEELE, Mary Q. *The True Men.* See Chapter 1, Allegory and Fable.

STEVENSON, Robert Louis. *The Touchstone.* See Chapter 1, Allegory and Fable.

TOLKIEN, J. R. R. *The Hobbit; or There and Back Again.* See Chapter 4, Good versus Evil.

TURNBULL, Ann. *The Wolf King.* See Chapter 8H, Fairies.

WAECHTER, Friedrich, and EILERT, Bernd. *The Crown Snatchers.* Pantheon, 1975. Tr. by Edite Kroll. Illus. by the authors. 160 pp. Gr. 4–6. [A]
Three children escape from the clutches of the Pig King, and cause his

downfall, only to learn that the new king is also a tyrant. (BL 71: 697; KR 43: 377; SLJ Apr'75 p. 60)

WARBURG, Sandol. *On the Way Home.* See Chapter 1, Allegory and Fable.

Alternative Worlds: Out-of-Print Works

SILVERBERG, Robert. *The Gate of the Worlds.* Holt, 1967. 244 pp. Gr. 7–10. (BL 64: 250; CCBB 21: 18; KR 35: 609; LJ 92: 3204; TLS 1978 p. 1396)

ZIMNIK, Reiner. *The Crane.* See Chapter 1, Allegory and Fable: Out-of-Print Works.

B. IMAGINARY LANDS

ABELL, Kathleen. *King Orville and the Bullfrogs.* Little, 1974. Illus. by Errol Le Cain. 48 pp. Gr. 2–4. [A]
Three young princes are changed into frogs and banished after they outdo their father-in-law, King Orville, in a bagpipe contest. (BL 70: 871; KR 42: 239; LJ 99: 1463)

AIKEN, Joan. *The Kingdom and the Cave.* (Orig. pub. 1960) Doubleday, 1974. Illus. by Victor Ambrus. 160 pp. Gr. 5–6. [R]
Prince Michael's cat is kidnapped after Michael uncovers the invasion plans of the people Down Under. (Adv: 181; Arb: 236; BL 70: 871; HB 50: 146; KR 42: 108; LJ 99: 2258)

AIKEN, Joan. *A Necklace of Raindrops and Other Stories.* See Chapter 2, Collected Tales.

AIKEN, Joan. *The Whispering Mountain.* (Orig. pub. 1969) Dell, 1971 (pap.). Illus. by Frank Bozzo. 240 pp. Gr. 5–8. [R]
Owen is falsely accused of stealing the legendary Golden Harp of Teirtu (Arb: 229; BL 66: 563; CC: 477; CCBB 23: 123; HB 46: 39; JHC: 379; KR 37: 1146; LJ 94: 4610; Suth: 5)

ALDEN, Raymond. *Why the Chimes Rang and Other Stories.* See Chapter 2, Collected Tales.

ALEXANDER, Lloyd. *The Marvelous Misadventures of Sebastian: Grand Extravaganza, Including a Performance by the Entire Cast of the Gallimaufry Theatricus.* Dutton, 1970. 204 pp. Gr. 4–6. [R]
Caught in a revolution, Sebastian saves a cat from a witch, rescues a princess, and kills the regent by playing a magical violin. National Book Award. (Arb: 207; BL 67: 266 and 659; CC: 478; CCBB 24: 85; HB 46: 628; KR 38: 949; LJ 95: 4040 and 4324; Suth: 7)

ALEXANDER, Lloyd. *The Truthful Harp.* Holt, 1967. Illus. by Evaline Ness. Unp. Gr. 2–4. [R]

King Fflewddur is embarrassed to find that the strings of his harp break whenever he tells a lie. (CC: 478; CCBB 21: 89; HB 44: 58; KR 35: 1268; LJ 92: 4608; Suth: 7)

ALEXANDER, Lloyd. *The Wizard in the Tree.* See Chapter 13, Witches, Wizards, Sorcerers, and Magicians.

ANDERSEN, Hans Christian. *Dulac's The Snow Queen and Other Stories from Hans Andersen.* See Chapter 2, Collected Tales.

ANDERSEN, Hans Christian. *The Emperor's New Clothes.* See Chapter 1, Allegory and Fable.

ANDERSEN, Hans Christian. *The Nightingale.* See Chapter 1, Allegory and Fable.

BABBITT, Natalie. *The Search for Delicious.* Farrar, 1969. 167 pp. Gr. 3–6. [R]
While polling inhabitants on the exact definition of "delicious," Gaylen uncovers a plot by the queen's brother to take over the kingdom. (Arb: 216; BL 66: 53; CC: 482; CCBB 23: 21; HB 45: 407; KR 37: 373; LJ 95: 3603; TLS 1975 p. 365)

BAKER, Betty. *Save Sirrushany! (Also Agotha, Princess Gwyn and All the Fearsome Beasts).* Macmillan, 1978. Illus. by Erick Ingraham. 134 pp. Gr. 5–6. [A]
A dragon, a rare snail, and a girl named Agotha restore the fortunes of the Kingdom of Sirrushany. (CCBB 32: 22; KR 46: 496; SLJ May'78 p. 62)

BANKS, Lynne Reid. *The Farthest-Away Mountain.* Doubleday, 1977. Illus. by Victor Ambrus. 140 pp. Gr. 4–6. [A]
A prince-turned-frog accompanies Dakin on her quest to free an unreachable mountain from three gargoyles and a witch's spell. (BL 74: 809; CCBB 31: 122; KR 46: 2; SLJ Feb'78 p. 54; TLS 1976 p. 1553)

BIEGEL, Paul. *The King of the Copper Mountains.* Dent, 1977 (dist. Biblio; repr. of 1969 ed.). Tr. by Gillian Hume and Paul Biegel. Illus. by Babs Van Wely. 176 pp. Gr. 4–6. [A]
While awaiting the arrival of a doctor to save the king's life, several animals tell stories to distract the king. (CCBB 23: 141; LJ 95: 1632; Suth: 38; TLS 1968 p. 1373)

BOMANS, Godfried. *The Wily Witch and All the Other Fairy Tales and Fables.* See Chapter 2, Collected Tales.

BUCHWALD, Emilie. *Gildaen: The Heroic Adventures of a Most Unusual Rabbit.* Harcourt, 1973. Illus. by Barbara Flynn. 189 pp. Gr. 4–8. [R]
Gildaen Rabbit sets out on a quest to save the kingdom and to restore the memory of his friend, who changes from an owl to a prince to a peasant

woman. (Adv: 95; Arb: 236; BL 69: 1019; CC: 491; CCBB 26: 167; KR 41: 455; LJ 98: 2191)

BYFIELD, Barbara. *Andrew and the Alchemist.* See Chapter 13, Witches, Wizards, Sorcerers, and Magicians.

CARTER, Angela. *The Donkey Prince.* Simon, 1970. Illus. by Eros Keith. 40 pp. Gr. 1–5. [A]
To save the queen's life, Prince Bruno, who has been changed into a donkey, must find her magic apple. (Adv: 95; BL 67: 662; CCBB 24: 103; KR 38: 1145; LJ 96: 256)

COATSWORTH, Elizabeth. *The Enchanted: An Incredible Tale.* (Orig. pub. 1951) Pantheon, 1968. Illus. by Mary Frank. 151 pp. Gr. 7 up. [R]
David Ross doesn't believe the Indian legends that the animals of the Enchanted Forest can assume human form, and he buys an abandoned farm on the very edge of it. (BL 47: 381; HB 27: 316; KR 19: 233, 36: 343; LJ 76: 1236, 93: 2119)

COATSWORTH, Elizabeth. *The Princess and the Lion.* Pantheon, 1963. Illus. by Evaline Ness. 77 pp. Gr. 4–6. [R]
After the king surprises his court by naming Prince Michael heir to the throne, Princess Miriam journeys to the Prison of Princes to prevent Michael's escape. (BL 60: 39; CC: 503; Eakin: 77; HB 39: 281; LJ 88: 2549)

DE CAYLUS, Compte. *Heart of Ice.* Pantheon, 1977. Adapt. by Benjamin Appel. Illus. by J. K. Lambert. 58 pp. Gr. 2–3. [A]
Cursed at birth, a tiny manikin prince scales the Ice Mountain and wins the hand of Princess Sabella. (BL 74: 158; CCBB 31: 76; KR 45: 669; SLJ Oct'77 p. 109)

DICKENS, Charles. *The Magic Fishbone.* Vanguard, 1953. Illus. by Louis Slobodkin. Unp. Gr. 3–5. [A]
Exhausted from caring for her nineteen brothers and sisters, Princess Alice is given a magic fishbone that will grant one wish. (CC: 511; Eakin: 99; TLS 1971 p. 774)

ENRIGHT, Elizabeth. *Tatsinda.* Harcourt, 1963. Illus. by Irene Haas. 80 pp. Gr. 3–5. [R]
In love with an outcast girl named Tatsinda, Prince Tackatan of Tatrajan determines to rescue her from the horrible giant who has kidnapped her. (Arb: 238; BL 59: 896; CC: 515; Eakin: 109; HB 39: 382; LJ 88: 2774; TLS 1964 p. 1081)

FARBER, Norma. *Six Impossible Things before Breakfast.* See Chapter 2, Collected Tales.

GARDNER, John. *Dragon, Dragon, and Other Tales.* See Chapter 2, Collected Tales.

GARDNER, John. *Gudgekin the Thistle Girl and Other Tales.* See Chapter 2, Collected Tales.

GRAHAME, Kenneth. *The Reluctant Dragon.* See Chapter 8E, Dragons.

GUILLOT, René. *The Three Hundred Ninety-Seventh White Elephant* (British title: *The Elephants of Sargabal*). Philips, 1957. Tr. by Gwen Marsh. Illus. by Moyra Leatham. 94 pp. Gr. 3–6. [A]
The young king is cured of his illness by Hong-Mo the Magnificent, a mysterious white elephant who becomes leader of the royal herd. Two British sequels are: *Master of the Elephants* and *Great Land of the Elephant.* (BL 53: 434; HB 33: 221; KR 25: 176; LJ 82: 1102)

HAUFF, Wilhelm. *The Adventures of Little Mouk.* Macmillan, 1975. Tr. and adapt. by Elizabeth Shub. Illus. by Monika Laimgruber. 36 pp. Gr. 3–4. [A]
Mouk finds a magic walking stick and shoes that help him serve the king. (BL 71: 866; CCBB 29: 10; HB 51: 257; KR 43: 18; SLJ Apr'75 p. 53)

HAYWOOD, Carolyn. *A Valentine Fantasy.* See Chapter 1, Allegory and Fable.

HEWETT, Anita. *The Bull beneath the Walnut Tree and Other Stories.* See Chapter 2, Collected Tales.

HORWITZ, Elinor. *The Strange Story of the Frog Who Became a Prince.* See Chapter 13, Witches, Wizards, Sorcerers, and Magicians.

HOUSMAN, Lawrence. *The Rat-Catcher's Daughter: A Collection of Stories.* See Chapter 2, Collected Tales.

HUGHES, Peter. *The Emperor's Oblong Pancake.* (Orig. pub. 1961) British Book Center, 1976 (pap.). Illus. by Gerald Rose. Unp. Gr. 2–4. [M]
Impressed by the oblong shape of his birthday pancake, the emperor decrees that all round things must be made oblong. (KR 30: 5; LJ 87: 838; TLS 1962 p. 400)

INGRAM, Tom. *Garranane* (British title: *The Hungry Cloud*). Bradbury, 1972. Illus. by Bill Geldart. 191 pp. Gr. 4–6. [A]
Prince Kai and Princess Flor discover that Miss Fenrir has trapped their parents in the pictures she draws so they run away and plot to save their kingdom. (BL 69: 302; KR 40: 623; LJ 98: 261; TLS 1971 p. 767)

JOHNSON, Crockett (pseud. of David Leisk). *The Frowning Prince.* Bookstore Press, 1974 (Repr. of 1959 ed.). Illus. by the author. 32 pp. Gr. 2–3. [A]
The king, upon learning that his son has an immovable frown, sends for all the entertainers in the kingdom to make the prince smile. (KR 27: 6; LJ 84: 1330)

JOHNSON, Sally, ed. *The Princesses: Sixteen Stories about Princesses* (British title: *The Book of Princesses*). Harper, 1962. Illus. by Beni Montresor. 318 pp. Gr. 4–6. [R]

One tale each by sixteen authors, including Andersen, de Morgan, Maugham, de la Mare, Farjeon, Sawyer, and Kipling. (BL 59: 396; CC: 586; Eakin: 178; HB 38: 603)

KENNEDY, Richard. *The Blue Stone.* See Chapter 6, Magic Adventure.

KENNEDY, Richard. *The Dark Princess.* See Chapter 1, Allegory and Fable.

KRENSKY, Stephen. *A Big Day for Scepters.* Atheneum, 1977. Illus. by Bruce Degen. 112 pp. Gr. 4–6. [A]
A boy named Corey teams up with Calandar, a magician, to oppose the villainous Prince Grogol in a race for possession of a powerful evil scepter. (BL 73: 1576; KR 45: 352; SLJ Apr'77 p. 68)

KRENSKY, Stephen. *The Perils of Putney.* Atheneum, 1978. Illus. by Jürg Obrist. 116 pp. Gr. 5–7. [A]
A peace-loving giant, pressed into a search for a missing Fair Damsel and captured by a band of dwarfs, encounters a dragon, a witch, and a wizard. (BL 75: 477; KR 46: 1189; SLJ Oct'78 p. 146)

LANG, Andrew. *Prince Prigio and Prince Ricardo: The Chronicles of Pantouflia.* (Orig. pub. 1889 and 1893) Garland, 1976. Illus. by D. J. Watkins-Pitchford. 171 pp. Gr. 4–6. [A]
Prince Prigio and its sequel *Prince Ricardo* were originally published separately. (BL 39: 144; HB 18: 423; LJ 67: 1069)

LAWRENCE, Ann. *The Half Brothers.* Walck, 1973. 172 pp. Gr. 5–8. [R]
All three of Duchess Ambra's cousins want to marry her, but only one is willing to let her be herself. (BL 70: 341; CCBB 27: 97; HB 50: 51; LJ 99: 891; TLS 1973 p. 685)

LEE, Tanith. *The Dragon Hoard.* Farrar, 1971. Illus. by Graham Oakley. 162 pp. Gr. 4–6. [A]
The witch Maligna's angry gift to Prince Jasleth—that he become a raven one hour every day—comes in handy after he joins a quest for the Dragon Hoard treasure. (HB 48: 49; KR 39: 1120; TLS 1971 p. 1511)

LEE, Tanith. *Princess Hynchatti and Some Other Surprises.* See Chapter 2, Collected Tales.

LLOYD, Norris. *The Desperate Dragons.* See Chapter 8E, Dragons.

MACDONALD, George. *The Light Princess.* See Chapter 1, Allegory and Fable.

MACDONALD, George. *The Lost Princess: A Double Story* (Orig. title: *The Wise Woman*). (Orig. pub. 1875) Dent, 1975 (dist. Biblio). Illus. by D. J. Watkins-Pitchford. 142 pp. Gr. 5–7. [A]
The paths of two little girls converge at the home of the Wise Woman, who changes both their lives. (HB 42: 306; TLS 1965 p. 1150)

MACDONALD, George. *The Princess and the Goblin.* (Orig. pub. 1872)
Penguin, 1964 (pap.). Illus. by Arthur Hughes. 207 pp. Gr. 5–7. [R]
Curdie, a miner's son, overhears a plot by Goblins to flood the mines and take
over the kingdom. *The Princess and Curdie* (Macmillan, 1954; orig. pub.
1882) is the sequel. (Arb: 210; BL 5: 64; CC: 547; HB 27: 261)

McGINLEY, Phyllis. *The Plain Princess.* See Chapter 1, Allegory and Fable.

McKINLEY, Robin. *Beauty: A Retelling of the Story of Beauty and the
Beast.* Harper, 1978. 245 pp. Gr. 5–9. [R]
A beautiful girl marries a Beast and grows to love him in this novel-length
version of the old tale. (BL 75: 222; CCBB 32: 67; HB 55: 201; KR 46: 1307;
SLJ Nov'78 p. 65)

MULOCK, Dinah (pseud. of Dinah Craik). *The Little Lame Prince.* (Orig.
pub. 1874) Collins, 1975. Illus. by Jon Nielson. 135 pp. Gr. 4–5. [A]
Prince Dolor, lame from an accident he had as a baby, uses magic to escape his
greedy uncle and to gain his rightful throne. (BL 6: 142, 45: 145; CC: 553)

MURPHY, Shirley R. *Silver Woven in My Hair.* Atheneum, 1977. Illus. by
Alan Tiegreen. 121 pp. Gr. 4–6. [R]
In an extended version of the Cinderella story, orphaned Thursey is abused by
her stepmother and stepsisters until her friend the goatherd turns out to be a
long-lost prince. (BL 73: 1355; CCBB 31: 51; HB 53: 316; KR 45: 224; SLJ
Sept'77 p. 134)

NESBIT, E. *The Complete Book of Dragons.* See Chapter 8E, Dragons.

NESBIT, E. *The Magic World.* See Chapter 2, Collected Tales.

NEWMAN, Sharon. *Dagda's Harp.* St. Martin's, 1977. 192 pp. Gr. 5–7. [M]
The land of Ierne can be saved only if Michael can win the magical harp from
the malevolent Queen Maebdh. (BL 73: 610; KR 44: 1175)

NYE, Robert. *The Mathematical Princess and Other Stories.* See Chapter 2,
Collected Tales.

NYE, Robert. *Wishing Gold.* Hill, 1971. Illus. by Helen Craig. 109 pp. Gr.
3–5. [A]
Wishing Gold, lost son of the King of Ireland, saves his father's life and battles
the evil queen and her three cowardly sons. (KR 39: 52; LJ 96: 1507; TLS 1970
p. 714)

PICARD, Barbara Leonie. *The Faun and the Woodcutter's Daughter.* See
Chapter 2, Collected Tales.

PUSHKIN, Alexander. *The Tale of Czar Saltan, or the Prince and the
Swan Princess* (British title: *The Tale of Tsar Saltan*). Crowell, 1975. Tr. by
Patricia Lowe. Illus. by I. Bilibin. 24 pp. Gr. 3–5. [R]
An enchanted swan helps Czar Saltan's son outsmart his father's wicked

advisors and reunite his family. (Adv: 100; BL 72: 167; SLJ Nov'75 p. 82; TLS 1974 p. 1382)

PYLE, Howard. *King Stork*. See Chapter 13, Witches, Wizards, Sorcerers, and Magicians.

PYLE, Howard. *The Wonder Clock*. See Chapter 2, Collected Tales.

RUSKIN, John. *The King of the Golden River, or the Black Brothers*. See Chapter 1, Allegory and Fable.

SELFRIDGE, Oliver. *The Trouble with Dragons*. Addison-Wesley, 1978. Illus. by Shirley Hughes. 86 pp. Gr. 4–6. [R]
Although her older sisters' attempts at dragon-slaying failed, Princess Celia succeeds and wins a prince's love in the bargain. (BL 74: 1556; CCBB 31: 184; SLJ Sept'78 p. 148)

* SEUSS, Dr. (pseud. of Theodor Geisel). *The 500 Hats of Bartholomew Cubbins*. Hale, 1938. Illus. by the author. 45 pp. Gr. 2–5.
Even the King of Didd's most able wise men and sorcerers cannot take off all of Bartholomew's hats. *Bartholomew and the Oobleck* (Random, 1949) and *The King's Stilts* (Random, 1939) are the sequels. (Adv: 94; Arb: 227; BL 35: 102; CC: 651; HB 14: 365 and 377; LJ 63: 818 and 890)

SHURA, Mary. *The Nearsighted Knight*. Knopf, 1964. Illus. by Adrienne Adams. 111 pp. Gr. 4–6. [A]
After learning that his sister must marry before he can leave home, Prince Todd decides to help the Knight Before Glasses kill a dragon and win his sister's hand. (HB 40: 284; LJ 89: 1454)

SINGER, Isaac Bashevis. *Alone in the Wild Forest*. Farrar, 1971. Tr. by the author and Elizabeth Shub. Illus. by Margot Zemach. 79 pp. Gr. 4–6. [A]
Orphaned Joseph dreams of meeting and winning Princess Chassidah, but wicked Bal Makane plots against him. (CCBB 25: 97; KR 39: 1015; LJ 97: 285)

SOLBERT, Ronni. *The Song That Sings Itself*. Bobbs-Merrill, 1972. Illus. by the author. Unp. Gr. 2–4. [A]
A shepherd boy solves the king's riddle and inherits the kingdom. (KR 40: 1023; LJ 98: 639)

TERLOUW, Jan. *How to Become King*. Hastings, 1977. 128 pp. Gr. 6–8. [R]
Seventeen-year-old Stark demands to know how he can become king, so the Ministers of Katoren devise seven impossible tasks for him including silencing the Birds of Decibel, destroying the Dragon of Smog, and outwitting the Wizard of Equilibrium. (BL 74: 1111; CC 1979 Suppl. p. 55; CCBB 31: 135; SLJ Mar'78 p. 134)

THACKERAY, William M. *The Rose and the Ring; or the History of Prince Giglio and Prince Bulbo*. (Orig. pub. 1855) Pierpont Morgan, 1947. Illus. by the author, John Gilbert, and Paul Hogarth. 212 pp. Gr. 6 up. [A]

Princess Rosealba and Prince Giglio are restored to their rightful thrones through the good offices of Fairy Blackstick. (BL 20: 65; HB 23: 14, 35: 480)

THURBER, James. *The Great Quillow.* Harcourt, 1944. Illus. by Doris Lee. 54 pp. Gr. 3–4. [R]
Quillow the toymaker saves the town by outwitting an unruly giant named Hunder. (Arb: 205; BL 41: 95; CC: 573; HB 20: 469 and 482; KR 12: 449; LJ 69: 866 and 1004)

THURBER, James. *Many Moons.* Harcourt, 1943. Illus. by Louis Slobodkin, 46 pp. Gr. K–4. [R]
Only the court jester is wise enough to cure Princess Lenore's illness by "giving" her the moon. (Adv: 273; Arb: 205; BL 40: 20; CC: 573; HB 19: 318 and 422, 20: 21; LJ 68: 672 and 818)

THURBER, James. *The 13 Clocks.* See Chapter 1, Allegory and Fable.

THURBER, James. *The White Deer.* See Chapter 1, Allegory and Fable.

TOLKIEN, J. R. R. *Farmer Giles of Ham.* See Chapter 8E, Dragons.

WHITE, T(erence) H(anbury). *The Sword in the Stone.* Putnam, 1939. Illus. by the author. 312 pp. Gr. 5 up. [R]
Merlyn, the sorcerer, teaches young King Arthur about magic and history. *The Once and Future King* (1958) is the sequel. (BL 35: 191; JHC: 439; TLS 1938 p. 571)

WILDE, Oscar. *The Happy Prince.* See Chapter 1, Allegory and Fable.

WILLIAMS, Jay. *The Practical Princess.* Parents, 1969. Illus. by Friso Henstra. 40 pp. Gr. 2–4. [R]
A fairy's gift of common sense enables a princess to rid herself of a dragon and an unwanted suitor and to find the prince she really wants. (BL 65: 1129; CC: 579; CCBB 23: 68; KR 37: 1774, 2073 and 4583)

YOLEN, Jane. *The Bird of Time.* Crowell, 1971. Illus. by Mercer Mayer. 32 pp. Gr. 2–4. [A]
The magical Bird of Time helps Pieter to rescue a princess captured by a giant. (BL 68: 509; CCBB 25: 83; LJ 97: 770)

YOLEN, Jane. *The Girl Who Cried Flowers and Other Tales.* See Chapter 2, Collected Tales.

YOLEN, Jane. *The Magic Three of Solatia.* Crowell, 1974. Illus. by Julia Noonan. 172 pp. Gr. 5–6. [R]
A wisewoman named Sianna and her son, Lann, use three magic buttons to keep out of danger's way and to rescue an enchanted bird-girl from a wizard-king. (Arb: 243; BL 71: 574; CCBB 28: 172; KR 42: 1207; SLJ Jan'75 p. 51)

YOLEN, Jane. *The Moon Ribbon and Other Tales.* See Chapter 2, Collected Tales.

Imaginary Lands: Out-of-Print Works

AIKEN, Joan. *Smoke from Cromwell's Time and Other Stories.* See Chapter 2, Collected Tales: Out-of-Print Works.

ANDERSEN, Hans Christian. *The Wild Swans.* Scribner, 1963. Tr. by M. R. James. Illus. by Marcia Brown. 80 pp. Gr. 3–6. (Arb: 236; BL 60: 416; CC: 480; HB 39: 601)

ANDERSON, Mildred. *A Gift for Merimond.* Oxford, 1953. Illus. by J. Paget-Fredericks. 84 pp. Gr. 4–6. (BL 49: 273; HB 29: 119; KR 21: 114; LJ 78: 737)

ANDERSON, Mildred. *Sandra and the Right Prince.* Oxford, 1951. Illus. by J. Paget-Fredericks. 72 pp. Gr. 3–5. (BL 47: 369; HB 27: 179 and 238; LJ 76: 781)

BOWEN, William. *The Enchanted Forest.* See Chapter 2, Collected Tales: Out-of-Print Works.

BRENTANO, Clemens. *Schoolmaster Whackwell's Wonderful Sons.* Random, 1963. Tr. by Doris Orgel. Illus. by Maurice Sendak. 88 pp. Gr. 3–6. (BL 59: 490; HB 39: 58)

BULLA, Clyde. *The Moon Singer.* See Chapter 1, Allegory and Fable: Out-of-Print Works.

CLAUDINE. *Rabash.* Macmillan, 1966. Illus. by the author. 39 pp. Gr. 1–3. (HB 42: 51)

COATSWORTH, Elizabeth. *Cricket and the Emperor's Son.* (Orig. pub. 1932) Norton, 1965. Illus. by Juliette Palmer. 126 pp. Gr. 3–6. (Arb: 216; BL 29: 118, 61: 873; CCBB 18: 144; Eakin: 77; HB 41: 275; KR 33: 310; LJ 90: 2402)

COLUM, Padraic. *The Boy Apprenticed to an Enchanter.* See Chapter 13, Witches, Wizards, Sorcerers, and Magicians: Out-of-Print Works.

COLUM, Padraic. *The Stone of Victory and Other Tales.* See Chapter 2, Collected Tales: Out-of-Print Works.

COOPER, Margaret. *The Ice Palace.* Macmillan, 1966. Illus. by Harold Goodwin. 50 pp. Gr. 4–6. (CCBB 20: 136; KR 34: 574; LJ 91: 4329)

CRAIG, M. Jean. *Pomando: The Story of a Royal Artist.* See Chapter 1, Allegory and Fable: Out-of-Print Works.

DE REGNIERS, Beatrice. *Penny.* See Chapter 8Q, Miniature People: Out-of-Print Works.

DICKINSON, Peter. *The Iron Lion.* Little, 1972. Illus. by Marc Brown. Unp. Gr. 2–4. (Adv: 185; CCBB 25: 120; KR 40: 135; LJ 97: 1594; TLS 1973 p. 1431)

DILLON, Eilis. *King Big Ears.* Norton, 1963. Illus. by Tom Hamil. 48 pp. Gr. 3–4. (HB 39: 286; KR 31: 3)

ELIOT, Ethel. *The Wind Boy.* See Chapter 1, Allegory and Fable: Out-of-Print Works.

FARJEON, Eleanor. *The Glass Slipper.* Viking, 1956. Illus. by Ernest Shepard. 187 pp. Gr. 3–6. (BL 52: 282; HB 32: 120; KR 24: 43; LJ 81: 1309)

FARJEON, Eleanor. *The Little Bookroom: Eleanor Farjeon's Short Stories for Children Chosen by Herself.* See Chapter 2, Collected Tales: Out-of-Print Works.

FARJEON, Eleanor. *Martin Pippin in the Apple Orchard.* (Orig. pub. 1922) Lippincott, 1961. Illus. by Richard Kennedy. 305 pp. Gr. 6–9. *Martin Pippin in the Daisy Field* (1937, 1963) is the sequel. (BL 19: 53, 58: 112; CC: 585; HB 37: 557; KR 29: 670)

FARJEON, Eleanor. *The Silver Curlew.* Viking, 1954. Illus. by Ernest Shepard. 162 pp. Gr. 3–6. (BL 50: 345; HB 30: 174; KR 22: 114; LJ 79: 1064)

FENTON, Edward. *The Nine Questions.* Doubleday, 1959. Illus. by C. Walter Hodges. 235 pp. Gr. 4–7. (BL 56: 125; HB 36: 129; KR 27: 495; LJ 85: 1302)

FENWICK, Elizabeth. *Cockleberry Castle.* Pantheon, 1963. Illus. by Fabio Rieti. 73 pp. Gr. 3–5. (KR 32: 3)

FLETCHER, David. *Mother O'Pearl: Three Tales.* See Chapter 2, Collected Tales: Out-of-Print Works.

FOSTER, Malcolm. *The Prince with a Hundred Dragons.* See Chapter 8E, Dragons: Out-of-Print Works.

FREEMAN, Barbara. *Broom-Adelaide.* Little, 1965. Illus. by the author. 124 pp. Gr. 4–6. (BL 62: 219; HB 41: 490; KR 33: 626; LJ 90: 3790; TLS 1963 p. 980)

FREEMAN, Barbara. *Timi: The Tale of a Griffin.* See Chapter 8M, Griffins: Out-of-Print Works.

FRIEDRICH, Priscilla and Otto. *Sir Alva and the Wicked Wizard.* Lothrop, 1960. Illus. by Talivaldis Stubis. 34 pp. Gr. 3–4. (LJ 85: 2036)

GARNETT, David. *Two by Two: A Story of Survival.* Atheneum, 1964. 143 pp. Gr. 8 up. (BL 60: 489; LJ 89: 653; TLS 1963 p. 781)

GIBSON, Katherine. *Cinders.* McKay, 1939. Illus. by Vera Bock. 133 pp. Gr. 4–5. (BL 36: 17; HB 15: 296; LJ 64: 712)

GRAY, Nicholas. *Mainly in Moonlight: Ten Stories of Sorcery and the Supernatural.* See Chapter 2, Collected Tales: Out-of-Print Works.

GRIPARI, Pierre. *Tales of the Rue Broca.* See Chapter 2, Collected Tales: Out-of-Print Works.

HALLOWELL, Priscilla. *The Long-Nosed Princess: A Fairy Tale.* Viking, 1959. Illus. by Rita Fava. 61 pp. Gr. 3–5. (BL 55: 633; HB 35: 299; KR 27: 88; LJ 84: 2086)

HAUFF, Wilhelm. *Dwarf Long-Nose.* See Chapter 8F, Dwarfs: Out-of-Print Works.

HODGES, Elizabeth. *The Three Princes of Serendip.* Atheneum, 1964. Illus. by Joan Berg. 158 pp. Gr. 4–6. *Serendipity Tales* (1966) is the sequel. (HB 40: 281; LJ 89: 2219)

HOLLANDER, John. *The Quest of the Gole.* Atheneum, 1966. Illus. by Reginald Pollack. 116 pp. Gr. 6–9. (BL 63: 418; HB 42: 562; KR 34: 982; LJ 91: 4352)

HOLT, Isabella. *The Adventures of Rinaldo.* Little, 1959. Illus. by Erik Blegvad. 142 pp. Gr. 4–6. (BL 55: 458; HB 35: 131; KR 27: 7)

HOUSMAN, Lawrence. *Cotton-Wooleena.* See Chapter 8H, Fairies: Out-of-Print Works.

IPCAR, Dahlov. *The Warlock of Night.* See Chapter 13, Witches, Wizards, Sorcerers, and Magicians: Out-of-Print Works.

JOHNSON, Elizabeth. *The Little Knight.* Little, 1957. Illus. by Ronni Solbert. 56 pp. Gr. 3–5. (BL 54: 28; HB 33: 400; KR 25: 412; LJ 82: 2191)

JUSTER, Norton. *Alberic the Wise and Other Journeys.* See Chapter 2, Collected Tales: Out-of-Print Works.

KELLOGG, Steven. *The Wicked Kings of Bloon.* Prentice-Hall, 1970. Illus. by the author. Unp. Gr. 2–4. (KR 38: 1188; LJ 96: 1495)

LANCASTER, Osbert. *The Saracen's Head; or, the Reluctant Crusader.* Houghton, 1949. Illus. by the author. 67 pp. Gr. 4–6. (BL 46: 101; HB 25: 533; KR 17: 302; LJ 74: 1466; TLS 1948 p. 712)

LEE, Tanith. *Animal Castle.* Farrar, 1972. Illus. by Helen Craig. 37 pp. Gr. K–3. (BL 69: 948; KR 40: 1094; LJ 97: 3797; TLS 1972 p. 808)

LEICHMAN, Seymour. *The Boy Who Could Sing Pictures.* See Chapter 1, Allegory and Fable: Out-of-Print Works.

LEWIS, Beth (pseud. of Beth Lipkin). *The Blue Mountain.* Knopf, 1956. Illus. by Adrienne Adams. 59 pp. Gr. 3–5. (HB 32: 35; KR 24: 519)

LIFTON, Betty. *The Dwarf Pine Tree.* See Chapter 1, Allegory and Fable: Out-of-Print Works.

LONGMAN, Harold. *Andron and the Magician.* Seabury, 1971. Illus. by Richard Cuffari. 143 pp. Gr. 4–7. (Adv: 99; KR 39: 1071; LJ 97: 1607)

LOVETT, Margaret. *The Great and Terrible Quest.* Holt, 1967. 187 pp. Gr. 4–6. (BL 64: 546; CCBB 21: 30; HB 43: 597; KR 35: 879; LJ 92: 4614; TLS 1967 p. 451)

McKENZIE, Ellen. *Taash and the Jesters.* Holt, 1968. 233 pp. Gr. 4–6. (BL 65: 451 and 901)

MAUGHAM, W. Somerset. *Princess September.* See Chapter 1, Allegory and Fable: Out-of-Print Works.

MERRILL, Jean. *The Superlative Horse: A Tale of Ancient China.* See Chapter 1, Allegory and Fable: Out-of-Print Works.

MILNE, A(lan) A(lexander). *Once on a Time.* (Orig. pub. 1917) New York Graphic Society, 1962. Illus. by Susan Perl. 242 pp. Gr. 5–7. (KR 29: 1086; LJ 87: 842)

MILNE, A. A. *Prince Rabbit and the Princess Who Could Not Laugh.* Dutton, 1966. Illus. by Mary Shepard. 72 pp. Gr. 3–5. (CCBB 20: 61; LJ 92: 329)

MOLESWORTH, Mary. *Fairy Stories.* See Chapter 2, Collected Tales: Out-of-Print Works.

MONTROSE, Anne. *The Winter Flower and Other Fairy Stories.* See Chapter 2, Collected Tales: Out-of-Print Works.

NEWMAN, Robert. *Merlin's Mistake.* See Chapter 13, Witches, Wizards, Sorcerers, and Magicians: Out-of-Print Works.

ORMONDROYD, Edward. *The Tale of Alain.* See Chapter 1, Allegory and Fable: Out-of-Print Works.

PALMER, Mary. *The Magic Knight.* Hale, 1964. Illus. by Bill Sokol. 93 pp. Gr. 3–5. (CCBB 18: 91; LJ 90: 382)

PARKER, Edgar. *The Enchantress.* Pantheon, 1960. Illus. by the author. 36 pp. Gr. 3–5. (BL 57: 249; HB 36: 407; KR 28: 816; LJ 85: 3866)

PEARCE, (Ann) Philippa. *The Squirrel Wife.* See Chapter 1, Allegory and Fable: Out-of-Print Works.

PICARD, Barbara. *The Goldfinch Garden: Seven Tales.* See Chapter 2, Collected Tales: Out-of-Print Works.

PICARD, Barbara. *The Lady of the Linden Tree.* See Chapter 2, Collected Tales: Out-of-Print Works.

PICARD, Barbara. *The Mermaid and the Simpleton.* See Chapter 2, Collected Tales: Out-of-Print Works.

POLLAND, Madeleine. *Deirdre.* Doubleday, 1967. Illus. by Seon Morrison. 166 pp. Gr. 7–9. (BL 63: 1050; CCBB 21: 16; HB 43: 465; KR 35: 424; TLS 1967 p. 1133; TN 24: 324)

POSTGATE, Oliver, and FIRMIN, Peter. *King of the Nogs.* Holiday, 1968. Illus. by the authors. 48 pp. Gr. 2–4. The sequels are *Noggin and the Whale* (1967), *The Ice Dragon* (1968), *Nogbad and the Elephants* (1967), and *Noggin and the Moon Mouse* (1967). (KR 36: 1220; LJ 94: 1772; TLS 1965 p. 1149)

READ, Elfreida. *The Magical Egg.* Lippincott, 1965. Illus. by Alison Green. 95 pp. Gr. 4–6. *The Spell of Chuchu-Chan* (World, 1966) is the sequel. (LJ 90: 2887)

REEVES, James. *The Cold Flame.* Meredith, 1967. Illus. by Charles Keeping. 137 pp. Gr. 5–7. (HB 45: 419; LJ 94: 1799; TLS 1967 p. 1142)

REID, Alastair. *Fairwater.* Houghton, 1957. Illus. by Walter Lorraine. 47 pp. Gr. 3–5. *Allth* (1958) is the sequel. (Eakin: 269; HB 33: 222; KR 25: 330; LJ 82: 2192)

SCHLEIN, Miriam. *The Raggle Taggle Fellow.* Abelard-Schuman, 1959. Illus. by Harvey Weiss. 62 pp. Gr. 2–4. (BL 55: 544; Eakin: 286; HB 35: 286; KR 27: 134; LJ 84: 1690)

SCHMIDT, Werner. *The Forests of Adventure.* Atlantic-Little, 1963. Illus. by Artur Marokvia. 161 pp. Gr. 5–6. (HB 39: 174; LJ 88: 2554)

SCHRANK, Joseph. *The Plain Princess and the Lazy Prince.* Day, 1958. Illus. by Mircea Vasiliu. 57 pp. Gr. 3–5. (KR 26: 498; LJ 83: 3012)

SHAPIRO, Irwin. *Twice upon a Time.* Scribner, 1973. Illus. by Adrienne Adams. 35 pp. Gr. 2–4. (Adv: 200; CCBB 27: 86; HB 50: 40; KR 41: 1032; LJ 98: 3703; TN 30: 206)

STOCKTON, Frank R. *The Griffin and the Minor Canon.* See Chapter 8M, Griffins: Out-of-Print Works.

VOEGELI, Max. *The Wonderful Lamp.* Oxford, 1955. Tr. by E. M. Prince. Illus. by Felix Hoffmann. 228 pp. Gr. 5–7. The sequel is *The Prince of Hindustan* (1961). (BL 51: 455; HB 31: 260; KR 23: 358)

WATSON, Sally. *Magic at Wynchwood.* Knopf, 1970. Illus. by Frank Bozzo. 127 pp. Gr. 4–6. (LJ 95: 2537 and 4327)

WEIR, Rosemary. *Albert the Dragon.* See Chapter 8E, Dragons: Out-of-Print Works.

WEISS, Renee K. *The Bird from the Sea*. See Chapter 1, Allegory and Fable: Out-of-Print Works.

WERSBA, Barbara. *A Song for Clowns*. Atheneum, 1965. Illus. by Mario Rivoli. 100 pp. Gr. 4–6. (CCBB 19: 53; HB 41: 629; KR 33: 677; LJ 90: 3797; TLS 1966 p. 1087)

WILLIAMS, Jay. *A Box Full of Infinity*. Grosset, 1970. Illus. by Robin Laurie. Unp. Gr. 2–4. (KR 38: 1247; LJ 96: 720)

WILLIAMS, Jay. *The Magical Storybook*. See Chapter 2, Collected Tales: Out-of-Print Works.

WILLIAMS, Jay. *Petronella*. Parents, 1973. Illus. by Friso Henstra. 33 pp. Gr. 2–4. (BL 70: 176; CC: 579; KR 41: 454; LJ 98: 2646)

YOLEN, Jane. *The Seventh Mandarin*. See Chapter 1, Allegory and Fable: Out-of-Print Works.

YOUNG, Ella. *The Unicorn with Silver Shoes*. McKay, 1932. Illus. by Robert Lawson. 213 pp. Gr. 5–7. (BL 29: 80; HB 34: 124; TLS 1932 p. 893)

ZEMACH, Harve. *The Tricks of Master Dabble*. Holt, 1965. Illus. by Margot Zemach. 32 pp. Gr. K–3. (BL 62: 164; HB 41: 166; KR 33: 3; LJ 90: 1546)

6
Magic Adventure

The majority of these books are about ordinary people who either gain magical powers or come in contact with magical objects, creatures, or events. A lighthearted tone usually prevails in this type of fantasy. Most tales involving extrasensory perception (ESP) or the occult have been excluded.

ᐯAIKEN, Joan. *The Faithless Lollybird.* See Chapter 2, Collected Tales.

ALLEN, Judy. *The Spring on the Mountain.* Farrar, 1973. 153 pp. Gr. 5–8. [R]
An old woman sends Peter, Emma, and Michael in search of a magical, knowledge-giving spring that she once found herself. (BL 70: 653; JHC: 379; LJ 98: 3142; TLS 1973 p. 1114)

BABBITT, Natalie. *Tuck Everlasting.* See Chapter 1, Allegory and Fable.

BACON, Peggy. *The Ghost of Opalina, or Nine Lives.* See Chapter 3, Ghosts.

BACON, Peggy. *The Magic Touch.* Little, 1968. Illus. by the author. 112 pp. Gr. 3–4. [A]
Recipes from a witch's cookbook change Ben, Esther, and Ted into animals. (BL 63: 183; HB 44: 556; KR 36: 690; LJ 94: 292)

BARRIE, Sir J. M. *Peter Pan.* See Chapter 12, Travel to Another World.

BEACHCROFT, Nina. *Well Met by Witchlight.* See Chapter 13, Witches, Wizards, Sorcerers, and Magicians.

BENCHLEY, Nathaniel. *The Magic Sled* (British title: *The Magic Sledge*). Harper, 1972. Illus. by Mel Furukawa. 44 pp. Gr. 3–5. [A]
No snow for his new sled? Fred finds that magic can make more snow than he ever dreamed of. (BL 68: 1002; CCBB 25: 134; KR 40: 68; LJ 97: 1593)

BERESFORD, Elizabeth. *Awkward Magic* (Orig. U.S. title: *The Magic World*, 1964). Granada, 1978. 153 pp. Gr. 4–6. [M]
During school vacation Joe goes treasure hunting with a stray dog that turns out to be a talking, flying griffin. (HB 41: 390; KR 33: 107)

BETHANCOURT, T. Ernesto (pseud. of Tom Paisley). *The Dog Days of Arthur Cane.* Holiday, 1976. 160 pp. Gr. 6–9. [R]
Arthur is changed into a stray mutt by a classmate he has ridiculed. (HB 53: 157; JHC 1977 Suppl. p. 41; KR 44: 848; SLJ Jan'77 p. 99; TLS 1978 p. 1082)

BOSTON, L(ucy) M(aud). *The Children of Green Knowe.* Harcourt, 1967. Illus. by Peter Boston. 157 pp. Gr. 4–7. [R]
With the help of three of his ancestors, Tolly lifts the curse on his family's ancient home, Green Knowe. Tolly's adventures continue in *The Treasure of Green Knowe* (British title: *The Chimneys of Green Knowe*) (1958), *An Enemy at Green Knowe* (1964), and *The Stones of Green Knowe* (Atheneum, 1976). *The River at Green Knowe* (1959) and *A Stranger at Green Knowe* (1961) are related stories, although the latter is not a fantasy. (Arb: 213; BL 52: 37; CC: 490; Eakin: 40; HB 31: 375; KR 23: 357; LJ 80: 1965)

BOSTON, L. M. *The Fossil Snake.* Atheneum, 1976. Illus. by Peter Boston. 53 pp. Gr. 4–6. [A]
The fossilized prehistoric snake that Rob hid under his radiator comes alive and begins to grow. (Adv: 182; BL 72: 1259; CC 1977 Suppl. p. 60; HB 52: 287; KR 44: 199; SLJ May'76 p. 56; TLS 1975 p. 1060)

BOSTON, L. M. *The Guardians of the House.* See Chapter 12, Travel to Another World.

BOSTON, L. M. *Nothing Said.* Harcourt, 1971. 64 pp. Gr. 3–5. [R]
Libby perceives that the garden and river surrounding an old country cottage are inhabited by nymphs and dryads. (Arb: 237; BL 67: 746; CCBB 25: 2; HB 47: 286; LJ 96: 2128; TLS 1971 p. 1317)

BOSTON, L. M. *The Sea Egg.* Harcourt, 1967. Illus. by Peter Boston. 94 pp. Gr. 3–5. [R]
Toby and Joe find a green, egg-shaped stone that hatches into a sea boy. (Arb: 237; BL 63: 1045; CCBB 21: 1; HB 43: 460; KR 35: 498; LJ 92: 2647; Suth: 47; TLS 1967 p. 1133)

BRADBURY, Ray. *The Halloween Tree.* See Chapter 11, Time Travel.

BROCK, Betty. *No Flying in the House.* Harper, 1970. Illus. by Wallace Tripp. 139 pp. Gr. 3–5. [R]
Annabel, a half-mortal, half-fairy child, is tempted by a wicked fairy to misuse her magic powers. (Arb: 237; BL 66: 1340; CC: 491; CCBB 24: 38; KR 38: 450; LJ 95: 2531; Suth: 52)

BROCK, Betty. *The Shades.* See Chapter 3, Ghosts.

BRÖGER, Achim. *Outrageous Kasimir.* See Chapter 8Q, Miniature People.

BROWN, Palmer. *Beyond the Pawpaw Trees; the Story of Anna Lavinia.* (Orig. pub. 1954) Avon, 1973 (pap.). Illus. by the author. 121 pp. Gr. 4–6. [A]
Anna Lavinia's many strange adventures on the road to her aunt's house include finding her long-lost father. *The Silver Nutmeg* (1956) is the sequel. (HB 30: 343; KR 22: 385; LJ 99: 2254)

BYARS, Betsy. *The Winged Colt of Casa Mia.* Viking, 1973. Illus. by Richard Cuffari. 128 pp. Gr. 5–7. [A]
The colt Charles is given when he comes to live on his Uncle Coot's ranch is quite special—it has wings! (CCBB 27: 107; HB 50: 47; LJ 98: 3448)

CARLSEN, Ruth. *Sam Bottleby.* Houghton, 1968. Illus. by Wallace Tripp. 151 pp. Gr. 4–6. [A]
When they are accidentally stranded at the airport, Trygve and Solveig are taken care of by their fairy godfather. (KR 36: 1282; LJ 94: 1324)

CARROLL, Lewis. *Alice's Adventures in Wonderland.* See Chapter 12, Travel to Another World.

CHESNUTT, Charles. *Conjure Tales.* See Chapter 2, Collected Tales.

CHEW, Ruth. *The Trouble with Magic.* Dodd, 1976. Illus. by the author. 112 pp. Gr. 3–5. [M]
Harrison Peabody's umbrella works magic in the rain. (BL 73: 664; CCBB 30: 119; SLJ Jan'77 p. 88)

CHEW, Ruth. *A Witch in the House.* Hastings, 1976. Illus. by the author. 112 pp. Gr. 3–6. [M]
Laura and Jane fly off on a magic bathmat to find a cure for Sally, a witch turned upside-down. (SLJ Feb'77 p. 62)

CHEW, Ruth. *The Witch's Broom.* Dodd, 1977. Illus. by the author. 128 pp. Gr. 3–5. [M]
Amy and Jean use a magic broom to undo a spell that transformed Beryl, the witch, into a bird. (BL 74: 745; SLJ Dec'77 p. 43)

CHEW, Ruth. *The Would-Be Witch.* Hastings, 1977. Illus. by the author. 112 pp. Gr. 3–5. [M]
Miniaturized by a magic cream, Robin and Andy make midnight flights on a dustpan to rescue their friend, Zelda. (BL 74: 745; SLJ Dec'77 p. 43)

CLARKE, Pauline. *The Return of the Twelves*. See Chapter 7, Magical Toys.

CLARKE, Pauline. *The Two Faces of Silenus*. Coward, 1972. 160 pp. Gr. 5–7. [A]
Drusilla and Rufus make a wish at an Italian fountain that brings the carved head of the ancient god Silenus to life. (CCBB 26: 73; HB 48: 594; KR 40: 1244; TLS 1972 p. 1325)

COATSWORTH, Elizabeth. *Pure Magic* (paper title: *The Werefox*). Macmillan, 1973. Illus. by Ingrid Fetz. 68 pp. Gr. 4–5. [R]
Johnny's new friend, Giles, has a secret: he can change into a fox, which proves dangerous when fox-hunting season begins. (Adv: 184; Arb: 237; BL 70: 385; HB 49: 464; KR 41: 642; LJ 98: 2649)

COATSWORTH, Elizabeth. *The Snow Parlor and Other Bedtime Stories*. See Chapter 2, Collected Tales.

COBLENTZ, Catherine. *The Blue Cat of Castle Town*. (Orig. pub. 1949) Countryman, 1974 (pap.). Illus. by Janice Holland. 123 pp. Gr. 4–6. [A]
A blue cat steps from a rug and wanders through the town of Castleton. (BL 46: 15; HB 25: 412; LJ 74: 1105)

COLLODI, Carlo. *The Adventures of Pinocchio*. See Chapter 7, Magical Toys.

COOPER, Susan. *Over Sea, under Stone*. See Chapter 4, Good versus Evil.

CORBETT, Scott. *The Great Custard Pie Panic*. See Chapter 13, Witches, Wizards, Sorcerers, and Magicians.

CORBETT, Scott. *The Lemonade Trick*. Little, 1960. Illus. by Paul Galdone. 103 pp. Gr. 4–6. [R]
Kirby's new chemistry set can change a person's character, but his fun ends when it changes his friend into a bully. The sequels are: *The Mailbox Trick* (1961), *The Disappearing Dog Trick* (1963), *The Limerick Trick* (1964), *The Turnabout Trick* (1967), *The Hairy Horror Trick* (1969), *The Hateful Plateful Trick* (1971), *The Home Run Trick* (1973), and *The Black Mask Trick* (1976). (Arb: 229; BL 56: 633; CC: 505; HB 36: 128; KR 28: 90; LJ 85: 2035)

CRESSWELL, Helen. *The Beachcombers*. Macmillan, 1972. 133 pp. Gr. 6–8. [R]
On holiday at the coast, Ned is caught in a feud between the beachcombing Pickerings and the scavenging Dallakers. (BL 69: 646; CCBB 26: 74; HB 49: 52)

CRESSWELL, Helen. *The Bongleweed*. Macmillan, 1973. 138 pp. Gr. 5–7. [R]
The magic seeds Becky plants change neatly-manicured Pew Gardens into a jungle of bongleweed. (Arb: 238; BL 70: 540; CCBB 27: 174; KR 41: 1159; LJ 98: 3143; TLS 1973 p. 1428)

CRESSWELL, Helen. *The Night Watchmen.* Macmillan, 1970. Illus. by Gareth Floyd. 122 pp. Gr. 4–6. [R]
Two tramps named Josh and Caleb tell Henry the secret of the Night Train. (BL 67: 371; CC: 507; CCBB 24: 121; HB 46: 615; KR 38: 1146; LJ 96: 2128; Suth: 94)

CRESSWELL, Helen. *Up the Pier.* See Chapter 11, Time Travel.

ČTVRTEK, Václav. *The Little Chalk Man.* Knopf, 1970. Illus. by Muriel Batherman. 81 pp. Gr. 2–4. [M]
A chalk man appears on the wall of the storyteller's house, comes to life, and begins a series of adventures in a magical chalk world. (CC: 507; KR 38: 1248)

CURLEY, Daniel. *Ann's Spring.* Crowell, 1977. Illus. by Donna Diamond. 48 pp. Gr. 4–6. [A]
Spring reverts to winter when neighborhood boys lock Mother Nature's children in an old truck and prevent them from supervising the coming of spring. (CCBB 31: 12; KR 45: 46; SLJ Jan'77 p. 90)

CURLEY, Daniel. *Billy Beg and the Bull.* Crowell, 1978. Illus. by Frank Bozzo. 127 pp. Gr. 3–5. [A]
Billy Beg flees his wicked stepmother and, with his friend the bull, sets out on an adventure-filled journey from Ireland to China. (A retelling of tales from Irish folklore.) (BL 74: 1677; HB 54: 289; KR 46: 243; SLJ May'78 p. 65)

CURRY, Jane. *Mindy's Mysterious Miniature.* See Chapter 8Q, Miniature People.

DAHL, Roald. *Charlie and the Chocolate Factory.* Knopf, 1964. Illus. by Joseph Schindelman. 161 pp. Gr. 3–6. [A]
Charlie Bucket is one of five lucky children who win a tour of Wonka's wonderful chocolate factory. *Charlie and the Great Glass Elevator* (1972) is the sequel. Dahl's depiction of Wonka's black helpers has provoked controversy. (Adv: 425; Arb: 234; CCBB 18: 115; LJ 89: 5004; TLS 1978 p. 1398)

DAHL, Roald. *James and the Giant Peach, a Children's Story.* Knopf, 1961. Illus. by Nancy Eckholm Burkert. 118 pp. Gr. 3–5. [A]
A magic potion enables James to escape his cruel aunts and travel across the ocean in a huge peach, with human-sized insects as traveling companions. (Arb: 235; CC: 507; KR 29: 727; LJ 86: 4036)

DAHL, Roald. *The Magic Finger.* Harper, 1966. Illus. by William Pène du Bois. 40 pp. Gr. 3–5. [R]
Zak puts the Magic Finger on her teacher and her duck-hunting neighbors, which changes the former into a cat, and the latter into bird-sized people hunted by huge ducks. (Arb: 234; BL 63: 264; KR 34: 830; LJ 91: 5224)

DE REGNIERS, Beatrice. *The Boy, the Rat, and the Butterfly.* Atheneum, 1971. Illus. by Haig and Regina Shekerjian. 40 pp. Gr. 3–4. [A]
Peter's worries about the short life of his friend the butterfly are over when he

finds a jar of magical wish-granting bubble solution. (CCBB 25: 104; HB 47: 475; KR 39: 805)

* EAGER, Edward. *Half Magic*. Harcourt, 1954. Illus. by N. M. Bodecker. 217 pp. Gr. 3–6.
Jane, Mark, Katharine, and Martha find a coin that grants half of every wish they make. *Magic by the Lake* (1957) is the sequel, and *Knight's Castle* (1956) and *Time Garden* (1958) relate the magical adventures of their children. (Arb: 235; BL 50: 363; CC: 513; HB 30: 174; KR 22: 232; LJ 79: 784; TLS Nov 19, 1954 p. vii)

EAGER, Edward. *Magic or Not?* Harcourt, 1959. Illus. by N. M. Bodecker. 190 pp. Gr. 4–6. [R]
Did Laura, James, Lydia, and Kip's wishes come true because of magic or was it only coincidence? *The Well-Wishers* (1960) is the sequel. (Arb: 235; BL 55: 424; CC: 513; HB 35: 213; KR 26: 906; LJ 84: 1332; TLS Dec 4, 1959 p. xiv)

EAGER, Edward. *Seven Day Magic*. Harcourt, 1962. Illus. by N. M. Bodecker. 156 pp. Gr. 5–7. [A]
The main characters in Susan's library book turn out to be Susan herself and her friends who take part in seven magic adventures. (CC: 513; HB 38: 602; LJ 88: 863; TLS 1963 p. 427)

ESTES, Eleanor. *The Witch Family*. See Chapter 13, Witches, Wizards, Sorcerers, and Magicians.

FARBER, Norma. *Six Impossible Things before Breakfast*. See Chapter 2, Collected Tales.

FARMER, Penelope. *A Castle of Bone*. See Chapter 1, Allegory and Fable.

FARMER, Penelope. *William and Mary: A Story*. See Chapter 12, Travel to Another World.

FARTHING, Alison. *The Mystical Beast*. See Chapter 12, Travel to Another World.

FEYDY, Anne. *Osprey Island*. Houghton, 1974. Illus. by Maggie Smith. 164 pp. Gr. 4–6. [A]
Through magic, Lizzie, Charles, and Amy enter identical paintings in their houses and meet on an island called Carmar-Ogali-Retne. (CCBB 28: 128; HB 51: 146; KR 42: 1201; LJ 98: 3045)

FOSTER, Elizabeth. *Lyrico: The Only Horse of His Kind*. See Chapter 8O, Magical Horses.

GAGE, Wilson (pseud. of Mary Q. Steele). *Miss Osborne-the-Mop*. Collins, 1963. Illus. by Paul Galdone. 156 pp. Gr. 4–6. [R]
Jody's magic abilities bring a dust mop to life, but she soon regrets her actions. (Arb: 226; BL 59: 747; Eakin: 133; HB 39: 382; LJ 88: 2143)

GORDON, John. *The Giant under the Snow: A Story of Suspense.* (Orig. pub. 1970) Harper, 1975 (pap.). Illus. by Rocco Negri. 200 pp. Gr. 5–7. [A]
An ancient brooch enables Jonquil, Bill, and Arthur to fly while attempting to keep the seal of power from the Warlord, who is the master of a huge Green Man. (BL 67: 492; KR 38: 1037; LJ 95: 4374)

GOUDGE, Elizabeth. *Linnets and Valerians.* (Orig. pub. 1964) Avon, 1978 (pap.). Illus. by Ian Ribbons. 290 pp. Gr. 5–7. [R]
After Mrs. Valerian takes in the runaway Linnet children, they decide to search for her long-lost son to repay her kindness. On the way, they encounter a witch, giants, and magic cats. (BL 61: 578; CCBB 18: 74; Eakin: 145; HB 40: 615; TLS 1964 p. 1077)

GOUDGE, Elizabeth. *The Little White Horse.* (Orig. pub. 1946) Avon, 1978 (pap.). Illus. by C. Walter Hodges. 280 pp. Gr. 6–9. [R]
Maria meets magical beings who help her to fight the evil Black Men of the forest. Carnegie Medal. (BL 43: 349; HB 23: 212; KR 15: 167; LJ 72: 738)

GRAY, Nicholas. *The Apple Stone.* Hawthorn, 1969. Illus. by Charles Keeping. 230 pp. Gr. 5–7. [A]
The golden Apple Stone that Missie, Jeremy, Jo, Nigel, and Douglas find brings a stuffed bird, a model rocket, a leopardskin rug, and a stone gargoyle to life. (BL 66: 408; CCBB 23: 128; KR 37: 777; LJ 94: 4582 and 4606; TLS 1965 p. 1131)

GREENWALD, Sheila. *Willie Bryant and the Flying Otis.* See Chapter 10, Tall Tales.

GROSSER, Morton. *The Snake Horn.* Atheneum, 1973. Illus. by David Stone. 131 pp. Gr. 5–7. [A]
When Danny Johnson blows his antique horn, a seventeenth-century music master appears and teaches Danny's father some "new" music that starts him on the road to fame. (Adv: 188; BL 70: 50; CCBB 26: 171; KR 41: 114; LJ 98: 1387)

HAAS, Dorothy. *The Bears Up Stairs.* See Chapter 9, Talking Animals.

HARRIS, Rosemary. *Sea Magic and Other Stories of Enchantment.* See Chapter 2, Collected Tales.

HAUFF, Wilhelm. *The Adventures of Little Mouk.* See Chapter 5B, Imaginary Lands.

HENDRICH, Paula. *Who Says So?* Lothrop, 1972. Illus. by Trina Schart Hyman. 160 pp. Gr. 4–6. [A]
Lucinda, using her book of magic spells, conjures up an apparition named Janaka to be her playmate, and then decides to enter Janaka in the county fair as part of a science project. (CCBB 26: 56; KR 40: 259; LJ 98: 644)

HILL, Elizabeth. *Ever-After Island.* Dutton, 1977. 160 pp. Gr. 4–5. [A]
Ryan and Sara must search the Cavern of the Winds to find the magic jewel
that will free their father from the spell of the evil Hepzibah. (BL 73: 1497;
CCBB 31: 34; KR 45: 575; SLJ Sept'77 p. 130)

HOUSMAN, Laurence. *The Rat-Catcher's Daughter: A Collection of
Stories.* See Chapter 2, Collected Tales.

HUNTER, Mollie. *The Walking Stones: A Story of Suspense.* See Chapter
13, Witches, Wizards, Sorcerers, and Magicians.

HUNTER, Mollie. *The Wicked One.* See Chapter 8C, Demons, Devils, and
Imps.

IPCAR, Dahlov. *A Dark Horn Blowing.* See Chapter 12, Travel to Another
World.

IRVING, Washington. *Rip Van Winkle.* (Orig. pub. 1848) Lippincott, 1967.
Illus. by Leonard Fisher. 44 pp. Gr. 5–8. [R]
After a drinking bout with some strange little men, Rip falls asleep for twenty
years. (BL 63: 586; CC: 534; LJ 92: 350)

ISH-KISHOR, Sulamith. *The Master of Miracle: A New Novel of the Golem.*
See Chapter 1, Allegory and Fable.

JARRELL, Randall. *Fly by Night.* Farrar, 1976. Illus. by Maurice Sendak. 31
pp. Gr. 2–4. [R]
A young boy floats out into the night and sees into dreams, listens to animals
talking, and visits an owl's nest to hear a bedtime poem-story. (Adv: 191; BL
73: 474; CC 1977 Suppl. p. 65; CCBB 30: 92; HB 53: 52; KR 44: 1137; SLJ
Nov'76 p. 59)

JESCHKE, Susan. *Rima and Zeppo.* See Chapter 13, Witches, Wizards,
Sorcerers, and Magicians.

JOHNSON, Elizabeth. *Break a Magic Circle.* Little, 1971. Illus. by Trina
Schart Hyman. 70 pp. Gr. 3–5. [R]
An invisible boy follows Tilly home and asks her to help him become visible
again. (BL 68: 109; CC: 536; CCBB 25: 27; HB 47: 482; KR 39: 676)

JONES, Adrienne. *The Mural Master.* See Chapter 12, Travel to Another
World.

* JONES, Diana Wynne. *The Ogre Downstairs.* Dutton, 1975. 191 pp. Gr.
6–8.
Amazing things happen when Johnny and Malcolm use the chemistry sets
given to them by "The Ogre," their new stepfather. (Arb: 240; BL 71: 1075;
CCBB 28: 179; HB 51: 464; KR 43: 453; SLJ Sept'75 p. 105)

JONES, Elizabeth. *Twig.* See Chapter 8H, Fairies.

KENNEDY, Richard. *The Blue Stone*. Holiday, 1976. Illus. by Ronald Himler. 93 pp. Gr. 3–6. [R]
The blue stone that fell from the sky brings magic into the peaceful lives of Bertie and Jack by turning people into animals, making poems come true, and changing a sparrow into a baby angel. (BL 73: 323; CC 1977 Suppl. p. 65; CCBB 30: 127; KR 44: 1094; SLJ Nov'76 p. 60)

KENNY, Herbert A. *Dear Dolphin*. See Chapter 12, Travel to Another World.

KIRKEGAARD, Ole. *Otto Is a Rhino*. Addison-Wesley, 1976. Tr. by Joan Tate. Illus. by the author. 96 pp. Gr. 4–6. [M]
The rhinoceros that Topper draws on his bedroom wall comes alive and promptly falls through the floor. (KR 44: 795; SLJ Oct'76 p. 108)

KOOIKER, Leonie. *The Magic Stone*. See Chapter 13, Witches, Wizards, Sorcerers, and Magicians.

KRENSKY, Stephen. *Dragon Circle*. See Chapter 8E, Dragons.

LAMORISSE, Albert. *The Red Balloon*. See Chapter 1, Allegory and Fable.

LANGTON, Jane. *The Diamond in the Window*. Harper, 1962. Illus. by Erik Blegvad. 256 pp. Gr. 5–7. [A]
The mysterious disappearance of two children and an Indian prince intrigues Eleanor and Eddie, who decide to find the key to the mystery: the Star of India Diamond. *The Swing in the Summerhouse* (1967) and *The Astonishing Stereoscope* (1971) are sequels. (Arb: 215; HB 38: 481; LJ 87: 3895)

LEWIS, C. S. *The Lion, the Witch and the Wardrobe*. See Chapter 12, Travel to Another World.

LEWIS, Hilda. *The Ship That Flew*. See Chapter 11, Time Travel.

LINDGREN, Astrid. *Karlsson-on-the-Roof*. See Chapter 8Q, Miniature People.

LIVELY, Penelope. *The Whispering Knights*. Dutton, 1976. Illus. by Gareth Floyd. 160 pp. Gr. 5–7. [R]
William, Martha, and Susie inadvertently bring the sorceress Morgan le Fay to life. (BL 72: 1467; CCBB 30: 13; HB 52: 499; KR 44: 593; SLJ Sept'76 p. 121; TLS 1971 p. 774)

LOFTING, Hugh. *The Twilight of Magic*. Lippincott, 1967 (Repr. of 1930 ed.). Illus. by Lois Lenski. 303 pp. Gr. 5–7. [M]
Anne and Giles learn about magic from Agnes the wise woman, whom many call a witch. (BL 27: 367; KR 35: 60)

LOVEJOY, Jack. *The Rebel Witch*. See Chapter 13, Witches, Wizards, Sorcerers, and Magicians.

MacDONALD, Betty. *Mrs. Piggle-Wiggle.* See Chapter 10, Tall Tales.

McHARGUE, Georgess. *Stoneflight.* Viking, 1975. Illus. by Arvis Stewart. 222 pp. Gr. 5–7. [R]
Just as Jane's home life is becoming unbearable, she discovers the joys of night flight on the back of a stone griffin come to life. (Arb: 240; BL 71: 762; CC 1977 Suppl. p. 66; CCBB 29: 50; HB 51: 268; KR 43: 239; SLJ Mar'75 p. 98)

MAGUIRE, Gregory. *Lightning Time.* See Chapter 11, Time Travel.

MAIDEN, Cecil. *Speaking of Mrs. McCluskie: A Story.* Vanguard, 1962. Illus. by Hilary Knight. 43 pp. Gr. 3–5. [M]
Poor Mrs. McCluskie was looking forward to a quiet retirement until she found an old broom that carried her up over the village and into a lot of trouble. (HB 39: 172)

MAYNE, William. *The Glass Ball.* Dutton, 1962. Illus. by Janet Duchesne. 63 pp. Gr. 4–6. [R]
Max and Niko find a glass ball in the sea and follow it as it rolls across their island. (BL 58: 796; Eakin: 228; HB 38: 374; LJ 87: 2026)

MAYNE, William. *A Grass Rope.* Dutton, 1962. Illus. by Lynton Lamb. 166 pp. Gr. 4–6. [R]
Four children weave a special rope to capture a unicorn. Carnegie Medal. (Eakin: 224; HB 38: 600; LJ 87: 4622)

MILES, Patricia. *The Gods in Winter.* See Chapter 1, Allegory and Fable.

MOLESWORTH, Mary. *The Cuckoo Clock.* See Chapter 12, Travel to Another World.

NESBIT, E. *The Complete Book of Dragons.* See Chapter 8E, Dragons.

NESBIT, E. (pseud. of Edith Bland). *The Enchanted Castle.* (Orig. pub. 1907) Dent, 1968 (dist. by Biblio). Illus. by Cecil Leslie. 231 pp. Gr. 5–7. [A]
A magical ring transports Gerald, Jimmy, and Cathy to a garden of stone monsters surrounding a castle. (BL 30: 24)

NESBIT, E. *The Five Children and It.* (Orig. pub. 1902) British Book Center, 1974. Illus. by J. S. Goodall. 253 pp. Gr. 5–7. [R]
Anthea, Jane, Robert, Cyril, and the Baby uncover a Psammead, or Sand Fairy, who reluctantly agrees to grant their wishes. *The Phoenix and the Carpet* (Orig. pub. 1904; British Book Center, 1974) and *The Story of the Amulet* (Orig. pub. 1906; British Book Center, 1974) are the sequels. (BL 27: 215; HB 25: 297 and 579)

NESBIT, E. *The House of Arden.* See Chapter 11, Time Travel.

NESBIT, E. *The Magic World.* See Chapter 2, Collected Tales.

NESBIT, E. *The Wonderful Garden; or the Three C's.* (Orig. pub. 1911) British Book Center, 1974. Illus. by H. R. Millar. 293 pp. Gr. 4–6. [A] Carolyn, Charlotte, and Charles find an old book of magic that convinces them the flowers in their uncle's garden are magical. (BL 32: 80, 57: 32; HB 11: 296, 36: 309; LJ 60: 830)

NICHOLS, Ruth. *The Left-handed Spirit.* Atheneum, 1978. 260 pp. Gr. 8–10. [A]
Because of her magical healing powers, Mariana is kidnapped by the Chinese ambassador and taken to China to save the life of the ambassador's twin brother. (BL 75: 469; CCBB 32: 85; KR 46: 1254; SLJ Oct'78 p. 158)

NORTON, André (pseud. of Alice Mary Norton). *Fur Magic.* (Orig. pub. 1968) Archway, 1978 (pap.). Illus. by John Kaufmann. 174 pp. Gr. 5–7. [A] Corey is afraid of everything on his foster-uncle's ranch until the Changer, part coyote and part man, turns him into a beaver named Yellow Shell. (HB 45: 172; KR 36: 1164; LJ 94: 877; TLS 1969 p. 689)

NORTON, André. *Lavender Green Magic.* See Chapter 11, Time Travel.

* NORTON, Mary. *Bedknob and Broomstick* (British titles: *The Magic Bedknob* and *Bonfires and Broomsticks*). (Orig. pub. 1943) Harcourt, 1957. Illus. by Erik Blegvad. 189 pp. Gr. 4–6.
A two-part story, in which a witch gives Paul, Carey, and Charles a magic bedknob that makes their bed fly through time. (Arb: 241; BL 54: 177; CC: 555; HB 33: 489; KR 25: 638; LJ 82: 3248; TLS Nov 15, 1957 p. iii)

O'HANLON, Jacklyn. *The Door.* See Chapter 12, Travel to Another World.

OPPENHEIM, Shulamith. *The Selchie's Seed.* See Chapter 8T, Seal People.

ORMONDROYD, Edward. *Time at the Top.* See Chapter 11, Time Travel.

PARKER, Richard. *M for Mischief.* Hawthorn, 1966. Illus. by Charles Geer. 90 pp. Gr. 3–5. [A]
The old stove in the garden house, which has a dial that can be set for O (ordinary) or M (magic) baking, enables the children to create eggs that, when eaten, make people invisible and cupcakes that change them into animals. (HB 42: 307; KR 34: 57; LJ 91: 2697; TLS 1965 p. 513)

PARKER, Richard. *The Old Powder Line.* See Chapter 11, Time Travel.

PARKER, Richard. *Spell Seven.* Nelson, 1971. Illus. by Trevor Ridley. 127 pp. Gr. 4–6. [A]
The wand Carolyn gives her brother, Norman, is a wand that grants wishes spoken in rhyme. (HB 47: 385; LJ 96: 2920; TLS 1971 p. 774)

PEARCE, A. Philippa. *Tom's Midnight Garden.* See Chapter 11, Time Travel.

PECK, Robert. *The King of Kazoo.* See Chapter 10, Tall Tales.

PINKWATER, D. Manus. *Wingman.* See Chapter 11, Time Travel.

POMER ANTZ, Charlotte. *The Downtown Fairy Godmother.* Addison-Wesley, 1978. Illus. by Susanna Natti. 45 pp. Gr. 3–5. [A]
Olivia's fairy godmother turns out to be an amateur who needs a lot of practice to perfect her wish-granting abilities. (CCBB 32: 70; KR 46: 1190; SLJ Nov'78 p. 67)

PROYSEN, Alf. *Little Old Mrs. Pepperpot and Other Stories.* See Chapter 2, Collected Tales.

PYLE, Howard. *King Stork.* See Chapter 13, Witches, Wizards, Sorcerers, and Magicians.

RAWLINGS, Marjorie. *The Secret River.* Scribner, 1955 (pap.). Illus. by Leonard Weisgard. Unp. Gr. 2–4. [R]
Calpurnia discovers a lovely river that disappears when she tries to find it again. (BL 51: 436; HB 31: 254 and 258; KR 23: 327; LJ 80: 1508)

ROCKWELL, Thomas. *Tin Cans.* Bradbury, 1975. Illus. by Saul Lambert. 70 pp. Gr. 6–7. [A]
David and Jane find a magic soup can that brings them jewels, money, and food, but also puts them on the police "Wanted" list. (BL 72: 240; KR 43: 714; SLJ Oct'75 p. 101)

SAUER, Julia. *Fog Magic.* See Chapter 11, Time Travel.

SELDEN, George (pseud. of George Selden Thompson). *The Genie of Sutton Place.* Farrar, 1973. 175 pp. Gr. 4–6. [R]
Nothing is quite the same after Abdulla, the genie, is released from 1000 years of captivity in an Arabian carpet. (Adv: 200; Arb: 241; BL 69: 861; CC: 563; CCBB 26: 176; HB 49: 382; JHC: 427; KR 41: 116; LJ 98: 1398 and 1656; TN 30: 206)

SINGER, Isaac Bashevis. *Alone in the Wild Forest.* See Chapter 5B, Imaginary Lands.

SINGER, Isaac Bashevis. *The Fearsome Inn.* Scribner, 1967. Tr. by the author and Elizabeth Shub. Illus. by Nonny Hogrogian. 45 pp. Gr. 4–6. [R]
With his piece of magic chalk, Liebel, a young Cabala student, rescues three young girls held by a witch and a devil. (Arb: 242; BL 64: 338; CC: 565; CCBB 21: 67; HB 43: 751; KR 35: 880; LJ 92: 3190; Suth: 367; TN 24: 324)

SINGER, Isaac Bashevis. *A Tale of Three Wishes.* See Chapter 1, Allegory and Fable.

SNYDER, Zilpha Keatley. *Black and Blue Magic*. Atheneum, 1966. Illus. by Gene Holtan. 186 pp. Gr. 4–6. [R]
Mr. Mazzeek's magic lotion makes Harry Houdini Marco sprout wings. (BL 62: 878; CC: 567; CCBB 20: 48; HB 42: 308; KR 34: 108; LJ 91: 2214; Suth: 371)

SNYDER, Zilpha Keatley. *A Season of Ponies*. Atheneum, 1964. Illus. by Alton Raible. 133 pp. Gr. 5–7. [A]
Her father's amulet enables Pamela to make friends with a beautiful pastel pony and to escape from the pig woman in the swamp. (HB 40: 284; LJ 89: 1862)

STEELE, Mary Q. *Because of the Sand Witches There*. Greenwillow-Morrow, 1975. Illus. by Paul Galdone. 183 pp. Gr. 5–7. [A]
The Sand Witch grants Mil and Hamish's wishes, which always lead to trouble. (Adv: 201; BL 72: 242; KR 75: 778; SLJ Sept'75 p. 112; TLS 1976 p. 882)

STORR, Catherine. *Thursday*. See Chapter 8H, Fairies.

SYKES, Pamela. *Mirror of Danger*. See Chapter 11, Time Travel.

THEROUX, Paul. *A Christmas Card*. See Chapter 1, Allegory and Fable.

TOLKIEN, J(ohn) R(onald) R(euel). *Smith of Wootton Major*. (Orig. pub. 1967) Houghton, 1978. Illus. by Pauline Baynes. 64 pp. Gr. 5 up. [A]
After the blacksmith's son finds a magical star buried in a piece of cake, his life is completely changed. (HB 44: 63; KR 35: 1164; LJ 92: 4175; TLS 1967: 1153)

TOWNE, Mary. *Goldenrod*. Atheneum, 1977. 180 pp. Gr. 5–7. [A]
Goldenrod, the Madder children's babysitter, can transport them to any spot they choose, as long as its name begins with the first letter of one of theirs. (CCBB 31: 149; KR 45: 852; SLJ Nov'77 p. 64)

TRAVERS, P(amela) L. *Mary Poppins*. (Orig. pub. 1934) Harcourt, 1962. Illus. by Mary Shepard. 206 pp. Gr. 5–7. [R]
Mary Poppins blows in on an east wind and becomes the Banks children's Nanny, bringing hilarious and magical adventures. These adventures are continued in *Mary Poppins Comes Back* (1935, 1963), *Mary Poppins in the Park* (1952), *Mary Poppins Opens the Door* (1943), and *Mary Poppins from A to Z* (1962). (Arb: 226; BL 31: 178; CC: 575; TLS 1934 p. 637)

WILLIAMS, Jay. *The Hawkstone*. Walck, 1971. 141 pp. Gr. 4–6. [M]
Colin Hyatt finds a green stone that brings him in contact with "Other People" from the past. (KR 39: 1073; LJ 97: 2240)

WILLIAMS, Jay. *The Hero from Otherwhere*. See Chapter 12, Travel to Another World.

WRIGHTSON, Patricia. *An Older Kind of Magic.* Harcourt, 1972. Illus. by Noela Young. 186 pp. Gr. 4–7. [R]
On the night a comet streaks through the sky, aboriginal spirits appear and Rupert, Selina, and Benny save the Botanical Gardens by using ancient spells. (BL 69: 247; CCBB 26: 35; HB 48: 472; KR 40: 1100; LJ 97: 3458; TLS 1972 p. 1325)

YOLEN, Jane. *The Mermaid's Three Wisdoms.* Collins + World, 1978. Illus. by Laura Rader. 112 pp. Gr. 4–6. [A]
Jess comes to terms with her deafness with the help of Melusina, an exiled mermaid who is unable to speak. (BL 74: 1738; KR 46: 638; SLJ Nov'78 p. 71)

YOLEN, Jane, ed. *Shape Shifters: Fantasy and Science Fiction Tales about Humans Who Can Change Their Shapes.* See Chapter 2, Collected Tales.

YOLEN, Jane. *The Transfigured Hart.* See Chapter 1, Allegory and Fable.

Magic Adventure: Out-of-Print Works

AIKEN, Joan. *Smoke from Cromwell's Time and Other Stories.* See Chapter 2, Collected Tales: Out-of-Print Works.

ALLFREY, Katherine. *The Golden Island.* See Chapter 12, Travel to Another World: Out-of-Print Works.

ANCKARSVÄRD, Karin. *Bonifacius the Green.* See Chapter 8E, Dragons: Out-of-Print Works.

ANDREWS, Frank. *The Upside-Down Town.* See Chapter 10, Tall Tales: Out-of-Print Works.

BACON, Martha. *The Third Road.* See Chapter 11, Time Travel: Out-of-Print Works.

BAKER, Margaret Joyce. *The Magic Sea Shell.* Holt, 1960. Illus. by Susan Elson. 122 pp. Gr. 3–5. (KR 28: 6; LJ 85: 2033; TLS Dec 4, 1959 p. xxii)

BAKER, Margaret Joyce. *Porterhouse Major.* Prentice-Hall, 1967. Illus. by Shirley Hughes. 116 pp. Gr. 4–6. (CCBB 21: 105 and 121; Suth: 26; TLS 1967 p. 451)

BAKER, Olaf. *Bengey and the Beast.* Dodd, 1947. Illus. by Victor Dowling. 243 pp. Gr. 5–7. (BL 43: 260; HB 23: 212; LJ 72: 466)

BERESFORD, Elizabeth. *Invisible Magic.* See Chapter 11, Time Travel: Out-of-Print Works.

BERESFORD, Elizabeth. *Travelling Magic.* See Chapter 11, Time Travel: Out-of-Print Works.

BINNS, Archie. *The Radio Imp.* Winston, 1950. Illus. by Rafaello Busoni. 216 pp. Gr. 4–7. (BL 46: 266; HB 26: 193; KR 18: 69; LJ 75: 706)

* BOSTON, L(ucy) M(aud). *The Castle of Yew* (British title: *Yew Hall*). Harcourt, 1965. Illus. by Margery Gill. 57 pp. Gr. 3–5. (Arb: 237; BL 62: 327; CCBB 19: 42; HB 42: 192; KR 33: 903; LJ 90: 4609; TLS 1965 p. 513)

BOWEN, William. *The Old Tobacco Shop: A True Account of What Befell a Little Boy in Search of Adventure.* Macmillan, 1921. 236 pp. Gr. 4–6. (BL 18: 159)

BRAND, Christianna (pseud. of Mary Lewis). *Nurse Matilda.* Dutton, 1964. Illus. by Edward Ardizzone. 127 pp. Gr. 2–5. *Nurse Matilda Goes to Town* (1967) is the sequel. *Nurse Matilda Goes to the Hospital* is the British sequel. (BL 61: 436; HB 40: 497; KR 32: 732; LJ 89: 3468; TLS 1964 p. 589)

CALHOUN, Mary. *Magic in the Alley.* Atheneum, 1970. Illus. by Wendy Watson. 167 pp. Gr. 4–6. (BL 67: 55; HB 46: 295; KR 38: 242; LJ 95: 1939)

CARLSEN, Ruth. *Mr. Pudgins.* Houghton, 1951. Illus. by Margaret Bradfield. 163 pp. Gr. 3–6. (BL 47: 240; HB 27: 1; LJ 76: 415)

CARLSEN, Ruth. *Monty and the Tree House.* Houghton, 1967. Illus. by Leonard Shortall. 183 pp. Gr. 4–6. (KR 35: 364; LJ 93: 288)

CHASE, Mary. *Loretta Mason Potts.* Lippincott, 1958. Illus. by Harold Berson. 221 pp. Gr. 4–6. (BL 55: 189; KR 26: 711; LJ 84: 248)

COATSWORTH, Elizabeth. *Cricket and the Emperor's Son.* See Chapter 5B, Imaginary Lands: Out-of-Print Works.

CURRY, Jane. *Beneath the Hill.* Harcourt, 1967. Illus. by Imero Gobbato. 255 pp. Gr. 5–7. A related story is *The Change Child* (1969). (BL 63: 1146; CC: 507; CCBB 21: 25; HB 43: 461; KR 35: 61; LJ 92: 2020; TLS 1968 p. 1113; TN 24: 223)

DAWSON, Carley. *Mr. Wicker's Window.* See Chapter 11, Time Travel: Out-of-Print Works.

DE LA MARE, Walter. *The Magic Jacket.* See Chapter 2, Collected Tales: Out-of-Print Works.

DOLBIER, Maurice. *The Half-Pint Jinni, and Other Stories.* See Chapter 2, Collected Tales: Out-of-Print Works.

DOLBIER, Maurice. *The Magic Shop.* Random, 1946. Illus. by Fritz Eichenberg. 74 pp. Gr. 3–5. (BL 43: 19; HB 22: 350 and 456; KR 14: 324; LJ 71: 1046)

DRUON, Maurice. *Tistou of the Green Thumbs.* See Chapter 1, Allegory and Fable: Out-of-Print Works.

ELKIN, Benjamin. *Al and the Magic Lamp.* Harper, 1963. Illus. by William Wiesner. 31 pp. Gr. 3–4. (BL 60: 207; CCBB 16: 125)

ERWIN, Betty. *Aggie, Maggie, and Tish.* See Chapter 13, Witches, Wizards, Sorcerers, and Magicians: Out-of-Print Works.

FARALLA, Dana. *The Singing Cupboard.* Lippincott, 1963. Illus. by Edward Ardizzone. 94 pp. Gr. 3–5. (BL 60: 630; HB 40: 174; LJ 88: 4852; TLS 1962 p. 900)

FARALLA, Dana. *The Wonderful Flying-Go-Round.* World, 1965. Illus. by Harold Berson. 94 pp. Gr. 4–6. (BL 62: 528; CCBB 20: 24; HB 42: 52; KR 33: 905; LJ 90: 5076)

FARMER, Penelope. *The Magic Stone.* Harcourt, 1964. Illus. by John Kaufmann. 233 pp. Gr. 6–8. (HB 41: 52; KR 32: 898; LJ 89: 4446; TLS 1965 p. 513)

FEAGLES, Anita. *The Genie and Joe Maloney.* Scott, 1962. Illus. by Don Sibley. 62 pp. Gr. 3–4. (KR 30: 175; LJ 87: 2416)

FLETCHER, David. *Mother O'Pearl: Three Tales.* See Chapter 2, Collected Tales: Out-of-Print Works.

FORBUS, Ina. *The Magic Pin.* Viking, 1956. Illus. by Corydon Bell. 138 pp. Gr. 4–6. (KR 24: 435)

FRAZIER, Neta. *The Magic Ring.* Longmans, 1959. Illus. by Kathleen Voute. 149 pp. Gr. 4–7. (BL 56: 247; HB 35: 382; KR 27: 402; LJ 84: 3926)

FRITZ, Jean. *Magic to Burn.* Coward, 1964. Illus. by Beth and Joe Krush. 255 pp. Gr. 4–6. (BL 61: 711; CCBB 18: 74)

GREEN, Roger. *A Cavalcade of Magicians.* See Chapter 13, Witches, Wizards, Sorcerers, and Magicians: Out-of-Print Works.

GUILLOT, René. *Nicolette and the Mill.* Abelard-Schuman, 1960. Tr. by Gwen Marsh. Illus. by Charles Mozley. 79 pp. Gr. 3–4. (KR 28: 949; LJ 86: 373; TLS May 20, 1960 p. vii)

HANLEY, Eve. *The Enchanted Toby Jug.* Washburn, 1965. Illus. by Nora Unwin. 134 pp. Gr. 4–5. (KR 33: 6; LJ 90: 960; TLS 1964 p. 602)

HARRISON, Ada. *The Doubling Rod.* Harcourt, 1958. Illus. by Christine Price. 192 pp. Gr. 4–7. (BL 54: 509; KR 26: 283; LJ 83: 1944)

HAUFF, Wilhelm. *The Heart of Stone: A Fairy Tale.* Macmillan, 1964. Retold by Doris Orgel. Illus. by David Levine. 66 pp. Gr. 4–6. (HB 40: 610; LJ 89: 4640)

HEAL, Edith. *What Happened to Jenny.* Atheneum, 1962. Illus. by Abbi Giventer. 62 pp. Gr. 3–5. (HB 39: 53 and 76; KR 30: 559)

HENRY, Jan. *Tiger's Chance.* Harcourt, 1957. Illus. by Hilary Knight. 138 pp. Gr. 3–6. (BL 53: 460; Eakin: 156; HB 33: 222; KR 25: 218; LJ 82: 2190)

HOFFMAN, Eleanor. *Mischief in Fez.* Holiday, 1943. Illus. by Fritz Eichenberg. 109 pp. Gr. 4–7. (BL 39: 373; HB 19: 170; LJ 68: 433 and 825)

HOPP, Zinken. *The Magic Chalk.* McKay, 1959. Tr. by Suzanne Bergensdahl. Illus. by Malvin Neset. 127 pp. Gr. 4–5. (KR 27: 492; LJ 85: 844; TLS Nov 25, 1960 p. x)

HORSEMAN, Elaine. *The Hubbles' Bubble.* Norton, 1964. Illus. by John Sergeant. 220 pp. Gr. 5–7. The British sequels are: *The Hubbles' Treasure Hunt* and *The Hubbles and the Robot.* (LJ 89: 4196; TLS 1964 p. 602)

HOUGH, Charlotte. *Red Biddy and Other Stories.* See Chapter 2, Collected Tales: Out-of-Print Works.

HOWARD, Joan. *The Oldest Secret.* See Chapter 12, Travel to Another World: Out-of-Print Works.

HOWARD, Joan (pseud. of Patricia Gordon). *The Thirteenth Is Magic.* Lothrop, 1950. Illus. by Adrienne Adams. 170 pp. Gr. 5–7. *The Summer is Magic* (1952) is the sequel. (BL 47: 224; HB 27: 31; KR 18: 725; LJ 76: 338)

HUNTER, Mollie. *The Ferlie.* See Chapter 8H, Fairies: Out-of-Print Works.

JOHNSON, Elizabeth. *No Magic, Thank You.* Little, 1964. Illus. by Garrett Price. 55 pp. Gr. 3–4. (CCBB 18: 119; HB 40: 499)

JOHNSON, Elizabeth. *Stuck with Luck.* See Chapter 8N, Leprechauns: Out-of-Print Works.

KASSIRER, Norma. *Magic Elizabeth.* See Chapter 11, Time Travel: Out-of-Print Works.

KELLAM, Ian. *The First Summer Year.* See Chapter 12, Travel to Another World: Out-of-Print Works.

KOTZWINKLE, William. *The Oldest Man and Other Timeless Stories.* See Chapter 2, Collected Tales: Out-of-Print Works.

LANCASTER, Clay. *Periwinkle Steamboat.* Viking, 1961. Illus. by author. 54 pp. Gr. 2–4. (HB 37: 261)

LATHROP, Dorothy P. *The Dog in the Tapestry Garden.* Macmillan, 1962. Illus. by the author. 40 pp. Gr. 2–4. (HB 38: 481)

LAWRENCE, Ann. *Tom Ass: Or the Second Gift.* Walck, 1973. Illus. by Mila Lazarevich. 132 pp. Gr. 4–7. (BL 70: 173; CCBB 27: 46; HB 49: 378; KR 41: 600)

LAWRENCE, Harriet. *Philip Birdsong's ESP.* Addison-Wesley, 1969. Illus. by Sandy Huffaker. 303 pp. Gr. 5–8. (BL 66: 138; LJ 94: 3221)

LEADABRAND, Russ. *Between the 16th and 17th Floors.* Ritchie, 1974. Illus. by Jay Rivkin. 40 pp. Gr. 3–5. (LJ 99: 3268)

LINDE, Gunnel. *The White Stone.* Harcourt, 1966. Tr. by Richard and Clara Winston. Illus. by Imero Gobbado. 185 pp. Gr. 4–6. (BL 63: 734; CCBB 20: 156; HB 42: 717; KR 34: 1053; LJ 91: 5232)

LIVELY, Penelope. *The Wild Hunt of the Ghost Hounds.* See Chapter 4, Good versus Evil: Out-of-Print Works.

McDONALD, Greville. *Billy Barnicoat.* Dutton, 1923. 230 pp. Gr. 6–8. (BL 20: 146)

MacFARLANE, Stephen. *The Other Side of Green Hills.* See Chapter 12, Travel to Another World: Out-of-Print Works.

McNEILL, Janet. *Tom's Tower.* See Chapter 12, Travel to Another World: Out-of-Print Works.

McNEILL, Janet. *Various Specs.* (Orig. pub. 1961) Nelson, 1971. Illus. by Rowel Friers. 127 pp. Gr. 4–6. *Best Specs* is the British sequel. (KR 39: 366; LJ 96: 3469)

MASEFIELD, John. *The Midnight Folk: A Novel.* (Orig. pub. 1927) Macmillan, 1932. Illus. by Rowland Hilder. 282 pp. Gr. 4–6. The sequel is *The Box of Delights, or When the Wolves Were Running* (1935). (BL 24: 284 and 287, 28: 396 and 401; TLS 1927 p. 906)

MAYNE, William. *The Blue Boat.* Dutton, 1960. Illus. by Geraldine Spence. 173 pp. Gr. 4–6. (BL 56: 609; KR 28: 49; LJ 85: 2479)

MEIGS, Cornelia. *The Wonderful Locomotive.* Macmillan, 1928. 104 pp. Gr. 3–5. (HB 20: 347)

MONATH, Elizabeth. *Topper and the Giant.* Viking, 1960. Illus. by the author. 60 pp. Gr. 4–6. (HB 36: 216; KR 28: 144; LJ 85: 2029)

MORETON, John. *Punky, Mouse for a Day.* Putnam, 1965. Illus. by Murray Tinkelman. 60 pp. Gr. 3–5. (LJ 90: 963; TLS 1962 p. 391)

NORTH, Joan. *The Cloud Forest.* Farrar, 1966. 180 pp. Gr. 5–8. (BL 63: 326; CCBB 20: 96; HB 42: 564; Suth: 297; TLS 1965 p. 1133)

PALMER, Mary. *The Teaspoon Tree.* Houghton, 1963. Illus. by Carlota Dodge. 114 pp. Gr. 3–5. (HB 39: 174; LJ 88: 1769)

PEARCE, (Ann) Philippa. *Mrs. Cockle's Cat.* Lippincott, 1962. Illus. by

Antony Maitland. 32 pp. Gr. 2–4. (BL 58: 694; HB 38: 172; LJ 87: 2026; TLS Dec 1, 1961 p. xiv)

RINKOFF, Barbara. *The Dragon's Handbook.* See Chapter 8E, Dragons: Out-of-Print Works.

SAWYER, Ruth. *The Enchanted Schoolhouse.* See Chapter 8N, Leprechauns: Out-of-Print Works.

SCHMIDT, Annie. *Wiplala.* Abelard, 1962. Tr. by Henrietta Anthony. Illus. by Jerry Dalenoord. 160 pp. Gr. 5–7. (HB 38: 605)

SEREDY, Kate. *Lazy Tinka.* See Chapter 1, Allegory and Fable: Out-of-Print Works.

SHURA, Mary. *A Shoe Full of Shamrock.* Atheneum, 1965. Illus. by N. M. Bodecker. 64 pp. Gr. 3–5. (BL 62: 222; CCBB 19: 68; Eakin: 299; HB 41: 500; KR 33: 677; LJ 90: 4622)

SLEIGH, Barbara. *Carbonel: The King of the Cats.* See Chapter 9, Talking Animals: Out-of-Print Works.

TARN, Sir William. *Treasure of the Isle of Mist: A Tale of the Isle of Skye.* (Orig. pub. 1920) Putnam, 1934. Illus. by Robert Lawson. 192 pp. Gr. 4–6. (BL 17: 119, 31: 38; TLS 1919 p. 740)

URQUHART, Elizabeth. *Horace.* See Chapter 8E, Dragons: Out-of-Print Works.

WARD, Patricia. *The Secret Pencil.* Random, 1960. Illus. by Nicole Hornby. 277 pp. Gr. 5–7. (HB 36: 217; KR 28: 90; LJ 85: 2045)

WATSON, Sally. *Magic at Wynchwood.* See Chapter 5B, Imaginary Lands: Out-of-Print Works.

WHITE, T. H. *Mistress Masham's Repose.* See Chapter 8Q, Miniature People: Out-of-Print Works.

WILLIAMS, Ursula Moray. *The Moonball.* (Orig. pub. 1958) Hawthorne, 1967. Illus. by Jane Paton. 138 pp. Gr. 3–5. (Arb: 243; BL 63: 1194; CCBB 21: 19; HB 43: 344; KR 35: 201; LJ 92: 2024; Suth: 425)

WUORIO, Eva-Lis. *The Happiness Flower.* World, 1969. Illus. by Don Bolognese. 78 pp. Gr. 3–5. (BL 65: 1228; LJ 94: 2507)

WUORIO, Eva-Lis. *Tal and the Magic Barruget.* World, 1965. Illus. by Bettina. 76 pp. Gr. 3–5. (BL 62: 414; HB 41: 630; KR 33: 981; LJ 91: 430)

YOLEN, Jane. *The Wizard of Washington Square.* See Chapter 13, Witches, Wizards, Sorcerers, and Magicians: Out-of-Print Works.

YORK, Carol. *Miss Know-It-All: A Butterfield Square Story.* Watts, 1966. Illus. by Victoria de Larrea. 87 pp. Gr. 3–5. The sequels are *The Christmas Dolls* (1967) and *Miss Know-It-All Returns* (1972). (CCBB 20: 52; LJ 91: 4345)

ZOLOTOW, Charlotte. *The Man with Purple Eyes.* Abelard-Shuman, 1961. Illus. by Joe Lasker. 60 pp. Gr. 2–4. (HB 37: 340)

7

Magical Toys

Tales of toys that talk or exhibit other magical abilities are listed in this chapter. Most are about dolls, but there are a few about carousel horses, stuffed animals, toy soldiers, and windup toys. This type of fantasy seems to have been more common in the past; this is the only category in which there are more entries in the out-of-print list at the of the chapter than in the inprint section.

ANASTASIO, Dina. *A Question of Time.* See Chapter 3, Ghosts.

AVERY, Gillian, ed. *Victorian Doll Stories, by Brenda, Mrs. Gatty and Frances Hodgson Burnett* (British title: *Victoria-Bess and Others*). Schocken, 1969. 141 pp. Gr. 3–6. [A]
Three British doll stories from the Victorian era: *Victoria-Bess* by Smith (n.d.), *Aunt Sally's Life* by Gatty (1862), and *Racketty-Packetty House* by Burnett (1907). (LJ 95: 1192; TLS 1968 p. 589)

BACON, Martha. *Moth Manor: A Gothic Tale.* Atlantic-Little, 1978. Illus. by Gail Burroughs. 160 pp. Gr. 5–7. [A]
A ghostly moth sparks Monica's interest in the mystery surrounding her great-aunt's dollhouse. (BL 75: 42; CCBB 32: 93; KR 46: 1188; SLJ Sept'78 p. 130)

BAILEY, Carolyn S. *Miss Hickory.* Viking, 1946. Illus. by Ruth Gannett. 123 pp. Gr. 3–5. [R]
Miss Hickory, a doll with a hickory-nut head, forgotten by her family, has a winter full of adventure. Newbery Medal. (Arb: 226; BL 43: 74; CC: 482; HB 22: 465; KR 14: 387; LJ 71: 1544)

BIANCO, Margery Williams. *The Little Wooden Doll.* Macmillan, 1925. Illus. by Pamela Bianco. 65 pp. Gr. 2–4. [A]
A lonely doll found in the attic becomes a princess doll. (BL 22: 121; CC: 487)

* BIANCO, Margery Williams. *The Velveteen Rabbit; or, How Toys Became Real.* (Orig. pub. 1926) Doubleday, 1958. Illus. by William Nicholson. 44 pp. Gr. 1–4.
A worn-out velveteen rabbit becomes real after it has been thrown away. (Adv: 203; Arb: 236; CC: 579)

BURNETT, Frances Hodgson. *Racketty-Packetty House.* See Chapter 8H, Fairies.

CLARKE, Pauline. *The Return of the Twelves* (British title: *The Twelve and the Genii*). Coward, 1963. Illus. by Bernarda Bryson. 251 pp. Gr. 3–6. [R]
Max Morley discovers that his twelve toy soldiers are alive, and he helps them reach their ancestral home. Carnegie Medal. (Arb: 226; BL 60: 701; CC: 500; Eakin: 74; HB 39: 602; LJ 89: 390; TLS 1962 p. 901)

COATSWORTH, Elizabeth. *All-of-a-Sudden Susan.* Macmillan, 1974. Illus. by Richard Cuffari. 74 pp. Gr. 3–5. [A]
Susan and her magic doll, Emelida, are lost during a flood. (BL 71: 506; CCBB 28: 128; KR 42: 1303; SLJ Mar'75 p. 86)

COATSWORTH, Elizabeth. *The Snow Parlor and Other Bedtime Stories.* See Chapter 2, Collected Tales.

COLLODI, Carlo (pseud. of Carlo Lorenzini). *The Adventures of Pinocchio.* (Orig. pub. 1882) Macmillan, 1969. Tr. by Carol Della Chiesa. Illus. by Attilio Mussino. 310 pp. Gr. 4 up. [R]
Pinocchio, a wooden puppet, yearns to be a real boy. (Arb: 223; BL 12: 299, 21: 238, 60: 387; CC: 504; HB 27: 260)

ESTES, Eleanor. *The Witch Family.* See Chapter 13, Witches, Wizards, Sorcerers, and Magicians.

FIELD, Rachel. *Hitty, Her First Hundred Years.* (Orig. pub. 1929) Macmillan, 1937. Illus. by Dorothy Lathrop. 207 pp. Gr. 4–6. [R]
The adventures of a carved-wood doll named Hitty include being shipwrecked while traveling from Maine to the South Seas. Newbery Medal. (Arb: 226; BL 26: 125; CC: 517; HB 5: 53, 6: 22)

GREENWALD, Sheila (pseud. of Sheila Green). *The Secret Museum.* Lippincott, 1974. Illus. by the author. 127 pp. Gr. 3–5. [A]
Jennifer comes upon some antique dolls who agree to take part in plays to earn money to help Jennifer's parents. (Adv: 239; BL 70: 1104; CCBB 27: 177; KR 42: 424; LJ 99: 1473)

HAYES, Geoffrey. *Patrick Comes to Puttyville and Other Stories.* Harper, 1978. Illus. by the author. 118 pp. Gr. K–4. [M]
A toy bear named Patrick moves to the country with his mother after his father deserts them. This is the sequel to *Bear by Himself* (1976). (BL 75: 546; CCBB 32: 117; KR 46: 1357; SLJ Oct'78 p. 145)

HOBAN, Russell. *The Mouse and His Child.* See Chapter 1, Allegory and Fable.

JONES, Elizabeth Orton. *Big Susan.* (Orig. pub. 1947) Macmillan, 1967. Illus. by the author. 82 pp. Gr. 2–4. [R]
The dolls in Susan's dollhouse give her a surprise on Christmas Eve. (BL 44: 138; CC: 536; HB 24: 39; KR 15: 547; LJ 72: 1692)

KROEBER, Theodora. *Carrousel.* Atheneum, 1977. Illus. by Douglas Tait. 91 pp. Gr. 2–4. [A]
When Pegason, the winged horse, falls into a giant city, his friends Gryphon and Pyggon must rescue him. (CCBB 31: 97; HB 53: 664; KR 45: 1198; SLJ Nov'77 p. 49)

LAMORISSE, Albert. *The Red Balloon.* See Chapter 1, Allegory and Fable.

* MILNE, A(lan) A(lexander). *Winnie-the-Pooh.* (Orig. pub. 1926) Dutton, 1954. Illus. by Ernest Shepard. 161 pp. Gr. 2–4.
The adventures of Christopher Robin and his friends, Winnie-the-Pooh, Tigger, Eeyore, Piglet, Rabbit, Owl, Kanga, and Baby Roo; including the times Pooh tangles with some honeybees, and Piglet meets a Heffalump. The sequels are: *The House at Pooh Corner* (1961; orig. pub. 1928) and *The Hums of Pooh* (1930); collections of tales about Pooh include *The World of Pooh* (1957), *The Pooh Story Book* (1965), and *The Christopher Robin Story Book* (1966). (Adv: 273; Arb: 223; BL 23: 137; CC: 552; KR 39: 1213; TLS 1926 p. 861, 1971 p. 1614)

O'CONNELL, Jean. *The Dollhouse Caper.* Crowell, 1976. Illus. by Erik Blegvad. 87 pp. Gr. 4–6. [R]
Although the Dollhouse family is unable to warn the Humans about an upcoming robbery, they manage to scare the burglars off by themselves. (Arb: 226; BL 72: 1049; CC 1977 Suppl. p. 67; CCBB 29: 149; HB 52: 291; KR 44: 70; SLJ Apr'76 p. 63)

SHECTER, Ben. *The Stocking Child.* Harper, 1976. Illus. by the author. 32 pp. Gr. 2–3. [A]

Sam and his friend, Epaphroditus, search for a missing button eye far and wide and wind up at Sam's own house. (BL 73: 669; CCBB 30: 114; KR 44: 1038; SLJ Jan'77 p. 85)

SLEATOR, William. *Among the Dolls.* Dutton, 1975. Illus. by Trina Schart Hyman. 70 pp. Gr. 4–6. [R]
Vicky learns a painful lesson when she shrinks to doll size and must suffer the ill-temper of the dolls she had mistreated. (Adv: 201; BL 72: 628; CCBB 29: 118; HB 52: 53; KR 43: 1186; SLJ Dec'75 p. 55)

SLOBODKIN, Louis. *The Adventures of Arab.* (Orig. pub. 1946) Vanguard, 1967. 123 pp. Gr. 3–4. [A]
Arab is not happy as a merry-go-round horse, so he changes places with a coach horse. (BL 43: 158; HB 22: 349; KR 14: 386)

TREGARTHEN, Enys. *The Doll Who Came Alive.* Day, 1972 (Repr. of 1942 ed.). Ed. by Elizabeth Yates. Illus. by Nora Unwin. 75 pp. Gr. 3–5. [R]
A little girl's great love for her wooden doll brings it to life. (BL 69: 911; CCBB 26: 33; HB 48: 596; KR 40: 860; LJ 98: 1009; TLS 1973 p. 387)

YORK, Susannah. *Lark's Castle.* See Chapter 13, Witches, Wizards, Sorcerers, and Magicians.

YOUNG, Miriam. *The Witch Mobile.* See Chapter 13, Witches, Wizards, Sorcerers, and Magicians.

Magical Toys: Out-of-Print Works

ALBRECHT, Lillie. *Deborah Remembers.* Hastings, 1959. Illus. by Rita Newton. 111 pp. Gr. 4–6. (BL 56: 246; HB 38: 381; KR 27: 548)

AVERILL, Esther. *The Adventures of Jack Ninepins.* Harper, 1944. 63 pp. Gr. 3–4. (HB 20: 471 and 480; KR 12: 399; LJ 69: 863 and 1104)

BAKER, Margaret Joyce. *The Shoe Shop Bears.* Ariel, 1965. 96 pp. Gr. 4–5. The sequels are *Hannibal and the Bears* (1966), *Bears Back in Business* (1967), and *Hi Jinks Joins the Bears* (1969). (CCBB 19: 41; LJ 90: 3785; TLS 1964 p. 605)

BANÉR, Skulda V. *Pims, Adventures of a Dala Horse.* McKay, 1964. Illus. by Vera Bock. 148 pp. Gr. 4–5. (KR 32: 738)

BEMELMANS, Ludwig. *The Happy Place.* Little, 1952. Illus. by the author. 58 pp. Gr. 2–4. (KR 20: 499; LJ 77: 1661)

BIANCO, Margery Williams. *Poor Cecco.* (Orig. pub. 1925) Doubleday, 1945. Illus. by Arthur Rackham. 175 pp. Gr. 2–4. (BL 22: 121; HB 2: 13, 19 and 21; TLS 1925 p. 809)

BIANCO, Pamela. *Little Houses Far Away.* Oxford, 1951. Illus. by the author. 87 pp. Gr. 1–4. (BL 48: 174; HB 27: 324; KR 19: 614; LJ 76: 2009)

BIANCO, Pamela. *Toy Rose.* Lippincott, 1957. 91 pp. Gr. 3–4. (HB 33: 398; KR 25: 479; LJ 82: 3241)

BLOCH, Marie. *The Dollhouse Story.* Walck, 1961. Illus. by Walter Erhard. 63 pp. Gr. 3–5. (BL 58: 488; HB 38: 176)

BRINK, Carol. *Andy Buckram's Tin Men.* See Chapter 10, Tall Tales: Out-of-Print Works.

BROWN, Abbie. *The Lonesomest Doll.* (Orig. pub. 1901) Houghton, 1928. 80 pp. Gr. 2–4. (BL 25: 173)

BUCK, David. *The Small Adventures of Dog.* Watts, 1969. Illus. by the author. 76 pp. Gr. 3–5. (CCBB 24: 5; LJ 95: 778; TLS 1968 p. 1376)

BYARS, Betsy. *Clementine.* Houghton, 1962. Illus. by Charles Wilton. 70 pp. Gr. 3–4. (KR 30: 280)

CLARE, Helen (pseud. of Pauline Clarke). *Five Dolls in a House.* Prentice-Hall, 1965. Illus. by Aliki (Brandenberg). 143 pp. Gr. 3–5. The sequels are *Five Dolls in the Snow* (1967), *Five Dolls and Their Friends* (British), *Five Dolls and the Duke* (British), and *Five Dolls and the Monkey* (British). (CCBB 19: 145; HB 41: 627; LJ 91: 1696; TLS 1961 p. 451)

FAIRSTAR, Mrs. (pseud. of Richard Horne). *Memoirs of a London Doll, Written by Herself.* (Orig. pub. 1846). Macmillan, 1968. Illus. by Margaret Gillies and Richard Smith. 143 pp. Gr. 4–6. (Arb: 239; BL 65: 257; CCBB 22: 79; HB 44: 560; KR 36: 642; TLS 1967 p. 1143)

FARJEON, Eleanor. *The Little Bookroom: Eleanor Farjeon's Short Stories for Children Chosen by Herself.* See Chapter 2, Collected Tales: Out-of-Print Works.

FLETCHER, David. *The Village of Hidden Wishes.* Pantheon, 1960. Illus. by Dorothea Stefula. 157 pp. Gr. 3–5. (KR 28: 185; LJ 85: 2477)

GODDEN, Rumer. *Candy Floss.* Viking, 1959. Illus. by Adrienne Adams. 63 pp. Gr. 2–4. (Arb: 225; BL 56: 633; Eakin: 141; HB 36: 212; KR 28: 144; LJ 85: 247; TLS Nov 25, 1960 p. iv)

GODDEN, Rumer. *The Dolls' House.* (Orig. pub. 1947) Viking, 1962. Illus. by Tasha Tudor. 136 pp. Gr. 3–5. (Arb: 225; BL 45: 53, 59: 292; CC: 524; Eakin: 141; HB 24: 347 and 457, 39: 75; KR 16: 363; LJ 73: 1097; TLS 1947 p. 636)

GODDEN, Rumer. *The Fairy Doll.* Viking, 1956. Illus. by Adrienne Adams.

67 pp. Gr. 2–4. (Arb: 225; BL 53: 51; HB 34: 453; KR 24: 431; TLS Nov 23, 1956 p. xv)

GODDEN, Rumer. *Home Is the Sailor.* Viking, 1964. Illus. by Jean Primrose. 128 pp. Gr. 3–5. (Arb: 225; CC: 524; Eakin: 141; HB 41: 56; LJ 90: 960; TLS 1964 p. 1081)

GODDEN, Rumer. *Impunity Jane: The Story of a Pocket Doll.* Viking, 1954. Illus. by Adrienne Adams. 47 pp. Gr. 2–4. (Arb: 225; BL 51: 47; CC: 524; Eakin: 142; HB 30: 330; KR 22: 383)

GODDEN, Rumer. *Miss Happiness and Miss Flower.* Viking, 1961. Illus. by Jean Primrose. 81 pp. Gr. 3–5. The sequel is *Little Plum* (1962). (Arb: 225; BL 57: 580; Eakin: 142; HB 37: 269; KR 29: 328; LJ 86: 1983; TLS May 19, 1961 p. iv)

GODDEN, Rumer. *The Story of Holly and Ivy.* Viking, 1957. Illus. by Adrienne Adams. 64 pp. Gr. 2–4. (Arb: 225; BL 55: 53; Eakin: 143; HB 34: 461; KR 26: 453; LJ 83: 3572; TLS Nov 21, 1958 p. xv)

JOHNSON, Crockett. *Ellen's Lion: Twelve Stories.* See Chapter 2, Collected Tales: Out-of-Print Works.

LATHROP, Dorothy. *An Angel in the Woods.* (Orig. pub. 1947) Macmillan, 1955. 42 pp. Gr. 2–4. (BL 44: 156; HB 24: 37; KR 15: 578; LJ 72: 1784)

McGAVIN, Moyra. *The House in the Attic.* Coward, 1966. Illus. by Eileen Armitage. 96 pp. Gr. 4–6. (HB 42: 711)

NESBIT, E. *The Magic City.* See Chapter 12, Travel to Another World: Out-of-Print Works.

PARRISH, Anne. *Floating Island.* Harper, 1930. Illus. by the author. 265 pp. Gr. 3–6. (BL 27: 214; HB 7: 60; TLS 1930 p. 1043)

SYMONDS, John. *Away to the Moon.* Lippincott, 1956. Illus. by Pamela Bianco. 64 pp. Gr. 2–4. (BL 53: 101; HB 32: 349; KR 24: 571)

WILLIAMS, Ursula Moray. *Adventures of the Little Wooden Horse.* Lippincott, 1939. Illus. by Joyce Brisley. 204 pp. Gr. 5–7. (LJ 65: 37)

WILLIAMS, Ursula Moray. *The Toymaker's Daughter.* Meredith, 1969. Illus. by Shirley Hughes. 134 pp. Gr. 4–6. *The Three Toymakers* (Nelson, 1971) and *Malkin's Mountain* (Nelson, 1972) are the sequels. (Arb: 243; CCBB 23: 68; HB 45: 538; KR 37: 507; LJ 94: 3209; TLS 1968 p. 1377)

8

Mythical Beings and Creatures

Many fantasies present characters that exist only in folktales, myth, or the author's imagination. For easy access to books about specific creatures, this chapter has been subdivided into twenty-three sections. Categories with less than three books are grouped together in a final subsection. Tales of dinosaurs living in modern times have been included in this chapter.

The subdivisions are: angels, brownies, demons, devils, and imps, dinosaurs, dragons, dwarfs, elves, fairies (faery people, fair folk, ferlies, little people), genies, giants, gnomes, goblins, griffins, leprechauns, magical horses, mermaids and sea people (kelpies, water nymphs, water sprites, undines), miniature people, monsters and sea serpents, the phoenix, seal people, trolls (peikkos), unicorns, and other mythical beings and creatures.

A. ANGELS

CAMPBELL, Hope. *Peter's Angel: A Story about Monsters.* See Chapter 9, Talking Animals.

KENNEDY, Richard. *The Blue Stone.* See Chapter 6, Magic Adventure.

TAZEWELL, Charles. *The Littlest Angel.* See Chapter 1, Allegory and Fable.

Angels: Out-of-Print Works

VASILIU, Mircea. *Hark the Little Angel.* Day, 1965. Illus. by the author. 48 pp. Gr. 3–5. (CCBB 19: 71; KR 33: 979; LJ 90: 4530)

B. BROWNIES

HUNTER, Mollie. *A Furl of Fairy Wind: Four Stories.* See Chapter 8H, Fairies.

Brownies: Out-of-Print Works

McGOWEN, Tom. *Sir Machinery.* See Chapter 13, Witches, Wizards, Sorcerers, and Magicians: Out-of-Print Works.

MULOCK, Diana (pseud. of Dinah Craik). *The Adventures of a Brownie as Told to My Child.* (Orig. pub. 1872) Macmillan, 1952. Illus. by Mary Seaman. 122 pp. Gr. 3–5. (BL 15: 153, 20: 224; HB 28: 422)

C. DEMONS, DEVILS, AND IMPS

* BABBITT, Natalie. *The Devil's Storybook.* Farrar, 1974. Illus. by the author. 101 pp. Gr. 4–6.
Ten tales of Satan's battles with humans. (Adv: 182; Arb: 236; BL 71: 37 and 765; CC: 584; CCBB 28: 58; HB 50: 134; KR 42: 679; TLS 1976 p. 882)

HOKE, Helen, ed. *Devils, Devils, Devils.* Watts, 1976. Illus. by Carol Barker. 216 pp. Gr. 5–8. [A]
This devilish collection includes "The Devil and Daniel Webster" by Benet, "The Bottle Imp" by Stevenson, "The Devil in the Churchyard" by Lovecraft, and French, Italian, Jewish, and Welsh folktales. (BL 72: 1184; JHC 1976 Suppl. p. 59; SLJ Sept'76 p. 117)

HUNTER, Mollie (pseud. of Maureen McIlwraith). *The Wicked One.* Harper, 1977. 128 pp. Gr. 5–9. [R]
Scottsman Colin Grant moves his family to America to avoid the devilish tricks of the Grollican, only to find that the Grollican has followed them. (BL 73: 1339 and 1352; CC 1978 Suppl. p. 51; CCBB 30: 160; HB 53: 442; KR 45: 426; SLJ May'77 pp. 36 and 62)

NORTON, André. *Here Abide Monsters.* See Chapter 12, Travel to Another World.

PRICE, Susan. *The Devil's Piper.* See Chapter 4, Good versus Evil.

SINGER, Isaac Bashevis. *Naftali the Storyteller and His Horse, Sus, and Other Stories.* See Chapter 2, Collected Tales.

SINGER, Isaac Bashevis. *Zlateh the Goat and Other Stories.* See Chapter 2, Collected Tales.

Demons, Devils, and Imps: Out-of-Print Works

BINNS, Archie. *The Radio Imp*. See Chapter 6, Magic Adventure: Out-of-Print Works.

GRIPARI, Pierre. *Tales of the Rue Broca*. See Chapter 2, Collected Tales: Out-of-Print Works.

McGOWEN, Tom. *Sir Machinery*. See Chapter 13, Witches, Wizards, Sorcerers, and Magicians: Out-of-Print Works.

D. DINOSAURS

BONHAM, Frank. *The Friends of the Loony Lake Monster*. Dutton, 1972. 135 pp. Gr. 4-6. [R]
The baby dinosaur hatched from an orange egg adopts Gussie as its mother. (BL 69: 711; CC: 489; CCBB 26: 71; KR 40: 1097; LJ 97: 3803)

BUTTERWORTH, Oliver. *The Enormous Egg*. Little, 1956. Illus. by Louis Darling. 187 pp. Gr. 4-7. [R]
Nate Twitchell's new pet, hatched from a leatherlike egg, turns out, to the amazement of the world's scientists, to be a baby Triceratops. *The Narrow Passage* (1973) is the sequel. (Arb: 228; BL 52: 298; Eakin: 56; HB 32: 187; KR 24: 45; LJ 81: 1042)

LAMPMAN, Evelyn. *The Shy Stegosaurus of Cricket Creek*. Doubleday, 1955. Illus. by Hubert Buel. 218 pp. Gr. 5-8. [R]
A shy dinosaur named George helps Joey and Joan capture a thief on their Oregon ranch. *The Shy Stegosaurus of Indian Springs* (1962) is the sequel. (BL 52: 150; CC: 540; HB 31: 377; LJ 80: 2386)

Dinosaurs: Out-of-Print Works

CORBETT, Scott. *Ever Ride a Dinosaur?* Holt, 1969. Illus. by Mircea Vasiliu. 128 pp. Gr. 4-6. (Arb: 228; CCBB 23: 41; HB 45: 409; KR 37: 558; LJ 94: 2111; Suth: 91)

PALMER, Mary. *The Teaspoon Tree*. See Chapter 6, Magic Adventure: Out-of-Print Works.

E. DRAGONS

BAKER, Betty. *Save Sirrushany!* (*Also Agotha, Princess Gwyn and All the Fearsome Beasts*). See Chapter 5B, Imaginary Lands.

BROUN, Heywood. *The Fifty-first Dragon*. Prentice-Hall, 1968. Illus. by Ed Emberley. 48 pp. Gr. 3 up [M]
Gwain Le Coeur-Hardy's magic talisman helps him slay fifty dragons, but his luck changes when he goes after the fifty-first. (HB 45: 176; KR 36: 1216; LJ 94: 3816)

CURLEY, Daniel. *Billy Beg and the Bull*. See Chapter 6, Magic Adventure.

DAWSON, Mary. *Tegwyn, the Last of the Welsh Dragons*. Parents, 1967. Illus. by Ingrid Fetz. 92 pp. Gr. 4–5. [A]
Megan and Hugh adopt a baby dragon who hatched from an egg at the bottom of a Welsh lake. (HB 43: 461; LJ 92: 2648)

GANNETT, Ruth. *My Father's Dragon*. Random, 1948. Illus. by the author. 86 pp. Gr. 3–5. [R]
When a stray alley cat tells him of a captive baby dragon, Elmer Elevator decides to run away and rescue it. *Elmer and the Dragon* (1950) and *The Dragons of Blueland* (1951) are the sequels. (BL 44: 320; CC: 522; HB 24: 266; KR 16: 194; LJ 73: 824)

GARDNER, John. *Dragon, Dragon, and Other Tales*. See Chapter 2, Collected Tales.

* GRAHAME, Kenneth. *The Reluctant Dragon*. (Orig. pub. 1938) Holiday, 1953. Illus. by Ernest Shepard. Unp. Gr. 4–6.
St. George and his young friend find a dragon that is not at all like the one they had intended to slay. (Arb: 239; BL 35: 143; CC: 525; Eakin: 146; HB 15: 29; LJ 64: 118)

HUGHES, Ted. *The Iron Giant: A Story in Five Nights*. See Chapter 8J, Giants.

KIMMEL, Margaret. *Magic in the Mist*. See Chapter 13, Witches, Wizards, Sorcerers, and Magicians.

KRENSKY, Stephen. *The Dragon Circle*. Atheneum, 1977. Illus. by A. Delaney. 116 pp. Gr. 4–6. [A]
The Wynd children are kidnapped by five dragons who plan to use the children's magic powers to search for treasure. (BL 74: 477; CCBB 31: 97; KR 45: 728; SLJ Oct'77 p. 115)

KRENSKY, Stephen. *The Perils of Putney*. See Chapter 5B, Imaginary Lands.

LEE, Tanith. *The Dragon Hoard*. See Chapter 5B, Imaginary Lands.

LINDGREN, Astrid. *The Brothers Lionheart*. See Chapter 1, Allegory and Fable.

LIVELY, Penelope. *The Whispering Knights*. See Chapter 6, Magic Adventure.

LLOYD, Norris. *The Desperate Dragons*. Hastings, 1960. Illus. by Joan Payne. 64 pp. Gr. 2–4. [A]
A young cowherd shows up all the knights of Rondo by chasing the last twelve

dragons on earth out of the kingdom. (HB 36: 289; KR 28: 88; LJ 85: 2041)

McCAFFREY, Anne. *Dragonsong*. Atheneum, 1976. 204 pp. Gr. 6-9. [R] Angered by her people's refusal to let a "mere woman" become a harper, Menolly runs away to make her home with a family of fire dragons. *Dragonsinger* (1977) and *Dragondrums* (1979) are the sequels, and *Dragonflight* (1968), *Dragonquest* (1975), and *The White Dragon* (1978) are adult novels set in the land of Pern. (BL 72: 1253 and 1266; CC 1977 Suppl. p. 66; CCBB 29: 177; HB 52: 406; JHC 1977 Suppl. p. 45; KR 44: 391; SLJ Apr'76 p. 91)

NESBIT, E. (pseud. of Edith Bland). *The Complete Book of Dragons*. (Orig. pub. 1899) Macmillan, 1973. Illus. by Erik Blegvad. 198 pp. Gr. 4-6. [R] Nine tales about children confronting dragons, including "The Ice Dragon," "The Dragon Tamers," and "The Last of the Dragons." (BL 69: 911; CC: 587; CCBB 26: 142; HB 49: 272; KR 41: 6)

NORTON, André. *Dragon Magic*. See Chapter 11, Time Travel.

POMERANTZ, Charlotte. *Detective Poufy's First Case: Or the Missing Battery-Operated Pepper Grinder*. See Chapter 10, Tall Tales.

REIT, Seymour. *Benvenuto*. Addison-Wesley, 1974. Illus. by Will Winslow. 126 pp. Gr. 4-5. [A]
The Bruno family apartment is not exactly the best place to raise a baby dragon, as Paolo finds out after he brings one home from camp. (BL 70: 878; KR 42: 301; LJ 99: 2276)

SELFRIDGE, Oliver. *The Trouble with Dragons*. See Chapter 5B, Imaginary Lands.

SHURA, Mary. *The Nearsighted Knight*. See Chapter 5B, Imaginary Lands.

SILVERBERG, Barbara. *Phoenix Feathers: A Collection of Mythical Monsters*. See Chapter 2, Collected Tales.

STEARNS, Pamela. *Into the Painted Bear Lair*. See Chapter 12, Travel to Another World.

TERLOUW, Jan. *How to Become King*. See Chapter 5B, Imaginary Lands.

TOLKIEN, J(ohn) R(onald) R(euel). *Farmer Giles of Ham*. (Orig. pub. 1949) Houghton, 1978. Illus. by Pauline Baynes. 78 pp. Gr. 5 up [A]
Farmer Giles leads a simple life until the day he finds himself protecting his village from dragons. (Arb: 242; HB 26: 287; LJ 75: 2084)

TOLKIEN, J. R. R. *The Hobbit; or There and Back Again*. See Chapter 4, Good versus Evil.

WILLIAMS, Jay. *The Practical Princess*. See Chapter 5B, Imaginary Lands.

Dragons: Out-of-Print Works

ANCKARSVÄRD, Karin. *Bonifacius the Green*. (Orig. pub. 1952) Abelard-Schuman, 1961. Tr. by C. M. Anckarsvärd and K. H. Beales. Illus. by Ingrid Rossell. 95 pp. Gr. 3–5. (KR 30: 7; LJ 87: 1314; TLS Dec 4, 1961 p. vii)

BENDICK, Jeanne. *The Goodknight Ghost*. See Chapter 3, Ghosts: Out-of-Print Works.

BRIGHT, Robert. *Richard Brown and the Dragon*. Doubleday, 1952. Retold from an anecdote by Samuel Clemens. 81 pp. Gr. 2–4. (BL 49: 18; HB 28: 319; KR 20: 498; LJ 77: 1661)

COOPER, Paul Fenimore. *Dindle*. Putnam, 1963. Illus. by Marion Cooper. 64 pp. Gr. 3–5. (HB 40: 174; LJ 89: 951)

DILLON, Eilis. *King Big Ears*. See Chapter 5B, Imaginary Lands: Out-of-Print Works.

FORESTER, Cecil. *Poo Poo and the Dragons*. See Chapter 10, Tall Tales: Out-of-Print Works.

FOSTER, Malcolm. *The Prince with a Hundred Dragons*. Doubleday, 1963. Illus. by Barbara Remington. 60 pp. Gr. 3–5. (KR 31: 656; LJ 88: 4083)

HILDICK, E(dmond) W. *The Dragon That Lived under Manhattan*. Crown, 1970. Illus. by Harold Berson. 62 pp. Gr. 3–4. (BL 67: 420; KR 38: 1143; LJ 95: 4337)

HODGES, Elizabeth. *The Three Princes of Serendip*. See Chapter 5B, Imaginary Lands: Out-of-Print Works.

HOUGH, Charlotte. *Red Biddy and Other Stories*. See Chapter 2, Collected Tales: Out-of-Print Works.

JOHNSON, Elizabeth. *The Little Knight*. See Chapter 5B, Imaginary Lands: Out-of-Print Works.

MANNING, Rosemary. *Green Smoke*. Doubleday, 1957. Illus. by Constance Marshall. 160 pp. Gr. 4–6. The sequels are *Dragon in Danger* (1959), *The Dragon's Quest* (1962), and a British sequel, *Dragon in Summer*. (KR 26: 378; LJ 83: 310)

MONTROSE, Anne. *The Winter Flower and Other Fairy Stories*. See Chapter 2, Collected Tales: Out-of-Print Works.

PALMER, Mary. *The Magic Knight*. See Chapter 5B, Imaginary Lands: Out-of-Print Works.

PARKER, Edgar. *The Question of a Dragon*. Pantheon, 1964. Illus. by the author. 43 pp. Gr. 3–5. (CCBB 19: 16; HB 40: 283; LJ 89: 2661)

READ, Elfrieda. *The Magical Egg*. See Chapter 5B, Imaginary Lands: Out-of-Print Works.

RINKOFF, Barbara. *The Dragon's Handbook*. Nelson, 1966. Illus. by Kelly Oechsli. 112 pp. Gr. 4–6. (KR 34: 753; LJ 91: 5238)

SAWYER, Ruth. *The Year of the Christmas Dragon*. Viking, 1960. Illus. by Hugh Troy. 88 pp. Gr. 4–6. (BL 57: 249; Eakin: 283; HB 36: 504; KR 28: 556; LJ 85: 4570)

SCHRANK, Joseph. *The Plain Princess and the Lazy Prince*. See Chapter 5B, Imaginary Lands: Out-of-Print Works.

URQUHART, Elizabeth. *Horace*. Dutton, 1951. Illus. by Rosita Pastor. 116 pp. Gr. 3–5. (BL 48: 38; HB 27: 325; KR 19: 387; LJ 76: 1433)

WEIR, Rosemary. *Albert the Dragon*. Abelard-Schuman, 1961. Illus. by Quentin Blake. 107 pp. Gr. 4–6. The sequels are *Further Adventures of Albert the Dragon* (1964) and *Albert the Dragon and the Centaur* (1968). *Albert and the Dragonettes* is the British sequel. (KR 29: 669)

WILLIAMS, Jay. *The Magical Storybook*. See Chapter 2, Collected Tales: Out-of-Print Works.

F. DWARFS

GARNER, Alan. *The Weirdstone of Brisingamen*. See Chapter 4, Good versus Evil.

KRENSKY, Stephen. *The Perils of Putney*. See Chapter 5B, Imaginary Lands.

TOLKIEN, J. R. R. *The Hobbit; or There and Back Again*. See Chapter 4, Good versus Evil.

Dwarfs: Out-of-Print Works

COOPER, Paul. *Dindle*. See Chapter 8E, Dragons: Out-of-Print Works.

HAUFF, Wilhelm. *Dwarf Long-Nose*. Random, 1960. Tr. by Doris Orgel. Illus. by Maurice Sendak. 60 pp. Gr. 3–5. (BL 57: 128; CC: 528; Eakin: 151; HB 36: 510; LJ 85: 3862)

G. ELVES

AIKEN, Joan. *A Necklace of Raindrops and Other Stories*. See Chapter 2, Collected Tales.

DAWSON, Mary. *Tinker Tales: A Humpty Dumpty Book*. Parents, 1973. Illus. by Jacqueline Chwast. 68 pp. Gr. 3–5. [M]

Eight adventures of an elf named Tinker and his friends, who try using witch remover on a Halloween pumpkin. (KR 41: 1157; LJ 99: 198)

DOLBIER, Maurice. *Torten's Christmas Secret.* Little, 1951. Illus. by Robert Henneberger. 61 pp. Gr. 2-4. [R]
Torten, one of Santa's elves, decides to make his own gifts for the not-so-good children overlooked by Santa. (Arb: 238; BL 48: 51; HB 27: 401 and 415; KR 19: 388; LJ 76: 1342)

HILL, Elizabeth. *Ever-After Island.* See Chapter 6, Magic Adventure.

Elves: Out-of-Print Works

BOWEN, William. *The Enchanted Forest.* See Chapter 2, Collected Tales: Out-of-Print Works.

CALHOUN, Mary. *Magic in the Alley.* See Chapter 6, Magic Adventure: Out-of-Print Works.

LAGERLÖF, Selma. *The Wonderful Adventures of Nils.* See Chapter 8Q, Miniature People: Out-of-Print Works.

LAWRENCE, Ann. *Tom Ass: Or the Second Gift.* See Chapter 6, Magic Adventure: Out-of-Print Works.

SLEIGH, Barbara. *Stirabout Stories, Brewed in Her Own Cauldron.* See Chapter 2, Collected Tales: Out-of-Print Works.

STOLZ, Mary. *The Leftover Elf.* Harper, 1952. Illus. by Peggy Bacon. 57 pp. Gr. 3-5. (HB 28: 172; KR 20: 188)

WUORIO, Eva-Lis. *Tal and the Magic Barruget.* See Chapter 6, Magic Adventure: Out-of-Print Works.

H. Fairies

AIKEN, Joan. *The Whispering Mountain.* See Chapter 5B, Imaginary Lands.

BARRIE, Sir J. M. *Peter Pan.* See Chapter 12, Travel to Another World.

BROCK, Betty. *No Flying in the House.* See Chapter 6, Magic Adventure.

BURNETT, Frances Hodgson. *Racketty-Packetty House.* (Orig. pub. 1906) Lippincott, 1975. Illus. by Holly Johnson. 60 pp. Gr. 3-5. [R]
When Cynthia replaces her tumbledown doll house with an elegant new one, Queen Crosspatch of the fairies steps in to save the old discarded dolls. This is the sequel to *Queen Silverbell* (Century, 1906). (Adv: 183; BL 2: 249, 72: 362; KR 43: 1065; LJ 95: 1192; SLJ Nov'75 p. 42; TLS 1968 p. 589)

ENRIGHT, Elizabeth. *Zeee.* Harcourt, 1965. Illus. by Irene Haas. 46 pp. Gr. 2-4. [R]

Careless humans always destroy Zeee's homes, until the temperamental fairy finds the perfect one in a most unlikely place. (Arb: 238; CC: 515; CCBB 18: 127; HB 41: 276; KR 33: 309; LJ 90: 2883)

GOUDGE, Elizabeth. *Smoky-House*. Buccaneer, 1976 (Repr. of 1940 ed.). Illus. by Richard Floethe. 286 pp. Gr. 5-8. [A]
Fairies help the Trequddick children save their father and neighbors from accusations of smuggling. (BL 37: 94; HB 16: 343 and 430; LJ 65: 849 and 878; TLS 1940 p. 634)

GREAVES, Margaret. *The Dagger and the Bird: A Story of Suspense*. Harper, 1975. Illus. by Laszlo Kubinyi. 144 pp. Gr. 4-7. [R]
When Bridget and Luke discover that their brother, Simon, is actually a fairy changeling, they journey to the Kingdom of the Good People to find their real brother. (BL 71: 618; HB 51: 147; KR 43: 374; SLJ May'75 p. 70)

HILL, Elizabeth. *Ever-After Island*. See Chapter 6, Magic Adventure.

HUNTER, Mollie (pseud. of Maureen McIlwraith). *A Furl of Fairy Wind: Four Stories*. Harper, 1977. Illus. by Stephen Gammell. 58 pp. Gr. 2-4. [R]
Four Scottish tales involving the fairy world: "The Brownie," "The Enchanted Boy," "Hi Johnny," and "A Furl of Fairy Wind." (BL 74: 613; CC 1978 Suppl. p. 57; CCBB 31: 142; HB 54: 47; KR 45: 1097; SLJ Sept'77 p. 109)

HUNTER, Mollie. *The Haunted Mountain: A Story of Suspense*. Harper, 1972. Illus. by Laszlo Kubinyi. 125 pp. Gr. 4-7. [R]
A stubborn Highlander named MacAllister, enslaved by the fairy folk for refusing to pay a tithe, is rescued by his dog and his son. (BL 68: 909; CC: 534; CCBB 26: 9; HB 48: 269; KR 40: 401; LJ 97: 1928; Suth: 203; TLS 1972 p. 1323)

INGELOW, Jean. *Mopsa the Fairy*. (Orig. pub. 1869) Dutton, 1964. Illus. by Dora Curtis and Diana Stanley. 142 pp. Gr. 4-6.
A boy named Jack crawls into the hollow of an old thorn tree and finds himself in Fairyland. (BL 60: 882; HB 40: 377)

IPCAR, Dahlov. *The Queen of Spells*. (Orig. pub. 1973) Dell, 1975 (pap.). 128 pp. Gr. 6-9. [R]
Janet can enter the Green World to save her lover only on Halloween night. (Adv: 190; BL 70: 51; CCBB 27: 45; KR 41: 396; LJ 98: 2665)

JOHNSON, Elizabeth. *Break a Magic Circle*. See Chapter 6, Magic Adventure.

JONES, Elizabeth. *Twig*. Macmillan, 1942. 152 pp. Gr. 3-5. [R]
A little girl named Twig, who believes in fairies, meets one who lives in a tomato can. (Arb: 240; BL 39: 256; CC: 537; HB 19: 102; LJ 67: 884, 68: 173)

KINGSLEY, Charles. *The Water Babies*. (Orig. pub. 1863) Garland, 1976. Illus. by Linley Sambourne. 372 pp. Gr. 4-6. [A]
After running away from his cruel master, Tom, an apprentice chimney sweep, is taken in by fairies who change him into a tiny water baby. (Arb: 210; BL 58: 352; HB 37: 549)

LYNCH, Patricia. *Brogeen Follows the Magic Tune*. See Chapter 8N, Leprechauns.

MAYNE, William. *A Grass Rope*. See Chapter 6, Magic Adventure.

MAYNE, William. *A Year and a Day*. Dutton, 1976. 86 pp. Gr. 4-6. [R]
Sara and Rebecca find a fairy changeling boy who brings happiness to their family, but only for a year and a day. (BL 72: 1528; CC 1977 Suppl. p. 66; CCBB 29: 178; HB 52: 398; KR 44: 391; SLJ Apr'76 p. 76; TLS 1976 p. 1241)

NESBIT, E. *The Five Children and It*. See Chapter 6, Magic Adventure.

NEWMAN, Sharon. *Dagda's Harp*. See Chapter 5B, Imaginary Lands.

* POPE, Elizabeth. *The Perilous Gard*. Houghton, 1974. Illus. by Richard Cuffari. 280 pp. Gr. 5-7.
The centuries-old spell surrounding the castle of Perilous Gard envelops Kate Sutton and she is enslaved by the Fairy Folk. (Adv: 197; BL 70: 1201; CC: 558; HB 50: 287; KR 42: 433; LJ 99: 1484)

STORR, Catherine. *Thursday*. Harper, 1972. 274 pp. Gr. 7-10. [A]
Bee Earnshaw believes that it was Thursday Townsend's involvement with the fairy folk, and not a nervous breakdown, that made him so lonely and withdrawn. (BL 69: 303; HB 49: 148; KR 40: 730; LJ 97: 3465)

THACKERAY, William M. *The Rose and the Ring; or the History of Prince Giglio and Prince Bulbo*. See Chapter 5B, Imaginary Lands.

TOLKIEN, J. R. R. *Smith of Wootton Major*. See Chapter 6, Magic Adventure.

TREGARTHEN, Enys. *The Doll Who Came Alive*. See Chapter 7, Magical Toys.

TURNBULL, Ann. *The Wolf King*. Seabury, 1976. 141 pp. Gr. 5-7. [R]
Grayla and Coll search the wolf-infested forest for their father and brother, aided by the Dark People and the magical Elder Folk. (Adv: 202; BL 72: 1339; JHC 1977 Suppl. p. 47; KR 44: 473; SLJ Sept'76 p. 126; TLS 1975 p. 1450)

WILLIAMS, Jay. *The Practical Princess*. See Chapter 5B, Imaginary Lands.

Fairies: Out-of-Print Works

ANDERSON, Mildred. *A Gift for Merimond*. See Chapter 5B, Imaginary Lands: Out-of-Print Works.

BAKER, Michael. *The Mountain and the Summer Stars: An Old Tale Newly Ended.* Harcourt, 1969. Illus. by Erika Weihs. 124 pp. Gr. 4–6. (BL 65: 1122; CCBB 23: 21; HB 45: 303; KR 37: 303; LJ 94: 1178; TLS 1968 p. 1113)

BERGENGREN, Ralph. *Susan and the Butterbees.* Longmans, 1947. Illus. by Anne Vaughan. 175 pp. Gr. 4–6. (HB 23: 212; KR 15: 163; LJ 72: 643)

BOWEN, William. *The Enchanted Forest.* See Chapter 2, Collected Tales: Out-of-Print Works.

COLUM, Padraic. *The Stone of Victory and Other Tales.* See Chapter 2, Collected Tales: Out-of-Print Works.

CREGAN, Mairin. *Old John.* Macmillan, 1936. Illus. by Helen Sewell. 184 pp. Gr. 2–5. (BL 32: 330; HB 12: 153; LJ 61: 457 and 809)

FISCHER, Marjorie. *Red Feather.* Messner, 1950. Illus. by Davine. 149 pp. Gr. 3–5. (BL 34: 112)

FOLLETT, Barbara. *The House without Windows and Eepersip's Life There.* See Chapter 1, Allegory and Fable: Out-of-Print Works.

FRY, Rosalie. *The Mountain Door.* Dutton, 1961. Illus. by the author. 128 pp. Gr. 4–6. (BL 57: 612; HB 37: 269; KR 29: 163; LJ 86: 1983; TLS Nov 25, 1960 p. x)

FRY, Rosalie. *The Wind Call.* Dutton, 1955. Illus. by the author. 115 pp. Gr. 2–4. (HB 32: 30)

GREEN, Kathleen. *Philip and the Pooka and Other Irish Fairy Tales.* See Chapter 2, Collected Tales: Out-of-Print Works.

HOUGH, Charlotte. *Red Biddy and Other Stories.* See Chapter 2, Collected Tales: Out-of-Print Works.

HOUSMAN, Laurence. *Cotton-Wooleena.* Doubleday, 1974. Illus. by Robert Binks. 58 pp. Gr. 3–5. (BL 70: 1056; KR 42: 425; LJ 99: 2270)

HOWARD, Joan. *The Oldest Secret.* See Chapter 12, Travel to Another World: Out-of-Print Works.

HUNTER, Mollie (pseud. of Maureen McIlwraith). *The Ferlie.* Funk, 1968. Illus. by Joseph Cellini. 128 pp. Gr. 4–6. (BL 65: 498; CCBB 22: 95; HB 45: 55)

HUNTER, Mollie. *The Smartest Man in Ireland* (British title: *Patrick Kentigen Keenan*). Funk, 1965. Illus. by Charles Keeping. 95 pp. Gr. 4–6. (BL 62: 487; HB 41: 629; KR 33: 821; TLS 1963 p. 427)

KIPLING, Rudyard. *Puck of Pook's Hill.* Doubleday, 1906. 251 pp. Gr. 5–8. The sequel is *Rewards and Fairies* (1910). (TLS 1906 p. 536)

KOTZWINKLE, William. *The Oldest Man and Other Timeless Stories.* See Chapter 2, Collected Tales: Out-of-Print Works.

MacALPINE, Margaret. *The Black Gull of Corie Lochan.* Prentice-Hall, 1965. 105 pp. Gr. 4–6. (CCBB 19: 102; KR 33: 627; LJ 91: 427; TLS 1964 p. 602)

MASON, Arthur. *The Wee Men of Ballywooden.* Doubleday, 1930. Illus. by Robert Lawson. 266 pp.; Viking, 1952. 214 pp. Gr. 4–6. (BL 27: 167; HB 29: 62)

MOLESWORTH, Mary. *Fairy Stories.* See Chapter 2, Collected Tales: Out-of-Print Works.

O'FAOLAIN, Eileen. *Miss Pennyfeather and the Pooka.* See Chapter 8N, Leprechauns: Out-of-Print Works.

PEARCE, A. Philippa. *The Squirrel Wife.* See Chapter 1, Allegory and Fable: Out-of-Print Works.

SAWYER, Ruth. *This Way to Christmas.* (Orig. pub. 1916) Harper, 1952. Rev. ed. 1967. Illus. by Maginel Barney. 175 pp. Gr. 3–5. (BL 13: 185)

SLEIGH, Barbara. *Stirabout Stories, Brewed in Her Own Cauldron.* See Chapter 2, Collected Tales: Out-of-Print Works.

WATSON, Sally. *Magic at Wynchwood.* See Chapter 5B, Imaginary Lands: Out-of-Print Works.

I. GENIES

SELDEN, George. *The Genie of Sutton Place.* See Chapter 6, Magic Adventure.

Genies: Out-of-Print Works

ELKIN, Benjamin. *Al and the Magic Lamp.* See Chapter 6, Magic Adventure: Out-of-Print Works.

FEAGLES, Anita. *The Genie and Joe Maloney.* See Chapter 6, Magic Adventure: Out-of-Print Works.

J. GIANTS

ALDEN, Raymond. *Why the Chimes Rang and Other Stories.* See Chapter 2, Collected Tales.

CURLEY, Daniel. *Billy Beg and the Bull.* See Chapter 6, Magic Adventure.

ENRIGHT, Elizabeth. *Tatsinda*. See Chapter 5B, Imaginary Lands.

ESTES, Eleanor. *The Sleeping Giant and Other Stories*. See Chapter 2, Collected Tales.

GARDNER, John. *Dragon, Dragon, and Other Tales*. See Chapter 2, Collected Tales.

GORDON, John. *The Giant under the Snow: A Story of Suspense*. See Chapter 6, Magic Adventure.

GOUDGE, Elizabeth. *Linnets and Valerians*. See Chapter 6, Magic Adventure.

HEARNE, Betsy. *South Star*. Atheneum, 1977. Illus. by Trina Schart Hyman. 84 pp. Gr. 3–6. [A]
After her parents' murder, Megan, a girl giant, flees the Screamer and follows the South Star across a vast plain and plateau toward a colony of giants. *Home* (1979) is the sequel. (BL 74: 375; CCBB 31: 78; HB 53: 662; KR 45: 990; SLJ Oct'77 p. 112)

HUGHES, Ted. *The Iron Giant: A Story in Five Nights* (British title: *The Iron Man*). Harper, 1968. Illus. by Robert Nadler. 56 pp. Gr. 3–6. [A]
The people of Australia ask the Iron Giant for help when a voraciously hungry space-bat-angel-dragon terrorizes the populace. (BL 65: 496; KR 36: 114; TLS 1968 p. 256)

JONES, Diana Wynne. *The Power of Three*. See Chapter 5A, Alternative Worlds.

KRENSKY, Stephen. *The Perils of Putney*. See Chapter 5B, Imaginary Lands.

NORTON, Mary. *Are All the Giants Dead?* See Chapter 12, Travel to Another World.

SWIFT, Jonathan. *Gulliver's Travels*. See Chapter 12, Travel to Another World.

THURBER, James. *The Great Quillow*. See Chapter 5B, Imaginary Lands.

WANGERIN, Walter, Jr. *The Book of the Dun Cow*. See Chapter 1, Allegory and Fable.

WILDE, Oscar. *The Happy Prince and Other Stories*. See Chapter 2, Collected Tales.

WILDE, Oscar. *The Selfish Giant*. See Chapter 1, Allegory and Fable.

YOLEN, Jane. *The Bird of Time*. See Chapter 5B, Imaginary Lands.

Giants: Out-of-Print Works

BOURLIAGUET, Léonce. *The Giant Who Drank from His Shoe and Other Stories.* See Chapter 2, Collected Tales: Out-of-Print Works.

DU BOIS, William Pène. *The Giant.* Viking, 1954. Illus. by the author. 124 pp. Gr. 4–8. (BL 51: 114; CC: 512; Eakin: 103; HB 30: 434; KR 22: 529; Suth: 212)

FARJEON, Eleanor. *The Little Bookroom: Eleanor Farjeon's Short Stories for Children Chosen by Herself.* See Chapter 2, Collected Tales: Out-of-Print Works.

HOUGH, Charlotte. *Red Biddy and Other Stores.* See Chapter 2, Collected Tales: Out-of-Print Works.

JOHNSON, Elizabeth. *The Little Knight.* See Chapter 5B, Imaginary Lands: Out-of-Print Works.

MANNING, Rosemary. *Green Smoke.* See Chapter 8E, Dragons: Out-of-Print Works.

MAYNE, William. *The Blue Boat.* See Chapter 6, Magic Adventure: Out-of-Print Works.

MONATH, Elizabeth. *Topper and the Giant.* See Chapter 6, Magic Adventure: Out-of-Print Works.

SHURA, Mary. *The Valley of the Frost Giants.* Lothrop, 1971. Illus. by Charles Keeping. 48 pp. Gr. 3–5. (KR 39: 175; LJ 96: 1806)

WIESNER, William. *Pin, the Reluctant Knight.* Norton, 1967. Illus. by the author. Unp. Gr. 3–4. (LJ 92: 4607)

WILLIAMS, Jay. *The Magical Storybook.* See Chapter 2, Collected Tales: Out-of-Print Works.

K. GNOMES

D'AULAIRE, Ingri and Edgar. *D'Aulaires' Trolls.* See Chapter 8U, Trolls.

FORST, S. *Pipkin.* Delacorte, 1970. Illus. by Robin Jacques. 144 pp. Gr. 1–4. [A]
Pipkin, prince of the gnomes, finds his way into the Ladybug Kingdom and is proclaimed king. (HB 46: 476; LJ 96: 1007)

HOUSMAN, Laurence. *The Rat-Catcher's Daughter: A Collection of Stories.* See Chapter 2, Collected Tales.

JANSSON, Tove. *Finn Family Moomintroll.* (Orig. pub. 1958) Avon, 1975 (pap.). Tr. by Elizabeth Portch. Illus. by the author. 170 pp. Gr. 4–6. [R]

Trouble comes to Moominvalley, home of the gnomelike Moomins, when Moomintroll, Sniff, and Snufkin bring home a hobgoblin's hat. The sequels are *Moominsummer Madness* (1961), *Moominland in Midwinter* (1962), *Tales from Moominvalley* (1964), *The Exploits of Moominpappa* (1966), *Moominpappa at Sea* (1967), *A Comet in Moominland* (1968), and *Moominvalley in November* (1971). *Moomin, Mymble and Little My* is the British sequel. (Adv: 190; Arb: 230; CC: 535)

Gnomes: Out-of-Print Works

HUNT, Marigold. *Hester and the Gnomes*. Whittlesey, 1955. Illus. by Jean Charlot. 124 pp. Gr. 2–5. (HB 31: 377; KR 23: 417; LJ 80: 2645)

WATKINS-PITCHFORD, Denys J. *The Little Grey Men*. Scribner, 1949. Illus. by the author. 249 pp. Gr. 4–6. (BL 46: 105; HB 25: 533; KR 17: 28)

L. GOBLINS

BRIGGS, Katherine. *Hobberdy Dick*. (Orig. pub. 1955) Greenwillow, 1977. 239 pp. Gr. 5–8. [R]
A hobgoblin named Hobberdy Dick uses his magic to help the children of the manor. (BL 73: 1417; CCBB 31: 7; HB 53: 311; KR 45: 166; SLJ May'77 p. 59)

KRENSKY, Stephen. *A Big Day for Scepters*. See Chapter 5B, Imaginary Lands.

MACDONALD, George. *The Princess and the Goblin*. See Chapter 5B, Imaginary Lands.

Goblins: Out-of-Print Works

CARRYL, Charles. *Davy and the Goblin, or What Followed Reading "Alice's Adventures in Wonderland."* See Chapter 12, Travel to Another World: Out-of-Print Works.

MAYNE, William. *The Blue Boat*. See Chapter 6, Magic Adventure: Out-of-Print Works.

M. GRIFFINS

BERESFORD, Elizabeth. *Awkward Magic*. See Chapter 6, Magic Adventure.

KROEBER, Theodora. *Carrousel*. See Chapter 7, Magical Toys.

McHARGUE, Georgess. *Stoneflight*. See Chapter 6, Magic Adventure.

SILVERBERG, Barbara. *Phoenix Feathers: A Collection of Mythical Monsters*. See Chapter 2, Collected Tales.

Griffins: Out-of-Print Works

FREEMAN, Barbara. *Timi: The Tale of a Griffin*. Grosset, 1970. Illus. by Marvin Bileck. 48 pp. Gr. 2-6. (LJ 96: 257)

STOCKTON, Frank R. *The Griffin and the Minor Canon*. Holt, 1963. Illus. by Maurice Sendak. 55 pp. Gr. 3-5. (Arb: 242; BL 59: 900; CC: 570; Eakin: 313; HB 39: 384; LJ 88: 2555)

N. LEPRECHAUNS

LYNCH, Patricia. *Brogeen Follows the Magic Tune*. Macmillan, 1968. Illus. by Ralph Pinto. 165 pp. Gr. 4-6. [A]
Brogeen the leprechaun sets out to get back the fairies' magic tune from the human fiddler who stole it. This story is preceded by *Brogeen and the Lost Castle* (1956), *Brogeen and the Black Enchanter* (1958), and *Brogeen and the Little Wind* (1963), and the sequels are *Brogeen and the Bronze Lizard* (1970) and *Brogeen and the Red Fez* (British). (BL 65: 837; KR 36: 1163; LJ 94: 302)

NEWMAN, Sharon. *Dagda's Harp*. See Chapter 5B, Imaginary Lands.

PATTEN, Brian. *Mr. Moon's Last Case*. Scribner, 1976. Illus. by Mary Moore. 158 pp. Gr. 6-9. [A]
A leprechaun named Nameon, who accidentally entered the human world, is pursued by a detective named Mr. Moon and aided by the members of the Secret Society for the Protection of Leprechauns as he tries desperately to get home. (BL 73: 410; CCBB 30: 111; HB 52: 626; KR 44: 974; SLJ Feb'77 p. 67)

PAYNE, Joan. *The Leprechaun of Bayou Luce*. Hastings, 1957. Illus. by the author. 60 pp. Gr. 2-4. [A]
Pirate ghosts have stolen a leprechaun's gold, and Josh Turnipseed agrees to help win it back. (BL 54: 208; HB 33: 489; KR 25: 689)

Leprechauns: Out-of-Print Works

FROST, Frances. *Then Came Timothy*. Whittlesey, 1950. Illus. by Richard Bennett. 155 pp. Gr. 4-6. (BL 47: 47; HB 26: 375; KR 18: 418; LJ 75: 1834)

JOHNSON, Elizabeth. *Stuck with Luck*. Little, 1967. Illus. by Trina Schart Hyman. 88 pp. Gr. 3-5. (BL 64: 198; HB 43: 589; KR 35: 740; LJ 92: 3187; TN 24: 223)

McKIM, Audrey. *Andy and the Gopher*. See Chapter 9, Talking Animals: Out-of-Print Works.

O'FAOLAIN, Eileen. *Miss Pennyfeather and the Pooka*. Random, 1946. Illus. by Aldren Watson. 154 pp. Gr. 4-7. (BL 42: 369; HB 22: 266; LJ 71: 983)

SAWYER, Ruth. *The Enchanted Schoolhouse*. Viking, 1956. Illus. by Hugh Troy. 128 pp. Gr. 4-6. (BL 53: 182; HB 32: 450; KR 24: 70)

SHURA, Mary. *A Shoe Full of Shamrock*. See Chapter 6, Magic Adventure: Out-of-Print Works.

WIBBERLEY, Leonard. *McGillicuddy McGotham*. Morrow, 1956, Illus. by Aldren Watson. 111 pp. Gr. 5 up. (BL 52: 312; KR 24: 55; LJ 81: 833)

O. MAGICAL HORSES

BAXTER, Caroline. *The Stolen Telesm*. Lippincott, 1976. 192 pp. Gr. 4-6. [A]
Telesm, a winged colt, helps David and Lucy escape the evil magic of Marada the sorceress. (KR 44: 794; SLJ Oct'76 p. 104; TLS 1975 p. 1457)

BYARS, Betsy. *The Winged Colt of Casa Mia*. See Chapter 6, Magic Adventure.

FOSTER, Elizabeth. *Lyrico: The Only Horse of His Kind*. Gambit, 1970. Illus. by Joy Buba. 230 pp. Gr. 4-7. [M]
Lyrico, Philippa's small, winged horse, becomes ill from polluted city air, so the Poppadou family must find a new home out west. (BL 67: 663)

GOUDGE, Elizabeth. *The Little White Horse*. See Chapter 6, Magic Adventure.

KROEBER, Theodora. *Carrousel*. See Chapter 7, Magical Toys.

MURPHY, Shirley Rousseau. *The Ring of Fire*. See Chapter 5A, Alternative Worlds.

SNYDER, Zilpha. *A Season of Ponies*. See Chapter 6, Magic Adventure.

Magical Horses: Out-of-Print Works

GREEN, Kathleen. *Philip and the Pooka and Other Irish Fairy Tales*. See Chapter 2, Collected Tales: Out-of-Print Works.

O'FAOLAIN, Eileen. *Miss Pennyfeather and the Pooka*. See Chapter 8N, Leprechauns: Out-of-Print Works.

P. MERMAIDS AND SEA PEOPLE

AIKEN, Joan. *The Faithless Lollybird*. See Chapter 2, Collected Tales.

AINSWORTH, Ruth. *The Bear Who Liked Hugging People and Other Stories*. See Chapter 2, Collected Tales.

ANDERSEN, Hans Christian. *Dulac's The Snow Queen and Other Stories from Hans Andersen*. See Chapter 2, Collected Tales.

BABBITT, Natalie. *The Search for Delicious*. See Chapter 5B, Imaginary Lands.

BOSTON, L. M. *The Sea Egg*. See Chapter 6, Magic Adventure.

DUGGAN, Maurice. *Falter Tom and the Water Boy*. Phillips, 1959. Illus. by Kenneth Rowell. 61 pp. Gr. 3-5. [A]
A sea-boy invites an old sailor named Falter Tom to come and live in the realm of the sea kings. (HB 36: 128; LJ 84: 3925; TLS 1975 p. 365)

HILL, Elizabeth. *Ever-After Island*. See Chapter 6, Magic Adventure.

HUNTER, Mollie (pseud. of Maureen McIlwraith). *The Kelpie's Pearls*. (Orig. pub. 1966) Harper, 1976. 112 pp. Gr. 4-6. [R]
The pearl necklace that a water sprite gives to Morag MacLeod causes the old woman to be accused of witchcraft. (Arb: 209; BL 63: 451; CC: 534; CCBB 20: 109; HB 42: 710; KR 34: 688; LJ 91: 5231; TLS 1964 p. 1081)

JARRELL, Randall. *The Animal Family*. See Chapter 1, Allegory and Fable.

LA MOTTE FOUQUÉ, Friedrich de. *Undine*. See Chapter 1, Allegory and Fable.

POLESE, Carolyn. *Something about a Mermaid*. Dutton, 1978. Illus. by Gail Owens. 27 pp. Gr. 2-4. [M]
The mermaid Janie finds at the beach does not adjust well to life in an apartment. (BL 75: 867; KR 47: 66)

POPHAM, Hugh. *The Fabulous Voyage of the Pegasus*. See Chapter 10, Tall Tales.

WILDE, Oscar. *The Happy Prince and Other Stories*. See Chapter 2, Collected Tales.

YOLEN, Jane. *The Mermaid's Three Wisdoms*. See Chapter 6, Magic Adventure.

Mermaids and Sea People: Out-of-Print Works

BAKER, Margaret Joyce. *The Magic Sea Shell*. See Chapter 6, Magic Adventure: Out-of-Print Works.

BAUM, L(yman) Frank. *The Sea Fairies*. (Orig. pub. 1911) Contemporary Books, 1969. 239 pp. Gr. 4-6. *Sky Island* (1912, 1970) is the sequel. (LJ 95: 1936)

CALHOUN, Mary. *Magic in the Alley*. See Chapter 6, Magic Adventure: Out-of-Print Works.

MacKELLAR, William. *The Smallest Monster in the World.* See Chapter 8R, Monsters and Sea Serpents: Out-of-Print Works.

MANNING, Rosemary. *Green Smoke.* See Chapter 8E, Dragons: Out-of-Print Works.

NATHAN, Robert. *The Snowflake and the Starfish.* See Chapter 13, Witches, Wizards, Sorcerers, and Magicians: Out-of-Print Works.

NESBIT, E. (pseud. of Edith Bland). *Wet Magic.* (Orig. pub. 1910) Coward, 1960. Illus. by H. R. Millar. 244 pp. Gr. 4-6. (BL 57: 32; HB 13: 378, 36: 309; LJ 62: 881)

PICARD, Barbara L. *The Mermaid and the Simpleton.* See Chapter 2, Collected Tales: Out-of-Print Works.

YOUNG, Ella. *The Unicorn with Silver Shoes.* See Chapter 5B, Imaginary Lands: Out-of-Print Works.

Q. MINIATURE PEOPLE

ANDERSEN, Hans Christian. *Thumbelina.* Scribner, 1961. Tr. by R. P. Keigwin. Illus. by Adrienne Adams. 56 pp. Gr. 1-4. [R]
Thumbelina, a girl "no taller than your thumb," is carried off by a frog, taken in by a fieldmouse, and almost married to a mole before she reaches the land of the flower people. (Arb: 236; BL 58: 228; CC: 480; HB 38: 41; KR 29: 953; LJ 86: 4357)

BRÖGER, Achim. *Outrageous Kasimir.* Morrow, 1976. Tr. by Hilda Van Stockum. Illus. by Susan Jeschke. 187 pp. Gr. 5-7. [M]
The police accuse a tiny magician of a series of robberies. (BL 73: 894; KR 44: 1169; SLJ Jan'77 p. 87)

CHEW, Ruth. *The Wednesday Witch.* See Chapter 13, Witches, Wizards, Sorcerers, and Magicians.

CHEW, Ruth. *The Would-Be Witch.* See Chapter 6, Magic Adventure.

CLAPP, Patricia. *King of the Doll House.* Lothrop, 1974. Illus. by Judith Brown. 94 pp. Gr. 3-5. [A]
King Borra Borra, Queen Griselda, and their eleven children move into Ellie's dollhouse for the summer. (CCBB 28: 74; KR 42: 680; LJ 99: 2738)

CURRY, Jane. *Mindy's Mysterious Miniature* (British title: *The House-napper*). Harcourt, 1970. Illus. by Charles Robinson. 157 pp. Gr. 3-5. [R]
Mindy and her neighbor, Mrs. Bright, are captured and shrunk to miniature size by Mr. Putt's miniaturizing machine. The "reducer" strikes again in *The Lost Farm* (1974). (Arb: 238; BL 67: 340; HB 46: 616; KR 38: 1146; LJ 95: 4374; Suth: 96; TLS 1971 p. 774)

DAHL, Roald. *The Magic Finger.* See Chapter 6, Magic Adventure.

DE CAYLUS, Compte. *Heart of Ice*. See Chapter 5B, Imaginary Lands.

GRIMSHAW, Nigel. *Bluntstone and the Wildkeepers*. Faber (dist. by Merrimack), 1978. 152 pp. Gr. 5–7. [A]
When the Wildkeepers are threatened by a builder named Bluntstone and his "yellow soil-eating monsters," the little people call on dark magic to save themselves. *The Wildkeepers' Guest* (1978) is the sequel. (BL 75: 1090; TLS 1974 p. 721)

IRVING, Washington. *Rip Van Winkle*. See Chapter 6, Magic Adventure.

KÄSTNER, Erich. *The Little Man*. Knopf, 1966. Tr. by James Kirkup. Illus. by Rick Schreiter. 183 pp. Gr. 4–6. [R]
Two-inch-tall Maxie Pichelsteiner gains fame by becoming Professor Hokus Von Pokus's Invisible Right-Hand Man. *The Little Man and the Big Thief* (1970) is the sequel. *The Little Man and the Little Miss* is a British sequel. (Arb: 240; BL 63: 728; CC: 537; CCBB 20: 124; KR 34: 1101; LJ 91: 6192; Suth: 220; TLS 1966 p. 1077)

* KENDALL, Carol. *The Gammage Cup* (British title: *The Minnipins*). Harcourt, 1959. Illus. by Erik Blegvad. 221 pp. Gr. 4–7.
Four nonconformists banished to the mountains by their fellow Minnipins risk their lives to save the country when it is invaded by the Mushroom People. *A Whisper of Glocken* (1965) is the sequel. (Adv: 273; Arb: 240; BL 56: 248; CC: 537; Eakin: 187; HB 34: 477; LJ 85: 845)

LINDGREN, Astrid. *Karlsson-on-the-Roof* (Orig. pub. 1955) Viking, 1971. Tr. by Marianne Turner. Illus. by Jan Pyk. 128 pp. Gr. 3–5. [A]
No one believes Eric that the trouble he gets into is all caused by the little flying man who lives on his roof. *Karlson Flies Again* and *Erik and Karlson on the Roof* are the British sequels. (CCBB 26: 28; KR 39: 1156; LJ 97: 1168; TLS 1975 p. 373)

McGOWEN, Tom. *The Spirit of the Wild*. Little, 1976. 104 pp. Gr. 5–7. [M]
Amy Nelson is captured by the Puk Wudj Ininees, little people who live beneath the earth. (BL 73: 40; KR 44: 535; SLJ Oct'76 p. 109)

* NORTON, Mary. *The Borrowers*. (Orig. pub. 1952) Harcourt, 1965 (pap.). Illus. by Beth and Joe Krush. 180 pp. Gr. 3–7.
The Clocks, a family of tiny people who subsist by "borrowing" from humans, must flee for their lives because of their daughter's friendship with a human boy. The sequels are *The Borrowers Afield* (1955), *The Borrowers Afloat* (1959), *The Borrowers Aloft* (1961), and *Poor Stainless* (1971). Carnegie Medal. (Arb: 212; BL 50: 4 and 40; CC: 555; Eakin: 249; HB 29: 456; KR 21: 483; LJ 78: 1699)

PROYSEN, Alf. *Little Old Mrs. Pepperpot and Other Stories*. See Chapter 2, Collected Tales.

SWIFT, Jonathan. *Gulliver's Travels*. See Chapter 12, Travel to Another World.

TOLKIEN, J. R. R. *The Hobbit; or There and Back Again*. See Chapter 4, Good versus Evil.

WERSBA, Barbara. *Let Me Fall before I Fly*. See Chapter 1, Allegory and Fable.

WINTERFELD, Henry. *Castaways in Lilliput*. See Chapter 12, Travel to Another World.

Miniature People: Out-of-Print Works

BERTON, Pierre. *The Secret World of Og*. See Chapter 12, Travel to Another World: Out-of-Print Works.

BOSTON, L. M. *The Castle of Yew*. See Chapter 6, Magic Adventure: Out-of-Print Works.

CHASE, Mary. *Loretta Mason Potts*. See Chapter 6, Magic Adventure: Out-of-Print Works.

DE REGNIERS, Beatrice. *Penny*. Viking, 1966. Illus. by Marvin Bileck. 66 pp. Gr. K–3. (CCBB 20: 107; HB 42: 705; KR 34: 1096; LJ 91: 6184)

FARJEON, Eleanor. *Mr. Garden*. Walck, 1966. Illus. by Jane Paton. 39 pp. Gr. 4–6. (CCBB 20: 139; HB 42: 429; LJ 91: 4312; TLS 1966 p. 448)

HOUGH, Charlotte. *Red Biddy and Other Stories*. See Chapter 2, Collected Tales: Out-of-Print Works.

KELLAM, Ian. *The First Summer Year*. See Chapter 12, Travel to Another World: Out-of-Print Works.

LAGERLÖF, Selma. *The Wonderful Adventures of Nils*. (Orig. pub. 1908) Pantheon, 1947. Tr. by Velma Howard. Illus. by H. Baumhauer. 539 pp. Gr. 5–7. Included in this edition is *The Further Adventures of Nils* (1908). (BL 4: 22, 44: 118; CC: 540; HB 23: 451)

LAWSON, Robert. *The Fabulous Flight*. Little, 1949. Illus. by the author. 152 pp. Gr. 4–6. (BL 46: 37; HB 25: 410; KR 17: 394; LJ 94: 1542 and 1682)

MORGAN, Helen. *Satchkin Patchkin*. (Orig. pub. 1966) Smith, 1970. Illus. by Shirley Hughes. 64 pp. Gr. 3–5. (Arb: 241; CCBB 24: 63; LJ 95: 4340; TLS 1966 p. 1092)

SCHMIDT, Annie. *Wiplala*. See Chapter 6, Magic Adventure: Out-of-Print Works.

WHITE, T(erence) H(anbury). *Mistress Masham's Repose.* Putnam, 1946. Illus. by Fritz Eichenberg. 255 pp. Gr. 5-7. (BL 43: 36; KR 14: 529; LJ 71: 2107)

YOLEN, Jane. *The Wizard of Washington Square.* See Chapter 13, Witches, Wizards, Sorcerers, and Magicians: Out-of-Print Works.

R. Monsters and Sea Serpents

BABBITT, Natalie. *Kneeknock Rise.* See Chapter 1, Allegory and Fable.

CAMERON, Eleanor. *The Terrible Churnadryne.* Little, 1959. Illus. by Beth and Joe Krush. 125 pp. Gr. 4-6. [R]
Few people believed the stories of a tremendous beast seen near Redwood Cove, so Tom and Jennifer decide to track it down themselves. (BL 56: 247; CC: 495; Eakin: 58; HB 35: 481; KR 27: 701; LJ 84: 3629)

CAMPBELL, Hope. *Peter's Angel: A Story about Monsters.* See Chapter 9, Talking Animals.

CHEW, Ruth. *The Trouble with Magic.* See Chapter 6, Magic Adventure.

FRY, Rosalie. *Mungo.* Farrar, 1972. Illus. by Velma Ilsley. 123 pp. Gr. 3-5. [A]
Richie's summer adventures with a sea monster take him to an uncharted isle inhabited by a shipwrecked sailor. (BL 68: 1004; HB 48: 370; KR 40: 324)

HARRIS, Rosemary. *Sea Magic and Other Stories of Enchantment.* See Chapter 2, Collected Tales.

HAYES, Geoffrey. *The Alligator and His Uncle Tooth: A Novel of the Sea.* See Chapter 9, Talking Animals.

KENNY, Herbert A. *Dear Dolphin.* See Chapter 12, Travel to Another World.

LITTLE, Jane. *Danger at Sneaker Hill.* See Chapter 13, Witches, Wizards, Sorcerers, and Magicians.

McNEILL, Janet. *A Monster Too Many.* Little, 1972. Illus. by Ingrid Fetz. 60 pp. Gr. 3-5. [A]
Sam and Joe prevent their sea monster from being sent to a zoo and return it to the sea. (BL 68: 1004; KR 40: 136; LJ 97: 2232)

MAYNE, William. *A Game of Dark.* See Chapter 11, Time Travel.

MENDOZA, George. *Gwot! Horribly Funny Hairticklers.* Harper, 1967. Illus. by Steven Kellogg. Unp. Gr. 5-7. [A]
Three ghastly monster tales: a huge black snake that grows bigger each time its

head is chopped off, an old woman who eats a hairy toe, and the hunt for the horrible Gumberoo. (KR 35: 1048; LJ 92: 4615)

NESBIT, E. *The Enchanted Castle.* See Chapter 6, Magic Adventure.

PHIPSON, Joan. *The Way Home.* See Chapter 11, Time Travel.

TROTT, Susan. *The Sea Serpent of Horse.* See Chapter 12, Travel to Another World.

WARBURG, Sandol. *On the Way Home.* See Chapter 1, Allegory and Fable.

WRIGHTSON, Patricia. *The Nargun and the Stars.* See Chapter 4, Good versus Evil.

Monsters and Sea Serpents: Out-of-Print Works

BENDICK, Jeanne. *The Blonk from beneath the Sea.* Watts, 1958. Illus. by the author. 55 pp. Gr. 3–5. (HB 34: 265; KR 26: 133; LJ 83: 1940)

DARLING, Lois and Louis. *The Sea Serpents Around Us.* Little, 1965. Illus. by Louis Darling. 69 pp. Gr. 3–4. (KR 33: 626; LJ 90: 3788)

GRIMBLE, Rosemary. *Jonothon and Large.* Bobbs-Merrill, 1966. Illus. by the author. 88 pp. Gr. 2–4. (KR 38: 340; LJ 92: 2014; TLS 1965 p. 1131)

KELLOGG, Steven. *The Wicked Kings of Bloon.* See Chapter 5B, Imaginary Lands: Out-of-Print Works.

LARSON, Jean. *The Silkspinners.* Scribner, 1967. Illus. by Uri Shulevitz. 93 pp. Gr. 3–5. (BL 64: 448; CCBB 21: 112; KR 35: 1047; LJ 92: 3852; Suth: 239)

LEITCH, Patricia. *The Black Loch.* Funk, 1968. Illus. by Janet Duchesne. 160 pp. Gr. 6–8. (BL 64: 1095; KR 36: 467; LJ 93: 1800)

MacKELLAR, William. *The Smallest Monster in the World.* McKay, 1969. Illus. by Ursula Koering. 113 pp. Gr. 4–5. (BL 66: 621; HB 46: 36; KR 37: 1064; LJ 95: 1628)

ORMONDROYD, Edward. *David and the Phoenix.* See Chapter 8S, Phoenix: Out-of-Print Works.

PALMER, Mary. *The Magic Knight.* See Chapter 5B, Imaginary Lands: Out-of-Print Works.

PALMER, Mary. *The Teaspoon Tree.* See Chapter 6, Magic Adventure: Out-of-Print Works.

SLEIGH, Barbara. *Stirabout Stories, Brewed in Her Own Cauldron.* See Chapter 2, Collected Tales: Out-of-Print Works.

S. The Phoenix

SILVERBERG, Barbara. *Phoenix Feathers: A Collection of Mythical Monsters.* See Chapter 2, Collected Tales.

The Phoenix: Out-of-Print Works

McNEILL, Janet. *Various Specs.* See Chapter 6, Magic Adventure: Out-of-Print Works.

ORMONDROYD, Edward. *David and the Phoenix.* Follett, 1957. Illus. by Joan Raysor. 173 pp. Gr. 7-9. (BL 54: 113; HB 33: 401; KR 25: 583; LJ 82: 3249)

T. Seal People

COATSWORTH, Elizabeth. *Marra's World.* Greenwillow/Morrow, 1975. Illus. by Krystyna Turska. 83 pp. Gr. 2-4. [R]
Marra doesn't understand her grandmother's hatred or her father's disinterest until she discovers that her mother was a selkie, or seal-woman, who went back to live in the sea. (Arb: 237; BL 72: 448; CC 1977 Suppl. p. 61; CCBB 29: 107; HB 52: 48; KR 43: 1129; SLJ Apr'76 p. 70)

HARRIS, Rosemary. *The Seal-Singing.* Macmillan, 1971. 245 pp. Gr. 7-10. [R]
Miranda's eerie resemblance to an infamous Scottish ancestor portends her own supernatural power over the seals. (Arb: 210; BL 68: 364; CCBB 25: 57; HB 48: 57; KR 39: 954; LJ 96: 4190; Suth: 169; TLS 1971 p. 1318)

HUNTER, Mollie (pseud. of Maureen McIlwraith). *A Stranger Came Ashore.* Harper, 1975. 192 pp. Gr. 6-8. [R]
No one but Robbie suspects that the handsome stranger who wishes to marry his sister may actually be the Great Selkie, a legendary seal-man who carries young girls off to the bottom of the sea. (Adv: 189; Arb: 209: BL 72: 303; CC 1977 Suppl. p. 66; CCBB 29: 79; HB 51: 592; JHC 1976 Suppl. p. 53; KR 43: 1067; SLJ Dec'75 p. 31; TLS 1975 p. 1053)

LOCKLEY, Ronald. *The Seal-Woman.* Bradbury, 1975. 178 pp. Gr. 8 up. [A]
An Irish girl named Shian, who believes she is princess of the seals, awaits the coming of her sea-prince. (BL 72: 228, 1038; KR 43: 869; SLJ Nov'75 p. 96; TLS 1974 p. 1405; TN 32: 284)

OPPENHEIM, Shulamith. *The Selchie's Seed.* Bradbury, 1975. Illus. by Diane Goode. 83 pp. Gr. 4-6. [R]
Marian never suspected that her ancestors were seal people until the night she is drawn to a white whale in the ocean near her island home. (BL 72: 580; CC 1977 Suppl. p. 67; CCBB 29: 129; KR 43: 1287; SLJ Jan'76 p. 49)

Seal People: Out-of-Print Works

FRY, Rosalie. *The Secret of the Ron Mor Skerry* (British title: *Child of the Western Isles*). Dutton, 1959. Illus. by the author. 95 pp. Gr. 4-6. (BL 55: 513; HB 35: 214; KR 27: 39; LJ 84: 1696)

GARD, Joyce. *Talargain*. Holt, 1965. 251 pp. Gr. 6-8. (Arb: 239; BL 61: 1029; CCBB 19: 8; Eakin: 134; HB 41: 175; KR 33: 243; LJ 90: 1558)

U. TROLLS

BANKS, Lynne Reid. *The Farthest-Away Mountain*. See Chapter 5B, Imaginary Lands.

D'AULAIRE, Ingri and Edgar. *D'Aulaires' Trolls*. Doubleday, 1972. Illus. by the authors. 62 pp. Gr. 3-6. [A]
In the mountains, forests, and waterways of Norway live bands of little people called trolls, gnomes, and hulder-people. (BL 69: 404; HB 48: 592; KR 40: 1415; Suth: 22)

JANSSON, Tove. *Finn Family Moomintroll*. See Chapter 8K, Gnomes.

Trolls: Out-of-Print Works

WUORIO, Eva-Lis. *The Happiness Flower*. See Chapter 6, Magic Adventure: Out-of-Print Works.

V. UNICORNS

FARBER, Norma. *Six Impossible Things before Breakfast*. See Chapter 2, Collected Tales.

L'ENGLE, Madeleine. *A Swiftly Tilting Planet*. See Chapter 11, Time Travel.

LITTLE, Jane. *Danger at Sneaker Hill*. See Chapter 13, Witches, Wizards, Sorcerers, and Magicians.

MAYNE, William. *A Grass Rope.* See Chapter 6, Magic Adventure.

SILVERBERG, Barbara. *Phoenix Feathers: A Collection of Mythical Monsters*. See Chapter 2, Collected Tales.

Unicorns: Out-of-Print Works

WILLIAMS, Anne. *Secret of the Round Tower*. Random, 1968. Illus. by J. C. Kocsis. 87 pp. Gr. 5-6. (HB 45: 47; KR 36: 820; LJ 94: 880)

YOUNG, Ella. *The Unicorn with Silver Shoes*. See Chapter 5B, Imaginary Lands: Out-of-Print Works.

W. OTHER MYTHICAL BEINGS AND CREATURES

BOSTON, L. M. *Nothing Said*. See Chapter 6, Magic Adventure.

DAVIES, Valentine. *The Miracle on 34th Street*. See Chapter 10, Tall Tales.

DURRELL, Gerald. *The Talking Parcel*. See Chapter 12, Travel to Another World.

ISH-KISHOR, Sulamith. *The Master of Miracle: A New Novel of the Golem*. See Chapter 1, Allegory and Fable.

KENNEDY, Richard. *Come Again in the Spring*. See Chapter 1, Allegory and Fable.

NORTON, André. *Here Abide Monsters*. See Chapter 12, Travel to Another World.

PICARD, Barbara. *The Faun and the Woodcutter's Daughter*. See Chapter 2, Collected Tales.

PRICE, Susan. *The Devil's Piper*. See Chapter 4, Good versus Evil.

SEREDY, Kate. *The White Stag*. Viking, 1937. Illus. by the author. 94 pp. Gr. 6-8. [R]
The white stag and the red eagle help guide Hunor, Magyar, Bendeguz, Attila, and their people to found Hungary. Newbery Medal. (BL 34: 197; CC: 564; HB 13: 366 and 378; LJ 62: 807, 63: 34)

Other Mythical Beings and Creatures: Out-of-Print Works

CHENAULT, Nell. *Parsifal the Poddley*. Little, 1960. Illus. by Vee Guthrie. 83 pp. Gr. 2-4. The sequel is *Parsifal Rides the Time Wave* (1962). (KR 28: 290; LJ 85: 2469)

DE JONG, Dola. *Sand for the Sandmen*. Scribner, 1946. Illus. by Natalie Norton. 87 pp. Gr. 3-5. (KR 14: 275; LJ 71: 982)

FRITZ, Jean. *Magic to Burn*. See Chapter 6, Magic Adventure: Out-of-Print Works.

HARTWICK, Harry. *Farewell to the Farivox*. See Chapter 1, Allegory and Fable: Out-of-Print Works.

HOWARD, Joan. *The Oldest Secret*. See Chapter 12, Travel to Another World: Out-of-Print Works.

JOHNSON, Elizabeth. *No Magic, Thank You*. See Chapter 6, Magic Adventure: Out-of-Print Works.

9
Talking Animals

There is sometimes only a fine line between realistic and fantastic portrayal of animals in literature. Thus, any tales in which the animal characters think or talk in a humanlike manner have been included in this list. This type of anthropomorphic depiction of animals seems to have been more common in the past than it is today.

ADAMS, Richard. *Shardik*. See Chapter 1, Allegory and Fable.

ADAMS, Richard. *Watership Down*. See Chapter 1, Allegory and Fable.

AIKEN, Joan. *The Kingdom and the Cave*. See Chapter 5B, Imaginary Lands.

AIKEN, Joan. *A Necklace of Raindrops and Other Stories*. See Chapter 2, Collected Tales.

AINSWORTH, Ruth. *The Bear Who Liked Hugging People and Other Stories*. See Chapter 2, Collected Tales.

ALEXANDER, Lloyd. *The Cat Who Wished to Be a Man*. Dutton, 1973. 107 pp. Gr. 4–6. [R]
Lionel nags the wizard Stephanus to change him from a cat into a human. Stephanus grants his wish, only to find that he cannot reverse the process. (Arb: 207; BL 70: 168; CC: 478; CCBB 27: 21; HB 49: 463; KR 41: 639; LJ 98: 2647; TN 30: 205)

ALEXANDER, Lloyd. *The Town Cats, and Other Tales.* See Chapter 2, Collected Tales.

ANDERSEN, Hans Christian. *Thumbelina.* See Chapter 8Q, Miniature People.

ANDERSON, Mary. *F*T*C* Superstar.* Atheneum, 1976. Illus. by Gail Owens. 156 pp. Gr. 4-6. [A]
Freddie the cat dreams of becoming an actor, but when Emma, his pigeon friend, helps him attain his dream, stardom goes to his head. *F*T*C* & Company* (1979) is the sequel. (BL 73: 140; KR 44: 320; SLJ Apr'76 p. 68)

ANNETT, Cora. *How the Witch Got Alf.* Watts, 1975. Illus. by Steven Kellogg. 47 pp. Gr. 3-5. [A]
Alf, the old folks' donkey, feels unloved and decides to take drastic measures. He runs away and his adventures begin. (Arb: 236; BL 71: 864; CCBB 29: 1; KR 43: 70; SJL Mar'75 p. 84)

ANNIXTER, Paul (pseud. of Paul Comfort). *The Best Nature Stories of Paul Annixter.* Ed. by Ruth Robinson. Hill, 1974. 181 pp. Gr. 6-8. [M]
Tales of animals with human thoughts. (JHC 1976 Suppl. p. 58)

ARKIN, Alan. *The Lemming Condition.* Harper, 1976. Illus. by Joan Sandin. 64 pp. Gr. 4-5. [R]
Bubber's family and friends undertake their unquestioning journey toward the sea and death. In order to live, Bubber must fight not only the other lemmings, but his own instincts as well. (Adv: 181; BL 72: 1182; HB 52: 394; KR 44: 389; SLJ Apr'76 p. 68)

AVERILL, Esther. *Captains of the City Streets: A Story of the Cat Club.* Harper, 1972. Illus. by the author. 147 pp. Gr. 3-4. [A]
Two tramp cats named Sinbad and the Duke move to New York City and become involved in a club run by the local cats. This is the sequel to *The Cat Club* (1944), *School for Cats* (1947), *How the Brothers Joined the Cat Club* (1953), and *The Hotel Cat* (1969), and is followed by *Jenny and the Cat Club* (1973). (BL 69: 809; CCBB 26: 149; HB 48: 47; KR 40: 1354; LJ 98: 1678)

AYMÉ, Marcel. *The Wonderful Farm.* Harper, 1951. Tr. by Norman Denny. Illus. by Maurice Sendak. 182 pp. Gr. 4-6. [A]
Marinette and Delphine don't know how to get around their parents' strict rules, but then the farm animals begin to talk to the girls and give them some unusual ideas. (BL 48: 161; HB 27: 406; LJ 76: 2009)

BACON, Peggy. *The Ghost of Opalina, or Nine Lives.* See Chapter 3, Ghosts.

BAKER, Betty. *Dupper.* Greenwillow/Morrow, 1976. Illus. by Chuck Eckart. 147 pp. Gr. 5-7. [R]

Dupper is an outcast in the prairie dog world until his search for the Great Ants leads to a solution to the killer rattlesnake problem. (Adv: 147; BL 73: 140; CCBB 30: 38; KR 44: 684; SLJ Feb'77 p. 60)

BANKS, Lynne Reid. *The Farthest-Away Mountain.* See Chapter 5B, Imaginary Lands.

BEEKS, Graydon. *Hosea Globe and the Fantastical Peg-Legged Chu.* See Chapter 10, Tall Tales.

BENCHLEY, Nathaniel. *Feldman Fieldmouse: A Fable.* Harper, 1971. Illus. by Hilary Knight. 96 pp. Gr. 3-6. [R]
Uncle Feldman's lessons in wild mouse survival are quite a change for Fendall, compared to his pampered life as a household pet. (BL 68: 55; CC: 487; CCBB 25: 54; HB 47: 285; KR 39: 500; LJ 96: 2128; Suth: 33)

BENCHLEY, Nathaniel. *Kilroy and the Gull.* Harper, 1977. Illus. by John Schoenherr. 118 pp. Gr. 5-7. [A]
Escaped from an aquarium after frustrating attempts to communicate with humans, Kilroy the killer whale and a seagull friend search the sea for Kilroy's family. (BL 73: 1086; CCBB 30: 138; HB 53: 309; KR 45: 3; SLJ Oct'77 p. 109)

BETHANCOURT, T. Ernesto. *The Dog Days of Arthur Cane.* See Chapter 6, Magic Adventure.

BIANCO, Margery Williams. *The Velveteen Rabbit; or, How Toys Became Real.* See Chapter 7, Magical Toys.

BIEGEL, Paul. *The King of the Copper Mountains.* See Chapter 5B, Imaginary Lands.

BODECKER, N. M. *The Mushroom Center Disaster.* Atheneum, 1974. Illus. by Erik Blegvad. 48 pp. Gr. 2-4. [R]
When the insect inhabitants of Mushroom Center find their peaceful community threatened by littering humans, William Beetle creates a "Garbage Emergency Plan" to recycle the debris. (BL 70: 1054; CC: 489; CCBB 28: 24; KR 42: 421; LJ 99: 1464)

* BOND, Michael. *A Bear Called Paddington.* Houghton, 1960. Illus. by Peggy Fortnum. 128 pp. Gr. 3-5.
The Brown family decides to adopt a little Peruvian bear they find at Paddington railroad station, but life with Paddington isn't always easy. The sequels are *Paddington Helps Out* (1961), *More about Paddington* (1962), *Paddington at Large* (1963), *Paddington Marches On* (1965), *Paddington at Work* (1967), *Paddington Goes to Town* (1968), *Paddington Takes the Air* (1971), *Paddington Abroad* (1972), *Paddington's Garden* (Random, 1973), *Paddington at the Circus* (Random, 1974), *Paddington's Lucky Day* (1974), *Paddington*

Takes to TV (1974), *Paddington on Top* (1975), *Paddington on Stage* (1977), *Paddington at the Seaside* (Random, 1978), and *Paddington at the Tower* (Random, 1978). The British sequels are *The Adventures of Paddington, Fun and Games with Paddington, Paddington Bear, Paddington Does It Himself, Paddington Goes Shopping, Paddington Goes to the Sales, Paddington Hits Out, Paddington in the Kitchen, Paddington's Birthday Party,* and *Paddington's "Blue Peter" Storybook.* (Arb: 222; CC: 489; HB 37: 53; KR 28: 676; LJ 85: 3856; TLS Nov 21, 1958 p. xiv; Suth: 42)

BOND, Michael. *Tales of Olga Da Polga.* Macmillan, 1973. Illus. by Hans Helweg. 113 pp. Gr. 3–5. [R]
Olga the guinea pig thinks very highly of herself, especially after she wins a pet show prize: Fattest Guinea Pig in the Show. The sequels are *Olga Meets Her Match* (Hastings, 1975), *Olga Carries On* (Hastings, 1977), *Olga Counts Her Blessings* (EMC, pap., 1977), *Olga Makes a Friend* (EMC, pap., 1977), *Olga Makes Her Mark* (EMC, pap., 1977), *Olga Takes a Bite* (EMC, pap., 1977), *Olga's New Home* (EMC, pap., 1977), *Olga's Second House* (EMC, pap., 1977), *Olga's Special Day* (EMC, pap., 1977), *Olga Makes a Wish* (EMC, pap., 1977), and a British sequel: *Olga Da Polga.* (Arb: 237; BL 69: 987, 70: 826; CC: 489; CCBB 27: 38; HB 49: 268; KR 41: 60 and 1349; LJ 98: 1384; TN 30: 8)

BRENNER, Barbara. *Hemi: A Mule.* Harper, 1973. Illus. by J. Higginbottom. 120 pp. Gr. 5–7. [A]
Hemionus, ex-farm mule and official mascot of West Point, runs away from army life to look for a farmhand who once befriended him. (BL 70: 539; KR 41: 1263; LJ 98: 3142)

BROOKS, Walter R. *Freddy the Detective.* Knopf, 1932. Illus. by Kurt Wiese. 263 pp. Gr. 5–7. [A]
Inspired by Sherlock Holmes, Freddy the Pig, the cleverest animal on Mr. Bean's farm, resolves to become a great detective. The sequels are *Freddy's Cousin Weedly* (1940), *Freddy and the Ignormus* (1941), *Freddy and the Perilous Adventure* (1942), *Freddy and the Bean Home News* (1943), *Freddy and Mr. Camphor* (1944), *Freddy and the Popinjay* (1945), *Freddy the Pied Piper* (1946), *Freddy the Magician* (1947), *Freddy Goes Camping* (1948), *Freddy Goes to Florida* (1949), *Freddy Plays Football* (1949), *Freddy Rides Again* (1951), *Freddy the Cowboy* (1951), *Freddy the Pilot* (1952), *Collected Poems of Freddy the Pig* (1953), *Freddy and the Space Ship* (1953), *Freddy and the Men from Mars* (1954), *Freddy and the Baseball Team from Mars* (1955), *Freddy and the Dragon* (1955), *Freddy and Simon the Dictator* (1956), and *Freddy and the Flying Saucer Plans* (1958). (Arb: 237; CC: 491; LJ 57: 865)

BROWN, Palmer. *Hickory.* Harper, 1978. Illus. by the author. 42 pp. Gr. K–3. [R]

Hickory the field mouse's youth inside a grandfather clock does not prepare him for life in the fields, but a friendly grasshopper helps overcome his loneliness. (CC: 1979 Suppl. p. 44; HB 55: 513; KR 46: 1137; SLJ Sept'78 p. 104)

BUCHWALD, Emilie. *Gildaen: The Heroic Adventures of a Most Unusual Rabbit.* See Chapter 5B, Imaginary Lands.

BURGESS, Thornton W(aldo). *Old Mother West Wind.* (Orig. pub. 1910) Little, 1960. Illus. by Harrison Caddy. 140 pp. Gr. 2-4. [A]
Tales of Johnny Chuck, Reddy Fox, and the other animals living near the Green Meadows, the Smiling Pool, the Laughing Brook, and the Lone Little Path through the woods. Other books in this series are *Mother West Wind's Children* (1911; Little, 1962), *Mother West Wind's Animal Friends* (1912; Grosset, 1940), *Mother West Wind's Neighbors* (1913; Little, 1968), *The Adventures of Johnny Chuck* (1913; Grosset, 1952), *The Adventures of Reddy Fox* (1913; Grosset, 1950), *Mother West Wind's "Why" Stories* (1915; Grosset, 1941), *Mother West Wind's "How" Stories* (1916; Grosset, 1941), *The Adventures of Buster Bear* (1916; Grosset, 1941), *Mother West Wind's "When" Stories* (1917; Grosset, 1941), *Mother West Wind's "Where" Stories* (1918; Grosset, 1941), *The Adventures of Old Granny Fox* (Grossett, 1943), *The Adventures of Lightfoot the Deer* (Grosset, 1944), *The Adventures of Whitefoot the Woodmouse* (Grosset, 1944), *The Adventures of Chatterer the Red Squirrel* (Grosset, 1949), *The Adventures of Prickly Porky* (Grosset, 1949), *The Adventures of Sammy Jay* (Grosset, 1949), *The Adventures of Danny Meadowmouse* (Grosset, 1950), *The Adventures of Peter Cottontail* (Grosset, 1950), *The Adventures of Jerry Muskrat* (Grosset, 1951), *The Adventures of Unc' Billy Possum* (Grosset, 1951), *The Adventures of Grandfather Frog* (Grosset, 1952), *The Adventures of Old Man Coyote* (Grosset, 1952), *The Adventures of Poor Mrs. Quack* (Grosset, 1953), *The Adventures of Bob White* (Grosset, 1954), *The Adventures of Bobby Coon* (Grosset, 1954), *The Adventures of Jimmy Skunk* (Grosset, 1954), and *The Adventures of Ol' Mistah Buzzard* (Grosset, 1957). (BL 7: 168; HB 36: 526)

BURMAN, Ben Lucien. *High Water at Catfish Bend.* (Orig. pub. 1952) Penguin, 1977 (pap.). Illus. by Alice Caddy. 121 pp. Gr. 5-7. [A]
The animals of Catfish Bend persuade the Army Corps of Engineers to build levees along the Mississippi River. The sequels are *Seven Stars for Catfish Bend* (1956, 1977), *The Owl Hoots Twice at Catfish Bend* (1961, 1977), *Blow a Wild Bugle for Catfish Bend* (1967, 1979), and *High Treason at Catfish Bend* (Vanguard, 1977). (BL 48: 344; HB 28: 174; KR 20: 224; LJ 77: 1018)

CAMPBELL, Hope. *Peter's Angel: A Story about Monsters.* Four Winds, 1976. Illus. by Lilian Obligado. 151 pp. Gr. 4-6. [A]
After the monster posters in Peter's room come to life, his two mouse friends

decide that an angel is needed to exorcise the creatures. (BL 72: 1525; KR 44: 467; SLJ Sept'76 p. 112)

CARLSON, Natalie. *Alphonse, That Bearded One.* See Chapter 10, Tall Tales.

CHRISTOPHER, Matthew. *The Pigeon with the Tennis Elbow.* Little, 1975. Illus. by Larry Johnson. 115 pp. Gr. 4-6. [M]
Kevin's confidence is restored by a talking pigeon (actually Kevin's reincarnated great-great-uncle Rickard), who helps him to win the town tennis championship. (KR 43: 1227; SLJ Jan'76 p. 44)

* CLEARY, Beverly. *The Mouse and the Motorcycle.* Morrow, 1965. Illus. by Louis Darling. 158 pp. Gr. 2-4.
Keith shows a mouse named Ralph the joys of cycling on a toy motorcycle. *Runaway Ralph* (1970) is the sequel. (Arb: 222; BL 62: 270; CC: 500; CCBB 19: 60; Eakin: 76; HB 41: 628; KR 33: 905; LJ 90: 5510)

CLEARY, Beverly. *Socks.* Morrow, 1973. Illus. by Beatrice Darwin. 156 pp. Gr. 3-5. [R]
The Brickers' new baby deprives a kitten named Socks of the family's undivided attention. (Adv: 148; CC: 501; CCBB 27: 23; KR 41: 599; LJ 98: 2185)

COATSWORTH, Elizabeth. *The Cat and the Captain.* (Orig. pub. 1927) Macmillan, 1974. Illus. by Bernice Loewenstein. 95 pp. Gr. 2-4. [R]
The captain's cat saves his master's house from burglary and earns a place in the housekeeper's heart. (BL 24: 210; CC: 503; CCBB 28: 40; HB 3: 12, 28: 421, 50: 395; KR 42: 364; LJ 99: 2242)

COATSWORTH, Elizabeth. *The Cat Who Went to Heaven.* See Chapter 1, Allegory and Fable.

COATSWORTH, Elizabeth. *The Enchanted: An Incredible Tale.* See Chapter 5B, Imaginary Lands.

COATSWORTH, Elizabeth. *The Snow Parlor and Other Bedtime Stories.* See Chapter 2, Collected Tales.

COBLENTZ, Catherine. *The Blue Cat of Castle Town.* See Chapter 6, Magic Adventure.

COOPER, Paul Fenimore. *Tal: His Marvelous Adventures with Noom-Zor-Noom.* See Chapter 12, Travel to Another World.

CUNNINGHAM, Julia. *Macaroon.* Pantheon, 1962. Illus. by Evaline Ness. 63 pp. Gr. 3-6. [R]
Macaroon, a raccoon who spends his winters in children's homes, decides one winter to choose the home of a selfish, surly child so that it won't be so hard to leave in the spring. (BL 59: 288; HB 38: 480; LJ 87: 4266; TLS 1963 p. 980)

CUNNINGHAM, Julia. *Maybe, a Mole*. Pantheon, 1974. Illus. by Cyndy Szekeres. 81 pp. Gr. 3-5. [R]
Five episodes about a mole named Maybe who is rejected by his own kind because he is not blind, but is befriended by a fox, a mouse, and a turtle. (Adv: 149; Arb: 238; BL 71: 506; CCBB 28: 109; HB 51: 51; KR 42: 1303)

CUSACK, Isabel. *Ivan the Great*. See Chapter 10, Tall Tales.

DAHL, Roald. *James and the Giant Peach, a Children's Story*. See Chapter 6, Magic Adventure.

DANA, Barbara. *Rutgers and the Watersnouts*. Harper, 1969. Illus. by Fred Brenner. 149 pp. Gr. 3-5. [A]
Rutgers the bulldog finds prickly creatures on the beach. When they disappear, Rutgers and his animal friends begin their search for the "watersnouts." (BL 65: 1075; KR 37: 53; LJ 94: 1324)

DAVIS, Robert. *Padre Porko; the Gentlemanly Pig*. (Orig. pub. 1939) Holiday, 1948. Illus. by Fritz Eichenberg. 197 pp. Gr. 5-7. [A]
Twelve tales about a pig who helps people and animals in distress. (BL 36: 308, 45: 17; HB 24: 379; LJ 74: 134)

DE REGNIERS, Beatrice. *The Boy, the Rat, and the Butterfly*. See Chapter 6, Magic Adventure.

DONOVAN, John. *Family: A Novel*. See Chapter 1, Allegory and Fable.

DRURY, Roger. *The Champion of Merrimack County*. Little, 1976. Illus. by Fritz Wegner. 198 pp. Gr. 3-5. [A]
O Crispin is champion mouse bicyclist until a sliver of soap on the Berryfields' bathtub causes a bicycle wreck and a dislocated tail. (BL 73: 1265; CCBB 30: 104; HB 53: 50; KR 44: 1092; SLJ Jan'77 p. 91)

DU BOIS, William Pène. *The Forbidden Forest*. See Chapter 10, Tall Tales.

DU BOIS, William Pène. *The Great Geppy*. See Chapter 10, Tall Tales.

DURRELL, Gerald. *The Talking Parcel*. See Chapter 12, Travel to Another World.

EDMONDS, Walter. *Beaver Valley*. Little, 1971. Illus. by Leslie Morrill. 70 pp. Gr. 4-6. [R]
A young deermouse watches helplessly as the dams built by an ambitious beaver family destroy or displace the other wild creatures of the valley. (BL 67: 797; CC: 513; HB 47: 286; KR 39: 432; LJ 96: 2363)

EDMONDS, Walter. *Time to Go House*. Little, 1969. Illus. by Joan Victor. 137 pp. Gr. 4-6. [A]
Smalleata belongs to a band of field mice that takes over a vacant human house, but her life changes when she falls in love with a house mouse named Raffles. (BL 66: 296; HB 45: 535; KR 37: 776; LJ 94: 4284)

EDMONDSON, Madeline. *The Witch's Egg*. See Chapter 13, Witches, Wizards, Sorcerers, and Magicians.

ERICKSON, Russell. *A Toad for Tuesday*. Lothrop, 1974. Illus. by Laurence Di Fiori. 63 pp. Gr. 3–4. [R]
Captured by an owl, Warton the toad becomes his housekeeper to avoid being eaten as birthday dinner. *Warton and Morton* (1976), *Warton's Christmas Eve Adventure* (1977), *Warton and the King of the Skies* (1978), and *Warton and the Traders* (1979) are the sequels. (BL 71: 98; CC: 515; CCBB 28: 76; HB 51: 48; KR 42: 681; LJ 99: 2244)

EZO, (pseud.). *Avril*. (Orig. pub. 1967) British Book Center, 1976. Tr. by John Buchanan-Brown. Illus. by Douglas Bissot. 94 pp. Gr. 4–6. [A]
Avril leaves her foster parents' home and runs away to the mountains. She brings along Lamb, Cat, a bear named Farou, and a baby ghost. (KR 35: 1046; LJ 92: 4612)

FEAGLES, Anita. *Casey, the Utterly Impossible Horse*. (Orig. pub. 1960) Scholastic, 1962 (pap.). Illus. by Dagmar Wilson. 95 pp. Gr. 2–4. [M]
Mike isn't totally pleased when Casey the talking horse chooses him as a pet. (LJ 85: 4566)

FLACK, Marjorie. *Walter the Lazy Mouse*. (Orig. pub. 1937) Doubleday, 1963. Illus. by Cyndy Szekeres. 95 pp. Gr. 2–4. [A]
Left behind during his family's move, Walter is befriended by Turtle and the three Frogs while he searches for his family. (CC: 518; HB 13: 284; LJ 62: 782)

FORST, S. *Pipkin*. See Chapter 8K, Gnomes.

FORT, John. *June the Tiger*. Little, 1975. Illus. by Bernice Loewenstein. 59 pp. Gr. 4–7. [R]
Mrs. Pinckney's feisty dog, June, and her friend, Billy the Bull, declare war on a bear named Scratch who has ravaged Mrs. Pinckney's house. (BL 72: 855; CCBB 29: 143; HB 52: 48; KR 43: 1397; SLJ Mar'76 p. 102)

FOX, Paula. *Dear Prosper*. White, 1968. Illus. by Steve McLachlin. 67 pp. Gr. 3–5. [A]
A dog named Chien writes his life story in a letter to the boy who was his first master. (KR 36: 393; LJ 93: 2733)

FOX, Paula. *The Little Swineherd and Other Tales*. See Chapter 2, Collected Tales.

FRANKO, Ivan, and MELNYK, Bohdan. *Fox Mykyta*. Tundra (dist. by Scribner), 1978. Tr. by Bodhan Melnyk. Illus. by William Kurelek. 148 pp. Gr. 4–5. [A]
All of the animals in Lion's court are out to get Fox Mykyta, but this wily animal manages to save himself every time. (BL 75: 933; HB 55: 191)

FRESCHET, Bernice. *Bernard of Scotland Yard.* Scribner, 1978. Illus. by Gina Freschet. 48 pp. Gr. 2-3. [R]
Bernard the mouse helps his cousin Foster of Scotland Yard break up a gang of robber moles who are planning a heist of the crown jewels. This is the sequel to *Bernard Sees the World* (1976). (BL 75: 750; CCBB 32: 135; KR 47: 3; SLJ Mar'79 p. 121)

GALLICO, Paul. *The Abandoned* (British title: *Jennie*). (Orig. pub. 1950) Avon, 1977 (pap.). 307 pp. Gr. 8 up. [A]
Injured in an auto accident, a boy named Peter imagines his transformation into a homeless cat, befriended by a worldly and gallant cat named Jenny. (BL 47: 2 and 39; HB 26: 501; KR 18: 394; LJ 75: 2161)

GATES, Doris. *The Cat and Mrs. Cary.* Viking, 1962. Illus. by Peggy Bacon. 216 pp. Gr. 5-7. [A]
Mrs. Cary understands the language of the Cat, who helps solve a mystery. (CC: 523; Eakin: 135; HB 38: 598; LJ 88: 864)

GODDEN, Rumer. *Mouse House.* Illus. by Adrienne Adams. Viking, 1957. 63 pp. Gr. K-3. [R]
Mary makes sure that her miniature house gets the right kind of tenants: a family of mice. (BL 54: 28; CC: 524; HB 33: 483; KR 25: 480; LJ 82: 2693)

GODDEN, Rumer. *The Mousewife.* See Chapter 1, Allegory and Fable.

GOODWIN, Harold. *Top Secret: Alligators!* Bradbury, 1975. Illus. by the author. 94 pp. Gr. 4-5. [A]
Beneath our cities, abandoned pet alligators are uniting to escape sewer life and return to the swamps. (BL 72: 233; KR 43: 711; SLJ Nov'75 p. 77)

GOUDGE, Elizabeth. *Smoky-House.* See Chapter 8H, Fairies.

GUILLOT, René. *The Three Hundred Ninety-Seventh White Elephant.* See Chapter 5B, Imaginary Lands.

* GRAHAME, Kenneth. *The Wind in the Willows.* (Orig. pub. 1908) Scribner, 1954. Illus. by Ernest Shepard. 259 pp.; Heritage, 1940. Illus. by Arthur Rackham. 190 pp. Gr. 4 up.
Ratty, Mole, and Toad fight the weasels and stoats that have taken over Toad Hall. (Adv: 273; Arb: 218; BL 50: 20; CC: 525; HB 30: 83)

GRAY, Nicholas. *Grimbold's Other World.* See Chapter 12, Travel to Another World.

HAAS, Dorothy. *The Bears Up Stairs.* Greenwillow/Morrow, 1978. 192 pp. Gr. 5-7. [A]
Wendy befriends Otto and Ursula Ma'am, two bears hiding in her apartment building while they wait for transportation to the planet Brun. (BL 75: 49; CCBB 32: 44; KR 46: 1248; SLJ Oct'78 p. 144)

HAYES, Geoffrey. *The Alligator and His Uncle Tooth: A Novel of the Sea.*
Harper, 1977. Illus. by the author. 88 pp. Gr. 3–5. [R]
Uncle Tooth's adventure-filled tales convince the old sea captain to sail again,
with Corduroy as mate. (BL 73: 1420; CC 1978 Suppl. p. 50; CCBB 31: 33;
HB 53: 441; KR 45: 350; SLJ Sept'77 p. 109; TLS 1977 p. 1414)

HEWETT, Anita. *The Bull beneath the Walnut Tree and Other Stories.* See
Chapter 2, Collected Tales.

HIMLER, Ronald and Ann. *Little Owl, Keeper of the Trees.* Harper, 1974.
Illus. by Ronald Himler. 63 pp. Gr. K–3. [A]
Although Little Owl is afraid of high places, his favorite spot is the highest
branch of the old Sycamore Tree, where he dreams of being the mighty
guardian of the forest. (BL 71: 570; CCBB 28: 148; KR 42: 1103; SLJ Jan'75
p. 39)

HOBAN, Russell. *The Mouse and His Child.* See Chapter 1, Allegory and
Fable.

HOBAN, Russell. *The Sea-Thing Child.* Harper, 1972. Illus. by Abrom
Hoban. 35 pp. Gr. 2–4. [A]
A newborn sea-thing is cast ashore where the friendly shore creatures ease
its fear of flying. (CCBB 26: 92; KR 40: 1188 and 1412; LJ 98: 644; TLS
1972 p. 1323)

HOLMAN, Felice. *The Cricket Winter.* (Orig. pub. 1967) Dell, 1973 (pap.).
Illus. by Ralph Pinto. 112 pp. Gr. 3–5. [A]
A boy and a cricket communicate in Morse code in order to catch a thieving
rat who is threatening a mouse family. (BL 64: 784; CCBB 21: 111; LJ 92:
3849; Suth: 193)

HORWITZ, Elinor. *The Strange Story of the Frog Who Became a Prince.*
See Chapter 13, Witches, Wizards, Sorcerers, and Magicians.

JARRELL, Randall. *The Bat-Poet.* Macmillan, 1964. Illus. by Maurice
Sendak. 42 pp. Gr. 3–5. [A]
A young bat writes poetry about day-creatures to convince his nocturnal
friends to stay awake during the day. (Arb: 221; CC: 536; LJ 89: 2210)

JARRELL, Randall. *Fly by Night.* See Chapter 6, Magic Adventure.

JONES, Diana Wynne. *Dogsbody.* Greenwillow/ Morrow, 1977. 242 pp. Gr.
6–8. [A]
Visiting Earth in search of a sacred object that fell from the sky, Sirius, the
Dog Star, takes on a dog's form and befriends a lonely human girl. (BL 73:
1414 and 1421; CCBB 30: 176; HB 53: 319; KR 45: 95; SLJ May'77
p. 62; TLS 1976 p. 383)

KENNEDY, Richard. *Come Again in the Spring.* See Chapter 1, Allegory and
Fable.

KENNY, Herbert A. *Dear Dolphin*. See Chapter 12, Travel to Another World.

KIPLING, Rudyard. *The Jungle Book*. See Chapter 2, Collected Tales.

KIPLING, Rudyard. *Just So Stories*. See Chapter 2, Collected Tales.

KRENSKY, Stephen. *Woodland Crossings*. See Chapter 2, Collected Tales.

LAWSON, John S. *You Better Come Home with Me*. See Chapter 1, Allegory and Fable.

LAWSON, Robert. *Ben and Me: A New and Astonishing Life of Benjamin Franklin As Written by His Good Mouse, Amos: Lately Discovered*. (Orig. pub. 1939) Little, 1951. Illus. by the author, 114 pp. Gr. 4–8. [R]
Amos Mouse discloses the fact that most of Ben Franklin's inventions were actually Amos's ideas, and describes their adventures together. (Arb: 219; BL 36: 117; CC: 541; HB 15: 388, 16: 28; LJ 65: 125)

LAWSON, Robert. *Captain Kidd's Cat: Being the True and Dolorous Chronicle of Wm. Kidd, Gentleman and Merchant of New York; Late Captain of the Adventure Galley; Of the Vicissitudes Attending His Unfortunate Cruise in Eastern Waters, Of His Unjust Trial and Execution, As Narrated by His Faithful Cat, McDermot, Who Ought to Know*. Little, 1956. Illus. by the author. 151 pp. Gr. 5–8. [R]
McDermot doesn't think Captain Kidd deserves to be called a pirate. (BL 52: 282; Eakin: 203; HB 32: 121; KR 24: 3; LJ 81: 767)

LAWSON, Robert. *I Discover Columbus: A True Chronicle of the Great Admiral and His Finding of the New World, Narrated by the Venerable Parrot Aurelio, Who Shared in the Glorious Venture*. Little, 1941. Illus. by the author. 110 pp. Gr. 5–8. [A]
Aurelio, a Caribbean parrot stranded in Spain, convinces Columbus to make a voyage of discovery to the New World. (BL 38: 58; HB 17: 366 and 453; LJ 66: 908)

LAWSON, Robert. *Mr. Revere and I: Being an Account of Certain Episodes in the Career of Paul Revere, Esq., As Recently Revealed by His Horse, Scheherazade, Late Pride of His Royal Majesty's 14th Regiment of Foot*. Little, 1953. Illus. by the author. 152 pp. Gr. 5 up. [R]
Scheherazade, a former cavalry horse rescued by Sam Adams from the glue factory, tells of her subsequent life with Paul Revere's family. (BL 50: 84; CC: 541; Eakin: 204; HB 29: 464; KR 21: 357; LJ 78: 1858)

LAWSON, Robert. *Rabbit Hill*. Viking, 1944. Illus. by the author. 127 pp. Gr. 3–6. [R]
Although they are happy that a new family is moving into the empty farmhouse, the animals on Rabbit Hill worry that the people might bring traps and guns. The sequels are *Robbut: A Tale of Tails* (1948) and *The*

Tough Winter (1954). Newbery Medal. (Arb: 219; BL 41: 62; CC: 541; HB 20: 487; KR 12: 403; LJ 69: 866 and 886)

LAZARUS, Keo. *The Shark in the Window*. See Chapter 10, Tall Tales.

LEWIS, C. S. *The Lion, the Witch and the Wardrobe*. See Chapter 12, Travel to Another World.

LITTLE, Jane. *Danger at Sneaker Hill*. See Chapter 13, Witches, Wizards, Sorcerers, and Magicians.

LOFTING, Hugh. *The Story of Mrs. Tubbs*. (Orig. pub. 1923) Lippincott, 1968. Illus. by the author. 91 pp. Gr. 2-4. [A]
Peter Punk the dog, Polly Ponk the duck, and Patrick Ping the pig take care of old Mrs. Tubbs until she can come home to her farm. (BL 20: 63; KR 36: 393)

McGOWEN, Tom. *Odyssey from River Bend*. Little, 1975. 166 pp. Gr. 4-6. [R]
Kip the badger leads a group of animals from River Bend into the Haunted Land to search for the secrets of the ancients. (BL 72: 44; CCBB 29: 82; KR 43: 513; SLJ Sept'75 p. 107)

McPHAIL, David. *Henry Bear's Park*. Little, 1976. Illus. by the author. 47 pp. Gr. 2-4. [R]
During the long wait for his balloonist father's return, Henry the Bear devotes himself to beautifying their park. Stanley Raccoon's life story is told in the companion volume, *Stanley, Henry Bear's Friend* (1979). (BL 72: 1408; KR 44: 589; SLJ Sept'76 p. 102)

MARSHALL, James. *A Summer in the South*. Houghton, 1977. Illus. by the author. 97 pp. Gr. 2-4. [A]
Eleanor Owl, famous detective, solves the case of the ghostly figure frightening Marietta Chicken. (KR 45: 1144; SLJ Dec'77 p. 61)

MERRILL, Jean. *The Black Sheep*. Pantheon, 1969. Illus. by Ronni Solbert. 73 pp. Gr. 4-6. [A]
A black sheep born into a community of white ones refuses to conform: Instead of knitting sweaters, he wears his own shaggy coat and spends his time gardening. (CCBB 23: 131; LJ 95: 1641, 1912 and 3603; Suth: 279)

MOLESWORTH, Mary. *The Cuckoo Clock*. See Chapter 12, Travel to Another World.

MURPHY, Shirley R. *Flight of the Fox*. Atheneum, 1978. Illus. by Donald Sibley, based on original designs by Richard Cuffari. 164 pp. Gr. 5-7. [A]
A kangaroo rat and a pet lemming ask a boy named Charlie to help them pilot a motorized model airplane. (BL 75: 384; CCBB 32: 142; KR 46: 1358; SLJ Jan'79 p. 56)

NEWMAN, Robert. *The Shattered Stone.* See Chapter 4, Good versus Evil.

NEWMAN, Sharon. *Dagda's Harp.* See Chapter 5B, Imaginary Lands.

NICKL, Peter. *Crocodile, Crocodile* (British title: *The Crocodile*). Tundra, 1976. Tr. by Ebbitt Cutler. Illus. by Binette Schroeder. Unp. Gr. 5–7. [A]
Omar the crocodile is excited over his trip to Paris to visit the crocodile store. But his excitement turns to horror when he discovers that he has come to a shop full of crocodile leather goods. (BL 73: 898; CCBB 30: 178; KR 44: 1262; SLJ Jan'77 p. 94)

NIXON, Joan. *Muffie Mouse and the Busy Birthday.* Seabury, 1978. Illus. by Geoffrey Hayes. 46 pp. Gr. 2–4. [A]
Muffie's plans for her mother's birthday go awry: Constant interruptions keep her from finishing the decorations, visits by friends disrupt the cookie-making, and the special birthday breakfast ends up on the floor. (BL 75: 617; KR 47: 63; SLJ Jan'79 p. 45)

NORTON, André. *Fur Magic.* See Chapter 6, Magic Adventure.

O'BRIEN, Robert C. (pseud. of Robert Conly). *Mrs. Frisby and the Rats of NIMH.* Atheneum, 1971. Illus. by Zena Bernstein. 233 pp. Gr. 4–7. [R]
Mrs. Frisby, a field mouse with a problem, is befriended by a group of superintelligent laboratory rats, and manages to save their lives. Newbery Medal. (Arb: 221; BL 67: 955, 68: 670; CC: 555; CCBB 25: 29; HB 47: 385; LJ 96: 4159 and 4186; Suth: 298; TLS 1972 p. 1317; TN 28: 74)

PEET, Bill. *Big Bad Bruce.* Houghton, 1977. Illus. by the author. 38 pp. Gr. 2–4. [A]
Bruce the bear bully is put in his place by a witch named Roxy who shrinks him to chipmunk size. (BL 73: 1172; CCBB 30: 163; HB 53: 302; KR 45: 163)

PEET, Bill. *The Whingdingdilly.* Houghton, 1970. Illus. by the author. 60 pp. Gr. 2–4. [A]
Wishing to become a famous horse, Orvie's dog Scamp changes into a creature that is part elephant, camel, zebra, rhinoceros, and giraffe. (BL 66: 1280; HB 46: 291; KR 38: 317; LJ 95: 2309; TLS 1971 p. 1515)

PINKWATER, D(aniel) Manus. *Blue Moose.* Dodd, 1975. Illus. by the author. 47 pp. Gr. 3–5. [R]
The maitre d' of Mr. Breton's gourmet restaurant in the wild is a talking blue moose. *Return of the Moose* (1979) is the sequel. (BL 72: 45; CCBB 29: 84; HB 52: 46; KR 43: 661; SLJ Sept'75 p. 88)

PINKWATER, D. Manus. *The Hoboken Chicken Emergency.* See Chapter 10, Tall Tales.

PINKWATER, D. Manus. *Lizard Music.* See Chapter 10, Tall Tales.

POTTER, Beatrix. *The Fairy Caravan.* (Orig. pub. 1929) Warne, 1951. 225 pp. Gr. 4–6. [A]
The animal caravan traveling through the English countryside includes Tuppeny the long-haired guinea pig, Pony Billy, Jenny Ferret, and Princess Xarifa the doormouse. (BL 47: 278; HB 5: 48, 28: 163)

POTTER, Beatrix. *The Tale of the Faithful Dove.* (Orig. pub. 1956) Warne, 1970. Illus. by Marie Angel. 2nd ed. Unp. Gr. 2–4. [A]
A mother dove fleeing a falcon becomes trapped in a chimney, but a mouse family and a boy help her to escape. (CC: 558; CCBB 24: 112; HB 46: 604; KR 38: 1141; LJ 96: 1498; TLS 1971 p. 768)

PUSHKIN, Alexander. *The Tale of Czar Saltan, or the Prince and the Swan Princess.* See Chapter 5B, Imaginary Lands.

ROBERTSON, Keith. *Tales of Myrtle the Turtle.* Viking, 1974. Illus. by Peter Parnall. 121 pp. Gr. 3–6. [M]
Aunt Myrtle recounts the spectacular achievements of Uncle Herman the turtle to Gloria and Witherspoon, including his invention of the light bulb, landing on the moon, and scaling of the Matterhorn. (KR 42: 944; LJ 99: 2276)

ROBERTSON, Mary. *Jemimalee.* McGraw, 1977. Illus. by Judith Brown. 122 pp. Gr. 4–7. [M].
Jemimalee the cat poet's biggest problem is a huge barn rat named Orzo. (KR 45: 991; SLJ Dec'77 p. 50)

SCHICK, Alice, and ALLEN, Marjorie. *The Remarkable Ride of Israel Bissell as Related by Molly the Crow: Being the True Account of an Extraordinary Post Rider Who Persevered.* See Chapter 10, Tall Tales.

SELDEN, George (pseud. of George Selden Thompson). *The Cricket in Times Square.* Farrar, 1960. Illus. by Garth Williams. 151 pp. Gr. 2–7. [R]
Chester Cricket's beautiful music (as managed by Tucker Mouse) brings fame to Chester and fortune to the subway-station newspaper stand where they live. The sequels are *Tucker's Countryside* (1969) and *Harry Cat's Pet Puppy* (1974). (Arb: 220; BL 57: 250; CC: 563; Eakin: 288; HB 36: 407; LJ 85: 4570)

SENDAK, Maurice. *Higglety Pigglety Pop! Or, There Must Be More to Life.* Harper, 1967. Illus. by the author. 69 pp. Gr. K–3. [R]
Bored by life at home, a dog named Jenny packs her bag and sets off to find happiness as the leading lady in the World Mother Goose Theatre. (Arb: 214; BL 64: 451; CC: 564; CCBB 21: 66; HB 44: 151 and 161; KR 35: 1209; LJ 92: 4618; Suth: 354)

* SHARP, Margery. *The Rescuers.* Little, 1959. Illus. by Garth Williams. 149 pp. Gr. 3–7.
Miss Bianca the mouse and two friends go on a dangerous mission to rescue a poet from imprisonment in a deep dungeon. The sequels are *Miss Bianca*

(1962), *The Turret* (1963), *Miss Bianca in the Salt Mines* (1966), *Miss Bianca in the Orient* (1970), *Miss Bianca in the Antarctic* (1971), *Miss Bianca and the Bridesmaid* (1972), *Bernard the Brave* (1977), and *Bernard into Battle* (1978). *Miss Bianca in the Arctic* is a British sequel. (Arb: 222; BL 56: 274; CC: 565; Eakin: 295; HB 36: 38; KR 27: 617; LJ 84: 3153; TLS Dec 4, 1959 p. xv)

SHEEDY, Alexandra. *She Was Nice to Mice: The Other Side of Elizabeth I's Character Never Before Revealed by Previous Historians.* McGraw, 1975. Illus. by Jessica Levy. 95 pp. Gr. 3–5. [A]
Esther Long Whiskers Gray Hair Wallgate the 42nd, a mouse with a literary mind, finds the memoirs of one of her ancestors who lived at the court of Queen Elizabeth I. (CCBB 29: 86; KR 43: 849; SLJ Oct'75 p. 108)

SMITH, Agnes. *An Edge of the Forest.* See Chapter 1, Allegory and Fable.

SMITH, Dodie (pseud. of Dorothy Smith). *The Hundred and One Dalmatians.* Viking, 1957. Illus. by Janet and Anne Grahame-Johnstone. 199 pp. Gr. 4–7. [R]
Pongo and Missis Dalmatian rescue their fifteen puppies from Cruella DeVil, who dognapped them to make into fur coats. *The Starlight Barking* (1967) is the sequel. (BL 53: 588; HB 33: 222; KR 25: 75; LJ 82: 1802)

SMITH, Emma. *Emily: The Traveling Guinea Pig.* Astor-Honor, 1960. Illus. by Katherine Wigglesworth. 76 pp. Gr. 3–5. [A]
Emily Guinea Pig sets off to see the ocean, leaving behind her brother Arthur to look after her tidy little house. *Emily's Voyage* (Harcourt, 1966) is the sequel. (HB 36: 287; KR 28: 232)

STEARNS, Pamela. *Into the Painted Bear Lair.* See Chapter 12, Travel to Another World.

* STEIG, William. *Abel's Island.* Farrar, 1976. Illus. by the author. 117 pp. Gr. 3–6.
A storm sweeps Abel the mouse away from his new bride, Amanda, to a deserted island, where he develops a talent for sculpting while waiting to go home. (Adv: 201; BL 73: 181; CC 1977 Suppl. p. 70; CCBB 30: 33; HB 52: 500; KR 44: 686; SLJ Oct' 76 p. 101; TLS 1977 p. 1248)

STEIG, William. *Dominic.* Farrar, 1972. Illus. by the author. 145 pp. Gr. 4–7. [R]
An adventurous dog named Dominic finds an enchanted garden, is given a fortune by an old pig, and helps fight the Doomsday Gang. (Arb: 222; BL 69: 531; CC: 569; CCBB 26: 31; HB 48: 470; KR 40: 1414; LJ 97: 2954; Suth: 378; TLS 1973 p. 386)

STEIG, William. *The Real Thief.* Farrar, 1973. Illus. by the author. 58 pp. Gr. 2–5. [R]
Angry over the theft of his jewels, the king accuses his loyal guard, Gawain the

goose, in spite of Gawain's pleas of innocence. (Adv: 201; Arb: 242; BL 70: 242 and 827; CC: 569; CCBB 27: 102; HB 49: 595; KR 41: 756; LJ 98: 3446; TN 30: 206)

STEVENSON, James. *Here Comes Herb's Hurricane!* Harper, 1973. 149 pp. Gr. 2–4. [A]
Herb Rabbit develops a hurricane warning system that refuses to work until a real hurricane comes along. (CCBB 27: 150; KR 41: 1310 and 1351; LJ 98: 3709)

STOLTZ, Mary. *Belling the Tiger*. Harper, 1961. Illus. by Beni Montresor. 64 pp. Gr. 2–3. [R]
Asa and Rambo the mouse are selected to put a bell on Siri, the tigerlike housecat, which starts their unexpected trip to a land of elephants and real tigers. The sequels are *The Great Rebellion* (1961), *Siri the Conquistador* (1963), and *Maximilian's World* (1966). (Arb: 242; BL 57: 644; Eakin: 314; HB 37: 339; KR 29: 326; LJ 86: 1989)

TITUS, Eve. *Basil of Baker Street*. (Orig. pub. 1958) Archway, n.d. (pap.). Illus. by Paul Galdone. 128 pp. Gr. 3–5. [A]
Basil, an English mouse detective who idolizes Sherlock Holmes, solves one of Mousedom's most baffling and mysterious kidnapping cases. The sequels are *Basil and the Lost Colony* (1964), *Basil and the Pygmy Cats* (1971), and *Basil in Mexico* (1975). (BL 54: 593; CC: 575; HB 34: 266; KR 26: 335; LJ 83: 1947)

TODD, Ruthven. *Space Cat*. Scribner, 1952. Illus. by Paul Galdone. 69 pp. Gr. 3–5. [A]
During Flyball the cat's trip to the moon, he makes an important scientific discovery and saves the pilot's life. The sequels are *Space Cat Visits Venus* (1955), *Space Cat Meets Mars* (1957), and *Space Cat and the Kittens* (1959). (Arb: 233 and 242; HB 28: 320; KR 20: 657; LJ 77: 1819)

TURKLE, Brinton. *Mooncoin Castle; or Skulduggery Rewarded*. See Chapter 3, Ghosts.

VAN LEEUWEN, Jean. *The Great Christmas Kidnapping Caper*. Dial, 1975. Illus. by Steven Kellogg. 133 pp. Gr. 3–5. [R]
The disappearance of Santa Claus mobilizes Marvin the Magnificent Mouse and his gang to the rescue. This is the sequel to *The Great Cheese Conspiracy* (Random, 1969). (BL 72: 169; CCBB 29: 54; KR 43: 778; SLJ Oct'75 p. 81)

WAECHTER, Friedrich, and EILERT, Bernd. *The Crown Snatchers*. See Chapter 5A, Alternative Worlds.

WAHL, Jan. *Pleasant Fieldmouse*. Harper, 1964. Illus. by Maurice Sendak. 65 pp. Gr. 2–4. [A]
Pleasant Fieldmouse becomes a firefighter and courageously rescues Anxious Squirrel's mother and Mrs. Worrywind Hedgehog. The sequels are *The Six

Voyages of Pleasant Fieldmouse (Delacorte, 1971), *Pleasant Fieldmouse's Halloween Party* (Putnam, 1974), and *The Pleasant Fieldmouse Storybook* (Prentice-Hall, 1977), *Pleasant Fieldmouse's Valentine Trick* (Dutton, 1977). (CCBB 18: 94; HB 40: 373; LJ 89: 3477; TLS 1969 p. 1387)

WALLACE, Barbara. *Palmer Patch*. Follett, 1976. Illus. by Lawrence Di Fiori. 128 pp. Gr. 4–6. [A]
The Patch family pets—skunk, cat, goat, duck, and dogs—run away from home, thinking they are no longer wanted. (BL 73: 671; CCBB 30: 116; SLJ Apr'77 p. 72)

WANGERIN, Walter, Jr. *The Book of the Dun Cow*. See Chapter 1, Allegory and Fable.

WENNING, Elizabeth. *The Christmas Mouse* (British title: *The Christmas Churchmouse*). Illus. by Barbara Remington. 44 pp. Gr. K–4. [A]
Kaspar Kleinmouse, a hungry little churchmouse, helps Herr Gruber write the Christmas carol "Silent Night." (BL 56: 225; HB 35: 471; KR 27: 756; LJ 84: 3627)

✓WHITE, Anne. *Junket*. (Orig. pub. 1955) Archway, 1976 (pap.). Illus. by Robert McCloskey. 183 pp. Gr. 4–6. [R]
Junket the Airedale needs an entire summer to teach his new owners about life on a farm. (BL 51: 287; CC: 577; Eakin: 348; HB 31: 114; KR 23: 81; LJ 80: 1259)

✓* WHITE, E(lwyn) B(rooks). *Charlotte's Web*. Harper, 1952. Illus. by Garth Williams. 184 pp. Gr. 3 up.
When Wilbur the pig is destined for the annual fall slaughtering, his resourceful friend, a spider named Charlotte, tries to save him. (Adv: 273; Arb: 220; BL 49: 2; CC: 577; Eakin: 348; HB 28: 394 and 407; KR 20: 501; LJ 77: 2185; TLS 1952 p. 7)

✓WHITE, E. B. *Stuart Little*. Harper, 1945. Illus. by Garth Williams. 131 pp. Gr. 4–6. [A]
Stuart Little is the second son of a normal Amerian family—except that Stuart turned out to be a mouse instead of a boy. (Arb: 220; CC: 578; HB 21: 455; KR 13: 314)

WHITE, E. B. *The Trumpet of the Swan*. Harper, 1970. Illus. by Edward Frascino. 210 pp. Gr. 4–6. [A]
Lewis's father buys him a trumpet to overcome his speech defect and starts the young swan on a career as a nightclub entertainer. (Arb: 220; BL 67: 59 and 661; CC: 578; CCBB 24: 35; HB 46: 391; KR 38: 455; LJ 95: 2537 and 4327; TLS 1970 p. 1458)

WIGGIN, Kate. *The Birds' Christmas Carol.* See Chapter 1, Allegory and Fable.

WILDE, Oscar. *The Happy Prince.* See Chapter 1, Allegory and Fable.

WILLIAMS, Garth. *The Adventures of Benjamin Pink.* (Orig. pub. 1952) Dell, 1971 (pap.). Illus. by the author. 152 pp. Gr. 2–4. [A]
A shipwrecked rabbit named Benjamin Pink has a more adventure-filled fishing trip than he'd originally planned. (HB 27: 400, 28: 27; KR 19: 347; LJ 76: 1710)

WILLIAMS, Ursula Moray. *Bogwoppit.* Nelson, 1978. 128 pp. Gr. 5–7. [R]
Samantha's crusade to save the furry creatures who live in the drains of her aunt's mansion takes a new turn when her aunt is kidnapped by the Bogwoppits. (BL 75: 54; CCBB 32: 128; KR 46: 879; SLJ Sept'78 p. 152; TLS 1978 p. 765)

WILLIAMS, Ursula Moray. *Tiger Nanny.* See Chapter 10, Tall Tales.

WILSON, Gahan. *Harry the Fat Bear Spy.* Scribner, 1973. Illus. by the author. 120 pp. Gr. 5–7. [A]
Harry would rather be a chef or a tap dancer than the bumbling spy he is, but he manages to solve the case of the green Bearmania macaroons. *Harry and the Sea Serpent* (1976) is the sequel. (Adv: 203; KR 41: 698; LJ 99: 2281)

WRIGGINS, Sally, ed. *The White Monkey King: A Chinese Fable.* See Chapter 1, Allegory and Fable.

YOLEN, Jane. *Hobo Toad and the Motorcycle Gang.* Collins + World, 1970. Illus. by Emily McCully. 62 pp. Gr. 3–5. [A]
An attempted bank robbery and kidnapping are foiled by Hobo Toad, a poetic truck driver, a waitress, and a boy. (BL 67: 149; HB 46: 391; KR 38: 455; LJ 95: 3056)

ZIMNIK, Reiner. *The Bear and the People.* See Chapter 1, Allegory and Fable.

Talking Animals: Out-of-Print Works

AGLE, Nan. *K Mouse and Bo Bixby.* Seabury, 1972. Illus. by Harold Berson. 96 pp. Gr. 4–5. (Adv: 180; CCBB 25: 149; KR 40: 134; LJ 97: 2235)

ALLFREY, Katherine. *The Golden Island.* See Chapter 6, Magic Adventure: Out-of-Print Works.

ANDERSEN, Hans Christian. *The Ugly Duckling.* See Chapter 1, Allegory and Fable: Out-of-Print Works.

ANNETT, Cora. *When the Porcupine Moved In.* Watts, 1971. Illus. by Peter Parnall. 40 pp. Gr. K–3. (BL 68: 626; CCBB 25: 70; LJ 97: 1593)

ANNIXTER, Paul (pseud. of Paul Comfort). *The Cat That Clumped.* Holiday, 1966. Illus. by Brinton Turkle. 41 pp. Gr. 2–4. (CCBB 19: 157; KR 34: 240; LJ 91: 1694)

ARUNDEL, Honor. *The Amazing Mr. Prothero.* Nelson, 1972. Illus. by Jane Paton. 80 pp. Gr. 3–5. (Adv: 182; BL 69: 200; CCBB 26: 101; KR 40: 30; LJ 97: 2928)

BABCOCK, Elisabeth. *The Expandable Pig.* See Chapter 10, Tall Tales: Out-of-Print Works.

BAILEY, Carolyn. *Finnegan II: His Nine Lives.* Viking, 1953. Illus. by Kate Seredy. 95 pp. Gr. 4–7. (BL 50: 150; CC: 482; HB 29: 455; LJ 78: 2225)

BAILEY, Carolyn. *Flickertail.* Walck, 1962. Illus. by Garry MacKenzie. 90 pp. Gr. 3–5. (HB 38: 368)

BAKER, Elizabeth. *Sunny-Boy Sim.* Rand, 1948. Illus. by Susanne Suba. 31 pp. Gr. 1–4. (BL 45: 320; HB 25: 285; KR 17: 177; LJ 74: 666)

BAKER, Margaret Joyce. *Homer Goes to Stratford.* Prentice-Hall, 1958. Illus. by W. T. Mars. 141 pp. Gr. 4–6. The British sequels are *Homer the Tortoise* and *Homer Sees the Queen.* (BL 55: 264; KR 26: 662; LJ 83: 3570)

BAKER, Margret Joyce. *Porterhouse Major.* See Chapter 6, Magic Adventure: Out-of-Print Works.

BAKER, Olaf. *Bengey and the Beast.* See Chapter 6, Magic Adventure: Out-of-Print Works.

BEECROFT, John. *What? Another Cat!* Dodd, 1966. Illus. by Kurt Wiese. Unp. Gr. 2–4. (KR 28: 753; LJ 85: 4557)

BEHN, Harry. *Roderick.* Harcourt, 1961. Illus. by Mel Silverman. 64 pp. Gr. 4–6. (HB 37: 340; LJ 86: 2353)

BERESFORD, Elizabeth. *The Wombles.* (Orig. pub. 1968) Penguin, 1975. Illus. by Margaret Gordon. 183 pp. Gr. 4–6. The British sequels are *MacWomble's Pipe Band, The Invisible Womble, The Snow Womble, The Wandering Wombles, The Wombles at Work, The Wombles Book, The Wombles go Round the World, The Wombles in Danger, The Wombles Make a Clean Sweep, The Wombles of Wimbledon,* and *The Wombles to the Rescue.* (KR 37: 1147; LJ 95: 1192; TLS 1968 p. 1376, 1973 p. 386)

BEST, Herbert. *Desmond's First Case.* Viking, 1961. Illus. by Ezra Jack Keats. 96 pp. Gr. 4–6. The sequels are *Desmond the Dog Detective: The Case of the Lone Stranger* (1962), *Desmond and the Peppermint Ghost; the Dog Detective's Third Case* (1965) and *Desmond and Dog Friday* (1968). (KR 29: 55; LJ 86: 1980)

BESTERMAN, Catherine. *The Quaint and Curious Quest of Johnny Long-foot, the Shoe King's Son.* Bobbs-Merrill, 1947. 147 pp. Gr. 5–7. (BL 44: 116; HB 23: 435, 24: 36; LJ 72: 1618)

BESTON, Henry (pseud. of Henry Beston Sheahan), and COATSWORTH, Elizabeth. *Chimney Farm Bedtime Stories.* (Orig. pub. 1938) Holt, 1966. Illus. by Maurice Day. 79 pp. Gr. 3–4. (HB 42: 707; KR 34: 1098; LJ 92: 371)

BIANCO, Margery Williams. *The Good Friends.* Viking, 1934. Illus. by Grace Paull. 142 pp. Gr. 4–6. (BL 31: 67; HB 10: 296)

BIANCO, Margery Williams. *Poor Cecco.* See Chapter 7, Magical Toys: Out-of-Print Works.

BLAISDELL, Mary Frances. *Bunny Rabbit's Diary.* (Orig. pub. 1915) Little, rev. ed., 1960. Illus. by Anne Jauss. 91 pp. Gr. 3–5. (KR 28: 89)

BOND, Michael. *Here Comes Thursday.* Lothrop, 1967. Illus. by Daphne Rowles. 126 pp. Gr. 3–5. The sequels are *Thursday Rides Again* (1969) and *Thursday Ahoy!* (1970). *Thursday in Paris* is a British sequel. (BL 64: 541; CCBB 21: 106; HB 43: 748; KR 35: 1204; LJ 93: 1301; TLS 1966 p. 1087)

BOSHINSKI, Blanche. *Aha and the Jewel of Mystery.* Parents, 1968. Illus. by Shirley Pulido. 155 pp. Gr. 5–7. (HB 45: 168; LJ 94: 868)

BOUTWELL, Edna. *Sailor Tom.* World, 1960. Illus. by Kurt Werth. 89 pp. Gr. 3–5. (KR 28: 185; LJ 85: 2034)

BOYLE, Kay. *The Youngest Camel.* See Chapter 1, Allegory and Fable: Out-of-Print Works.

BRO, Margueritte. *The Animal Friends of Peng-U.* Doubleday, 1965. Illus. by Seong Moy. 96 pp. Gr. 1–4. (BL 61: 956; HB 41: 274; KR 33: 173)

BROOKS, Walter. *To and Again.* Knopf, 1927. Illus. by Adolfo Best-Maugard. 196 pp. Gr. 4–6. (BL 24: 30; TLS 1927 p. 883)

BUTTERS, Dorothy C. *Papa Dolphin's Table.* Knopf, 1955. Illus. by Kurt Werth. 88 pp. Gr. 4–6. (BL 52: 171; Eakin: 56; KR 23: 597; LJ 80: 2640)

BUZZATI, Dino. *The Bears' Famous Invasion of Sicily.* Pantheon, 1947. Tr. by Frances Lobb. Illus. by the author. 146 pp. Gr. 4–6. (BL 44: 189; HB 24: 36; KR 15: 625; LJ 72: 1473)

CAPEK, Joseph. *Harum Scarum.* (Orig. pub. 1959) Norton, 1967. Tr. by Stephen Jolly. Illus. by the author. 95 pp. Gr. 2–5. (KR 35: 409; LJ 92: 2648)

CARLSON, Natalie. *Evangeline, Pigeon of Paris.* (British title: *Pigeon of Paris*). Harcourt, 1960. Illus. by Nicolas Mordvinoff. 72 pp. Gr. 4–6. (BL 56: 632; HB 36: 215; KR 28: 184; LJ 85: 2475)

CAUFIELD, Don and Joan. *The Incredible Detectives.* Harper, 1966. Illus. by Kiyo Komoda. 75 pp. Gr. 4–6. (Adv: 236; CCBB 20: 71; HB 42: 708; KR 34: 830; LJ 91: 5771; Suth: 67)

CLARK, Ann N. *Looking-for-Something: The Story of a Stray Burro of Ecuador.* Viking, 1952. Illus. by Leo Politi. 53 pp. Gr. 1–4. (BL 48: 236; HB 28: 96; KR 20: 123; LJ 77: 725)

CLIFFORD, Peggy. *Elliott.* Houghton, 1967. Illus. by Jacqueline Chwast. 119 pp. Gr. 4–6. (HB 44: 57; KR 35: 1365; LJ 93: 289)

COLUM, Padraic. *The White Sparrow.* (British title: *Sparrow Alone*). (Orig. pub. 1933) McGraw, 1972. Illus. by Joseph Low. 61 pp. Gr. 3–5. (BL 29: 344; KR 40: 1097; LJ 58: 805, 98: 259)

COOPER, Elizabeth. *The Wild Cats of Rome.* Golden Gate, 1972. Illus. by Don Freeman. 70 pp. Gr. 3–6. (Adv: 149; KR 40: 1025; LJ 98: 642)

CREGAN, Mairin. *Old John.* See Chapter 8H, Fairies: Out-of-Print Works.

CUNNINGHAM, Julia. *Candle Tales.* Pantheon, 1964. Illus. by Evaline Ness. 57 pp. Gr. 3–5. (HB 40: 376; LJ 89: 1448)

CUNNINGHAM, Julia. *Viollet.* Pantheon, 1966. Illus. by Alan Cober. 82 pp. Gr. 4–6. (CCBB 20: 86; KR 34: 1054; LJ 91: 6190)

DE LA MARE, Walter. *Mr. Bumps and His Monkey.* Holt, 1942. Illus. by Dorothy Lathrop. 69 pp. Gr. 4–6. (BL 39: 73; CC: 510; HB 18: 426; LJ 67: 884 and 955)

DE LA MARE, Walter. *Three Royal Monkeys* (Orig. title: *Three Mulla Mulgars,* 1919). Knopf, 1966. Illus. by Mildred Eldridge. 277 pp. Gr. 5–7. (Arb: 238; BL 45: 110)

DE LA ROCHE, Mazo. *The Song of Lambert.* Little, 1955. Illus. by Eileen Soper. 52 pp. Gr. 2–4. (KR 24: 431; LJ 81: 2038)

DOLBIER, Maurice. *A Lion in the Woods.* See Chapter 10, Tall Tales: Out-of-Print Works.

DU BOIS, William Pène. *Elizabeth the Cow Ghost.* See Chapter 3, Ghosts: Out-of-Print Works.

DU BOIS, William Pène. *The Squirrel Hotel.* See Chapter 10, Tall Tales: Out-of-Print Works.

DUMAS, Gerald. *Rabbits Rafferty.* Houghton, 1968. Illus. by Wallace Tripp. 196 pp. Gr. 4–6. (CCBB 22: 25; KR 36: 510; LJ 193: 68; TLS 1970 p. 414)

ERWIN, John. *Mrs. Fox.* Simon, 1969. Illus. by Wallace Tripp. 127 pp. Gr. 4–6. (CCBB 23: 6; KR 37: 99; LJ 94: 1780; Suth: 117)

ESTES, Eleanor. *Miranda the Great.* Harcourt, 1967. Illus. by Edward Ardizzone. 79 pp. Gr. 3–6. (BL 63: 948; CCBB 20: 120; HB 43: 201; KR 35: 130; LJ 92: 1315)

EZO (pseud.). *My Son-in-Law, the Hippopotamus.* Abelard-Schuman, 1962. Tr. by Hugh Shelley. Illus. by Quentin Blake. 160 pp. Gr. 4–6. (HB 38: 602)

FARALLA, Dana. *The Singing Cupboard.* See Chapter 6, Magic Adventure: Out-of-Print Works.

FORBUS, Ina. *The Magic Pin.* See Chapter 6, Magic Adventure: Out-of-Print Works.

FREEMAN, Barbara. *Broom-Adelaide.* See Chapter 5B, Imaginary Lands: Out-of-Print Works.

FRY, Rosalie. *The Wind Call.* See Chapter 8H, Fairies: Out-of-Print Works.

GALL, Alice, and CREW, Fleming. *Ringtail.* Oxford, 1933. Illus. by James Reid. 119 pp. Gr. 3–5. (BL 30: 88)

GAUNT, Michael. *Brim's Boat.* Coward, 1966. Illus. by Stuart Tresilian. 128 pp. Gr. 4–6. The sequels are *Brim Sails Out* (1966) and *Brim's Valley* (British). (BL 62: 831; HB 42: 305; KR 34: 56; LJ 91: 1063)

GOODWIN, Harold. *The Magic Number.* Bradbury, 1969. Illus. by the author. 97 pp. Gr. 4–6. (BL 66: 206; CCBB 23: 8; KR 37: 559; LJ 95: 3204 and 3603)

GOODWIN, Murray. *Alonzo and the Army of Ants.* Harper, 1966. Illus. by Kiyo Komoda. 104 pp. Gr. 4–6. (KR 34: 419; LJ 91: 3258)

GUILLOT, René. *Nicolette and the Mill.* See Chapter 6, Magic Adventure: Out-of-Print Works.

HARTWICK, Harry. *Farewell to the Farivox.* See Chapter 1, Allegory and Fable: Out-of-Print Works.

HEAL, Edith. *What Happened to Jenny.* See Chapter 6, Magic Adventure: Out-of-Print Works.

HEWETT, Anita. *A Hat for Rhinoceros and Other Stories.* Barnes, 1960. Illus. by Margery Gill. 80 pp. Gr. 3–5. (LJ 86: 878; TLS May 29, 1959 p. xvi)

HOFFMANN, Eleanor. *The Four Friends.* Macmillan, 1946. Illus. by Kurt Wiese. 105 pp. Gr. 3–6. (BL 43: 173; HB 22: 349; KR 14: 422; LJ 71: 1808)

HOUGH, Charlotte. *Red Biddy and Other Stories.* See Chapter 2, Collected Tales: Out-of-Print Works.

HOWARD, Joan (pseud. of Patricia Gordon). *The Taming of Giants.* Viking, 1950. Illus. by Garry MacKenzie. 57 pp. Gr. 1–4. (BL 47: 16; HB 26: 375; KR 18: 512)

HOWARD, Joan. *Uncle Sylvester.* Oxford, 1950. Illus. by Garry MacKenzie. 48 pp. Gr. 3-6. (HB 26: 194; KR 18: 176; LJ 75: 629 and 987)

HUGHES, Ted. *How the Whale Became.* See Chapter 2, Collected Tales: Out-of-Print Works.

HURT, Freda. *Mr. Twink and the Pirates.* Roy, 1960. Illus. by Nina Langley. 127 pp. Gr. 4-6. (HB 36: 215)

INCHFAWN, Fay. *Who Goes to the Wood.* Winston, 1942. Illus. by Diana Thorne. 229 pp. Gr. 4-6. (LJ 67: 884)

JOHNSTON, Johanna. *Great Gravity the Cat.* Knopf, 1958. Illus. by Kurt Wiese. 66 pp. Gr. 3-5. (HB 34: 195; KR 26: 74; LJ 83: 1602)

KÄSTNER, Erich. *The Animal's Conference.* See Chapter 1, Allegory and Fable: Out-of-Print Works.

KING, Alexander. *Memoirs cf a Certain Mouse.* McGraw, 1966. Illus. by Richard Erdoes. 95 pp. Gr. 3-5. (CCBB 20: 125; HB 42: 710; KR 34: 1048; LJ 92: 881)

KING, Clive. *The Town That Went South.* Macmillan, 1959. Illus. by Maurice Bartlett. 117 pp. Gr. 4-6. (HB 36: 130; LJ 85: 1305; TLS May 20, 1960 p. xv, 1969 p. 352)

KIPLING, Rudyard. *All the Mowgli Stories.* Doubleday, 1936. Illus. by Kurt Wiese. 299 pp. Gr. 6-9. (BL 32: 333; HB 12: 158; JHC: 448; LJ 61: 733)

KRÜSS, James. *The Happy Islands behind the Winds.* See Chapter 12, Travel to Another World: Out-of-Print Works.

LAGERLÖF, Selma. *The Wonderful Adventures of Nils.* See Chapter 8Q, Miniature People: Out-of-Print Works.

LAMPMAN, Evelyn. *The City under the Back Steps.* See Chapter 12, Travel to Another World: Out-of-Print Works.

LANCASTER, Clay. *Periwinkle Steamboat.* See Chapter 6, Magic Adventure: Out-of-Print Works.

LANIER, Sterling. *The War for the Lot: A Tale of Fantasy and Terror.* Follett, 1969. Illus. by Robert Baumgartner. 256 pp. Gr. 4-6. (BL 66: 928; CCBB 24: 61; HB 46: 162; LJ 95: 1945 and 3603)

LAURENCE, Margaret. *Jason's Quest.* Knopf, 1970. Illus. by Staffan Torell. 211 pp. Gr. 4-7. (Arb: 240; CCBB 24: 29; LJ 95: 3050; Suth: 240; TLS 1970 p. 1458)

LAWRENCE, Harriet. *Philip Birdsong's ESP.* See Chapter 6, Magic Adventure: Out-of-Print Works.

LAWSON, Robert. *Edward, Hoppy and Joe.* Knopf, 1952. Illus. by the author. 122 pp. Gr. 3–6. (BL 48: 303; HB 28: 107; KR 20: 224; LJ 77: 907)

LAWSON, Robert. *Mr. Twigg's Mistake.* Little, 1947. Illus. by the author. 141 pp. Gr. 5–7. (BL 44: 117; KR 15: 467; LJ 72: 1543)

LEE, Tanith. *Animal Castle.* See Chapter 5B, Imaginary Lands: Out-of-Print Works.

LEFEBURE, Molly. *Scratch and Co.: The Great Cat Expedition.* Meredith, 1969. Illus. by Charles Geer. 183 pp. Gr. 5–8. (KR 69: 1257; LJ 95: 1204; TLS 1968 p. 1111)

LEZRA, Giggy. *The Cat, the Horse, and the Miracle.* Atheneum, 1967. Illus. by Zena Bernstein. 114 pp. Gr. 4–6. (CCBB 20: 155; KR 35: 198; LJ 92: 1317; Suth: 250)

LIFTON, Betty. *The Cock and the Ghost Cat.* See Chapter 3, Ghosts: Out-of-Print Works.

LIFTON, Betty. *The Silver Crane.* Seabury, 1971. Illus. by Laszlo Kubinyi. 121 pp. Gr. 4–6. (HB 47: 613; LJ 97: 1170)

LINDOP, Audrey E. *The Adventures of the Wuffle.* McGraw, 1968. Illus. by William Stobbs. 126 pp. Gr. 4–6. (KR 36: 150; LJ 93: 2730; TLS 1966 p. 1087)

LINDSAY, Norman. *The Magic Pudding.* (Orig. pub. 1918) Farrar, 1936. Illus. by the author. 159 pp. Gr. 3–5. (LJ 61: 809, 62: 38; TLS 1936 p. 974)

McKIM, Audrey. *Andy and the Gopher.* Little, 1959. Illus. by Ronni Solbert. 119 pp. Gr. 3–5. (HB 35: 131)

MASEFIELD, John. *The Midnight Folk: A Novel.* See Chapter 6, Magic Adventure: Out-of-Print Works.

MASON, Miriam. *Hoppity.* (Orig. pub. 1947) Macmillan, 1962. Illus. by Cyndy Szekeres. 66 pp. Gr. 2–4. (BL 44: 117; HB 23: 34; KR 15: 427)

MATTHIESSEN, Peter. *The Seal Pool.* Doubleday, 1972. Illus. by William Pène Du Bois. 78 pp. Gr. 3–5. (CCBB 26: 80; KR 40: 724; LJ 98: 645)

MAYNE, William. *The Blue Boat.* See Chapter 6, Magic Adventure: Out-of-Print Works.

MILNE, A(lan) A(lexander). *Prince Rabbit and the Princess Who Could Not Laugh.* See Chapter 5B, Imaginary Lands: Out-of-Print Works.

MOON, Sheila. *Kneedeep in Thunder.* See Chapter 12, Travel to Another World: Out-of-Print Works.

MOORE, Margaret. *Willie Without.* Coward, 1952. Illus. by Nora S. Unwin. 92 pp. Gr. 4–6. (HB 28: 108; KR 20: 124)

MORETON, John. *Punky, Mouse for a Day.* See Chapter 6, Magic Adventure: Out-of-Print Works.

MORGAN, Alison. *River Song.* Harper, 1975. Illus. by John Schoenherr. 160 pp. Gr. 4–6. (BL 72: 457; HB 52: 52; KR 43: 1131; SLJ Sept'75 p. 108)

MURPHY, Shirley R. *Elmo Doolan and the Search for the Golden Mouse.* Viking, 1970. Illus. by Fritz Kredel. 125 pp. Gr. 3–6. (Adv: 194; KR 38: 1192; LJ 96: 2365)

NICKLESS, Will. *Owlglass.* Day, 1966. Illus. by the author. 158 pp. Gr. 4–6. The British sequel is *Dotted Lines.* (BL 62: 833; HB 42: 307; LJ 91: 2696)

NYGAARD, Jacob. *Tobias, the Magic Mouse.* Harcourt, 1968. Tr. by Edith McCormick. Illus. by Ib Spang Olsen. 55 pp. Gr. 3–5. (HB 45: 167; KR 36: 1049; LJ 94: 288)

OSBORNE, Maurice. *Ondine: The Story of a Bird Who Was Different.* Houghton, 1960. Illus. by Evaline Ness. 75 pp. Gr. 4–8. (BL 56: 690; Eakin: 251; HB 36: 290; LJ 85: 2683)

OSBORNE, Maurice. *Rudi and the Mayor of Naples.* Houghton, 1958. Illus. by Joseph Low. 48 pp. Gr. 2–4. (HB 35: 33)

PARKER, Edgar. *The Dream of the Doormouse.* Houghton, 1963. Illus. by the author. 48 pp. Gr. 2–5. (HB 39: 286; LJ 88: 2553)

PARKER, Edgar. *The Duke of Sycamore.* Houghton, 1959. 38 pp. Gr. 1–4. (BL 55: 488; HB 35: 214; KR 27: 264; LJ 84: 1699)

PARKER, Edgar. *The Flower of the Realm.* Houghton, 1966. Illus. by the author. 60 pp. Gr. 3–5. (HB 42: 564; KR 34: 831; LJ 91: 5236)

PARKER, Edgar. *The Question of a Dragon.* See Chapter 8E, Dragons: Out-of-Print Works.

PAYNE, Joan. *Ambrose.* Hastings, 1956. 48 pp. Gr. 2–4. (HB 32: 445; KR 24: 627)

PAYNE, Joan. *The Piebald Princess.* Farrar, 1954. Illus. by the author. 79 pp. Gr. 3–5. (BL 50: 327; HB 30: 95; KR 22: 229; LJ 79: 702 and 865)

PLENN, Doris. *The Green Song.* (Orig. pub. 1954) McKay, 1969. Illus. by Paul Galdone. 126 pp. Gr. 4–6. (KR 22: 152; LJ 79: 1238)

PLIMPTON, George. *The Rabbit's Umbrella.* See Chapter 10, Tall Tales: Out-of-Print Works.

POTTER, Miriam. *Queer, Dear Mrs. Goose.* (Orig. pub. 1941) Lippincott, 1959. Illus. by Zenas and Miriam Potter. 125 pp. Gr. 3–5. Other titles in this series are *Just Mrs. Goose* (n.d.), *Mrs. Goose and Three Ducks* (1936), *Mrs. Goose of Animal Town* (1939), *Hello, Mrs. Goose* (1947), *Here Comes Mrs.*

Goose (1953), *Our Friend, Mrs. Goose* (1956), *Goodness, Mrs. Goose* (1960), and *Mrs. Goose and Her Funny Friends* (1964). (KR 27: 135; LJ 84: 1688)

PURSCELL, Phyllis. *Old Boy's Tree House and Other "Deep Forest" Tales.* Weybright, 1968. Illus. by Ursala Arndt. Unp. Gr. 2–4. (KR 36: 691; LJ 93: 3292)

ROBINSON, Mabel. *Back-Seat Driver.* Random, 1949. Illus. by Leonard Shortall. Gr. 3–5. The sequels are *Skipper Riley* (1955) and *Riley Goes to Obedience School* (1956). (KR 17: 360; LJ 74: 1918)

ROCCA, Guido. *Gaetano the Pheasant: A Hunting Fable.* See Chapter 1, Allegory and Fable: Out-of-Print Works.

SANCHEZ-SILVA, José. *The Boy and the Whale.* See Chapter 1, Allegory and Fable: Out-of-Print Works.

SEEMAN, Elizabeth. *The Talking Dog and the Barking Man.* Watts, 1960. Illus. by James Flora. 186 pp. Gr. 3–5. (HB 36: 291; LJ 85: 2043)

SEIDLER, Rosalie. *Grumpus and the Venetian Cat.* Atheneum, 1964. Illus. by the author. 39 pp. Gr. 2–4. (KR 33: 731)

SEIDMAN, Mitzi. *Who Woke the Sun?* Macmillan, 1960. Illus. by Karla Kushkin. Unp. Gr. 2–4. (KR 28: 232; LJ 85: 2472; TLS Nov 25, 1960 p. iv)

SELDEN, George (pseud. of George Selden Thompson). *The Garden under the Sea.* Viking, 1957. Illus. by Garry MacKenzie. 190 pp. Gr. 4–7. (BL 53: 508; KR 25: 37; LJ 82: 1802)

SEREDY, Kate. *Lazy Tinka.* See Chapter 1, Allegory and Fable: Out-of-Print Works.

SHEEHAN, Carolyn and Edmond. *Magnifi-Cat.* Doubleday, 1972. 229 pp. Gr. 6 up. (BL 69: 551 and 570; KR 40: 887; LJ 97: 2756; TN 29: 258)

SHURA, Mary. *A Tale of Middle Length.* Atheneum, 1966. Illus. by Peter Parnall. 105 pp. Gr. 3–6. (BL 63: 268; CCBB 20: 48; HB 42: 566; KR 34: 687; LJ 91: 4343)

SIMONT, Marc. *Mimi.* Harper, 1954. Illus. by the author. 56 pp. Gr. 3–5. (HB 31: 111; KR 22: 726; LJ 80: 193)

SISSON, Rosemary. *The Adventures of Ambrose.* Dutton, 1952. Illus. by Astrid Walford. 118 pp. Gr. 2–4. (HB 28: 406; KR 20: 598; LJ 77: 1662)

SLEIGH, Barbara. *Carbonel: The King of the Cats* (British title: *Carbonel*). Bobbs, 1956. Illus. by V. H. Drummond. 253 pp. Gr. 4–7. The sequel is *The Kingdom of Carbonel* (1960). *Carbonel and Calidor* is a British sequel. (Arb: 242; BL 54: 30; CC: 566; Eakin: 300; HB 33: 408; LJ 82: 2702; TLS 1978 p. 765)

STOLZ, Mary. *Frédou.* Harper, 1962. Illus. by Tomi Ungerer. 118 pp. Gr. 4–6. (BL 59: 84; HB 38: 370; KR 30: 386; LJ 87: 2625)

STOLZ, Mary. *Pigeon Flight.* Harper, 1962. Illus. by Murray Tinkelman. 54 pp. Gr. 2–4. (Eakin: 317; HB 38: 607)

STONG, Philip. *Positive Pete!* Dodd, 1947. Illus. by Kurt Wiese. 64 pp. Gr. 2–4. (LJ 72: 1474)

STORR, Catherine. *The Adventures of Polly and the Wolf.* See Chapter 10, Tall Tales: Out-of-Print Works.

SYMONDS, John. *Elfrida and the Pig.* Watts, 1959. Illus. by Edward Ardizzone. 48 pp. Gr. 2–4. (HB 36: 292; LJ 85: 2044; TLS Dec 4, 1959 p. xv)

TARN, Sir William. *Treasure of the Isle of Mist: A Tale of the Isle of Skye.* See Chapter 6, Magic Adventure: Out-of-Print Works.

TREVOR, Elleston. *Deep Wood.* Longmans, 1947. Illus. by Stephen Voorhis. 282 pp. Gr. 4–6. (BL 44: 138; HB 23: 358; KR 45: 394)

UNWIN, Nora. *Two Too Many.* McKay, 1962. 54 pp. Gr. 2–4. (Eakin: 339; HB 38: 473; LJ 87: 4615; TLS 1965 p. 1141)

VILDRAC, Charles. *The Lion's Eyeglasses.* (Orig. pub. 1951) Coward, 1969. Tr. by Regina McDonnell. Illus. by Noelle Lavaivre. 116 pp. Gr. 3–5. (KR 37: 1002; LJ 95: 245)

WEIR, Rosemary. *Pyewacket.* Abelard-Schuman, 1967. Illus. by Charles Pickard. 123 pp. Gr. 3–5. (KR 35: 1210; LJ 93: 297; TLS 1967 p. 1153)

WHITE, Anne. *The Story of Serapina.* Viking, 1951. Illus. by Tony Palazzo. 128 pp. Gr. 3–6. (BL 47: 333; Eakin: 348; HB 27: 180; LJ 76: 970)

WILLIAMS, Ursula Moray. *Island Mackenzie* (British title: *The Nine Lives of Island Mackenzie*). Morrow, 1960. Illus. by Edward Ardizzone. 128 pp. Gr. 4–6. (Arb: 243; BL 57: 157; HB 36: 503; KR 28: 498; LJ 85: 3228; TLS Dec 4, 1959 p. xv)

WYNDHAM, Lee (pseud. of Jane Hyndman). *Mourka, the Mighty Cat.* Parents, 1969. Illus. by Charles Mikolaycak. Unp. Gr. 2–4. (HB 45: 529; LJ 95: 1192)

10

Tall Tales

In their use of humor and exaggeration, the stories in this chapter resemble the traditional tall tales of American folklore. However, the definition of "tall tale" has been broadened here to include a variety of humorous fantasies: those with fast-paced comic plots, tales of people with bizarre pets, amusing stories of inanimate objects that come to life, and others.

AIKEN, Joan. *Arabel's Raven* (British title: *Tales of Arabel's Raven*). Doubleday, 1974. Illus. by Quentin Blake. 118 pp. Gr. 4–7. [A]
Life in the Jones's house just isn't the same after Mr. Jones brings home a raven named Mortimer who enjoys eating stairs and sleeping in the refrigerator. (Adv: 180; CCBB 28: 1; HB 50: 278; KR 42: 478; LJ 99: 2258)

AIKEN, Joan. *The Whispering Mountain.* See Chapter 5B, Imaginary Lands.

AIKEN, Joan. *The Wolves of Willoughby Chase.* Doubleday, 1962. Illus. by Pat Marriott. 168 pp. Gr. 5–7. [R]
While Bonnie's parents travel, she and her cousin Sylvia are left with a sinister governess. The girls run away from home, are chased by wolves, and end up in an orphanage, from which they finally manage to escape and thwart the plans of the evil Miss Slighcarp. The sequels are *Black Hearts in Battersea* (1964), *Nightbirds on Nantucket* (1966), and *The Cuckoo Tree* (1971). (Arb: 229; CC: 477; Eakin: 3; LJ 88: 4076; TLS 1962 p. 901)

ATWATER, Richard and Florence. *Mr. Popper's Penguins.* Little, 1938. Illus. by Robert Lawson. 138 pp. Gr. 4–5. [R]
A paperhanger named Mr. Popper is given a penguin as a gift, but before he knows it, his problems multiply into twelve penguins. (Arb: 228; BL 35: 86; CC: 481; HB 14: 370; LJ 63: 818)

AVI (pseud. of Avi Wortis). *Emily Upham's Revenge: Or, How Deadwood Dick Saved the Banker's Niece: A Massachusetts Adventure.* Pantheon, 1978. Illus. by Paul Zelinsky. 172 pp. Gr. 4–6. [R]
Emily and her friend Seth need money to escape to Boston. Their plans to rob a bank go awry, but Emily triumphs in the end. (BL 74: 1098; CC 1979 Suppl. p. 41; CCBB 31: 170; KR 46: 304; SLJ Mar'78 p. 24)

BABBITT, Natalie. *Goody Hall.* Farrar, 1971. Illus. by the author. 176 pp. Gr. 4–6. [R]
The mystery surrounding the death of young Willet Goody's father is solved only after a seance visitation by Shakespeare and a nighttime visit to Mr. Goody's tomb. (BL 67: 954; CC: 482; CCBB 25: 21; HB 47: 380; KR 39: 431; LJ 96: 1780 and 1820; Suth: 23)

BAKER, Betty. *Save Sirrushany! (Also Agotha, Princess Gwyn and All the Fearsome Beasts).* See Chapter 5B, Imaginary Lands.

BAUM, Thomas. *It Looks Alive To Me!* Harper, 1976. 168 pp. Gr. 5–8. [A]
Accidentally locked inside the Museum of Natural History overnight, Burdick and Lola madly search for the moon rock that is bringing the museum specimens back to life. (BL 72: 1332; JHC 1977 Suppl. p. 40; KR 44: 403)

BEEKS, Graydon. *Hosea Globe and the Fantastical Peg-Legged Chu.* Atheneum, 1974. Illus. by Carol Nicklaus. 170 pp. Gr. 4–6. [A]
Hosea and his talking dog are ordered to bring a scientist who can control cyclones and typhoons to their secret island home. (Adv: 182; BL 71: 813; KR 43: 305; SLJ Oct'75 p. 94)

BRELIS, Nancy. *The Mummy Market.* (Orig. pub. 1966) Harper, 1975 (pap.). Illus. by Ben Shecter. 145 pp. Gr. 5–7. [R]
The Martin children find that selecting a new mother to replace their awful housekeeper, the Gloom, isn't easy. (CCBB 20: 38; HB 42: 707; KR 34: 757; LJ 91: 5222; Suth: 50)

BRÖGER, Achim. *Bruno.* Morrow, 1975. Tr. by Hilda Van Stockum. Illus. by Ronald Himler. 160 pp. Gr. 4–6. [A]
Amazing things keep happening to Bruno: a dinosaur comes for dinner, snowmen and statues talk to him, and in one day he meets forty-two doubles of himself. *Bruno Takes a Trip* (1978) is the sequel. (Adv: 182; BL 72: 622; KR 43: 1128; SLJ Nov'75 p. 71)

BRÖGER, Achim. *Outrageous Kasimir.* See Chapter 8Q, Miniature People.

BROWN, Jeff. *Flat Stanley.* Harper, 1964. Illus. by Tomi Ungerer. 48 pp. Gr. 1–4. [R]
Stanley Lambchop, flat as a pancake after a huge bulletin board falls on him, is lowered through sidewalk gratings, mailed to California, and disguised as a framed painting to capture art thieves. (BL 60: 875; HB 40: 274; LJ 89: 1850; TLS 1968 p. 583)

BURMAN, Ben Lucien. *High Water at Catfish Bend.* See Chapter 9, Talking Animals.

BURN, Doris, *The Tale of Lazy Lizard Canyon.* Putnam, 1977. Illus. by the author. 48 pp. Gr. 2–4. [A]
Bull Hokum and Bronco Burley's feud over the rights to Lazy Lizard Canyon is settled when their children, Lafe and Mattie Mae, decide to get married. (BL 73: 1495; KR 45: 425; SLJ Sept'77 p. 103)

BUTTERWORTH, Oliver. *The Enormous Egg.* See Chapter 8D, Dinosaurs.

BUTTERWORTH, Oliver. *The Trouble with Jenny's Ear.* Little, 1960. Illus. by Julian de Miskey. 275 pp. Gr. 4–7. [R]
When Jenny discovers that one of her ears is sensitive enough to hear other people's thoughts, her brothers concoct an ingenious money-making scheme. (Arb: 229; BL 56: 546; Eakin: 56; HB 36: 215; KR 28: 184; LJ 85: 2034)

BYFIELD, Barbara. *The Haunted Ghost.* See Chapter 3, Ghosts.

CALLEN, Larry. *Pinch.* Little, 1975. Illus. by Marvin Friedman. 179 pp. Gr. 5–8. [R]
Pinch Grimball trains his pet pig, Homer, to be the best bird-hunting pig in Four Corners, Louisiana. (Adv: 183; BL 72: 1260, 73: 1425; CCBB 30: 5; HB 52: 394; KR 44: 134; SLJ Apr'76 p. 70, May'76 p. 34)

CARLSEN, Ruth. *Henrietta Goes West.* Houghton, 1966. Illus. by Wallace Tripp. 185 pp. Gr. 5–6. [A]
The Nelson's trip in a 1925 automobile named Henrietta is enlivened by such unexpected occurrences as Aunt Em's backwards ride on a huge bear. (CCBB 19: 175; KR 34: 475; LJ 91: 3256)

CARLSEN, Ruth. *Sam Bottleby.* See Chapter 6, Magic Adventure.

CARLSON, Natalie. *Alphonse, That Bearded One.* Harcourt, 1954. Illus. by Nicolas. 78 pp. Gr. 3–5. [R]
Trained to take a clever woodsman's place as a soldier, Alphonse the bear causes chaos in the French Canadian army. (BL 50: 325; Eakin: 59; HB 30: 174; KR 22: 197; LJ 79: 783)

CHRISTOPHER, Matthew. *The Pigeon with the Tennis Elbow.* See Chapter 9, Talking Animals.

CLEARY, Beverly. *The Mouse and the Motorcycle.* See Chapter 9, Talking Animals.

COATSWORTH, Elizabeth. *Bob Bodden and the Good Ship Rover.* Garrard, 1968. 48 pp. Gr. 2–4. [M]
Having smashed his huge ship into the South Pole, Bob Bodden decides to leave it behind to be mistaken for a new continent. (CCBB 22: 139)

COBALT, Martin. *Pool of Swallows.* See Chapter 3, Ghosts.

CORBETT, Scott. *The Discontented Ghost.* See Chapter 3, Ghosts.

CORBETT, Scott. *The Great Custard Pie Panic.* See Chapter 13, Witches, Wizards, Sorcerers, and Magicians.

CORBETT, Scott. *The Lemonade Trick.* See Chapter 6, Magic Adventure.

COREN, Alan. *Arthur the Kid.* Little, 1978. Illus. by John Astrop. 74 pp. Gr. 3–5. [R]
Ten-year-old Arthur's career as leader of the gang of bank-robbing gunslingers takes an about-face when they save the bank from another gang. The sequels are *Buffalo Arthur* (1978), *The Lone Arthur* (1978), *Railroad Arthur* (1978), *Klondike Arthur* (1979) and *Arthur's Last Stand* (British). (BL 74: 1616; CC 1979 Suppl. p. 45; CCBB 32: 26; KR 46: 594; SLJ Sept'78 p. 133)

COX, Wally, and GREENBAUM, Everett. *The Tenth Life of Osiris Oaks.* Simon, 1972. Illus. by F. A. Fitzgerald. 125 pp. Gr. 3–5. [M]
After his mummified cat comes to life as a mind reader, Roger tries to help the police solve crimes, and decides to become a show biz star. (KR 40: 258; LJ 93: 3451)

CRESSWELL, Helen. *The Bongleweed.* See Chapter 6, Magic Adventure.

CURRY, Jane. *Mindy's Mysterious Miniature.* See Chapter 8Q, Miniature People.

CUSACK, Isabel. *Ivan the Great.* Crowell, 1978. Illus. by Carol Nicklaus. 45 pp. Gr. 2–4. [M]
Ivan the parrot gives Robbie advice and gets him into trouble with his mother, who doesn't believe in talking birds. (CCBB 32: 76; SLJ Mar'79 p. 138)

DAHL, Roald. *Charlie and the Chocolate Factory.* See Chapter 6, Magic Adventure.

DAHL, Roald. *The Magic Finger.* See Chapter 6, Magic Adventure.

DAVIES, Valentine. *The Miracle on 34th Street.* (Orig. pub. 1947) Harcourt, 1959. 120 pp. Gr. 7 up. [A]

Old Mr. Kringle tries to convince skeptics that he is Santa Claus and gets a job as Macy's Christmas Santa to prove it. (BL 43: 359; KR 15: 316; LJ 72: 1033)

DAWSON, Mary. *Tegwyn, the Last of the Welsh Dragons.* See Chapter 8E, Dragons.

DRURY, Roger. *The Champion of Merrimack County.* See Chapter 9, Talking Animals.

DRURY, Roger. *The Finches' Fabulous Furnace.* Little, 1971. Illus. by Erik Blegvad. 149 pp. Gr. 4–6. [R]
The Finch family tries to keep the volcano in their basement a secret, yet safeguard their town. (Arb: 238; BL 67: 907; CCBB 25: 4; HB 47: 382; LJ 97: 1169; Suth: 108)

DU BOIS, William Pène. *The Alligator Case.* Harper, 1965. Illus. by the author. 63 pp. Gr. 3–5. [R]
A case involving a circus alligator and three suspicious strangers is solved by a boy detective even before the crime is committed. *The Horse in the Camel Suit* (1967) is the sequel. (Arb: 238; BL 62: 330; CC: 512; CCBB 19: 31; Eakin: 103; HB 41: 497; KR 33: 827; LJ 90: 3788)

DU BOIS, William Pène. *Call Me Bandicoot.* Harper, 1970. Illus. by the author. 63 pp. Gr. 3–5. [R]
A tall tale about a young con artist named Ermine Bandicoot that explains how New York Harbor became tobacco brown. (Adv: 197; Arb: 238; CC: 512; CCBB 24: 105; KR 38: 1095; LJ 95: 4326 and 4354; Suth: 109)

DU BOIS, William Pène. *The Forbidden Forest.* Harper, 1978. Illus. by the author. 56 pp. Gr. 3–5. [R]
Lady Adelaide (a kangaroo), Buckingham the bulldog, and Spider Max the champion boxer are hailed as heroes for stopping World War I. (BL 75: 215; CC 1979 Suppl. p. 46; CCBB 32: 78; HB 55: 515; KR 46: 946; SLJ Sept'78 p. 122; TLS 1978 p. 1397)

DU BOIS, William Pène. *The Great Geppy.* (Orig. pub. 1940) Viking, 1946. Illus. by the author. 92 pp. Gr. 4–6. [R]
The special sleuth called in to investigate problems at the Bott Bros. Three-Ring Circus is a red-and-white-striped horse. (Arb: 238; BL 36: 368; HB 16: 166 and 175; LJ 65: 502 and 847)

DU BOIS, William Pène. *Peter Graves.* Viking, 1950. Illus. by the author. 168 pp. Gr. 6–9. [A]
Peter uses a retired inventor's antigravity alloy to try such feats as tightrope walking upside down and the Indian rope trick. (Arb: 238; BL 47: 140; HB 26: 375; KR 18: 518)

DU BOIS, William Pène. *The Three Policemen, or Young Bottsford of Farbe Island.* (Orig. pub. 1938) Viking, 1960. Illus. by the author. 95 pp. Gr. 4–6. [R]

The mystery of the stolen fishing nets on the fabulous island of Farbe is solved by three policemen, with the help of young Bottsford. (BL 57: 190; CC: 512; HB 14: 365 and 375, 36: 485; LJ 63: 818 and 978)

DU BOIS, William Pène. *The Twenty-One Balloons*. Viking, 1947. Illus. by the author. 180 pp. Gr. 5–7. [R]
Professor William Waterman Sherman is tired of teaching arithmetic. He sails off in a balloon to see the world and lands on the volcanic island of Krakatoa. Newbery Medal. (Adv: 273; Arb: 212; BL 43: 296; CC: 512; HB 23: 214; LJ 72: 819)

EVARTS, Hal. *Jay-Jay and the Peking Monster*. Scribner, 1978. 185 pp. Gr. 6–9. [A]
Aunt Hattie's experiments on ancient human bones bring a boy named Zurria to life, and involve Jay-Jay with the Marines, a Chinese attaché, and gangsters. (BL 74: 1492; HB 54: 401; KR 46: 500; SLJ May'78 p. 86)

FISHER, Leonard E. *Noonan: A Novel about Baseball, ESP, and Time Warps*. See Chapter 11, Time Travel.

FISHER, Leonard E. *Sweeney's Ghost*. See Chapter 3, Ghosts.

FLEISCHMAN, (Albert) Sid(ney). *By the Great Horn Spoon*. Little, 1963. Illus. by Eric Von Schmidt. 193 pp. Gr. 4–6. [R]
Jack Flagg runs away from home in Boston to make his fortune in the California gold fields, accompanied by Praiseworthy the butler. (Arb: 230; BL 60: 207; CC: 519; HB 39: 598; LJ 88: 3348)

FLEISCHMAN, Sid. *Chancy and the Grand Rascal*. Little, 1966. Illus. by Eric Von Schmidt. 179 pp. Gr. 4–6. [R]
Chancy, orphaned and searching for his long-lost sister Indiana, meets a tall-tale-telling uncle and a sly villain named Colonel Plugg. (BL 63: 119; CC: 519; CCBB 20: 41; HB 42: 569; KR 34: 625; LJ 91: 5226; Suth: 126; TLS 1967 p. 1145; TN 23: 291)

FLEISCHMAN, Sid. *The Ghost in the Noonday Sun*. See Chapter 3, Ghosts.

FLEISCHMAN, Sid. *The Ghost on Saturday Night*. Little, 1974. Illus. by Eric Von Schmidt. 57 pp. Gr. 3–5. [R]
Opie becomes a town hero when he exposes Dr. Pepper's traveling ghost-raising show as a front for bank robberies. (BL 70: 1252; CC: 519; CCBB 28: 61; HB 50: 379; KR 42: 535; LJ 99: 2267; TLS 1975 p. 770)

FLEISCHMAN, Sid. *Humbug Mountain*. Atlantic-Little, 1978. Illus. by Eric Von Schmidt. 149 pp. Gr. 4–6. [R]
Grandpa Flint's "property" in the boom town of Sunshine, Dakota, turns out to be no more than an abandoned riverboat in the ghost town of Sunshine, Nevada. But the family makes the best of it by setting off a gold rush. (BL 75: 477; CC 1979 Suppl. p. 47; CCBB 32: 113; HB 55: 640; KR 46: 1071; SLJ Sept'78 p. 136)

FLEISCHMAN, Sid. *Jim Bridger's Alarm Clock, and Other Tall Tales.* Dutton, 1978. Illus. by Eric Von Schmidt. 56 pp. Gr. 2–4. [R]
Three tall tales about an army scout and mountain man named Jim Bridger, including one in which he uses the echo of fireworks to outwit bank robbers. (BL 75: 808; CC 1979 Suppl. p. 57; HB 55: 191; KR 42: 124; SLJ Apr'79 p. 55)

FLEISCHMAN, Sid. *Jingo Django.* Little, 1971. Illus. by Eric Von Schmidt. 172 pp. Gr. 4–6. [R]
Orphaned Jingo Hawks and his benefactor, Mr. Peacock-Hemlock-Jones, travel from Boston to Mexico trying their hands at horse trading, river piloting, portrait painting, and treasure hunting. (BL 67: 954, 68: 669; CC: 519; HB 47: 383; KR 39: 432; LJ 96: 2916; TLS 1971 p. 1509)

FLEISCHMAN, Sid. *McBroom Tells the Truth* (British title: *McBroom's Wonderful One Acre Farm*). Grosset, 1966. Illus. by Kurt Werth. 47 pp. Gr. 3–5. [R]
Farmer McBroom's crops grow so fast that his eleven children can ride the pumpkins and use the cornstalks for pogo sticks. The sequels are *McBroom and the Big Wind* (1967), *McBroom's Ear* (1969), *McBroom's Ghost* (1971), *McBroom's Zoo* (1972), *McBroom the Rainmaker* (1973), *McBroom Tells a Lie* (Atlantic-Little, 1976; British title: *Here Comes McBroom!*), and *McBroom and the Beanstalk* (Atlantic-Little, 1978). (BL 62: 662; CCBB 19: 129; HB 42: 193; KR 33: 1187; LJ 91: 424; Suth: 127)

FLEISCHMAN, Sid. *Me and the Man on the Moon-Eyed Horse.* Atlantic-Little, 1977. Illus. by Eric Von Schmidt. 57 pp. Gr. 3–5. [R]
The circus train's visit to Furnace Flats is almost ruined by a desperado named Step-and-a-half Jackson, but young Clint saves the day. (BL 73: 1652; CC 1978 Suppl. p. 49; HB 53: 553; KR 45: 46; SLJ May'77 p. 61)

FLEISCHMAN, Sid. *Mister Mysterious and Company.* Little, 1962. Illus. by Eric Von Schmidt. 151 pp. Gr. 5–7. [R]
Mr. Mysterious and his magician family travel across the country in a covered wagon, entertaining people with wonderful feats of magic. (BL 58: 728; CC: 519; HB 38: 279)

FLEMING, Ian. *Chitty-Chitty Bang Bang: The Magical Car.* Random, 1964. Illus. by John Burningham. 111 pp. Gr. 4–6. [A]
The Pott family's rattletrap auto can both fly and float and takes them across the English Channel to the underground hideout of England's worst gangster. (Arb: 235; BL 61: 435; CCBB 22: 77; HB 41: 167)

FLORA, James. *Grandpa's Ghost Stories.* See Chapter 2, Collected Tales.

GATHORNE-HARDY, Jonathan. *Operation Peeg* (British title: *Jane's Adventures on the Island of Peeg*). (Orig. pub. 1968) Lippincott, 1974. Illus. by Glo Coalson. 192 pp. Gr. 5–7. [R]

After a rocket explosion sets the island of Peeg adrift on the Atlantic Ocean, two little girls and a housekeeper are caught up in a power struggle between two long-lost World War II soldiers and an evil billionaire. *The Airship Ladyship Adventure* (1977) and *Jane's Adventures In and Out of the Book* (British) are the sequels. (CCBB 28: 77; HB 51: 147; KR 42: 1060, 43: 6; LJ 9ᶜ: 2740; TLS 1968 p. 1377)

GOODWIN, Harold. *Top Secret: Alligators!* See Chapter 9, Talking Animals.

GRAY, Nicholas. *The Apple Stone.* See Chapter 6, Magic Adventure.

GREENWALD, Sheila (pseud. of Sheila Green). *Willie Bryant and the Flying Otis.* Grosset, 1971. 153 pp. Gr. 4-6. [M]
Willie Bryant's flying elevator continually saves the day for the Rose family, especially when Mrs. Rose finds she has nothing to serve unexpected dinner guests. (KR 39: 365; LJ 96: 2130)

GROCH, Judith. *Play the Bach, Dear!* Doubleday, 1978. 160 pp. Gr. 4-6. [M]
Did Hilary's piano teacher, Miss Orpheo, save the day at Hilary's recital by hiding inside the grand piano—or did Hilary succeed on her own? (CCBB 31: 159; KR 46: 107; SLJ Jan'78 p. 89)

GROSSER, Morton. *The Snake Horn.* See Chapter 6, Magic Adventure.

HALE, Lucretia. *The Complete Peterkin Papers* (British titles: *The Peterkin Papers* and *The Last of the Peterkins*). Houghton, 1960. Illus. by the author. 302 pp. Gr. 4-8. [R]
The Peterkin family's problems are solved by the common sense of the Lady from Philadelphia. (Arb: 226; BL 57: 190; CC: 527; KR 28: 905; LJ 85: 4567)

HAUFF, Wilhelm. *A Monkey's Uncle.* Farrar, 1969. Retold by Doris Orgel. Illus. by Mitchell Miller. 74 pp. Gr. 4-6. [A]
A newcomer to Gruenwiesel decides to teach town busybodies a lesson by introducing an orangutan as his nephew. (KR 37: 1109; LJ 95: 241)

HAYES, Geoffrey. *The Alligator and His Uncle Tooth: A Novel of the Sea.* See Chapter 9, Talking Animals.

HAYNES, Betsy, *The Ghost of the Gravestone Hearth.* See Chapter 3, Ghosts.

HEWETT, Anita. *The Bull beneath the Walnut Tree and Other Stories.* See Chapter 2, Collected Tales.

HOBAN, Russell. *How Tom Beat Captain Najork and His Hired Sportsmen.* Atheneum, 1974. Illus. by Quentin Blake. Unp. Gr. 3-5. [R]
Tom's Aunt Fidget Wonkham-Strong hires Captain Najork to teach Tom a lesson about foolish behavior, but even that doesn't stop him. *A Near Thing*

for Captain Najork (1976) is the sequel. (BL 71: 766; CCBB 28: 78; HB 51: 138; KR 42: 1299, 43: 2; LJ 99: 2733; TLS 1974 p. 718)

HOBAN, Russell. *The Twenty-Elephant Restaurant.* Atheneum, 1978. Illus. by Emily McCully. 37 pp. Gr. K–4. [R]
A wobbly table, strengthened enough for an elephant to dance on, inspires an old man to build a restaurant featuring twenty dancing elephants. (BL 74: 1494; CC 1979 Suppl. p. 49; CCBB 32: 10; KR 46: 299; SLJ May'78 p. 56)

HOLMAN, Felice. *The Blackmail Machine.* Macmillan, 1968. Illus. by Victoria de Larrea. 182 pp. Gr. 4–6. [R]
A flying treehouse enables Murk and Arabella to "blackmail" the government into preserving wildlife and bringing peace to the world. (BL 64: 995; CCBB 21: 129; HB 44: 173; KR 35: 1472; LJ 93: 870; TLS 1968 p. 1112)

HOLMAN, Felice. *The Escape of the Giant Hogstalk.* Scribner, 1974. Illus. by Ben Shecter. 96 pp. Gr. 3–6. [A]
The huge plant discovered by Anthony Wilson-Brown and his nephew, Lawrence, is donated to the Royal Botanic Gardens, but it grows out of control and causes a national emergency. (Adv: 189; CCBB 28: 28; HB 50: 283; KR 42: 363; LJ 99: 2270)

HUTCHINS, Pat. *Follow That Bus!* Greenwillow/Morrow, 1977. Illus. by Laurence Hutchins. 102 pp. Gr. 2–4. [R]
Their teacher and schoolbus hijacked by robbers, Miss Beaver's second-grade class rescues her and captures the bandits. (BL 73: 1498; CCBB 31: 48; HB 53: 442; KR 45: 351; SLJ Apr'77 p. 55; TLS 1977 p. 1412)

HUTCHINS, Pat. *The House That Sailed Away.* Greenwillow/Morrow, 1975. Illus. by Laurence Hutchins. 150 pp. Gr. 4–6. [R]
A house that floats out to sea, a battle with pirates, landing on a cannibal island, and the discovery of buried treasure are just some of the adventures in store for Morgan and his family. (Adv: 190; BL 72: 303; CCBB 29: 64; HB 51: 593; KR 43: 777; SLJ Sept'75 p. 84; TLS 1976 p. 882)

IBBOTSON, Eva. *The Great Ghost Rescue.* See Chapter 3, Ghosts.

JUSTER, Norton. *The Phantom Tollbooth.* See Chapter 12, Travel to Another World.

KÄSTNER, Erich. *The Little Man.* See Chapter 8Q, Miniature People.

KIRKEGAARD, Ole. *Otto Is a Rhino.* See Chapter 6, Magic Adventure.

LAMPMAN, Evelyn. *The Shy Stegosaurus of Cricket Creek.* See Chapter 8D, Dinosaurs.

LAWSON, Robert. *Ben and Me: A New and Astonishing Life of Benjamin Franklin As Written by His Good Mouse, Amos: Lately Discovered.* See Chapter 9, Talking Animals.

LAWSON, Robert. *Captain Kidd's Cat: Being the True and Dolorous Chronicle of Wm. Kidd, Gentleman and Merchant of New York; Late Captain of the Adventure Galley; Of the Vicissitudes Attending His Unfortunate Cruise in Eastern Waters, of His Unjust Trial and Execution, As Narrated by His Faithful Cat, McDermot, Who Ought to Know.* See Chapter 9, Talking Animals.

LAWSON, Robert. *I Discover Columbus: A True Chronicle of the Great Admiral and His Finding of the New World, Narrated by the Venerable Parrot Aurelio, Who Shared in the Glorious Venture.* See Chapter 9, Talking Animals.

LAWSON, Robert. *McWhinney's Jaunt.* Little, 1951. Illus. by the author. 76 pp. Gr. 6–9. [A]
Professor McWhinney powers his bicycle with Z-gas and flies off across the country to Hollywood. (BL 48: 16; KR 19: 294; LJ 76: 1341)

LAWSON, Robert. *Mr. Revere and I: Being an Account of Certain Episodes in the Career of Paul Revere, Esq., as Recently Revealed by His Horse, Scheherazade, Late Pride of His Royal Majesty's 14th Regiment of Foot.* See Chapter 9, Talking Animals.

LAZARUS, Keo. *The Shark in the Window.* Morrow, 1972. Illus. by Laurel Schindelman. 159 pp. Gr. 4–6. [A]
Shelly's new pet poses some problems: how to control a baby shark that swims in air instead of water, and how to find it the right kind of home. (BL 69: 357; CCBB 26: 45; KR 40: 940; LJ 97: 3806; Suth: 241)

LEVITIN, Sonia. *Jason and the Money Tree.* Harcourt, 1974. Illus. by Pat Porter. 121 pp. Gr. 4–7. [R]
The ten-dollar bill Jason's grandfather left him sprouts into a money tree but fills his life with problems as he attempts to account for his wealth. (Adv: 193; BL 70: 1057; CCBB 27: 180; KR 42: 300; LJ 99: 2274)

LIFTON, Betty. *The One-Legged Ghost.* Atheneum, 1968. Illus. by Fuku Akino. 37 pp. Gr. 1–4. [A]
Something round with one bamboo leg and forty wooden bones has fallen from the sky and the villagers decide it is a god. (BL 65: 314; KR 36: 1163; LJ 93: 4396; Suth: 251)

LINDGREN, Astrid. *Pippi Longstocking.* Viking, 1950. Tr. by Florence Lamborn. Illus. by Louis Glanzman. 158 pp. Gr. 4–6. [R]
Life is never dull for Annika and Tommy after the strongest child in the world moves in next door with her pet monkey and horse. The sequels are *Pippi Goes on Board* (1957) (British title: *Pippi Goes Abroad*), *Pippi in the South Seas* (1959), and *Pippi on the Run* (1976). (Adv: 273; Arb: 227; BL 47: 208; CC: 554; HB 26: 376; KR 18: 515)

LOFTING, Hugh. *The Story of Doctor Dolittle.* Lippincott, 1920. Illus. by the author. 172 pp. Gr. 3–6. [A]
When a great plague strikes the animals of Africa, Doctor Dolittle, the best animal doctor in the world, travels to Africa to save them. Lofting's depiction of Africans has been criticized. Newbery Medal. The sequels are *The Voyages of Doctor Dolittle* (1922), *Doctor Dolittle's Post Office* (1923), *Doctor Dolittle's Circus* (1924), *Doctor Dolittle's Zoo* (1925), *Doctor Dolittle's Caravan* (1926), *Doctor Dolittle's Garden* (1927), *Doctor Dolittle in the Moon* (1928), *Gub-Gub's Book: An Encyclopedia of Food* (1932), *Doctor Dolittle's Return* (1933), *Doctor Dolittle and the Secret Lake* (1948), *Doctor Dolittle and the Green Canary* (1950), and *Doctor Dolittle's Puddleby Adventures* (1952). (Arb: 233; BL 19: 193; CC: 546; HB 24: 341)

MacDONALD, Betty. *Mrs. Piggle-Wiggle.* (Orig. pub. 1947) Lippincott, 1957. Illus. by Hilary Knight. 118 pp. Gr. 2–5. [R]
Mrs. Piggle-Wiggle has magical cures for all children's ailments, including the won't-pick-up-toys cure, the answer-backer cure, and the selfishness cure. The sequels are *Mrs. Piggle-Wiggle's Farm* (1954), *Hello, Mrs. Piggle-Wiggle* (1957), and *Mrs. Piggle-Wiggle's Magic* (1957). (BL 43: 260; CC: 546; HB 23: 213; KR 15: 127; LJ 72: 739)

MacKELLAR, William. *Alfie and Me and the Ghost of Peter Stuyvesant.* See Chapter 3, Ghosts.

MacKELLAR, William. *The Kid Who Owned Manhattan Island.* Dodd, 1976. Illus. by David Stone. 192 pp. Gr. 5–7. [M]
Rusty's fast-talking Uncle Chester tries to give Manhattan Island back to the Indians, but gangster kidnappers snarl his plan to get New York City out of its financial difficulties. (CCBB 30: 109; SLJ Oct'76 p. 109)

MERRILL, Jean. *The Pushcart War.* Addison-Wesley, 1964. Illus. by Ronni Solbert. 222 pp. Gr. 5–8. [R]
Traffic congestion in New York City brings on a war between the truck drivers and the pushcart owners. (Adv: 273; Arb: 228; BL 61: 219; CC: 550; Eakin: 223; HB 40: 378; LJ 89: 2828)

MERRILL, Jean. *The Toothpaste Millionaire.* Houghton, 1974. 90 pp. Gr. 4–5. [R]
Eleven-year-old Lucas starts his own toothpaste factory to compete with higher-priced name brand toothpastes. (Adv: 168; BL 70: 1254; CC: 551; CCBB 28: 49; HB 50: 137; KR 42: 480)

NASH, Mary. *While Mrs. Coverlet Was Away.* Little, 1958. Illus. by Garrett Price. 133 pp. Gr. 4–6. [A]
Molly, Malcolm, and Toad Persever manage on their own after their housekeeper is called away while their father is out of town. The sequels are *Mrs. Coverlet's Magicians* (1961) and *Mrs. Coverlet's Detectives* (1965). (BL 55: 137; Eakin: 243; HB 34: 386; KR 26: 380; LJ 83: 2502)

NÖSTLINGER, Christine. *Konrad* (British title: *Conrad: The Hilarious Adventures of a Factory-made Child*). Watts, 1977. Tr. by Anthea Bell. Illus. by Carol Nicklaus. 135 pp. Gr. 5–6. [R]
Despite his unexpected arrival, a canned, mail-order child named Konrad is allowed to move in with Mrs. Bartolotti, but his perfect behavior angers his classmates and disturbs his new mother. (BL 74: 482; CC 1978 Suppl. p. 53; CCBB 31: 98; HB 53: 665; SLJ Nov'77 p. 60; TLS 1977 p. 348)

PASCAL, Francine. *Hangin' Out with Cici.* See Chapter 11, Time Travel.

PAYNE, Joan. *General Billycock's Pigs.* Hastings, 1961. Illus. by the author. 64 pp. Gr. 3–5. [A]
General Billycock's bullying ways are no match for the herd of wild pigs that devastates the crops in his fields. (HB 37: 270; KR 29: 161; LJ 86: 1986)

PECK, Richard. *The Ghost Belonged to Me: A Novel.* See Chapter 3, Ghosts.

PECK, Robert. *The King of Kazoo.* Knopf, 1976. Illus. by W. B. Park. 96 pp. Gr. 3–5. [M]
A cowless cowpuncher, an unemployed plumber, and a drumless drummer help out a ghost who gives them three magic kazoos and sends them in search of the King of Kazoo. (CCBB 30: 148; KR 44: 1138; SLJ Oct'76 p. 110)

PINKWATER, D. Manus. *Blue Moose.* See Chapter 9, Talking Animals.

PINKWATER, D(aniel) Manus. *The Hoboken Chicken Emergency.* Prentice-Hall, 1977. Illus. by the author. 83 pp. Gr. 3–5. [R]
Arthur Bobowicz's adoption of a 266-pound chicken meets with opposition from his parents, the mayor, and the townspeople. (BL 73: 1268; CCBB 30: 163; HB 53: 316; KR 45: 166; SLJ Sept'77 p. 134)

PINKWATER, D. Manus. *The Last Guru.* Dodd, 1978. Illus. by the author. 115 pp. Gr. 5–7. [R]
After twelve-year-old Harold Blatz invests his racetrack winnings in a hamburger chain and becomes a billionaire, the Blatz family tries to escape their newfound fame by moving to a castle in the Bavarian Alps and then to a village in India. (BL 75: 548; CC 1979 Suppl. p. 52; CCBB 32: 124; KR 46: 1189; SLJ Nov'78 p. 66)

PINKWATER, D. Manus. *Lizard Music.* Dodd, 1976. Illus. by the author. 157 pp. Gr. 4–6. [R]
Victor can't understand why lizards and the Chicken Man turn up wherever he goes, until he is taken to an invisible, lizard-run island. (BL 73: 41; CC 1977 Suppl. p. 68; CCBB 30: 112; HB 53: 161; KR 44: 846; SLJ Oct'76 p. 110)

POMERANTZ, Charlotte. *Detective Poufy's First Case: Or the Missing Battery-Operated Pepper Grinder.* Addison-Wesley, 1976. Illus. by Marty Norman. 64 pp. Gr. 3–5. [A]
A lonely dragon named Dragobert turns out to be the robber who broke into

Rosie Maloon's house and left all the electrical gadgets running. (BL 73: 476; KR 44: 796; SLJ Dec'76 p. 65)

POPHAM, Hugh. *The Fabulous Voyage of the Pegasus.* Phillips, 1959. Illus. by Graham Oakley. 150 pp. Gr. 5–6. [A]
Lee-O! and the crew of his yacht, *Pegasus,* encounter an assortment of legendary creatures during their voyage, including a Narwhal and the sea god, Poseidon. (HB 35: 301; KR 27: 176; LJ 84: 1700)

RASKIN, Ellen. *Figgs and Phantoms.* Dutton, 1974. Illus. by the author. 152 pp. Gr. 5–7. [R]
Mona Lisa Newton does not appreciate her kooky relatives—her tap-dancing mother, twin brothers Romulus and Remus, contortionist Truman Figg, and cousin Fido Figg—until her beloved uncle dies. (Adv: 198; BL 71: 46; CC: 558; CCBB 28: 98; HB 50: 138; KR 42: 425; LJ 99: 1451, 1475, and 3247)

RASKIN, Ellen. *The Mysterious Disappearance of Leon (I Mean Noel).* Dutton, 1971. Illus. by the author. 149 pp. Gr. 4–7. [R]
Married at five and seven years of age to solve their parents' business problems, Caroline (Little Dumpling) and Leon (Noel) Carillon don't see each other again until fourteen years full of clues, puzzles, and secret codes have passed. (Adv: 245; BL 68: 394 and 670; CC: 558; CCBB 25: 79; HB 48: 51; KR 39: 1122; LJ 96: 4160; Suth: 323; TN 28: 310)

REIT, Seymour. *Benvenuto.* See Chapter 8E, Dragons.

RICHLER, Mordecai. *Jacob Two-Two Meets the Hooded Fang.* Knopf, 1975. Illus. by Fritz Wegner. 87 pp. Gr. 3–5. [A]
Jacob is teased for his habit of saying everything twice, but he proves his courage after he is captured by the Slimers and their chief, the Hooded Fang. (Adv: 198; CCBB 28: 184; KR 43: 568; SLJ Sept'75 p. 90; TLS 1976 p. 376)

RINKOFF, Barbara. *Elbert, the Mind Reader.* Lothrop, 1967. Illus. by Paul Galdone. 112 pp. Gr. 4–6. [A]
Elbert's new filling enables him to tune in on people's thoughts, a talent he uses to impress the football coach so that he can join the team. (BL 64: 594; CCBB 21: 65; KR 35: 809; LJ 92: 3855)

* RODGERS, Mary. *Freaky Friday.* Harper, 1972. 155 pp. Gr. 4–7.
Annabel Adams wakes up one morning to discover that she has turned into her mother. *A Billion for Boris* (1974) is the sequel. (Arb: 241; BL 68: 910; CC: 561; CCBB 26: 15; HB 48: 378; JHC: 425; KR 40: 267; LJ 97: 1608)

ROUNDS, Glen. *The Day the Circus Came to Lone Tree.* Holiday, 1973. Illus. by the author. 39 pp. Gr. 3–4. [R]
The townspeople of Lone Tree are treated to some unwelcome entertainment when a circus lion and his trainer stampede all of the town's livestock. The sequels are *Mr. Yowder and the Lion Roar Capsules* (1976), *Mr. Yowder and*

the Steamboat (1977), and *Mr. Yowder and the Giant Bull Snake* (1978). (BL 70: 545; CCBB 27: 85; HB 52: 393; KR 41: 1155; LJ 99: 203)

SCHICK, Alice, and ALLEN, Marjorie. *The Remarkable Ride of Israel Bissell as Related by Molly the Crow: Being the True Account of an Extraordinary Post Rider Who Persevered.* Lippincott, 1976. Illus. by Joel Schick. 48 pp. Gr. 1–3. [A]
Israel's ride from Boston to Philadelphia with news of the Battle of Lexington is a journey fraught with setbacks. (BL 72: 982; CCBB 30: 47; KR 44: 254; SLJ Apr'76 p. 64)

SELDEN, George. *The Cricket in Times Square.* See Chapter 9, Talking Animals.

SENDAK, Maurice. *Higglety Pigglety Pop! Or, There Must Be More to Life.* See Chapter 9, Talking Animals.

SEUSS, Dr. *The 500 Hats of Bartholomew Cubbins.* See Chapter 5B, Imaginary Lands.

SINGER, Isaac Bashevis. *The Fools of Chelm and Their History.* Farrar, 1973. Tr. by the author and Elizabeth Shub. Illus. by Uri Shulevitz. 57 pp. Gr. 4–6. [R]
Angry that the whole world thinks them to be fools, the citizens of Chelm declare war, but they attack the wrong town and stage a revolution to depose the council of sages and replace them with thieves. (Adv: 200; CC: 565; CCBB 27: 101; HB 49: 593; KR 41: 1037; LJ 99: 213; TLS 1976 p. 376)

SINGER, Isaac Bashevis. *Naftali the Storyteller and His Horse, Sus, and Other Stories.* See Chapter 2, Collected Tales.

SINGER, Isaac Bashevis. *Zlateh the Goat and Other Stories.* See Chapter 2, Collected Tales.

SLOTE, Alfred. *My Robot Buddy.* Lippincott, 1975. 96 pp. Gr. 2–4. [A]
Jack is mistaken for his robot by a gang of robotnappers, but the robot rescues him from his captors. (BL 72: 460; CCBB 29: 102; KR 43: 999; SLJ Oct'75 p. 92)

STAHL, Ben. *Blackbeard's Ghost.* See Chapter 3, Ghosts.

STEELE, William O. *Andy Jackson's Water Well.* Harcourt, 1959. Illus. by Michael Ramos. 80 pp. Gr. 4–6. [R]
Andy Jackson and Chief Ticklepitcher are traveling to East Tennessee to fetch a water well for drought-stricken Nashville, but problems arise when Andy has trouble controlling his temper. (Arb: 242; BL 55: 426; Eakin: 307; HB 35: 214; KR 27: 224; LJ 84: 1700)

STEELE, William O. *Daniel Boone's Echo.* Harcourt, 1957. Illus. by Nicolas. 79 pp. Gr. 3–5. [A]

Aaron Adamsale is afraid of the Sling-Tailed Galootis and the One-Horned Sumpple of Kentucky, but Daniel Boone helps him conquer his fears. (BL 54: 146; HB 33: 490; KR 25: 771; LJ 82: 2976)

STEELE, William O. *Davy Crockett's Earthquake.* Harcourt, 1956. Illus. by Nicolas. 64 pp. Gr. 3–5. [A]
Davy meets up with a comet while out shooting bears in Tennessee. (BL 52: 346; Eakin: 308; HB 32: 188; KR 24: 242; LJ 81: 2045)

STEELE, William O. *The No-Name Man of the Mountain.* Harcourt, 1964. Illus. by Jack Davis. 79 pp. Gr. 4–7. [R]
Anxious to know his own name, a younger brother outwits his older brothers, who constantly plays tricks on him. (BL 61: 805; CCBB 18: 110; Eakin: 308; HB 41: 58)

SWAYNE, Samuel and Zoa. *Great Grandfather in the Honey Tree.* Viking, 1949. Illus. by the authors. 54 pp. Gr. K–4. [R]
With one round of ammunition and a net, Great-Grandfather captures a bear, a fish, twenty-four geese, a partridge, a deer, twelve turkeys, and a barrel of wild honey. (BL 46: 86; CC: 572; HB 25: 411; KR 17: 465; LJ 74: 1531, 75: 51)

THURBER, James. *The Wonderful O.* See Chapter 1, Allegory and Fable.

TODD, Ruthven. *Space Cat.* See Chapter 9, Talking Animals.

VAN LEEUWEN, Jean. *The Great Christmas Kidnapping Caper.* See Chapter 9, Talking Animals.

WAECHTER, Friedrich, and EILERT, Bernd. *The Crown Snatchers.* See Chapter 5A, Alternative Worlds.

WAHL, Jan. *The Furious Flycycle.* (Orig. pub. 1968) Dell, 1970 (pap.). 114 pp. Gr. 3–5. [M]
Determined to be liked for himself, not for his father's ice-cream factory, Melvin Spitznagle invents a flying bicycle. The sequel is *SOS Bobomobile!* (1973). (LJ 93: 3974)

WAHL, Jan. *The Screeching Door: Or, What Happened at the Elephant Hotel.* See Chapter 3, Ghosts.

WHITE, Anne. *Junket.* See Chapter 9, Talking Animals.

WHITE, E. B. *Stuart Little.* See Chapter 9, Talking Animals.

WHITE, E. B. *The Trumpet of the Swan.* See Chapter 9, Talking Animals.

WIBBERLEY, Leonard. *The Mouse That Roared.* Little, 1955. 279 pp. Gr. 7 up. [A]
Attempting to revive its national economy, the tiny duchy of Grand Fenwick declares war on the United States, hoping for a quick defeat and large war

reparations. But its twenty-three longbowmen not only win the war, they capture the top secret Q-Bomb! The sequels are *Beware of the Mouse* (1958), *The Mouse on the Moon* (1962), and *The Mouse on Wall Street* (1969). (BL 51: 190; KR 22: 788; LJ 79: 1506)

WILLIAMS, Ursula Moray. *Tiger Nanny* (British title: *Johnnie Tigerskin*). Nelson, 1974. Illus. by Gunvor Edwards. 128 pp. Gr. 4–6. [A]
The Harper children have the perfect nanny—efficient, responsible, and entertaining—only this nanny happens to be a tiger cub. (CCBB 28: 140; HB 51: 151; KR 42: 805; SLJ Jan'75 p. 42)

WRIGHTSON, Patricia. *An Older Kind of Magic.* See Chapter 6, Magic Adventure.

YOLEN, Jane. *Hobo Toad and the Motorcycle Gang.* See Chapter 9, Talking Animals.

YOLEN, Jane, ed. *Shape Shifters: Fantasy and Science Fiction Tales about Humans Who Can Change Their Shapes.* See Chapter 2, Collected Tales.

Tall Tales: Out-of-Print Works

AIKEN, Joan. *Armitage, Armitage, Fly Away Home.* Doubleday, 1968. Illus. by Betty Fraser. 214 pp. Gr. 4–7. (BL 65: 183; CCBB 22: 1; HB 44: 558; KR 36: 603; LJ 93: 3296)

ANDREWS, Frank. *The Upside-Down Town.* Little, 1958. Illus. by Louis Slobodkin. 60 pp. Gr. 3–5. (BL 54: 449; KR 26: 34; LJ 83: 1282)

BABCOCK, Elisabeth. *The Expandable Pig.* Scribner, 1949. Illus. by the author. 114 pp. Gr. 3–5. (HB 25: 410 and 436; KR 17: 323; LJ 74: 1541 and 1760)

BAKER, Margaret Joyce. *Porterhouse Major.* See Chapter 6, Magic Adventure: Out-of-Print Works.

BEATON-JONES, Cynon. *The Adventures of So Hi.* Vanguard, 1956. 179 pp. Gr. 5–7. (BL 53: 228; HB 32: 445)

BELL, Norman. *The Weightless Mother.* Follett, 1967. Illus. by W. T. Mars. 144 pp. Gr. 4–6. (BL 64: 384; HB 43: 459; KR 35: 339; LJ 92: 2647)

BENDICK, Jeanne. *The Blonk from beneath the Sea.* See Chapter 8R, Monsters and Sea Serpents: Out-of-Print Works.

BEST, Herbert. *Desmond's First Case.* See Chapter 9, Talking Animals: Out-of-Print Works.

BRIGHT, Robert. *Richard Brown and the Dragon.* See Chapter 8E, Dragons: Out-of-Print Works.

BRINK, Carol. *Andy Buckram's Tin Men.* Viking, 1966. Illus. by W. T. Mars. 192 pp. Gr. 4–6. (Arb: 233; BL 62: 774; CC: 491; CCBB 19: 143; KR 34: 245; LJ 91: 3255)

CARLSEN, Ruth. *Monty and the Tree House.* See Chapter 6, Magic Adventure: Out-of-Print Works.

CARLSEN, Ruth. *Mr. Pudgins.* See Chapter 6, Magic Adventure: Out-of-Print Works.

CARLSON, Natalie. *Evangeline, Pigeon of Paris.* See Chapter 9, Talking Animals: Out-of-Print Works.

CARLSON, Natalie. *Hortense, the Cow for a Queen.* Harcourt, 1957. Illus. by Nicolas. 95 pp. Gr. 4–6. (BL 53: 458; HB 33: 208 and 298; KR 25: 274; LJ 82: 1684)

CAUFIELD, Don and Joan. *The Incredible Detectives.* See Chapter 9, Talking Animals: Out-of-Print Works.

CORBETT, Scott. *Ever Ride a Dinosaur?* See Chapter 8D, Dinosaurs: Out-of-Print Works.

CRESSWELL, Helen. *The Piemakers.* Lippincott, 1967. Illus. by W. T. Mars. 142 pp. Gr. 4–6. (Arb: 238; BL 64: 1041; KR 36: 261; LJ 93: 2536; TLS 1967 p. 445)

DAVIES, Valentine. *It Happens Every Spring.* Farrar, 1949. 224 pp. Gr. 7 up. (BL 45: 359; KR 17: 238; LJ 74: 955 and 1031)

DOLBIER, Maurice. *A Lion in the Woods.* Little, 1955. Illus. by Robert Henneberger. 115 pp. Gr. 4–6. (BL 51: 301; HB 31: 111; LJ 80: 999)

DU BOIS, William Pène. *The Giant.* See Chapter 8J, Giants: Out-of-Print Works.

DU BOIS, William Pène. *The Squirrel Hotel.* Viking, 1952. Illus. by the author. 48 pp. Gr. 3–6. (BL 48: 269; HB 28: 106; KR 20: 71; LJ 77: 727)

EDMONDS, Walter. *Uncle Ben's Whale.* (Orig. pub. 1931) Dodd, 1955. Illus. by William Gropper. Unp. Gr. 4–6. (BL 52: 60; KR 23: 646; LJ 80: 2641)

EGNER, Thorbjorn. *The Singing Town.* (Orig. pub. 1955) Macmillan, 1959. Tr. by Evelyn Ramsden and Leila Berg. Illus. by the author. 105 pp. Gr. 4–6. (HB 35: 387; LJ 84: 3630; TLS Dec 4, 1959 p. iv)

EZO. *My Son-in-Law, the Hippopotamus.* See Chapter 9, Talking Animals: Out-of-Print Works.

FORESTER, Cecil. *Poo Poo and the Dragons.* Little, 1942. Illus. by Robert Lawson. 142 pp. Gr. 4–6. (HB 18: 332; LJ 67: 682; TLS 1942 p. 573)

FOSTER, John. *Marco and the Tiger*. Dodd, 1967. Illus. by Lorence Bjorklund. 128 pp. Gr. 4–6. (BL 64: 273; HB 43: 462; KR 35: 57; LJ 92: 2020)

GARNETT, David. *Two by Two: A Story of Survival*. See Chapter 5B, Imaginary Lands: Out-of-Print Works.

HILDICK, E. W. *The Dragon That Lived under Manhattan*. See Chapter 8E, Dragons: Out-of-Print Works.

HOLMAN, Felice. *The Future of Hooper Toote*. Scribner, 1972. Illus. by Gahan Wilson. 138 pp. Gr. 5–7. (BL 69: 529; CCBB 25: 171; KR 40: 259; LJ 97: 2951; Suth: 193)

HUNTER, Mollie. *The Smartest Man in Ireland*. See Chapter 8H, Fairies: Out-of-Print Works.

HUNTER, Mollie. *Thomas and the Warlock*. See Chapter 13, Witches, Wizards, Sorcerers, and Magicians: Out-of-Print Works.

JANEWAY, Elizabeth. *Ivanov Seven*. Harper, 1967. Illus. by Eros Keith. 176 pp. Gr. 5–8. (Arb: 239; BL 64: 502; CC: 535; HB 43: 750; KR 35: 1145; LJ 92: 4261)

JONSSON, Runer. *Viki Viking* (British title: *Vike the Viking*). World, 1968. Illus. by Ewert Karlsson. Tr. by Birgit Rogers and Patricia Lowe. 143 pp. Gr. 4–6. (BL 64: 1094; CCBB 21: 129; HB 44: 324; KR 35: 1473; LJ 93: 2114; TLS 1969 p. 689)

KING, Clive. *The Town That Went South*. See Chapter 9, Talking Animals: Out-of-Print Works.

KRÜSS, James. *The Happy Islands behind the Winds.* See Chapter 12, Travel to Another World: Out-of-Print Works.

LAMPMAN, Evelyn. *Captain Apple's Ghost*. See Chapter 3, Ghosts: Out-of-Print Works.

LAWSON, Robert. *The Fabulous Flight*. See Chapter 8Q, Miniature People: Out-of-Print Works.

LAWSON, Robert. *Mr. Twigg's Mistake*. See Chapter 9, Talking Animals: Out-of-Print Works.

LEE, Robert. *The Iron Arm of Michael Glenn*. Little, 1965. Illus. by Al Fiorentino. 153 pp. Gr. 5–9. The sequel is *The Day It Rained Forever* (1968). (KR 33: 752; LJ 90: 4636)

LE GRAND (pseud. of Le Grand Henderson). *How Baseball Began in Brooklyn*. Abingdon, 1958. Illus. by the author. 58 pp. Gr. 3–5. (BL 54: 540; Eakin: 205; HB 34: 108; LJ 83: 1604)

LE GRAND. *How Space Rockets Began.* Abingdon, 1960. 64 pp. Gr. 3–5. (HB 36: 289; KR 28: 89; LJ 85: 2040)

LE GRAND. *Matilda.* Abingdon, 1956. 63 pp. Gr. 4–6. (BL 53: 52; Eakin: 205; KR 24: 353; LJ 81: 2041)

LINDSAY, Norman. *The Magic Pudding.* See Chapter 9, Talking Animals: Out-of-Print Works.

LINKLATER, Eric. *The Pirates in the Deep Green Sea.* See Chapter 12, Travel to Another World: Out-of-Print Works.

McLAUGHLIN, Lorrie. *Shogomoc Sam.* St. Martin's, 1970. Illus. by Randy Jones. 61 pp. Gr. 4–6. (CCBB 24: 174)

MÜNCHHAUSEN, Karl. *Baron Münchhausen, His Wonderful Travels and Adventures.* (Orig. pub. 1785) Messner, 1957. Retold by Erich Kästner. Tr. by Richard and Clara Winston. Illus. by Walter Trier. 68 pp.; Pantheon, 1944. Illus. by Gustav Doré. 213 pp. Gr. 3–5. (BL 41: 157; KR 12: 483; LJ 69: 1006, 86: 576)

NYGAARD, Jacob. *Tobias, the Magic Mouse.* See Chapter 9, Talking Animals: Out-of-Print Works.

ORMONDROYD, Edward. *David and the Phoenix.* See Chapter 8S, The Phoenix: Out-of-Print Works.

PALMER, Mary. *The Dolmop of Dorkling.* See Chapter 12, Travel to Another World: Out-of-Print Works.

PARRISH, Anne. *The Story of Appleby Capple.* Harper, 1950. Illus. by the author. 184 pp. Gr. 2 up. (BL 47: 225; HB 26: 457 and 467, 27: 20; KR 18: 512; LJ 76: 338)

PETRIE, Stuart. *The Voyage of Barracks.* Meredith, 1968. Illus. by the author. 120 pp. Gr. 4–5. (BL 65: 754; KR 36: 643; LJ 93: 3308; TLS 1967 p. 1133)

PLIMPTON, George. *The Rabbit's Umbrella.* Viking, 1973. Illus. by William Pène Du Bois. 158 pp. Gr. 4–6. (KR 23: 414 and 516)

PREUSSLER, Otfried. *The Robber Hotzenplotz.* Abelard-Schuman, 1965. Illus. by F. J. Tripp. 126 pp. Gr. 5–7. *Further Adventures of the Robber Hotzenplotz* (1971) is the sequel. *The Final Adventures of the Robber Hotzenplotz* is a British sequel. (KR 33: 107; LJ 90: 2409; TLS 1964 p. 1081)

PREUSSLER, Otfried. *The Wise Men of Schilda.* Abelard-Schuman, 1963. Tr. by Anthea Bell. Illus. by F. J. Tripp. 185 pp. Gr. 4–6. (BL 60: 44; HB 39: 286)

RASKIN, Ellen. *The Tattooed Potato and Other Clues.* Dutton, 1975. 170 pp. Gr. 6–8. (Adv: 245; Arb: 367; BL 71: 967; CC: 559; CCBB 29: 52; HB 51: 271; KR 43: 457; SLJ Apr'75 p. 69, Dec'75 p. 32; TLS 1976 p. 1548)

RIOS, Tere. *The Fifteenth Pelican.* Doubleday, 1965. Illus. by Arthur King. 118 pp. Gr. 4 up. (KR 33: 782; LJ 90: 4076)

RUCK-PAUQUET, Gina. *Fourteen Cases of Dynamite.* Dial, 1968. Tr. by Edite Kroll. Illus. by Lilo Fromm. 84 pp. Gr. 3–6. (KR 36: 763; LJ 94: 304; TLS 1970 p. 415)

SHEEHAN, Carolyn and Edmond. *Magnifi-Cat.* See Chapter 9, Talking Animals: Out-of-Print Works.

SIMONT, Marc. *The Contest at Paca.* Harper, 1959. Illus. by the author. 60 pp. Gr. 3–5. (BL 55: 634; HB 35: 301; KR 27: 300; LJ 84: 2084; TLS Nov 25, 1960 p. iv)

SIMONT, Marc. *Mimi.* See Chapter 9, Talking Animals: Out-of-Print Works.

STORR, Catherine. *The Adventures of Polly and the Wolf* (British title: *Clever Polly and the Stupid Wolf*). (Orig. pub. 1957) Macrae, 1970. Illus. by Marjorie-Ann Watts. 94 pp. Gr. 3–6. The British sequel is *Polly and the Wolf Again.* (LJ 95: 3054)

TEAL, Mildred. *The Flight of the Kite Merriweather.* Atheneum, 1968. Illus. by Valli Van de Bovenkamp. 87 pp. Gr. 3–5. (KR 36: 902; LJ 93: 4409)

VASILIU, Mircea. *Hark, the Little Angel.* Day, 1965. See Chapter 8A, Angels: Out-of-Print Works.

WALKER, Kenneth, and BOUMPHREY, Geoffrey. *The Log of the Ark* (British title: *What Happened in the Arc*). (Orig. pub. 1926) Pantheon, 1960. 214 pp. Gr. 4–6. (BL 23: 139, 57: 33; HB 36: 217)

WEAVER, Jack. *Mr. O'Hara.* Viking, 1953. Illus. by the author. 160 pp. Gr. 5–7. (HB 29: 221; KR 21: 115)

WHITE, Anne. *The Story of Serapina.* See Chapter 9, Talking Animals: Out-of-Print Works.

WIBBERLEY, Leonard. *McGillicuddy McGotham.* See Chapter 8N, Leprechauns: Out-of-Print Works.

WIEMER, Rudolf O. *The Good Robber, Willibald.* (Orig. pub. 1965) Atheneum, 1968. Tr. by Barbara Gollob. Illus. by Marie Marcks. 65 pp. Gr. 3–5. (CCBB 21: 167; KR 36: 181; TLS 1969 p. 699)

WILLIAMS, Ursula Moray. *The Cruise of the Happy-Go-Gay.* Meredith, 1968. Illus. by Gunvor Edwards. 151 pp. Gr. 3–5. (BL 64: 1046; CCBB 22: 87; HB 44: 424; KR 35: 1474; LJ 93: 298; Suth: 424)

WILLIAMS, Ursula Moray. *Island Mackenzie.* See Chapter 9, Talking Animals: Out-of-Print Works.

11

Time Travel

Tales about people who step into another time can be the most memorable of all types of fantasy. This chapter includes books about travel from our time to the past and future, and stories in which travelers from the past or future visit the twentieth century. A few stories deal with two time periods that somehow touch, permitting glimpses into the past or future without any actual traveling. In fantasy, the means of time travel must be magical, not scientific. Tales of travelers to other worlds, rather than other times, will be found in Chapter 12, *Travel to Another World*.

ALEXANDER, Lloyd. *Time Cat: The Remarkable Journeys of Jason and Gareth* (British title: *Nine Lives*). (Orig. pub. 1963) Avon, 1975 (pap.). Illus. by Bill Sokol. 191 pp. Gr. 4–6. [M]
An orange-eyed black cat takes Gareth back into the eight periods of the cat's previous lives, including ancient Egypt, Rome, Britain, Peru, and Revolutionary America. (LJ 88: 2548; TLS 1963 p. 980)

ALLAN, Mabel. *Romansgrove*. Atheneum, 1975. Illus. by Gail Owens. 192 pp. Gr. 4–6. [R]
Wandering through the ruins of the old manor house called Romansgrove, Clare and Richard find themselves in the year 1902, attempting to save Emily Roman and her family from death by fire. (Adv: 181; BL 72: 295; CCBB 29: 89; HB 52: 54; KR 43: 776; SLJ Oct'75 p. 93)

ALLEN, Judy. *The Spring on the Mountain.* See Chapter 6, Magic Adventure.

AMOSS, Berthe. *The Chalk Cross.* Seabury, 1976. 136 pp. Gr. 5–8. [M]
Stephanie Martin envisions herself in the year 1832 and becomes Sidonie Laveau, daughter of a Voodoo Queen entangled in a struggle with Catholicism. (KR 44: 389; SLJ May'76 p. 65)

ANDERSON, Margaret. *In the Keep of Time.* Knopf, 1977. 151 pp. Gr. 4–6. [A]
An abandoned Scottish tower is the gateway into the fifteenth as well as the twenty-second centuries for Elinor, Andrew, Ian, and Ollie. *In the Circle of Time* (1979) is the sequel. (CCBB 30: 169; KR 45: 2; SLJ May'77 p. 66)

ANDERSON, Margaret. *To Nowhere and Back.* Knopf, 1975. 141 pp. Gr. 5–6. [A]
Elizabeth learns that a path near her house can take her into the 1870s, where she becomes a girl named Ann, but runs the risk of remaining permanently in the past. (BL 71: 961; CCBB 28: 157; HB 51: 379; KR 43: 181; SLJ Mar'75 p. 91)

ARTHUR, Ruth M. *On the Wasteland.* Atheneum, 1975. Illus. by Margery Gill. 159 pp. Gr. 5–7. [R]
When Betony travels into the past, she is transformed from a friendless orphan into Estrith, a Viking chief's daughter engaged to a Saxon prince. (Adv: 181; BL 72: 163; CC 1977 Suppl. p. 59; HB 51: 459; JHC 1976 Suppl. p. 47; KR 43: 710; SLJ Oct'75 p. 94; TLS 1975 p. 1455)

ARTHUR, Ruth M. *Requiem for a Princess.* Atheneum, 1967. Illus. by Margery Gill. 182 pp. Gr. 7–9. [R]
Willow Forrester's upsetting discovery that she is adopted causes her nightmares, in which she becomes a sixteenth-century Spanish girl fated to death by drowning. (Arb: 236; BL 63: 1098; CCBB 21: 138; HB 43: 211; JHC: 381; KR 35: 61; LJ 92: 1744; TLS 1967 p. 1141)

* BARBER, Antonia. *The Ghosts.* Farrar, 1969. 189 pp. Gr. 4–6.
Lucy and Jamie move to an old country house where they meet two ghostly children. They make a frightening journey into the past to save the ghosts from a fiery death. (BL 66: 563; CCBB 23: 92; HB 45: 532; KR 37: 854; LJ 95: 777; TLS 1969 p. 689)

BETHANCOURT, T. Ernesto (pseud. of Tom Paisley). *Tune In Yesterday.* Holiday, 1978. 156 pp. Gr. 8–10. [A]
A love for jazz propels two friends into the past to 1942, but racial prejudice and Nazi plots make life more complicated than they had anticipated. (BL 74: 1420; HB 54: 400; KR 46: 311; SLJ May'78 p. 73)

* BOND, Nancy. *A String in the Harp.* Atheneum, 1976. 370 pp. Gr. 6–8.
Unhappy over his mother's recent death and the family's move to Wales, Peter

Morgan is drawn into the sixth-century period of Taliesin by the tuning key of an ancient harp. (BL 72: 1108; CC 1976 Suppl. p. 60; CCBB 29: 171; HB 52: 287; JHC 1976 Suppl. p. 48; KR 44: 255; SLJ Apr'76 p. 84)

BOSTON, L. M. *The Children of Green Knowe.* See Chapter 6, Magic Adventure.

BRADBURY, Ray. *The Halloween Tree.* Knopf, 1972. Illus. by Joseph Mugnaini. 145 pp. Gr. 5–7. [A]
Eight Halloween-costumed boys search through ancient Egypt, druid Britain, Medieval Europe and Mexican catacombs for a friend who vanished from a haunted house. (BL 69: 404; KR 40: 801; LJ 97: 4086)

BRANDEL, Marc (pseud. of Marcus Beresford). *The Mine of Lost Days.* Lippincott, 1974. Illus. by John Verling. 185 pp. Gr. 4–7. [R]
Deep inside an abandoned Irish copper mine, Henry discovers four people who have lived without aging for over one hundred years, but who would die the moment they emerged into the modern world. (BL 71: 241; KR 42: 876; LJ 99: 2738)

BURFORD, Lolah. *The Vision of Stephen; an Elegy.* Macmillan, 1972. Illus. by Bill Greer. 192 pp. Gr. 7 up. [A]
Narrowly escaping execution by an Anglo-Saxon king, Prince Stephen flees from the seventh century into nineteenth-century England, where he is adopted by Margery and Peter's family. (BL 69: 26, 292 and 299; KR 40: 344; LJ 97: 2640 and 3473)

CAMERON, Eleanor. *The Court of the Stone Children.* See Chapter 3, Ghosts.

CAMERON, Eleanor. *Time and Mr. Bass: A Mushroom Planet Book.* Little, 1967. Illus. by Fred Meise. 247 pp. Gr. 4–6. [R]
Forces of evil reach through Mycetian history to ensnare Tyco Bass and his friends, Chuck and David, after they visit ancient Wales to translate an old scroll. *The Wonderful Flight to the Mushroom Planet* (1954), *Stowaway to The Mushroom Planet* (1956), *Mr. Bass's Planetoid* (1958), and *A Mystery for Mr. Bass* (1960) are science-fiction stories preceding this book. (BL 63: 988; CC: 495; HB 43: 460; KR 35: 56; LJ 92: 1314)

CHURCH, Richard. *The French Lieutenant: A Ghost Story.* See Chapter 3, Ghosts.

CRESSWELL, Helen. *A Game of Catch.* See Chapter 3, Ghosts.

* CRESSWELL, Helen. *Up the Pier.* Macmillan, 1971. Illus. by Gareth Floyd. 144 pp. Gr. 4–6.
Lonely Carrie meets the invisible Pontifex family, who were unwillingly transported from 1921 to the present and need Carrie's help to break the spell that holds them here. (BL 68: 1002; CC: 507; CCBB 26: 40; HB 48: 368; KR 40: 477; LJ 97: 4070; Suth: 94; TLS 1971 p. 1516)

CURRY, Jane. *The Bassumtyte Treasure.* Atheneum, 1978. 129 pp. Gr. 5–7. [R]
Clues to the lost family treasure lie in a cryptic riddle, two ancestral portraits, and an old medallion, but it is a sixteenth-century ghost named Lady Margaret who helps Tommy solve the family mystery. (BL 74: 1347; CC 1979 Suppl. p. 46; CCBB 32: 6; HB 54: 393; KR 46: 243; SLJ May'78 p. 84; TLS 1978 p. 1396)

CURRY, Jane. *The Daybreakers.* Harcourt, 1970. Illus. by Charles Robinson. 191 pp. Gr. 4–6. [R]
Researching the history of Apple Lock, Callie and her friends stumble into Abalok, an American Indian village of the past where the children help the inhabitants defeat their enemies. In this way they become part of their own town's history. The sequel is *The Birdstones* (1977). Both stories are related to *Over the Sea's Edge* (1971). (BL 66: 1406; CC: 507; HB 46: 296; KR 38: 452; LJ 95: 3626; TLS 1970 p. 1251)

CURRY, Jane. *Parsley, Sage, Rosemary and Time.* Atheneum, 1975. Illus. by Charles Robinson. 108 pp. Gr. 3–6. [A]
Thyme, a plant from her aunt's garden, sends Rosemary into Pilgrim times where she is put into the town jail for helping a woman accused of witchcraft. *The Magical Cupboard* (1976) is the sequel. (KR 43: 306; SLJ Apr'75 p. 51)

CURRY, Jane. *Poor Tom's Ghost.* Atheneum, 1977. 178 pp. Gr. 6–9. [R]
A hidden staircase is not the only secret held by the old house Roger's father inherits—ghostly sobbings and footsteps prove to be caused by Tom Garland, a seventeenth-century actor who involves Roger's family in danger. (BL 73: 1413 and 1419; CC 1978 Suppl. p. 49; CCBB 31: 12; HB 53: 439; JHC 1978 Suppl. p. 47; KR 45: 426; SLJ May'77 p. 67; TLS 1977 p. 864)

CURRY, Jane. *The Sleepers.* See Chapter 13, Witches, Wizards, Sorcerers, and Magicians.

CURRY, Jane. *The Watchers.* Atheneum, 1975. Illus. by Trina Schart Hyman. 235 pp. Gr. 6–8. [R]
Ray Silver joins the family battle against a coal company threatening their land, and when a stone splinter sends him sixteen hundred years into the past he becomes involved in a tragedy surrounding his ancestors. (Arb: 238; BL 72: 451; CC 1977 Suppl. p. 62; CCBB 29: 108; KR 43: 988; SLJ Nov'75 p. 73; TLS 1976 p. 392)

DUNLOP, Eileen. *Elizabeth, Elizabeth* (British title: *Robinsheugh*). Holt, 1977. Illus. by Peter Farmer. 185 pp. Gr. 6–9. [R]   .
On a lonely visit to her aunt at the Melville manor house, Elizabeth escapes through an old looking-glass into the eighteenth century, but she soon fears for her life. (BL 73: 1349; CCBB 30: 174; HB 53: 314; SLJ May'77 p. 67; TLS 1975 p. 733)

EVARTS, Hal. *Jay-Jay and the Peking Monster.* See Chapter 10, Tall Tales.

FARMER, Penelope. *A Castle of Bone.* See Chapter 1, Allegory and Fable.

* FARMER, Penelope. *Charlotte Sometimes.* Harcourt, 1969. Illus. by Chris Conor. 192 pp. Gr. 4–7.
Charlotte Makepeace discovers that she has a double named Claire who slept in the same boarding school bed in the year 1918, and that she and Claire can exchange places in time. This is the sequel to *The Summer Birds* (1962) and *Emma in Winter* (1966). (Arb: 214; BL 66: 457; CC: 516; CCBB 23: 158; HB 45: 675; KR 37: 1121; LJ 94: 4604; Suth: 120; TLS 1969 p. 1190; TN 26: 425)

FISHER, Leonard E. *Noonan: A Novel about Baseball, ESP, and Time Warps.* Doubleday, 1978. 125 pp. Gr. 6–9. [A]
In 1896, young hopeful Johnny Noonan, a baseball pitcher, is hit by a foul ball and sent one hundred years into the future, where his psychokinetic ability to control a baseball leads to stardom. (BL 74: 1733; CCBB ͻ2: 60; KR 46: 749; SLJ May'78 p. 87)

FREEMAN, Barbara. *The Other Face.* Dutton, 1976. Illus. by the author. 151 pp. Gr. 5–8. [A]
Betony Dovewood's discovery of a miniature china cottage transports her 150 years into the past, where she becomes involved in a romance between one of her ancestors and the housekeeper's daughter. (BL 73: 832; KR 44: 1169; SLJ Jan'77 p. 91; TLS 1975 p. 733)

FREEMAN, Barbara. *A Pocket of Silence.* Dutton, 1978. Decorations by the author. 171 pp. Gr. 7–9. [R]
Zilia spins a tale of romance, kidnapping, and murder for Caroline, who discovers that Zilia has come from two hundred years in the past to help solve a mystery. (BL 75: 804 and 809; HB 55: 192; KR 42: 132; SLJ Apr'79 p. 55; TLS 1977 p. 864)

GROSSER, Morton. *The Snake Horn.* See Chapter 6, Magic Adventure.

HAYNES, Betsy. *The Ghost of the Gravestone Hearth.* See Chapter 3, Ghosts.

HENDRICH, Paula. *The Girl Who Slipped through Time.* Lothrop, 1978. 117 pp. Gr. 5 up. [M]
When a twenty-first century girl named Para visits rural Kansas during the 1930s she becomes convinced of the need for ecological preservation and conservation of nature. (KR 46: 375; SLJ Mar'78 p. 129)

INGRAM, Tom. *The Night Rider.* Bradbury, 1975. 176 pp. Gr. 5–8. [R]
A cursed golden bracelet lures Laura to pre-Roman Britain where she becomes a girl called Merta, desperate to find the matching necklace and destroy it before the curse kills her. (BL 71: 1128; CCBB 29: 47; KR 43: 521; SLJ Sept'75 p. 105)

JONES, Diana Wynne. *A Charmed Life.* Greenwillow/Morrow, 1978. 217 pp. Gr. 5–8. [R]
After Cat and Gwen Chant are adopted by the mysterious Chrestomanei, Gwen uses witchcraft to change places with a twentieth-century girl, leaving Cat to fend for himself. (BL 74: 1009; CC 1979 Suppl. p. 49; CCBB 31: 113; HB 54: 396; KR 46: 177; SLJ Apr'78 p. 94; TLS 1977 p. 348)

KEY, Alexander. *The Sword of Aradel.* Westminster, 1977. 144 pp. Gr. 5–7. [A]
Escape into the future seems the only answer for Brian and Merra as they flee Duke Rupert and search for the magic sword of Aradel. (BL 73: 1728; CCBB 31: 35; SLJ Sept'77 p. 146)

LAWRENCE, Louise. *Sing and Scatter Daisies.* See Chapter 3, Ghosts.

LEE, Robert. *Once upon Another Time.* Nelson, 1977. 160 pp. Gr. 7–9. [A]
A car accident propels middle-aged Bob Crawford back into the 1940s, where he dates the girl he'd always been too shy to approach and is interrogated by the military because of his knowledge of the future. (CCBB 31: 35; KR 45: 436; SLJ Mar'77 p. 152)

L'ENGLE, Madeleine. *A Swiftly Tilting Planet.* Farrar, 1978. 278 pp. Gr. 6–9. [R]
When a South American dictator threatens global war, Charles Wallace travels back in time to change the course of history and save the world from destruction. This is the sequel to *A Wrinkle in Time* (1962) and *The Wind in the Door* (1973), two science-fiction novels. (BL 74: 1679; CC 1979 Suppl. p. 50; CCBB 32: 33; HB 55: 525; KR 46: 754; SLJ Sept'78 p. 160)

LEVIN, Betty. *The Sword of Culann.* Macmillan, 1973. 288 pp. Gr. 6–8. [A]
Claudia and Evan find an ancient sword hilt and disappear from Maine, to reappear in Iron Age Ireland where they become involved in magical battles. *A Griffon's Nest* (1975) and *The Forespoken* (1976) are the sequels. (KR 41: 1212; LJ 98: 3156)

LEWIS, Hilda. *The Ship That Flew.* (Orig. pub. 1939) Phillips, 1958. Illus. by Nora Lavrin. 246 pp. Gr. 5–7. [A]
A dwarf-made toy Viking ship takes four modern children to ancient Egypt, Norman Britain, and Sherwood Forest. (BL 54: 509; HB 34: 109; KR 26: 77; LJ 83: 1286)

LITTLE, Jane. *The Philosopher's Stone.* Atheneum, 1971. Illus. by Robin Hall. 123 pp. Gr. 4–6. [A]
A sorcerer named Nyvrem needs a rock from Stephen's collection to convert copper into gold, but he accidentally transports Stephen from Indiana to the twelfth century and Castle Mordemagne. (BL 68: 367; KR 39: 1121; LJ 96: 2918)

LIVELY, Penelope. *The Driftway*. Dutton, 1973. 140 pp. Gr. 5–7. [A]
Resentment against his father's remarriage causes Paul to take his sister on an
impulsive trip to their grandmother's. On the way they are involved in a
Viking raid, a Civil War battle, and an eighteenth-century highway robbery.
(BL 69: 813; CCBB 26: 172; HB 49: 271; KR 41: 188; LJ 98: 2003; TLS 1972 p.
812)

* LIVELY, Penelope. *The Ghost of Thomas Kempe*. Dutton, 1973. 186 pp.
Gr. 4–6.
James Harrison becomes the unwilling apprentice of a seventeenth-century
sorcerer and ends up taking the blame for the mischief caused when Thomas
Kempe decides to start life anew in the twentieth century. Carnegie Medal.
(Adv: 193; Arb: 215; BL 70: 388; CC: 545; CCBB 27: 81; HB 49: 591; KR 41:
883; LJ 99: 211; TLS 1973 p. 380)

LIVELY, Penelope. *The House in Norham Gardens*. Dutton, 1974. 154 pp.
Gr. 6–9. [R]
A New Guinean ceremonial shield brought home by Clare Mayfield's great-
grandfather has the power to transport Clare from present-day England to the
primitive jungles of New Guinea. (Arb: 215; BL 71: 767; CCBB 28: 96; HB 51:
55; KR 42: 1161; LJ 99: 3273; TLS 1974 p. 717)

LIVELY, Penelope. *A Stitch in Time*. See Chapter 3, Ghosts.

LIVELY, Penelope. *The Whispering Knights*. See Chapter 6, Magic
Adventure.

LUNN, Janet. *Twin Spell* (British title: *Double Spell*). (Orig. pub. 1968) Dell,
1971 (pap.). Illus. by Emily McCully. 158 pp. Gr. 5–6. [A]
An antique doll gives twins Jane and Elizabeth identical nightmares and
intertwines their lives with a pair of twins from the past. (CCBB 23: 101; HB
45: 675; KR 37: 1064; LJ 94: 3821)

MACE, Elisabeth. *The Ghost Diviners*. Nelson, 1977. 160 pp. Gr. 5–7. [A]
An aura of violence surrounds the metal rod found by Martin at the building
site of his family's new home, a feeling that is verified when Martin's sister,
Jackie, is sent back in time to witness a murder on that very site. (BL 74: 299;
KR 46: 3; SLJ Sept'77 p. 132; TLS 1977 p. 864)

MACE, Elisabeth. *The Rushton Inheritance*. Nelson, 1978. 173 pp. Gr. 5–7.
[A]
Steve's visits to the past initiate a search for treasure by two generations of
Rushtons: Tom and his sisters in the nineteenth century and Steve in the
twentieth. (BL 75: 1093; CCBB 32: 179; HB 55: 195; KR 42: 126; SLJ Dec'78
p. 54; TLS 1978 p. 1083)

McGRAW, Eloise. *A Really Weird Summer*. Atheneum, 1977. 218 pp. Gr.
6–8. [R]

While trying to cope with his parents' imminent divorce, Nels's secret friendship with Alan, a mysterious boy from the past, hurts his younger brother's feelings. (BL 73: 1421; CCBB 31: 62; HB 53: 532; KR 45: 427; SLJ Oct'77 p. 126)

MacKELLAR, William. *Alfie and Me and the Ghost of Peter Stuyvesant.* See Chapter 3, Ghosts.

McKILLIP, Patricia. *The House on Parchment Street.* See Chapter 3, Ghosts.

MAGUIRE, Gregory. *Lightning Time.* Farrar, 1978. 256 pp. Gr. 6–8. [A]
Daniel is distressed to learn of construction plans for the mountain where his grandmother lives, and where magic occurs whenever lightning strikes. (BL 74: 1680; CC 1979 Suppl. p. 51; HB 55: 517; KR 46: 750; SLJ Sept'78 p. 143)

* MAYNE, William. *Earthfasts.* Dutton, 1967. 154 pp. Gr. 5–8.
A curious cold-flamed candle is powerful enough to reverse time and endangers the lives of David and Keith when it brings King Arthur and his knights back to life. (Arb: 209; BL 68: 1050; CC: 549; CCBB 20: 172; HB 43: 343; KR 35: 508; LJ 92: 1750; Suth: 274; TLS 1966 p. 1080)

MAYNE, William. *A Game of Dark.* Dutton, 1971. 143 pp. Gr. 6–9. [R]
Feeling increasingly helpless and guilty over his father's critical illness, Donald finds himself traveling into the past to a land menaced by a huge man-eating worm that only he can destroy. (Arb: 209; BL 68: 629; CCBB 25: 61; HB 48: 58; KR 39: 1022; LJ 97: 2490; Suth: 274; TLS 1971 p. 1319)

MAZER, Norma. *Saturday, the Twelfth of October.* Delacorte, 1975. 247 pp. Gr. 6–9. [R]
Furious at her family, Zan Ford wishes so intensely to be elsewhere that she crosses the "river of time" into the Stone Age and is adopted by a tribe of cave-dwellers. (Arb: 240; BL 72: 44; CCBB 29: 67; JHC 1976 Suppl. p. 54; KR 43: 1195; SLJ Nov'75 p. 93)

NESBIT, E. (pseud. of Edith Bland). *The House of Arden.* (Orig. pub. 1908) Dutton, 1968. Illus. by Clarke Hutton. 244 pp. Gr. 4–6. [A]
In the ruins of Arden Castle lives a magical creature called Mouldiwarp with the power to send Edred and Elfrida into the past in search of lost Arden treasure. *Harding's Luck* (1910, 1960) is the sequel. (BL 57: 32; HB 36: 309)

NICHOLS, Ruth. *A Walk out of the World.* See Chapter 12, Travel to Another World.

NORTON, André (pseud. of Alice Mary Norton). *Dragon Magic.* Crowell, 1972. Illus. by Robin Jacques. 213 pp. Gr. 5–7. [A]
Four tales in one, this book describes the adventures of four boys who put together different sections of a dragon puzzle and are sent into the past, each

to a different ancient civilization. (BL 68: 1004; CCBB 25: 160; HB 48: 373; KR 40: 485; LJ 97: 2244)

NORTON, André. *Lavender Green Magic*. Crowell, 1974. Illus. by Judith Brown. 241 pp. Gr. 5–7. [A]
A maze at their grandparents' home causes Holly Wade and her brother and sister to travel back in time until they meet a good and an evil witch. (BL 71: 101; HB 50: 137; LJ 99: 2275)

NORTON, André. *Octagon Magic*. (Orig. pub. 1967) Archway, 1978 (pap.). Illus. by Mac Conner. 189 pp. Gr. 4–6. [A]
Lorrie enters a doll-sized replica of Octagon House and goes back in time to the Civil War period where she takes part in the Underground Railroad rescue of escaped slaves. (KR 35: 601; LJ 92: 2656; TLS 1968 p. 584)

NORTON, André. *Red Hart Magic*. Crowell, 1976. Illus. by Donna Diamond. 179 pp. Gr. 5–7. [A]
Mutual dreams of an old English inn draw Chris and Nan, stepbrother and sister, together as they travel through history and learn to deal with problems in their own lives. (BL 73: 610; CCBB 30: 110; HB 53: 160; KR 44: 974; SLJ Nov'76 p. 61)

NORTON, Mary. *Bedknob and Broomstick*. See Chapter 6, Magic Adventure.

ORMONDROYD, Edward. *Time at the Top*. Parnassus, 1963. Illus. by Peggie Bach. 176 pp. Gr. 4–6. [R]
Susan Shaw takes the elevator to the top floor of her apartment building and steps out into the world of 1881, where she helps two children search for lost treasure. *All in Good Time* (1975) is the sequel, describing what happens after Susan's father follows her into the past. (Arb: 241; BL 60: 262; CC: 555; Eakin: 251; HB 39: 603; LJ 88: 4478; TLS 1976 p. 392)

* PARKER, Richard. *The Old Powder Line*. Nelson, 1971. 143 pp. Gr. 5–8.
Brian Kane embarks on a dangerous journey when he boards an antiquated steam train to rescue his friend, Mr. Mincing, trapped somewhere in the past. (BL 68: 676; CCBB 25: 78; KR 39: 677; Suth: 306; TLS 1971 p. 744)

PARKER, Richard. *A Time to Choose: A Story of Suspense*. Harper, 1974. 151 pp. Gr. 6–9. [R]
Stephen and Mary have only brief glimpses, at first, of a peaceful, unpolluted world of the future, but they eventually choose between it and the unhappy twentieth-century life they know. (Arb: 241; CCBB 27: 183; HB 50: 385; JHC: 422; KR 42: 309; LJ 99: 1488; TLS 1973 p. 1434)

PASCAL, Francine. *Hangin' Out with Cici*. Viking, 1977. 152 pp. Gr. 7–9. [R]

After Victoria's smart mouth and disruptive behavior get her expelled from school, a bump on the head transports her to 1944 where she makes friends with a strangely familiar girl. (BL 73: 1355; CC 1978 Suppl. p. 53; HB 53: 541; KR 45: 99; SLJ Sept'77 p. 134)

* PEARCE, (Ann) Philippa. *Tom's Midnight Garden.* Lippincott, 1959. Illus. by Susan Einzig. 229 pp. Gr. 5–7.
When the grandfather clock strikes thirteen, Tom Long is able to enter an old-fashioned garden to meet Hatty, a mysterious girl who seems to have grown older each time he visits her. Carnegie Medal. (Arb: 213; BL 56: 126; CC: 557; Eakin: 254; HB 35: 478; KR 27: 492; LJ 84: 3930; TLS Nov 21, 1958 p. x)

PEYTON, K. M. *A Pattern of Roses.* See Chapter 3, Ghosts.

PHIPSON, Joan (pseud. of Joan Fitzhardinge). *The Way Home.* Atheneum, 1973. 184 pp. Gr. 5–7. [R]
Prue, Peter, and Richard are thrown over a cliff during a car accident and swept downstream into a world of enormous monsters and volcanic eruptions. (CC: 558; HB 50: 52; KR 41: 760; LJ 98: 2656; TLS 1973 p. 1114)

PINKWATER, D(aniel) Manus. *Wingman.* Dodd, 1975. Illus. by the author. 63 pp. Gr. 4–6. [A]
Donald Chen skips school to read comic books atop the George Washington Bridge in New York, until the day Wingman appears and carries him off to ancient China. (KR 43: 375; SLJ Sept'75 p. 109)

POPE, Elizabeth. *The Sherwood Ring.* Houghton, 1958. Illus. by Evaline Ness. 266 pp. Gr. 7 up. [R]
The American Revolutionary period comes alive for Peggy when she meets the ghost of her ancestor, Barbara Grahame, and sympathizes with Barbara's forbidden love affair with a British soldier. (BL 54: 567; Eakin: 265; HB 34: 613, 35: 399; KR 26: 38; LJ 83: 2073)

SAUER, Julia. *Fog Magic.* Viking, 1943. 107 pp. Gr. 4–6. [R]
In search of a friend her own age, Greta Addington wanders through the Nova Scotia fog and enters Blue Cove, a village from one hundred years in the past. (Adv: 273; BL 40: 83; CC: 563; HB 19: 405 and 422; LJ 68: 822 and 963; TLS 1977 p. 1409)

SELDEN, George. *The Genie of Sutton Place.* See Chapter 6, Magic Adventure.

SEVERN, David. *The Girl in the Grove.* See Chapter 3, Ghosts.

SHECTER, Ben. *The Whistling Whirligig.* See Chapter 3, Ghosts.

SHERBURNE, Zoa. *Why Have the Birds Stopped Singing?* Morrow, 1974. 189 pp. Gr. 5–7. [A]

An epileptic seizure at an ancestor's birthplace sends Katie into the nineteenth century where she becomes Kathryn, a girl imprisoned by her uncle. (BL 70: 1202; JHC: 428; LJ 99: 1488)

SNYDER, Zilpha. *The Truth about Stone Hollow*. See Chapter 3, Ghosts.

STEELE, Mary Q. *The First of the Penguins*. Macmillan, 1973. Illus. by Susan Jeffers. 160 pp. Gr. 6–9. [A]
Lonesome for his hospitalized father, Jim and his friend George go on frightening journeys to the North Pole, to a prehistoric jungle, and to an ancient shrine. (HB 50: 153; KR 41: 116; LJ 98: 3159; TLS 1974 p. 1005)

STOLZ, Mary. *The Cat in the Mirror*. Harper, 1975. 199 pp. Gr. 5–7. [R]
Difficulties in coping with a disinterested mother and unfriendly classmates lead to two lives for Erin Gandy, one in the twentieth century and the other in ancient Egypt. (Arb: 242; BL 72: 628; CC 1977 Suppl. p. 70; CCBB 29: 70; HB 51: 597; JHC 1976 Suppl. p. 57; KR 45: 999; SLJ Oct'75 p. 103)

SYKES, Pamela. *Mirror of Danger* (British title: *Come Back, Lucy*). Nelson, 1974. 175 pp. Gr. 5–6. [R]
Orphaned Lucy comes to live with distant cousins and is befriended by Alice, the ghost of a Victorian girl, who tries to trap Lucy permanently in the past. (BL 70: 1007; JHC 1976 Suppl. p. 57; LJ 99: 2742; TLS 1973 p. 1117)

SYMONS, Geraldine. *Crocuses Were Over, Hitler Was Dead* (British title: *Now and Then*). Lippincott, 1978. 158 pp. Gr. 5–7. [A]
Jassy travels back in time to the period of World War II, where she helps a British soldier accomplish a secret mission behind German lines. (BL 75: 550; CCBB 32: 145; KR 46: 1308; SLJ Oct'78 p. 151; TLS 1977 p. 864)

TOWNSEND, John Rowe. *The Visitors* (British title: *The Xanadu Manuscript*). Lippincott, 1977. Gr. 7–10. [R]
Katherine Wyatt and her parents are sent from the world of 2149 A.D. back into the twentieth century, but they need John Dunham's help to survive and to stay out of trouble. (BL 74: 34 and 45; CCBB 31: 87; HB 53: 671; JHC 1978 Suppl. p. 56; KR 45: 856; SLJ Nov'77 p. 75)

TWAIN, Mark (pseud. of Samuel Clemens). *A Connecticut Yankee in King Arthur's Court* (British title: *A Connecticut Yankee at the Court of King Arthur*). Harper, 1899. 450 pp. Gr. 6 up. [R]
An accidental blow on the head sends Hank Morgan 1300 years back through time to King Arthur's court, where he uses his knowledge of history and modern technology to replace Merlin as Court Magician. (BL 22: 170)

WALSH, Jill Paton. *A Chance Child*. Farrar, 1978. 186 pp. Gr. 6–9. [R]
Abused by his mother, Creep enters an even crueler time, that of the nineteenth century before child labor laws, where he and two runaways must

work to survive. (BL 75: 1215 and 1222; CCBB 32: 147; HB 55: 64; KR 46: 1359; SLJ Jan'79 p. 63)

WELDRICK, Valerie. *Time Sweep.* Lothrop, 1978. Illus. by Ron Brooks. 157 pp. Gr. 5–7. [A]
Laurie's bed is the means by which he travels from twentieth century Sydney, Australia, to 1862 London, where he and his new friend, Frank, avert a robbery. (CCBB 32: 127; HB 55: 196; KR 47: 7; SLJ Jan'78 p. 58)

WESTALL, Robert. *The Watch House.* Greenwillow/Morrow, 1978. 218 pp. Gr. 7–9. [R]
Ghosts from the past haunt a museum of shipwreck salvage and ensnare Anne in their quest for vengeance. (BL 74: 1356; CC 1979 Suppl. p. 56; CCBB 31: 187; HB 54: 405; KR 46: 381; SLJ Apr'78 p. 99, May'78 p. 36; TLS 1977 p. 1408)

* WESTALL, Robert. *The Wind Eye.* Greenwillow/Morrow, 1977. 213 pp. Gr. 7–9.
A boat that once belonged to a medieval monk carries Mike, Beth, and Sally across time into the seventh century, where St. Cuthbert changes both their lives and those of their parents. (BL 74: 370 and 381; CC 1978 Suppl. p. 56; CCBB 31: 103; HB 54: 56; KR 45: 1104; SLJ Nov'77 p. 77; TLS 1976 p. 1547)

WILLIAMS, Jay. *The Hawkstone.* See Chapter 6, Magic Adventure.

WILLIAMS, Ursula Moray. *Castle Merlin.* See Chapter 3, Ghosts.

Time Travel: Out-of-Print Works

ALLAN, Mabel. *Time to Go Back.* Abelard-Schuman, 1972. 134 pp. Gr. 5–8. (CCBB 26: 70; KR 40: 1105; LJ 98: 257)

ANDREWS, J. S. *The Green Hills of Nendrum* (British title: *The Bell of Nendrum*). Hawthorne, 1970. 214 pp. Gr. 6–8. (BL 67: 266; HB 46: 613; TLS 1969 p. 690; TN 27: 305)

ARTHUR, Ruth M. *The Autumn People.* Antheneum, 1973. Illus. by Margery Gill. 166 pp. Gr. 6–10. (BL 69: 1071; CCBB 27: 21; HB 49: 375; JHC: 381; KR 41: 122; LJ 98: 1702; TLS 1973 p. 680)

BACON, Martha. *The Third Road.* Little, 1971. Illus. by Robin Jacques. 188 pp. Gr. 5–8. (KR 39: 943; LJ 96: 4182)

BERESFORD, Elizabeth. *Invisible Magic.* Granada, 1977. Illus. by Reg Gray. 158 pp. Gr. 4–6. (BL 74: 1185; CCBB 32: 23; TLS 1975 p. 763)

BERESFORD, Elizabeth. *Travelling Magic.* (Orig. pub. 1965) Granada, 1977. Illus. by Judith Valpy. 163 pp. Gr. 4–6. (BL 74: 1185; TLS 1965 p. 1130)

BROWN, Bill and Rosalie. *The Department Store Ghost*. See Chapter 3, Ghosts: Out-of-Print Works.

BUCHAN, John. *Lake of Gold*. Houghton, 1941. Illus. by S. Levenson. 190 pp. Gr. 5–7. (HB 17: 367 and 476; LJ 66: 737)

CHASE, Mary. *The Wicked Pigeon Ladies in the Garden*. Knopf, 1968. Illus. by Don Bolognese. 115 pp. Gr. 4–7. (BL 65: 493; CCBB 22: 90; HB 45: 52; KR 36: 1162; LJ 94: 293; Suth: 69)

CHAUNCY, Nan. *The Secret Friends*. Watts, 1962. Illus. by Brian Wildsmith. 180 pp. Gr. 5–7. (HB 38: 275)

CHENAULT, Nell. *Parsifal the Poddley*. See Chapter 8W, Other Mythical Beings and Creatures: Out-of-Print Works.

DAWSON, Carley. *Mr. Wicker's Window*. Houghtor '952. Illus. by Lynd Ward. 272 pp. Gr. 5–7. The sequels are *The Sign of the Seven Seas* (1954) and *Dragon's Run* (1955). (BL 49: 160; HB 29: 53; LJ 78: 68)

EAGER, Frances. *Time Tangle*. Nelson, 1977. 172 pp. Gr. 5–7. (CCBB 31: 45; KR 45: 539; SLJ Oct'77 p. 88)

EMERSON, Caroline. *The Magic Tunnel: A Story of Old New York*. (Orig. pub. 1940) Four Winds, 1968. Illus. by Jerry Robinson. 122 pp. Gr. 4–6.
(LJ 65: 850)

GARD, Joyce. *Talargain*. See Chapter 8T, Seal People, Out-of-Print Works.

HOLM, Anne. *Peter*. Tr. by L. W. Kingsland. Harcourt, 1968. 224 pp. Gr. 6–8. (KR 36: 466; LJ 93: 2121)

HORSEMAN, Elaine. *The Hubbles' Bubble*. See Chapter 6, Magic Adventure: Out-of-Print Works.

KASSIRER, Norma. *Magic Elizabeth*. Illus. by Joe Krush. Viking, 1966. 173 pp. Gr. 4–6. (CCBB 20: 44; KR 34: 304; LJ 91: 3535)

KIPLING, Rudyard. *Puck of Pook's Hill*. See Chapter 8H, Fairies: Out-of-Print Works.

LAMPMAN, Evelyn. *Captain Apple's Ghost*. See Chapter 3, Ghosts: Out-of-Print Works.

LAWSON, John S. *The Spring Rider*. Crowell, 1968. 147 pp. Gr. 5–8 . (Arb: 240; BL 65: 254; HB 44: 564; KR 36: 699; Suth: 240)

LOVE, Edmund. *An End to Bugling*. Harper, 1963. Illus. by Bob Bugg. 150 pp. Gr. 8 up. (BL 59: 679 and 776)

MacKELLAR, William. *The Ghost in the Castle.* See Chapter 3, Ghosts: Out-of-Print Works.

MAYNE, William. *The Hill Road* (British title: *Over the Hills and Far Away*). Dutton, 1968. 144 pp. Gr. 4–6. (CCBB 22: 161; HB 45: 171; KR 37: 55; LJ 94: 1783)

MILLER, Eugenia. *The Sign of the Salamander.* Holt, 1967. 233 pp. Gr. 5–7. (HB 43: 464; KR 35: 600; LJ 92: 2022)

MORRESSY, John. *The Windows of Forever.* Walker, 1975. Illus. by Allen Atkinson. 86 pp. Gr. 4–7. (BL 72: 859; CCBB 29: 116; KR 43: 1229; SLJ Dec'75 p. 54)

NORTH, Joan. *The Whirling Shapes.* Farrar, 1967. 183 pp. Gr. 6–8. (CCBB 21: 82; LJ 92: 3202; Suth: 298)

PARDOE, M. *Curtain of Mist* (British title: *Argle's Mist*). Funk, 1957. Illus. by Leslie Atkinson. 246 pp. Gr. 6–8. *Argle's Oracle* is the British sequel. (HB 34: 38; KR 25: 485)

SEVERN, David. *Dream Gold.* Viking, 1952. Illus. by Isami Kashiwagi. 192 pp. Gr. 6–8. (HB 29: 53; KR 20: 412; LJ 77: 2079)

SLEIGH, Barbara. *Jessamy.* Bobbs-Merrill, 1967. 246 pp. Gr. 4–5. (BL 63: 1195; CCBB 21: 33; HB 43: 343; KR 35: 416; LJ 92: 2024; TLS 1967 p. 451)

UTTLEY, Alison. *A Traveller in Time.* (Orig. pub. 1939) Viking, 1964. Illus. by Christine Price. 287 pp. Gr. 6–9. (BL 61: 581; HB 40: 612; LJ 89: 4653)

WELCH, Ronald. *The Gauntlet.* Oxford, 1952. Illus. by T. R. Freeman. 248 pp. Gr. 7–9. (BL 49: 53; HB 29: 53; KR 20: 456; LJ 77: 1522)

12
Travel to Another World

Some of the most frequently read fantasy tales describe journeys across the boundaries of our world into entirely new and unfamiliar worlds. In these tales there is no manipulation of time, no indication of past or future, just a magical (not "scientific") transportation out of our world. Tales of travelers to other times will be found in Chapter 11, *Time Travel*.

* ALEXANDER, Lloyd. *The First Two Lives of Lukas-Kasha*. Dutton, 1978. 224 pp. Gr. 5–8.
Lukas volunteers to participate in a magic act, and unexpectedly ends up in the land of Abadan, where he is made king despite the objection of the Grand Vizier. (BL 75: 42; CC 1979 Suppl. p. 41; CCBB 32: 57; HB 55: 513; KR 46: 878; SLJ Oct'78 p. 141)

ALLEN, Judy. *The Lord of the Dance*. Dutton, 1977. 124 pp. Gr. 6–8. [A] Mike's exploration of an old well shaft in the rubble of the collapsed Civic Center leads to his meeting the sun king and the earth queen. (CCBB 31: 25; HB 53: 536; KR 45: 580; SLJ Sept'77 p. 139; TLS 1976 p. 1544)

ANDERSEN, Hans Christian. *The Snow Queen*. See Chapter 1, Allegory and Fable.

* BARRIE, Sir J(ames) M. *Peter Pan*. (Orig. pub. 1911) Scribner, 1950. Illus. by Nora Unwin. 242 pp. Gr. 3–6.

Peter teaches three children to fly to Never Never Land with him, but a jealous fairy named Tinkerbell betrays them to Captain Hook's pirate band. *Peter Pan in Kensington Gardens* (Orig. pub. 1906; Scribner, 1937) tells of Peter's infancy. (Arb: 211; BL 8: 171, 47: 18; CC: 483; HB 26: 387)

BAUM, L(yman) Frank. *The Wizard of Oz*. (Orig. pub. 1900) Reilly, 1956. Illus. by Evelyn Copelman, adapted from the illustrations of W. W. Denslow. 206 pp. Gr. 3–6. [R]
A cyclone blows Dorothy from Kansas to the Land of Oz. The price of her trip home is the death of the Wicked Witch of the West. The sequels are *The Land of Oz* (1904), *Ozma of Oz* (1907), *Dorothy and the Wizard in Oz* (1908), *The Road to Oz* (1909), *The Emerald City of Oz* (1910), *The Patchwork Girl of Oz* (1913), *Tik-tok of Oz* (1914), *The Scarecrow of Oz* (1915), *Rinkitink in Oz* (1916), *The Lost Princess of Oz* (1917), *The Tin Woodman of Oz* (1918), *The Magic of Oz* (1919), and *Glinda of Oz* (1920). (Arb: 233; CC: 484)

BOSTON, L(ucy) M(aud). *The Guardians of the House*. Atheneum, 1975. Illus. by Peter Boston. 52 pp. Gr. 4–6. [A]
A collection of peculiar masks and carved heads in an old mansion lures Tom Morgan to a jungle temple, a submerged Roman villa, and an Indian cave. (Arb: 237; CCBB 29: 3; HB 51: 265; KR 43: 121; SLJ May'75 p. 52; TLS 1974 p. 1373)

BOSTON, L. M. *The Sea Egg*. See Chapter 6, Magic Adventure.

BRADLEY, Michael. *The Shaping Room*. Dodd, 1978. 151 pp. Gr. 5–7. [A]
Professor Apollonius's Mindstone brings on Stephen's dreams, set in the paintings of his favorite artists, but the dreams become a terrifying nightmare. (BL 74: 1098; CCBB 31: 171; KR 46: 107; SLJ Mar'78 p. 136)

* CARROLL, Lewis (pseud. of Charles Dodgson). *Alice's Adventures in Wonderland*. (Orig. pub. 1865) Macmillan, 1963. Illus. by John Tenniel. 125 pp.; St. Martin's, 1977. Illus. by John Tenniel. 205 pp.; Watts, 1966. Illus. by Arthur Rackham. 161 pp.; Delacorte, 1977. Illus. by Tove Jansson. 120 pp. Gr. 4 up.
Alice has two adventures: First she follows a rabbit into a curious world where she meets the Mad Hatter and the Queen of Hearts. In *Through the Looking Glass and What Alice Found There* (written 1870; pub. 1899; Macmillan, 1963; St. Martin's, 1977) she steps through a mirror into a backwards world. (Arb: 210; BL 51: 210, 63: 189; CC: 496, 1978 Suppl. p. 47; HB 5: 48, 42: 76 and 326, 49: 284; LJ 91: 5258; TLS 1972 p. 1525)

CHANT, Joy. *Red Moon and Black Mountain: The End of the House of Kendreth*. (Orig. pub. 1973) Dutton, 1976. 277 pp. Gr. 7–10. [R]
A prophecy calls three children into the Starlit Land: Nick and Penelope to the Black Mountain lair of the sorcerer Fendarl, and Oliver to join a Warrior band and train to battle the Black Lord. *The Gray Mane of Morning* (1977) is the sequel. (BL 72: 1584 and 1594; CCBB 30: 22; KR 44: 600; SLJ Sept'76 p. 130; TLS 1970 p. 1449)

CLEMENTS, Bruce. *Two against the Tide.* Farrar, 1967. 199 pp. Gr. 5–7. [A]
Tom and Sharon are kidnapped and taken to an island whose inhabitants
have found the secret of everlasting youth. (BL 64: 542; HB 43: 587; KR 35:
966 and 1444; SLJ 93: 289)

COOPER, Paul Fenimore. *Tal: His Marvelous Adventures with Noom-Zor-
Noom.* Ungar, 1929. Illus. by Ruth Reeves. 305 pp. Gr. 4–6. [A]
Tal's journey to the kingdom of Troom ends with the discovery that he is the
king's long-lost son. (BL 26: 285; TLS 1930 p. 979)

DAHL, Roald. *James and the Giant Peach: A Children's Story.* See Chapter
6, Magic Adventure.

DUGGAN, Maurice. *Falter Tom and the Water Boy.* See Chapter 8P,
Mermaids and Sea People.

DURRELL, Gerald. *The Talking Parcel.* Lippincott, 1975. Illus. by Pamela
Johnson. 191 pp. Gr. 4–6. [A]
A parrot, a spider, and a toad enlist the help of three children to save
Mythologia after fire-breathing Cockatrices steal the books of magic. (BL 71:
1127; HB 51: 268; KR 43: 453; SLJ May'75 p. 54; TLS 1974 p. 1380)

FARMER, Penelope. *A Castle of Bone.* See Chapter 1, Allegory and Fable.

FARMER, Penelope. *William and Mary: A Story.* Atheneum, 1974. 160 pp.
Gr. 5–6. [R]
Mary and William find that a rare shell has the power to carry them into an
aquarium, back to the fall of Atlantis, and to a world beneath the sea. (Adv:
186; Arb: 239; BL 71: 168; CCBB 28: 93; HB 50: 690; KR 42: 1160; LJ 99: 3052;
TLS 1974 p. 1380)

FARTHING, Alison. *The Mystical Beast.* Hastings, 1978. Illus. by Anne
Mieke. 123 pp. Gr. 4–6. [A]
Sara and Henry enter the Other Side after meeting Lavinia, daughter of the
Hereditary Keeper of the Mystical Beast, and organize a hectic search for the
Beast, to avert a "terrible" occurrence. (CCBB 32: 42; SLJ Oct'78 p. 144; TLS
1976 p. 882)

FEYDY, Anne. *Osprey Island.* See Chapter 6, Magic Adventure.

FORST, S. *Pipkin.* See Chapter 8K, Gnomes.

FRY, Rosalie. *Mungo.* See Chapter 8R, Monsters and Sea Serpents.

GANNETT, Ruth. *My Father's Dragon.* See Chapter 8E, Dragons.

GARNER, Alan. *Elidor.* (Orig. pub. 1967) Collins + World, 1979. 186 pp. Gr.
4–6. [R]
Roland, Helen, Nicholas, and David unexpectedly stumble into the medieval
kingdom of Elidor, where they promise to protect four treasures from evil

beings able to follow them back into twentieth-century England. (BL 63: 1099; HB 43: 462; KR 35: 269; LJ 92: 2449; TLS 1965 p. 1131)

GRAY, Nicholas. *Grimbold's Other World.* (Orig. pub. 1968) Faber, 1979 (pap.; dist. by Merrimack). Illus. by Charles Keeping. 184 pp. Gr. 5–7. [A]
A goatherd named Muffler gets himself into trouble when he returns to a world of darkness shown him by Grimbold the cat. (BL 64: 1185; KR 36: 114; TLS 1963 p. 427)

GREAVES, Margaret. *The Dagger and the Bird: A Story of Suspense.* See Chapter 8H, Fairies.

GREGORIAN, Joyce Ballou. *The Broken Citadel.* Atheneum, 1975. Illus. by the author. 373 pp. Gr. 7–9. [A]
A shaft of sunlight in an abandoned house takes Sibby into the lands of Tredana and Treclere, where she joins Prince Leron in his fight against Queen Simirimia. The sequel is *Castledown* (1977). (Adv: 187; BL 72: 235; HB 52: 154; KR 75: 782; SLJ Nov'75 p. 90)

GRIPE, Maria. *The Glassblower's Children.* Delacorte, 1973. Tr. by Sheila LaFarge. Illus. by Harald Gripe. 170 pp. Gr. 4–7. [R]
Klas and Klara, kidnapped and imprisoned by the Lord of All Wishes Town, lose all hope of rescue until a sorceress named Flutter Mildweather arrives to help them. (Arb: 239; BL 70: 170; CC: 526; CCBB 27: 9; KR 41: 515 and 1350; LJ 98: 2194; TLS 1975 p. 365; TN 30: 434)

GRIPE, Maria. *The Land Beyond.* See Chapter 1, Allegory and Fable.

HILL, Elizabeth. *Ever-After Island.* See Chapter 6, Magic Adventure.

HILTON, James. *Lost Horizon.* (Repr. of 1922 ed.) Morrow, 1936. 211 pp. Gr. 8 up. [R]
Four survivors of a plane crash in Tibet find their way to the lamasery of Shangri-La, an oasis of eternal youth. But they long to return home. (BL 30: 79; TLS 1933 p. 648)

HUNTER, Mollie. *The Haunted Mountain: A Story of Suspense.* See Chapter 8H, Fairies.

INGELOW, Jean. *Mopsa the Fairy.* See Chapter 8H, Fairies.

IPCAR, Dahlov. *A Dark Horn Blowing.* Viking, 1978. 228 pp. Gr. 7–10. [A]
Magic brings Nora into an unknown kingdom to care for an infant prince, but despite her love for the young prince, she wants to return to her own family. (BL 74: 1610; KR 46: 510; SLJ Nov'78 p. 82)

IPCAR, Dahlov. *The Queen of Spells.* See Chapter 8H, Fairies.

JONES, Adrienne. *The Mural Master.* Houghton, 1974. Illus. by David White. 249 pp. Gr. 5–6. [A]

Carrie, Digby, Tonio, and Leo follow Til Pleeryn, the mural master, right through the scenes he paints into the land of Pawthania on a mission to free the captive king. (CCBB 28: 44; HB 50: 283; LJ 99: 2271)

JONES, Diana Wynne. *Dogsbody.* See Chapter 9, Talking Animals.

JUSTER, Norton. *The Phantom Tollbooth.* Random, 1961. Illus. by Jules Feiffer. 255 pp. Gr. 5–7. [R]
Finding a boy-sized car and tollbooth in his bedroom, Milo drives off to rescue the lost princesses, Rhyme and Reason, aided by the Spelling Bee and a watchdog named Tock. (Arb: 235; LJ 87: 332; TLS 1962 p. 892)

KENNY, Herbert A. *Dear Dolphin.* Pantheon, 1967. Illus. by Kelly Oechsli. 174 pp. Gr. 4–6. [M]
A talking dolphin takes Ann beneath the sea to meet a sea serpent and Davy Jones. (KR 35: 958; LJ 92: 3187)

KEY, Alexander. *The Forgotten Door.* Westminster, 1965. 126 pp. Gr. 6–9. [R]
Falling from another world into a remote mountain town, Jon's mind-reading ability generates fear and greed in the villagers who find him. (CC: 538; CCBB 18: 151; HB 41: 392; JHC: 412; KR 33: 117; LJ 90: 972; TLS 1966 p. 449)

KINGSLEY, Charles. *The Water Babies.* See Chapter 8H, Fairies.

LANGTON, Jane. *The Diamond in the Window.* See Chapter 6, Magic Adventure.

LAWRENCE, Louise. *Star Lord.* See Chapter 4, Good versus Evil.

* LEWIS, C(live) S(taples). *The Lion, the Witch and the Wardrobe.* Macmillan, 1951. Illus. by Pauline Baynes. 154 pp. Gr. 4–6.
The White Witch casts a spell over the Land of Narnia, ensnaring Edmund and drawing his brother and sisters into Narnia too, where they join Aslan's struggle to break the enchantment. Other titles in the Narnia series are *Prince Caspian* (1951), *The Voyage of the Dawn Treader* (1952), *The Silver Chair* (1953), *The Horse and His Boy* (1954), *The Magician's Nephew* (1955), and *The Last Battle* (1956; Carnegie Medal). (Arb: 206; BL 47: 208; CC: 543; HB 27: 54; KR 18: 514)

LITTLE, Jane. *Danger at Sneaker Hill.* See Chapter 13, Witches, Wizards, Sorcerers, and Magicians.

LOFTING, Hugh. *The Story of Doctor Dolittle.* See Chapter 10, Tall Tales.

LOVEJOY, Jack. *The Rebel Witch.* See Chapter 13, Witches, Wizards, Sorcerers, and Magicians.

MACDONALD, George. *At the Back of the North Wind.* See Chapter 1, Allegory and Fable.

MACDONALD, George. *The Golden Key.* See Chapter 1, Allegory and Fable.

McGOWEN, Tom. *Odyssey from River Bend.* See Chapter 9, Talking Animals.

McGOWEN, Tom. *The Spirit of the Wild.* See Chapter 8Q, Miniature People.

McKENZIE, Ellen. *Drujienna's Harp.* Dutton, 1971. 305 pp. Gr. 5–8. [A]
A San Francisco curio shop is the entrance to the terror-ridden land of T'Pahl, where Tha and Duncan attempt to topple a tyrant from power. (BL 67: 908; CCBB 25: 12; HB 47: 614; KR 39: 434; LJ 96: 1814; TN 28: 74)

MOLESWORTH, Mary. *The Cuckoo Clock.* (Orig. pub. 1877) Dutton, 1954. Illus. by Ernest Shepard. 165 pp. Gr. 4–6. [A]
The cuckoo in Griselda's new home takes her through its clock into a magical land. (BL 36: 118, 51: 48; HB 30: 324 and 344)

NICHOLS, Ruth. *The Marrow of the World.* Atheneum, 1972. Illus. by Trina Schart Hyman. 168 pp. Gr. 5–7. [A]
Linda, daughter of a witch, is summoned into another world by her dying half-sister and ordered to bring back the essence of life in exchange for her freedom. (Adv: 195; BL 69: 717; KR 40: 1191; LJ 98: 262)

NICHOLS, Ruth. *A Walk out of the World.* Harcourt, 1969. Illus. by Trina Schart Hyman.192 pp. Gr. 4–6. [R]
Judith and her brother Tobit follow a strange light into a world once ruled by their ancestors where they mastermind a plot to overthrow the hated King Hagerrak. (BL 65: 1178; CC: 554; CCBB 22: 180; HB 45: 412; KR 37: 304; LJ 94: 2677; TN 26: 308)

NORTON, André (pseud. of Alice Mary Norton). *Here Abide Monsters.* Atheneum, 1974. 215 pp. Gr. 7–12. [A]
Nick and Linda stumble into legendary Avalon where they become fugitives hunted by dangerous demons and mythical beasts. (BL 70: 485; JHC: 421; KR 41: 760; LJ 98: 3708)

NORTON, André. *Knave of Dreams.* Viking, 1975. 252 pp. Gr. 7 up. [A]
Crossing into a parallel world called Ulad, Ramsay Kimble becomes Kaskar, doomed son of the late emperor, embroiled in a vicious struggle for power. (BL 72: 294; KR 43: 856; SLJ Nov'75 p. 94; TLS 1976 p. 1242)

NORTON, André. *Steel Magic.* (Orig. pub. 1965) Archway, 1978 (pap.). Illus. by Robin Jacques. 155 pp. Gr. 5–7. [A]
Eric, Sara, and Greg Lowry enter Avalon through a miniature castle, where they search for Arthur's sword and Merlin's ring in order to save the land from evil. (CCBB 19: 151; HB 41: 629; LJ 90: 5519; TLS 1967 p. 451)

NORTON, André. *Wraiths of Time.* Atheneum, 1976. 210 pp. Gr. 7–12. [A]
Radiation from a curious artifact thrusts Tallahassee Mitford into the Nubian
kingdom of Meroë, where she takes on the memories and powers of Princess
Ashake to battle evil forces from another world. (BL 73: 138 and 180; CCBB
30: 96; KR 44: 740; SLJ Oct'76 p. 120)

NORTON, Mary. *Are All the Giants Dead?* Harcourt, 1975. Illus. by Brian
Froud. 123 pp. Gr. 4–6. [A]
James goes on a guided tour of fairy-tale land where he battles a giant to save
Princess Dulcibel from an ill-fated marriage to a frog. (Adv: 100; BL 72: 627;
CCBB 29: 129; HB 51: 465; KR 43: 1131; SLJ Sept'75 p. 107; TLS 1975 p.
1053)

O'BRIEN, Robert C. (pseud. of Robert Conly). *The Silver Crown.*
Atheneum, 1968. Illus. by Dale Payson. 247 pp. Gr. 5–6. [A]
Ellen's bejeweled crown saves her from death by fire but endangers her life
because of its potential for overthrowing the terrible Hieronymus Machine.
(HB 44: 174; LJ 93: 1802; TLS 1973 p. 1115)

O'HANLON, Jacklyn. *The Door.* Dial, 1978. 76 pp. Gr. 5–8. [A]
Rachel steps through "The Door" into a frightening world populated by
captives of Burt Pelf, who intends to keep Rachel under his power. (CCBB 32:
49; KR 46: 498; SLJ Apr'78 p. 87)

PATTEN, Brian. *Mr. Moon's Last Case.* See Chapter 8N, Leprechauns.

PINKWATER, D. Manus. *Lizard Music.* See Chapter 10, Tall Tales.

POPE, Elizabeth. *The Perilous Gard.* See Chapter 8H, Fairies.

SAINT-EXUPÉRY, Antoine de. *The Little Prince.* See Chapter 1, Allegory
and Fable.

SLEATOR, William. *Among the Dolls.* See Chapter 7, Magical Toys.

STEARNS, Pamela. *Into the Painted Bear Lair.* Houghton, 1976. Illus. by
Ann Strugnell. 153 pp. Gr. 4–6. [A]
A visit to a toy store takes Gregory into a fairy-tale kingdom where a hungry
bear and a knight help him rescue a princess from a dragon and awaken an
enchanted prince. (BL 73: 670; CCBB 30: 133; HB 53: 164; KR 44: 1170; SLJ
Dec'76 p. 56)

STEWART, Mary. *Ludo and the Star Horse.* See Chapter 1, Allegory and
Fable.

SWAHN, Sven. *The Island through the Gate.* Macmillan, 1974. Tr. by
Patricia Crampton. 183 pp. Gr. 6–8. [A]
Stranded on the isolated island of Oberair, Michael is prevented from leaving
by the superstitious islanders and their leader, Gourven the sorcerer. (BL 70:
1059; HB 50: 154; KR 42: 187; LJ 99: 2279)

SWIFT, Jonathan. *Gulliver's Travels.* (Orig. pub. 1726) Dutton, 1957. Illus. by Arthur Rackham. 210 pp.; Macmillan, 1962. Retold by Padraic Colum. Illus. by Willy Pogany. 260 pp. Gr. 6 up. [R]
Gulliver's adventures begin with a shipwreck on an island of miniature people called Lilliput and continue with his voyage to Brobdingnag, land of giants. (BL 44: 118, 45: 145; HB 39: 604; JHC: 432)

TOLKIEN, J. R. R. *Smith of Wootton Major.* See Chapter 6, Magic Adventure.

TOWNE, Mary. *Goldenrod.* See Chapter 6, Magic Adventure.

TROTT, Susan. *The Sea Serpent of Horse.* Little, 1973. Illus. by Irene Burns. 117 pp. Gr. 5–6. [A]
An unhappy girl decides whether to stay forever in an undersea world or return to her life on land. (BL 70: 546; KR 41: 1045 and 1358; LJ 99: 577)

WHEELER, Thomas. *Loose Chippings.* Phillips, 1969. 190 pp. Gr. 8–12. [A]
Stranded after his car breaks down in the village of Loose Chippings, Bob Vickery finds the town to be full of secrets. (BL 66: 50; KR 37: 247; LJ 94: 1802)

WHEELER, Thomas. *Lost Threshold: A Novel.* Phillips, 1968. 189 pp. Gr. 8–12. [A]
His father's disappearance brings James MacGregor into another world, where he leads an uprising against the tyrants in power and finds himself a wife. (BL 65: 167; KR 36: 467; LJ 93: 3328)

WILLARD, Nancy. *Sailing to Cythera, and Other Anatole Stories.* Harcourt, 1974. Illus. by David McPhail. 72 pp. Gr. 4–5. [A]
Three stories about a boy named Anatole and his journeys to magical lands, including one in which he enters the wallpaper of his bedroom to meet a creature named the Blimlim. *The Island of the Grass King: The Further Adventures of Anatole* (1979) is the sequel. (BL 71: 573; KR 43: 19; LJ 99: 2281)

WILLIAMS, Jay. *The Hero from Otherwhere.* Walck, 1972. 175 pp. Gr. 5–7. [A]
Jesse and Rich, sent to the principal's office for fighting, end up instead in the kingdom of Gwyliath, charged with finding a magic rope to shackle the fiendish wolf, Fenris. (BL 69: 407; CCBB 26: 99; KR 40: 1193; LJ 98: 1399)

WINTERFELD, Henry. *Castaways in Lilliput.* Harcourt, 1960. Tr. by Kyrill Schabert. Illus. by William Hutchinson. 188 pp. Gr. 4–6. [R]
Two hundred and fifty years after Gulliver's visit, the Lilliputians are again alarmed by the appearance of giants: three human children whose raft accidentally drifts to Lilliput. (BL 56: 577; CC: 579; Eakin: 355; HB 36: 292; LJ 85: 2484)

Travel to Another World: Out-of-Print Works

ALLFREY, Katherine. *The Golden Island* (British title: *On a Dolphin's Back*). Doubleday, 1966. Tr. by Edelgard von Heydekamph. Illus. by John Kaufmann. 160 pp. Gr. 4–6. (CCBB 20: 2; KR 34: 108; LJ 91: 2687; TLS 1967 p. 451)

BAKER, Michael. *The Mountain and the Summer Stars: An Old Tale Newly Ended.* See Chapter 8H, Fairies: Out-of-Print Works.

BAUM, L. Frank. *The Sea Fairies.* See Chapter 8P, Mermaids and Sea People: Out-of-Print Works.

BERTON, Pierre. *The Secret World of Og.* Little, 1962. Illus. by William Winter. 146 pp. Gr. 3–6. (BL 58: 688; HB 38: 176; KR 30: 181; LJ 87: 2020)

BIANCO, Pamela. *Little Houses Far Away.* See Chapter 7, Magical Toys: Out-of-Print Works.

BOSTON, L. M. *The Castle of Yew.* See Chapter 6, Magic Adventure: Out-of-Print Works.

BRYHER, Winifred. *A Visa for Avalon.* Harcourt, 1965. 119 pp. Gr. 8 up. (BL 61: 980; CCBB 18: 143; KR 33: 198; LJ 90: 1929)

CARLSEN, Ruth. *Ride a Wild Horse.* Houghton, 1970. Illus. by Beth and Joe Krush. 164 pp. Gr. 4–6. (BL 67: 338; KR 38: 1145; LJ 96: 264)

CARRYL, Charles. *Davy and the Goblin, or What Followed Reading "Alice's Adventures in Wonderland."* (Reprint of 1885 ed.; orig. pub. 1884) University Microfilms, 1967. Illus. by E. B. Bensell. 160 pp. Gr. 3–5. (BL 25: 173)

CHASE, Mary. *Loretta Mason Potts.* See Chapter 6, Magic Adventure: Out-of-Print Works.

DELL, Joan. *The Missing Boy.* Putnam, 1958. Illus. by Sheila Greenwald. 192 pp. Gr. 4–6. (HB 35: 130; KR 26: 819; LJ 84: 249)

GOUDGE, Elizabeth. *The Valley of Song.* See Chapter 1, Allegory and Fable: Out-of-Print Works.

HENRY, Jan. *Tiger's Chance.* See Chapter 6, Magic Adventure: Out-of-Print Works.

HOWARD, Joan (pseud. of Patricia Gordon). *The Oldest Secret.* Viking, 1953. Illus. by Garry MacKenzie. 128 pp. Gr. 6–8. (BL 50: 84; HB 29: 362; KR 21: 429)

HOWARD, Joan. *The Thirteenth Is Magic.* See Chapter 6, Magic Adventure: Out-of-Print Works.

JOHNSTON, Thomas. *The Fight for Arkenvald.* Doubleday, 1973. Illus. by Jane Walworth. 150 pp. Gr. 4–6. (KR 41: 1097; LJ 98: 3147; TLS 1970 p. 1264)

KELLAM, Ian. *The First Summer Year.* Crowell, 1974. Illus. by Robin Jacques. 275 pp. Gr. 5–8. (KR 42: 943; LJ 99: 3047)

KRÜSS, James. *The Happy Islands behind the Winds.* Atheneum, 1966. Tr. by Edelgard Brühl. Illus. by Eberhart Binder-Strassfurt. 153 pp. Gr. 3–6. *Return to the Happy Islands* (1967) is the sequel. (KR 34: 1097; LJ 91: 5750)

LAMPMAN, Evelyn. *The City under the Back Steps.* Doubleday, 1960. Illus. by Honoré Valintcourt. 210 pp. Gr. 4–6. (HB 36: 510; KR 28: 816; LJ 85: 4567)

LANCASTER, Clay. *Periwinkle Steamboat.* See Chapter 6, Magic Adventure: Out-of-Print Works.

LINDGREN, Astrid. *Mio, My Son.* Viking, 1956. Tr. by Marianne Turner. Illus. by Ilon Wikland. 179 pp. Gr. 4–6. (BL 53: 304; KR 24: 868; LJ 82: 588)

LINKLATER, Eric. *The Pirates in the Deep Green Sea.* Macmillan, 1949. Illus. by William Reeves. 398 pp. Gr. 5–8. (BL 46: 52; HB 25: 411; KR 17: 324; LJ 74: 1105; TLS July 15, 1949 p. iii)

MacFARLANE, Stephen (pseud. of John Kier Cross). *The Other Side of Green Hills* (British title: *The Owl and the Pussycat*). (Orig. pub. 1946) Coward, 1947. Illus. by Robin Jacques. 190 pp. Gr. 5 up. (HB 23: 443; LJ 72: 1475)

McNEILL, Janet. *Tom's Tower.* Little, 1967. Illus. by Mary Russon. 182 pp. Gr. 5–7. (HB 43: 464; KR 35: 132; TLS 1965 p. 513)

MANNING, Rosemary. *Green Smoke.* See Chapter 8E, Dragons: Out-of-Print Works.

MASEFIELD, John. *The Midnight Folk: A Novel.* See Chapter 6, Magic Adventure: Out-of-Print Works.

MOON, Sheila. *Kneedeep in Thunder.* Atheneum, 1967. Illus. by Peter Parnall. 307 pp. Gr. 6–9. The sequel is *Hunt Down the Prize* (1971). (Arb: 241; BL 64: 503; CCBB 21: 98; HB 43: 589; KR 35: 968; LJ 92: 3853; Suth: 285; TN 24: 324)

NATHAN, Robert. *The Snowflake and the Starfish.* See Chapter 13, Witches, Wizards, Sorcerers, and Magicians: Out-of-Print Works.

NESBIT, E. *The Magic City.* (Orig. pub. 1910) Coward, 1960. Illus. by H. R. Millar. 333 pp. Gr. 4–6. (BL 57: 32; HB 36: 309)

NESBIT, E. *Wet Magic.* See Chapter 8P, Mermaids and Sea People: Out-of-Print Works.

NORTH, Joan. *The Light Maze.* Farrar, 1971. 185 pp. Gr. 7–10. (BL 68: 392; CCBB 26: 12; HB 48: 156; JHC: 420; KR 39: 1132; LJ 96: 4192; Suth: 297; TLS 1972 p. 1329)

PALMER, Mary. *The Dolmop of Dorkling.* Houghton, 1967. Illus. by Fen Lasell. 155 pp. Gr. 3–5. (BL 64: 335; CCBB 21: 31; KR 35: 652; LJ 92: 2454)

REEVES, James. *The Strange Light.* Rand, 1966. Illus. by J. C. Kocsis. 152 pp. Gr. 4–6. (BL 63: 491; CCBB 20: 97; KR 34: 689; LJ 91: 5237; TLS 1964 p. 602)

SHURA, Mary. *The Valley of the Frost Giants.* See Chapter 8J, Giants: Out-of-Print Works.

TARN, Sir William. *Treasure of the Isle of Mist: A Tale of the Isle of Skye.* See Chapter 6, Magic Adventure: Out-of-Print Works.

WALKER, Gwen. *The Golden Stile.* Day, 1958. Illus. by C. Walter Hodges. 188 pp. Gr. 4–6. (HB 34: 479; KR 26: 606; LJ 83: 3304)

WICKENDEN, Dan. *The Amazing Vacation.* Harcourt, 1956. Illus. by Erik Blegvad. 216 pp. Gr. 6–8. (BL 53: 230; HB 32: 352; KR 24: 475)

13

Witches, Wizards, Sorcerers, and Magicians

These are tales of magic as practiced by witches and warlocks, enchanters and enchantresses, wizards and magicians. Most have a light-hearted quality, distinguishing them from the more serious and at times terrifying tales of the occult.

AIKEN, Joan. *The Faithless Lollybird.* See Chapter 2, Collected Tales.

AIKEN, Joan. *The Kingdom and the Cave.* See Chapter 5B, Imaginary Lands.

AINSWORTH, Ruth. *The Bear Who Liked Hugging People and Other Stories.* See Chapter 2, Collected Tales.

ALEXANDER, Lloyd. *The Cat Who Wished to Be a Man.* See Chapter 9, Talking Animals.

ALEXANDER, Lloyd. *The Marvelous Misadventures of Sebastian: Grand Extravaganza, Including a Performance by the Entire Cast of the Gallimaufry Theatricus.* See Chapter 5B, Imaginary Lands.

ALEXANDER, Lloyd. *The Wizard in the Tree.* Dutton, 1975. Illus. by Laszlo Kubinyi. 160 pp. Gr. 4–6. [R]

A firm belief in magic helps Mallory, an overworked, orphaned servant girl, to release a crotchety old wizard from imprisonment in an oak tree. (Adv: 181; Arb: 207; BL 71: 813; CC: 478; CCBB 28: 173; HB 51: 377; KR 43: 451; SLJ May'75 pp. 34 and 45)

ANDERSEN, Hans Christian. *The Snow Queen.* See Chapter 1, Allegory and Fable.

BACON, Peggy. *The Magic Touch.* See Chapter 6, Magic Adventure.

BANKS, Lynne Reid. *The Farthest-Away Mountain.* See Chapter 5B, Imaginary Lands.

BATO, Joseph. *The Sorcerer.* Ed. by Katherine Donnelly. McKay, 1976. Illus. by the author. 171 pp. Gr. 7–10. [A]
Cro-Magnon sorcerer Aoh's powers help him become his people's leader, but also bring about his downfall. (BL 73: 890 and 893; HB 53: 165; KR 44: 1174; SLJ Nov'76 p. 65)

BAUM, L. Frank. *The Wizard of Oz.* See Chapter 12, Travel to Another World.

BAXTER, Caroline. *The Stolen Telesm.* See Chapter 8O, Magical Horses.

BEACHCROFT, Nina. *Well Met by Witchlight.* Atheneum, 1973. 137 pp. Gr. 4–5. [A]
A good witch named Mary brings magic into the lives of Christopher, Sarah, and Lucy Fraser, until her powers are threatened by an evil witch named Mrs. Black. (BL 70: 595; KR 41: 1199; LJ 99: 205)

BELLAIRS, John. *The Face in the Frost.* Macmillan, 1969. Illus. by Marilyn Fitschen. 174 pp. Gr. 8 up. [A]
Two bumbling wizards, Prospero and Roger Bacon, search for an evil being that is causing eerie dreams, terrifying gray shadows, and frightening frost faces on windows in their land. (BL 65: 1209; KR 36: 1395; LJ 94: 776; TN 26: 209)

BELLAIRS, John. *The House with a Clock in Its Walls.* See Chapter 3, Ghosts.

BENARY-ISBERT, Margot. *The Wicked Enchantment.* See Chapter 1, Allegory and Fable.

BENNETT, Anna Elizabeth. *Little Witch.* Lippincott, 1953. Illus. by Helen Stone. 127 pp. Gr. 3–5. [R]
Even though she can perform all kinds of exciting and unusual feats, Miniken does not want to be a witch. She wants to go to school like a real little girl. (CC: 487; HB 29: 356; LJ 78: 1855)

BOMANS, Godfried. *The Wily Witch and All the Other Fairy Tales and Fables.* See Chapter 2, Collected Tales.

BRADBURY, Ray. *Something Wicked This Way Comes.* Simon, 1962. 317 pp. Gr. 8 up. [A]
Two boys attending a carnival freak show become the targets of an evil magician who imprisons them in the Wax Museum. (BL 59: 163; TLS 1963 p. 189)

BRIGGS, Katherine. *Hobberdy Dick.* See Chapter 8L, Goblins.

BRÖGER, Achim. *Outrageous Kasimir.* See Chapter 8Q, Miniature People.

BUCHWALD, Emilie. *Gildaen: The Heroic Adventures of a Most Unusual Rabbit.* See Chapter 5B, Imaginary Lands.

BYFIELD, Barbara. *Andrew and the Alchemist.* Doubleday, 1976. Illus. by Deanne Hollinger. 129 pp. Gr. 4–6. [R]
Andrew's "easy" job as apprentice to an alchemist goes wrong after he is accused of misusing his power and stealing the king's treasure. (BL 73: 128; CCBB 30: 172; HB 53: 312; KR 44: 1264; SLJ Jan'77 p. 88)

CHANT, Joy. *Red Moon and Black Mountain: The End of the House of Kendreth.* See Chapter 12, Travel to Another World.

CHESNUTT, Charles. *Conjure Tales.* See Chapter 2, Collected Tales.

CHEW, Ruth. *The Trouble with Magic.* See Chapter 6, Magic Adventure.

CHEW, Ruth. *The Wednesday Witch.* Holiday, 1972. 128 pp. Gr. 3–5. [M]
After Hilda the witch miniaturizes herself and moves into Mary Jane's dollhouse to make mischief, she finds that Mary Jane can be equally mischievous. (BL 69: 646; KR 40: 1190; LJ 98: 642)

CHEW, Ruth. *A Witch in the House.* See Chapter 6, Magic Adventure.

CHEW, Ruth. *The Witch's Broom.* See Chapter 6, Magic Adventure.

CHEW, Ruth. *The Would-Be Witch.* See Chapter 6, Magic Adventure.

COOMBS, Patricia. *Dorrie and the Blue Witch.* Lothrop, 1964. 42 pp. Gr. 2–4. [A]
Shrinking powder enables young Dorrie the witch to capture the bad blue witch and win the first prize for witch-catching. Other titles in this series are *Dorrie's Magic* (1962), *Dorrie's Play* (1965), *Dorrie and the Weather-Box* (1966), *Dorrie and the Witch Doctor* (1967), *Dorrie and the Wizard's Spell* (1968), *Dorrie and the Haunted House* (1970), *Dorrie and the Birthday Eggs* (1971), *Dorrie and the Goblin* (1972), *Dorrie and the Fortune Teller* (1973), *Dorrie and the Amazing Magic Elixir* (1974), *Dorrie and the Witch's Imp* (1975), *Dorrie and the Halloween Plot* (1976), *Dorrie and the Dreamyard Monsters* (1977), and *Dorrie and the Screebit Ghost* (1979). (HB 40: 488; LJ 89: 3458)

CORBETT, Scott. *The Great Custard Pie Panic.* Little, 1974. Illus. by Joe Mathieu. 47 pp. Gr. 2–4. [A]
Nick thwarts Dr. Merlin's diabolical plan to use Nick's dog's brain to create the smartest dog in the world. This is the sequel to *Dr. Merlin's Magic Shop* (1973) and is followed by *The Foolish Dinosaur Fiasco* (1978). (BL 70: 1252; CCBB 28: 26; KR 42: 580)

CURLEY, Daniel. *Billy Beg and the Bull.* See Chapter 6, Magic Adventure.

CURRY, Jane. *The Sleepers.* Harcourt, 1968. Illus. by Gareth Floyd. 255 pp. Gr. 5–7. [A]
Jennifer's meetings with Myrddin the sorcerer involve her and her brother in a plot to murder King Arthur and his knights in their sleep. (BL 65: 61; HB 44: 427; KR 36: 459; TLS 1969 p. 351)

DE CAYLUS, Compte. *Heart of Ice.* See Chapter 5B, Imaginary Lands.

DICKINSON, Peter. *The Weathermonger.* See Chapter 5A, Alternative Worlds.

EDMONDSON, Madeline. *The Witch's Egg.* Seabury, 1974. Illus. by Kay Chorao. 47 pp. Gr. 2–3 [A]
A crabby witch named Agatha who is living in an abandoned eagle's nest becomes the foster mother of a baby bird. (BL 70: 939; KR 42: 182; LJ 99: 1465)

EMBRY, Margaret. *The Blue-Nosed Witch.* Holiday, 1956. Illus. by Carl Rose. 45 pp. Gr. 1–4. [R]
On her way to the witches' Halloween flight meeting, a young witch named Blanche joins a group of trick-or-treating children. (BL 53: 154; CC: 514; HB 32: 366; KR 24: 514)

ESTES, Eleanor. *The Witch Family.* Harcourt, 1960. Illus. by Edward Ardizzone. 186 pp. Gr. 3–5. [R]
Two girls drawing witches are quite surprised when their drawings come to life. (Arb: 238; BL 57: 329; CC: 516; HB 36: 395; KR 28: 817; LJ 85: 4558; TLS 1962 p. 393)

FARTHING, Alison. *The Mystical Beast.* See Chapter 12, Travel to Another World.

FLORA, James. *Grandpa's Ghost Stories.* See Chapter 2, Collected Tales.

GARNER, Alan. *The Weirdstone of Brisingamen.* See Chapter 4, Good versus Evil.

GORDON, John. *The Giant under the Snow: A Story of Suspense.* See Chapter 6, Magic Adventure.

GOUDGE, Elizabeth. *Linnets and Valerians.* See Chapter 6, Magic Adventure.

GRIPE, Maria. *The Glassblower's Children.* See Chapter 12, Travel to Another World.

HEWETT, Anita. *The Bull beneath the Walnut Tree and Other Stories.* See Chapter 2, Collected Tales.

HILL, Elizabeth. *Ever-After Island.* See Chapter 6, Magic Adventure.

HORWITZ, Elinor. *The Strange Story of the Frog Who Became a Prince.* Delacorte, 1971. Illus. by John Heinly. 45 pp. Gr. 3–4. [A]
A witch changes a happy frog into a prince and can't understand his dissatisfaction, nor can she remember how to change him back. (HB 47: 282; KR 39: 428; LJ 96: 2906)

HUNTER, Mollie. *The Kelpie's Pearls.* See Chapter 8P, Mermaids and Sea People.

HUNTER, Mollie. *A Stranger Came Ashore.* See Chapter 8T, Seal People.

HUNTER, Mollie. (pseud. of Maureen McIlwraith). *The Walking Stones: A Story of Suspense* (British title: *The Bodach*). Harper, 1970. Illus. by Trina Schart Hyman. 143 pp. Gr. 4–6. [R]
An elderly Bodach (a sorcerer) lets Donald Campbell take over his magical powers in order to save his stone circle from the waters of a new hydroelectric plant. (Adv: 190; Arb: 209; BL 67: 228; CC: 534; CCBB 24: 157; HB 47: 51; KR 38: 800; LJ 95: 4375; Suth: 204; TLS 1970 p. 1251; TN 27: 305)

IPCAR, Dahlov. *The Queen of Spells.* See Chapter 8H, Fairies.

JESCHKE, Susan. *Rima and Zeppo.* Windmill, 1976. Illus. by the author. 32 pp. Gr. 2–4. [A]
After Rima, a witch's daughter, accidentally turns her friend Zeppo into a dog, she makes a pet of him until she can undo the magic. (BL 73: 608; CCBB 30: 92; SLJ Jan'77 p. 83)

JONES, Diana Wynne. *A Charmed Life.* See Chapter 11, Time Travel.

JONES, Diana Wynne. *Witch's Business* (British title: *Wilkin's Tooth*). Dutton, 1974. 168 pp. Gr. 5–7. [M]
Jess and Frank decide to earn some extra money by helping people obtain revenge, but they have competition from Biddy, the nasty local witch. (KR 42: 186; LJ 99: 1220)

KIMMEL, Margaret. *Magic in the Mist.* Atheneum, 1975. Illus. by Trina Schart Hyman. 31 pp. Gr. 2–4. [R]
Although he is studying to be a wizard, young Thomas's spells cannot even warm his own hut until his pet toad, Jeremy, leads him to a tiny dragon. (BL 71: 867; CC 1977 Suppl. p. 65; CCBB 29: 28; HB 51: 139; KR 43: 119; SLJ Apr'75 p. 46)

KOOIKER, Leonie. *The Magic Stone*. Morrow, 1978. Tr. by Richard and Clara Winston. Illus. by Carl Hollander. 224 pp. Gr. 4–6. [R]
Frank's grandmother's magic stone enables him to control other people's behavior, but when the witch's association wants the stone back, she is determined that he keep it. (BL 74: 1494; CCBB 32: 65; HB 54: 396; KR 46: 595; SLJ May'78 p. 68)

KRENSKY, Stephen. *A Big Day for Scepters*. See Chapter 5B, Imaginary Lands.

KRENSKY, Stephen. *The Dragon Circle*. See Chapter 8E, Dragons.

KRENSKY, Stephen. *The Perils of Putney*. See Chapter 5B, Imaginary Lands.

LAUGHLIN, Florence. *The Little Leftover Witch*. Macmillan, 1960. Illus. by Sheila Greenwald. 107 pp. Gr. 2–4. [A]
Felina the witch's broomstick breaks in midair. She falls out of the sky and is stranded on Earth for an entire year, causing problems for the Doon family who take her in. (BL 57: 362; HB 36: 396; KR 28: 496; LJ 85: 4226; TLS 1967 p. 1153)

LAWSON, John S. *You Better Come Home with Me*. See Chapter 1, Allegory and Fable.

LEACH, Maria. *The Thing at the Foot of the Bed and Other Scary Tales*. See Chapter 2, Collected Tales.

LEE, Tanith. *The Dragon Hoard*. See Chapter 5B, Imaginary Lands.

LEE, Tanith. *Princess Hynchatti and Some Other Surprises*. See Chapter 2, Collected Tales.

LE GUIN, Ursula. *A Wizard of Earthsea*. See Chapter 4, Good versus Evil.

LEWIS, C. S. *The Lion, the Witch and the Wardrobe*. See Chapter 12, Travel to Another World.

LITTLE, Jane. *Danger at Sneaker Hill* (Orig. title: *Sneaker Hill*, 1967). Archway, 1975 (pap.). Illus. by Nancy Grossman. 176 pp. Gr. 3–5. [A]
Mathew and Susan follow Mathew's scatterbrained mother into a magic land after she leaves for her Sisterhood of Witches membership test without her owl. (CCBB 21: 29; LJ 92: 1738)

LITTLE, Jane. *The Philosopher's Stone*. See Chapter 11, Time Travel.

LITTLE, Jane. *Spook*. (Orig. pub. 1965) Scholastic, 1971 (pap.). Illus. by Suzanne Larsen. 110 pp. Gr. 3–5. [A]
Grimalda the witch is allergic to cats and tries to make do with a small dog named Spook, but a boy named Jamie wants Spook too. (CCBB 19: 35; HB 41: 492; LJ 90: 3812)

LIVELY, Penelope. *The Ghost of Thomas Kempe*. See Chapter 11, Time Travel.

LIVELY, Penelope. *The Whispering Knights*. See Chapter 6, Magic Adventure.

LOFTING, Hugh. *The Twilight of Magic*. See Chapter 6, Magic Adventure.

LOVEJOY, Jack. *The Rebel Witch*. Lothrop/Morrow, 1978. Illus. by Judith Brown. 201 pp. Gr. 4–6. [A]
A magic wand enables Suzie, an apprentice witch, to enter the witch world of Veneficon to search for her teacher, Madame Mengo. (BL 75: 50; KR 46: 1248; SLJ Dec'78 p. 54)

MacKELLAR, William. *The Witch of Glen Gowrie*. Dodd, 1978. 134 pp. Gr. 5–7. [R]
Greedy Mr. Cuthbert attempts to find a witch's treasure but is thwarted by the ghost of old Meg herself, who intends the treasure for young Gavin Fraser. (BL 74: 1109; CC 1979 Suppl. p. 51; CCBB 32: 34; SLJ May'78 p. 85)

McKILLIP, Patricia. *The Forgotten Beasts of Eld*. See Chapter 5A, Alternative Worlds.

McKILLIP, Patricia. *The Riddle-Master of Hed*. See Chapter 5A, Alternative Worlds.

McLEOD, Emilie. *Clancy's Witch*. Little, 1959. Illus. by Lisl Weil. 38 pp. Gr. 2–4. [A]
Clancy's next-door neighbor at 13 Moody Street is a witch who is trying to "unhaunt" her house. (BL 55: 543; Eakin: 224; HB 35: 131; KR 26: 905; LJ 84: 1686)

MIAN, Mary. *Take Three Witches*. Houghton, 1971. Illus. by Eric Von Schmidt. 279 pp. Gr. 6–8. [A]
Three sixth graders, a ghost, and three witches take on the mayor to prevent their town from spraying insecticide and usurping land belonging to the Mexican-American community. *The Net to Catch War* (1975) is the sequel. (HB 47: 485; LJ 96: 2133)

NEWMAN, Robert. *The Shattered Stone*. See Chapter 4, Good versus Evil.

NEWMAN, Sharon. *Dagda's Harp*. See Chapter 5B, Imaginary Lands.

NICHOLS, Ruth. *The Marrow of the World*. See Chapter 12, Travel to Another World.

NORTON, André. *Lavender Green Magic*. See Chapter 11, Time Travel.

NORTON, Mary. *Bedknob and Broomstick*. See Chapter 6, Magic Adventure.

O'HANLON, Jacklyn. *The Door*. See Chapter 12, Travel to Another World.

PEET, Bill. *Big Bad Bruce*. See Chapter 9, Talking Animals.

PEET, Bill. *The Whingdingdilly*. See Chapter 9, Talking Animals.

PLACE, Marian T. *The Resident Witch*. (Orig. pub. 1970) Avon, 1973 (pap.). Illus. by Marilyn Miller. 119 pp. Gr. 3–5. [A]
Living with her aunt while her mother is away, Witcheena is working hard to become a Junior Witch when she makes the mistake of befriending some earthlings. (Adv: 197; CCBB 24: 65; KR 38: 244; LJ 95: 2309)

PLACE, Marian T. *The Witch Who Saved Halloween*. (Orig. pub. 1971) Avon, 1974 (pap.). 150 pp. Gr. 4–6. [A]
When pollution threatens both witches and humans, Witchard comes up with a plan to save them. (BL 75: 306; CCBB 25: 1281; KR 39: 1072; LJ 97: 284)

* PREUSSLER, Otfried. *The Satanic Mill*. Macmillan, 1973. Tr. by Anthea Bell. 250 pp. Gr. 5–8.
Krabat thinks he has been apprenticed to a miller, but discovers that the mill is actually a school of black magic run by an evil magician. (Adv: 198; Arb: 241; BL 69: 1073, 70: 827; CCBB 26: 143; HB 49: 147; JHC: 424; KR 41: 61 and 1351; LJ 98: 1398 and 1655; TLS 1972 p. 1489; TN 30: 206)

PYLE, Howard. *King Stork*. Little, 1973. Illus. by Trina Schart Hyman. 48 pp. Gr. 2–4. [R]
A beautiful but wicked witch is won and tamed by a poor drummer and King Stork's magic. (BL 70; 174; HB 49: 373; KR 41: 455; LJ 98: 2643)

SENDAK, Jack. *The Second Witch*. Harper, 1965. Illus. by Uri Shulevitz. 94 pp. Gr. 3–4. [A]
Andrew tries to save Vivian, an unpopular witch, from the wrath of the villagers. (KR 33: 751; LJ 90: 4620)

SINGER, Isaac Bashevis. *Alone in the Wild Forest*. See Chapter 5B, Imaginary Lands.

SINGER, Isaac Bashevis. *The Fearsome Inn*. See Chapter 6, Magic Adventure.

SNYDER, Zilpha Keatley. *A Season of Ponies*. See Chapter 6, Magic Adventure.

STEELE, Mary Q. *Because of the Sand Witches There*. See Chapter 6, Magic Adventure.

STEELE, Mary Q. *The Owl's Kiss: Three Stories*. See Chapter 2, Collected Tales.

STEWART, Mary. *The Little Broomstick*. Morrow, 1972. Illus. by Shirley Hughes. 192 pp. Gr. 3–5. [R]
Mary accidentally rubs the handle of a broomstick, which takes her and her black cat to a witch school where Mary learns magic to rescue her pet. (Adv: 202; BL 68: 822; CC: 570; CCBB 25: 146; HB 48: 271; KR 40: 5; LJ 97: 1690; Suth: 382)

STOCKTON, Frank R. *The Bee-Man of Orn.* See Chapter 1, Allegory and Fable.

SWAHN, Sven. *The Island through the Gate.* See Chapter 12, Travel to Another World.

TERLOUW, Jan. *How to Become King.* See Chapter 5B, Imaginary Lands.

TOLKIEN, J. R. R. *The Hobbit; or There and Back Again.* See Chapter 4, Good versus Evil.

TURKLE, Brinton. *Mooncoin Castle; or Skulduggery Rewarded.* See Chapter 3, Ghosts.

TURNBULL, Anne. *The Frightened Forest.* Seabury, 1975. Illus. by Gillian Gaze. 125 pp. Gr. 4–6. [R]
Responsible for unleashing a witch from an abandoned tunnel, Gillian and her cousins make a midnight attempt to recapture the malevolent witch. (BL 71: 1018; HB 51: 385; KR 43: 460; SLJ May'75 p. 59; TLS 1974 p. 714)

WHITE T. H. *The Sword in the Stone.* See Chapter 5B, Imaginary Lands.

WILDE, Oscar. *The Happy Prince and Other Stories.* See Chapter 2, Collected Tales.

WRIGGINS, Sally, ed. *The White Monkey King: A Chinese Fable.* See Chapter 1, Allegory and Fable.

WRIGHTSON, Patricia. *An Older Kind of Magic.* See Chapter 6, Magic Adventure.

YOLEN, Jane. *The Magic Three of Solatia.* See Chapter 5B, Imaginary Lands.

YORK, Susannah. *Lark's Castle.* McKay, 1976. Illus. by Michael Baldwin. 112 pp. Gr. 3–6. [M]
The Lifestone lost by Ermyntrude the witch brings a doll named Lark to life, but its loss threatens Ermyntrude with becoming mortal. (SLJ Mar'77 p. 149)

YOUNG, Miriam. *The Witch Mobile.* Lothrop, 1969. Illus. by Victoria Chess. Unp. Gr. 2–4. [A]
Nanette, the smallest witch on the toy-shop witch mobile, doesn't want to work revengeful spells like her sisters. (KR 37: 995; LJ 95: 1192)

Witches, Wizards, Sorcerers, and Magicians: Out-of-Print Works

AIKEN, Joan. *Smoke from Cromwell's Time and Other Stories.* See Chapter 2, Collected Tales: Out-of-Print Works.

BAUM, L. Frank. *The Sea Fairies.* See Chapter 8P, Mermaids and Sea People: Out-of-Print Works.

BERESFORD, Elizabeth. *Travelling Magic.* See Chapter 11, Time Travel: Out-of-Print Works.

CALHOUN, Mary. *Magic in the Alley.* See Chapter 6, Magic Adventure: Out-of-Print Works.

CHICHESTER, Imogen. *The Witch Child.* Coward, 1967. Illus. by Robert Bartelt. 189 pp. Gr. 3–5. (KR 34: 1221; LJ 92: 1728; TLS 1965 p. 1130)

COLUM, Padraic. *The Boy Apprenticed to an Enchanter.* (Orig. pub. 1920) Macmillan, 1966. Illus. by Edward Leight. 150 pp. Gr. 4–7. (BL 63: 493; HB 42: 708; LJ 72: 333)

COLUM, Padraic. *The Stone of Victory and Other Tales.* See Chapter 2, Collected Tales: Out-of-Print Works.

DAWSON, Carley. *Mr. Wicker's Window.* See Chapter 11, Time Travel: Out-of-Print Works.

DILLON, Eilis. *King Big Ears.* See Chapter 5B, Imaginary Lands: Out-of-Print Works.

ERWIN, Betty. *Aggie, Maggie, and Tish.* Little, 1965. Illus. by Paul Kennedy. 154 pp. Gr. 3–5. The sequel is *Where's Aggie?* (1967). (BL 62: 330; HB 41: 628; KR 33: 626; LJ 90: 4615)

FLETCHER, David. *Mother O'Pearl: Three Tales.* See Chapter 2, Collected Tales: Out-of-Print Works.

FREEMAN, Barbara. *Broom-Adelaide.* See Chapter 5B, Imaginary Lands: Out-of-Print Works.

FRIEDRICH, Priscilla and Otto. *Sir Alva and the Wicked Wizard.* See Chapter 5B, Imaginary Lands: Out-of-Print Works.

FROMAN, Elizabeth. *Eba, the Absent-Minded Witch.* World, 1965. Illus. by Dorothy Maas. 64 pp. Gr. 3–5. (CCBB 20: 24; HB 41: 491; KR 33: 824; LJ 90: 5514; TLS 1968 p. 256)

GARD, Joyce. *The Mermaid's Daughter.* Holt, 1969. 319 pp. Gr. 6–9. (BL 66: 564; CCBB 24: 176; HB 46: 166; LJ 95: 1202; Suth: 139; TLS 1969 p. 690)

GRAY, Nicholas. *Mainly in Moonlight: Ten Stories of Sorcery and the Supernatural.* See Chapter 2, Collected Tales: Out-of-Print Works.

GREEN, Kathleen. *Philip and the Pooka and Other Irish Fairy Tales.* See Chapter 2, Collected Tales: Out-of-Print Works.

GREEN, Roger. *A Cavalcade of Magicians* (British title: *A Book of Magicians*). Walck, 1973. Illus. by Victor Ambrus. 274 pp. Gr. 5–6. (Adv: 187; BL 70: 291; HB 49: 461; KR 41: 645; LJ 98: 2664; TLS 1973 p. 1115)

HOFFMAN, Eleanor. *Mischief in Fez.* See Chapter 6, Magic Adventure: Out-of-Print Works.

HOLMAN, Felice. *The Witch on the Corner.* Norton, 1966. Illus. by Arnold Lobel. 88 pp. Gr. 3–5. (CCBB 20: 108; KR 34: 1101; LJ 92: 335; TLS 1967 p. 1133)

HOPP, Zinken. *The Magic Chalk.* See Chapter 6, Magic Adventure: Out-of-Print Works.

HOUGH, Charlotte. *Red Biddy and Other Stories.* See Chapter 2, Collected Tales: Out-of-Print Works.

HOWARD, Joan (pseud. of Patricia Gordon). *The Witch of Scrapfaggot Green.* Viking, 1948. Illus. by William Pène Du Bois. 78 pp. Gr. 4–5. (BL 44: 228; HB 24: 191; KR 16: 49; LJ 73: 657)

HUNTER, Mollie. *The Ferlie.* See Chapter 8H, Fairies: Out-of-Print Works.

HUNTER, Mollie (pseud. of Maureen McIlwraith). *Thomas and the Warlock.* Funk, 1967. Illus. by Joseph Cellini. 128 pp. Gr. 4–6. (BL 64: 450; CCBB 21: 60; HB 43: 749; KR 35: 808; LJ 92: 3850; Suth: 204; TLS 1967 p. 451)

IPCAR, Dahlov. *The Warlock of Night.* Viking, 1969. 159 pp. Gr. 5–7. (KR 37: 1195; LJ 95: 789 and 1911)

LARSON, Jean. *The Silkspinners.* See Chapter 8R, Monsters and Sea Serpents: Out-of-Print Works.

LEE, Josephine. *Joy Is Not Herself.* Harcourt, 1963. Illus. by Pat Marriott. 154 pp. Gr. 5–7. (HB 39: 174; LJ 88: 1768; TLS 1962 p. 393)

McDONALD, Greville. *Billy Barnicoat.* See Chapter 6, Magic Adventure: Out-of-Print Works.

McGOWEN, Tom. *Sir Machinery.* Follett, 1971. Illus. by Trina Schart Hyman. 155 pp. Gr. 3–6. (BL 68: 367; HB 48: 49; KR 39: 1071; LJ 96: 4191)

McKENZIE, Ellen. *Taash and the Jesters.* See Chapter 5B, Imaginary Lands: Out-of-Print Works.

McNEILL, Janet. *Tom's Tower.* See Chapter 12, Travel to Another World: Out-of-Print Works.

MAYNE, William. *The Hill Road.* See Chapter 11, Time Travel: Out-of-Print Works.

MONTROSE, Anne. *The Winter Flower and Other Fairy Stories.* See Chapter 2, Collected Tales: Out-of-Print Works.

NATHAN, Robert. *The Snowflake and the Starfish.* Knopf, 1959. 68 pp. Gr. 3–4. (HB 35: 478; LJ 84: 3930)

NESS, Evaline. *The Girl and the Goatherd, or This and That and Thus and So.* See Chapter 1, Allegory and Fable: Out-of-Print Works.

NEWMAN, Robert. *Merlin's Mistake.* Atheneum, 1970. Illus. by Richard Lebenson. 237 pp. Gr. 5–8. (BL 66: 1162; HB 46: 298; KR 38: 174; LJ 95: 2309; TLS 1971 p. 390; TN 27: 432)

ORMONDROYD, Edward. *David and the Phoenix.* See Chapter 8S, The Phoenix: Out-of-Print Works.

PARKER, Edgar. *The Enchantress.* See Chapter 5B, Imaginary Lands: Out-of-Print Works.

PAYNE, Joan. *The Piebald Princess.* See Chapter 9, Talking Animals: Out-of-Print Works.

PICARD, Barbara. *The Goldfinch Garden: Seven Tales.* See Chapter 2, Collected Tales: Out-of-Print Works.

PICARD, Barbara. *The Mermaid and the Simpleton.* See Chapter 2, Collected Tales: Out-of-Print Works.

PREUSSLER, Otfried. *The Little Witch.* Abelard, 1961. Tr. by Anthea Bell. Illus. by Winnie Gayler. 127 pp. Gr. 3–6. (BL 58: 450; KR 29: 843; LJ 86: 4040; TLS May 19, 1961 p. iv)

PREUSSLER, Otfried. *The Robber Hotzenplotz.* See Chapter 10, Tall Tales: Out-of-Print Works.

READ, Elfrieda. *The Magical Egg.* See Chapter 5B, Imaginary Lands: Out-of-Print Works.

REEVES, James. *The Cold Flame.* See Chapter 5B, Imaginary Lands: Out-of-Print Works.

REID, Alastair. *Fairwater.* See Chapter 5B, Imaginary Lands: Out-of-Print Works.

SLEIGH, Barbara. *Carbonel: The King of the Cats.* See Chapter 9, Talking Animals: Out-of-Print Works.

SLEIGH, Barbara. *Stirabout Stories, Brewed in Her Own Cauldron.* See Chapter 2, Collected Tales: Out-of-Print Works.

TERRIS, Susan. *The Upstairs Witch and the Downstairs Witch.* Doubleday, 1970. Illus. by Olivia Cole. Unp. Gr. 2–4. (KR 38: 1033; LJ 95: 4039)

UNWIN, Nora. *Two Too Many.* See Chapter 9, Talking Animals: Out-of-Print Works.

WEALES, Gerald. *Miss Grimsbee Is a Witch.* Little, 1957. Illus. by Lita Scheel. 123 pp. Gr. 3–5. *Miss Grimsbee Takes a Vacation* (1965) is the sequel. (BL 53: 435; HB 33: 140; KR 25: 74: LJ 82: 884)

WICKENDEN, Dan. *The Amazing Vacation.* See Chapter 12, Travel to Another World: Out-of-Print Works.

WILLIAMS, Anne. *Secret of the Round Tower.* See Chapter 8V, Unicorns: Out-of-Print Works.

WILLIAMS, Jay. *A Box Full of Infinity.* See Chapter 5B, Imaginary Lands: Out-of-Print Works.

WILLIAMS, Jay. *Petronella.* See Chapter 5B, Imaginary Lands: Out-of-Print Works.

WILLIAMS, Ursula Moray. *The Toymaker's Daughter.* See Chapter 7, Magical Toys: Out-of-Print Works.

YOLEN, Jane. *The Wizard of Washington Square.* Collins + World, 1969. Illus. by Ray Cruz. 126 pp. Gr. 4–6. (CC: 581; CCBB 23: 170; KR 37: 1150; LJ 95: 783)

Titles Available in the United Kingdom

The publication information provided in the following list of titles available in the United Kingdom is based on *British Books in Print 1978*. Addresses for all British publishers and distributors listed here are included in the Directory of Publishers. Page numbers refer to the main entry for each title in the chapter listings.

Abell, Kathleen. *King Orville and the Bullfrog*. London: Faber, 1976. p. 45.

Adams, Richard. *Shardik*. London: Lane, 1974. p. 1.

_____. *Watership Down*. London: Collings, 1972; London: Kestrel, 1976. p. 1.

Aiken, Joan. *All and More* (New ed. of *All You've Ever Wanted and More Than You Bargained For*). London: Cape, 1971. p. 17.

_____. *Arabel's Raven*. London: BBC, 1972. p. 138.

_____. *Black Hearts in Battersea*. London: Cape, 1965. p. 138.

_____. *The Cuckoo Tree*. London: Cape, 1971. p. 138.

_____. *The Faithless Lollybird and Other Stories*. London: Cape, 1977. p. 16.

_____. *A Harp of Fishbones*. London: Cape, 1971. p. 17.

_____. *The Kingdom and the Cave*. London: Abelard-Schuman, 1973. p. 45.

_____. *A Necklace of Raindrops*. London: Cape, 1968. p. 16.

_____. *Night Birds on Nantucket*. London: Cape, 1966. p. 138.

_____. *A Small Pinch of Weather*. London: Cape, 1969. p. 17.

_____. *Tales of Arabel's Raven*. London: Cape, 1974. p. 138.

————. *The Whispering Mountain.* London: Cape, 1968. p. 45.

————. *The Wolves of Willoughby Chase.* London: Cape, 1962. p. 138.

Ainsworth, Ruth. *The Bear Who Liked Hugging People.* London: Heinemann, 1976. p. 17.

————. *The Phantom Roundabout.* London: Deutsch, 1977. p. 28.

Alexander, Lloyd. *The Black Cauldron.* London: Collins, 1973 (pap.). p. 41.

————. *The Book of Three.* London: Collins, 1973 (pap.). p. 41.

————. *The Castle of Llyr.* London: Armada, 1977 (pap.). p. 41.

Allan, Mabel. *Time to Go Back.* London: Abelard-Schuman, 1976. p. 170.

Allen, Judy. *The Lord of the Dance.* London: H. Hamilton, 1976. p. 173.

————. *The Spring on the Mountain.* London: Cape, 1973. p. 159.

Andersen, Hans Christian. *Classic Fairy Tales.* London: Gollancz, 1976. p. 18.

————. *The Complete Fairy Tales and Stories.* London: Gollancz, 1974. p. 17.

————. *The Emperor's New Clothes.* London: Abelard-Schuman, 1977; London: H. Hamilton, 1973. p. 1.

————. *Fairy Tales.* London: Collins, 1963; London: Dent, 1976. p. 24.

————. *The Fir Tree.* London: Kaye, 1971. p. 2.

————. *The Nightingale.* London: Kaye, 1972. p. 2.

————. *Seven Tales.* Tadsworth, Surrey: World's Work, 1972. p. 18.

————. *The Snow Queen.* London: Hodder, 1975. p. 2.

————. *Thumbelina.* London: Dobson, 1975; London: Kaye, 1973. p. 103.

————. *The Ugly Duckling.* London: Kaye, 1971. p. 12.

Annett, Cora. *How the Witch Got Alf.* London: Watts, 1977. p. 112.

Arthur, Ruth M. *The Autumn People.* London: Gollancz, 1973. p. 170.

————. *On the Wasteland.* London: Gollancz, 1975. p. 160.

————. *The Whistling Boy.* London: Gollancz, 1969. p. 28.

Arundel, Honor. *The Amazing Mr. Prothero.* London: H. Hamilton, 1968 (pap.). p. 129.

Averill, Esther. *Jenny and the Cat Club.* London: Collins, 1976 (pap.). p. 112.

Babbitt, Natalie. *The Devil's Storybook.* London: Chatto, 1976. p. 86.

————. *The Search for Delicious.* London: Armada, 1977 (pap.). p. 46.

————. *Tuck Everlasting.* London: Chatto, 1977. p. 3.

Bailey, Carolyn. *Miss Hickory.* London: Hodder, 1977. p. 80.

Baker, Margaret Joyce. *Bears Back in Business.* London: Harrap, 1967. p. 82.

————. *The Magic Seashell*. London: Hodder, 1976. p. 72.

————. *Porterhouse Major*. London: Methuen, 1967. p. 72.

Barber, Antonia. *The Ghosts*. London: Cape, 1969. p. 160.

Barrie, Sir J. M. *Peter Pan*. London: Brockhampton, 1971. p. 173.

————. *Peter Pan and Wendy*. London: Brockhampton, 1970; London: Hodder, 1976. p. 173.

————. *Peter Pan in Kensington Gardens*. London: Hodder, 1906; London: Brockhampton, 1970. p. 174.

Baum, L. Frank. *The Land of Oz*. London: Hutchinson, 1974. p. 174.

————. *The Lost Princess of Oz*. London: Hutchinson, 1974. p. 174.

————. *Ozma of Oz*. London: Hutchinson, 1974. p. 174.

————. *The Tin Woodman of Oz*. London: Hutchinson, 1974. p. 174.

————. *The Wizard of Oz*. London: Dent, 1965. p. 174.

Baxter, Carolyn. *The Stolen Telesm*. London: Cape, 1975. p. 101.

Beachcroft, Nina. *Well Met by Witchlight*. London: Heinemann, 1972. p. 185.

Benchley, Nathaniel. *Feldman Fieldmouse*. London: Abelard-Schuman, 1975. p. 113.

————. *The Magic Sledge*. London: Deutsch, 1974. p. 60.

Beresford, Elisabeth. *Awkward Magic*. St. Albans, Herts: Hart-Davis, 1976. p. 60.

————. *Invisible Magic*. St. Albans, Herts: Hart-Davis, 1975. p. 170.

————. *The Invisible Womble and Other Stories*. London: Benn, 1973. p. 129.

————. *MacWomble's Pipe Band*. London: Benn, 1976. p. 129.

————. *The Snow Womble*. London: Benn, 1975. p. 129.

————. *Travelling Magic*. St. Albans, Herts: Hart-Davis, 1976. p. 170.

————. *The Wandering Wombles*. London: Benn, 1970. p. 129.

————. *The Wombles*. London: Benn, 1968. p. 129.

————. *The Wombles at Work*. London: Benn, 1976. p. 129.

————. *The Wombles Book*. London: Benn, 1975. p. 129.

————. *The Wombles go Round the World*. London: Benn, 1976. p. 129.

————. *The Wombles in Danger*. Harmondsworth, Middx: Puffin, 1973 (pap.). p. 129.

————. *The Wombles Make a Clean Sweep*. Harmondsworth, Middx: Puffin, 1975 (pap.). p. 129.

————. *The Wombles of Wimbledon*. London: Benn, 1976. p. 129.

————. *The Wombles to the Rescue*. London: Benn, 1974. p. 129.

Bianco, Margery Williams. *Poor Cecco*. London: Deutsch, 1973. p. 82.

———. *The Velveteen Rabbit*. London: Heinemann, 1970. p. 80.

Biegel, Paul. *The King of the Copper Mountains*. London: Dent, 1968. p. 46.

Bomans, Godfried. *The Wily Wizard and the Wicked Witch and Other Weird Stories*. London: Dent, 1969. p. 18.

Bond, Michael. *The Adventures of Paddington*. London: Collins, 1965. p. 114.

———. *A Bear Called Paddington*. London: Collins, 1958. p. 113.

———. *Fun and Games with Paddington*. London: Collins, 1977. p. 114.

———. *More about Paddington*. London: Collins, 1959. p. 113.

———. *Olga Carries On*. London: Kestrel, 1976. p. 114.

———. *Olga Counts Her Blessings*. Hardmondsworth, Middx: Puffin, 1975 (pap.). p. 114.

———. *Olga Da Polga*. London: Longman Young Bks, 1975. p. 114.

———. *Olga Makes a Friend*. Harmondsworth, Middx: Puffin, 1975 (pap.). p. 114.

———. *Olga Makes a Wish*. Harmondsworth, Middx: Puffin, 1975 (pap.). p. 114.

———. *Olga Makes Her Mark*. Harmondsworth, Middx: Puffin, 1975 (pap.). p. 114.

———. *Olga Meets Her Match*. London: Longman Young Bks, 1973. p. 114.

———. *Olga Takes a Bite*. Harmondsworth, Middx: Puffin, 1975 (pap.). p. 114.

———. *Olga's New Home*. Harmondsworth, Middx: Puffin, 1975 (pap.). p. 114.

———. *Olga's Second House*. Harmondsworth, Middx: Puffin, 1975 (pap.). p. 114.

———. *Olga's Special Day*. Harmondsworth, Middx: Puffin, 1975 (pap.). p. 114.

———. *Paddington Abroad*. London: Collins, 1961. p. 113.

———. *Paddington at Large*. London: Collins, 1963. p. 113.

———. *Paddington at the Circus*. London: Collins, 1973. p. 113.

———. *Paddington at the Seaside*. London: Collins, 1975. p. 114.

———. *Paddington at the Tower*. London: Collins, 1975. p. 114.

———. *Paddington at Work*. London: Collins, 1966. p. 113.

———. *Paddington Bear*. London: Collins, 1972. p. 114.

———. *Paddington Does it Himself*. London: Collins, 1977. p. 114.

_____. *Paddington Goes Shopping*. London: Collins, 1973. p. 114.

_____. *Paddington Goes to the Sales*. London: Collins, 1976. p. 114.

_____. *Paddington Goes to Town*. London: Collins, 1968. p. 113.

_____. *Paddington Helps Out*. London: Collins, 1960. p. 113.

_____. *Paddington Hits Out*. London: Collins, 1977. p. 114.

_____. *Paddington in the Kitchen*. London: Collins, 1977. p. 114.

_____. *Paddington Marches On*. London: Collins, 1964. p. 113.

_____. *Paddington on Stage*. London: Collins, 1974. p. 114.

_____. *Paddington on Top*. London: Collins, 1974. p. 114.

_____. *Paddington Takes the Air*. London: Collins, 1970. p. 113.

_____. *Paddington's Birthday Party*. London: Collins, 1977. p. 114.

_____. *Paddington's "Blue Peter" Storybook*. London: Collins, 1973. p. 114.

_____. *Paddington's Garden*. London: Collins, 1972. p. 113.

_____. *Tales of Olga Da Polga*. London: Longman Young Bks, 1972. p. 114.

_____. *Thursday Ahoy!* Harmondsworth, Middx: Puffin, 1973 (pap.). p. 130.

_____. *Thursday in Paris*. Harmondsworth, Middx: Puffin, 1974 (pap.). p. 130.

Boston, L. M. *The Castle of Yew*. London: Bodley Head, 1965. p. 73.

_____. *The Children of Green Knowe*. London: Faber, 1954. p. 60.

_____. *The Chimneys of Green Knowe*. London: Faber, 1958. p. 60.

_____. *An Enemy at Green Knowe*. London: Faber, 1964. p. 60.

_____. *The Fossil Snake*. London: Bodley Head, 1975. p. 60.

_____. *The Guardians of the House*. London: Bodley Head, 1974. p. 174.

_____. *The River at Green Knowe*. London: Faber, 1959. p. 60.

_____. *The Sea Egg*. London: Faber, 1967. p. 60.

_____. *The Stones of Green Knowe*. London: Bodley Head, 1976. p. 60.

_____. *A Stranger at Green Knowe*. London: Faber, 1961. p. 60.

Bourliaguet, Léonce. *The Giant Who Drank from His Shoe*. London: Abelard-Schuman, 1974. p. 24.

Bradbury, Ray. *The Hallowe'en Tree*. London: Corgi, 1975. p. 161.

_____. *Something Wicked This Way Comes*. St. Albans, Herts: Hart-Davis, 1963. p. 186.

Brand, Christianna. *Nurse Matilda*. London: Brockhampton, 1973 (pap.). p. 73.

———. *Nurse Matilda Goes to the Hospital.* London: Brockhampton, 1974. p. 73.

———. *Nurse Matilda Goes to Town.* London: Brockhampton, 1967. p. 73.

Brandel, Marc. *The Mine of the Lost Days.* London: Cape, 1975, p. 161.

Briggs, Katharine. *Hobberdy Dick.* Harmondsworth, Middx: Puffin, 1972 (pap.). p. 99.

Brock, Betty. *No Flying in the House.* London: Harper, 1978. p. 61.

———. *The Shades.* London: Gollancz, 1973. p. 29.

Brown, Jeff. *Flat Stanley.* London: Methuen, 1974. p. 140.

Buck, David. *The Small Adventures of Dog.* London: Heinemann, 1968. p. 83.

Burman, Ben Lucien. *High Water at Catfish Bend, and Seven Stars for Catfish Bend.* London: Kestrel, 1975. p. 115.

———. *The Owl Hoots Twice at Catfish Bend.* London: Kestrel, 1975. p. 115.

Burnett, Frances Hodgson. *Racketty-Packetty House.* London: Evans, 1976. p. 92.

Butterworth, Oliver. *The Enormous Egg.* London: Sidgwick, 1975. p. 87.

Byars, Betsy. *The Winged Colt of Casa Mia.* London: Bodley Head, 1975. p. 61.

Capek, Josef. *Harum Scarum: The Adventures of Puss and Pup.* London: Transworld, 1975. p. 130.

Carlson, Natalie. *Pigeon of Paris.* Glasgow: Blackie, 1972. p. 130.

Carroll, Lewis. *Alice in Wonderland.* London: Collins, 1973; London: Bodley Head, 1974. p. 174.

———. *Alice in Wonderland and Through the Looking Glass.* London: Oxford, 1975; London: Dent, 1977; London: Macmillan, 1977. p. 174.

———. *Alice Through the Looking Glass.* London: Macmillan, n.d. p. 174.

Cervantes, Miguel de. *Don Quixote.* London: Oxford, 1973; London: Dent, n.d. p. 3.

Chant, Joy. *The Grey Mane of Morning.* London: Allen, 1977. p. 174.

———. *Red Moon and Black Mountain.* London: Allen, 1970. p. 174.

Chesnutt, Charles. *Conjure Tales.* London: Collins, 1975. p. 18.

Christopher, John. *Beyond the Burning Lands.* Harmondsworth, Middx: Penguin, 1973 (pap.). p. 42.

———. *The Prince in Waiting.* London: H. Hamilton, 1970. p. 42.

———. *The Sword of the Spirits.* London: H. Hamilton, 1970. p. 42.

Church, Richard. *The French Lieutenant*. London: Heinemann, 1971. p. 29.

Claire, Keith. *The Otherwise Girl*. London: Blond, 1976. p. 30.

Clare, Helen. *Five Dolls and Their Friends*. London: Bodley Head, 1972. p. 83.

_____. *Five Dolls in a House*. London: Bodley Head, 1972. p. 83.

Clarke, Pauline. *The Twelve and the Genii*. London: Faber, 1962. p. 80.

_____. *The Two Faces of Silenus*. London: Faber, 1972. p. 62.

Cleary, Beverly. *The Mouse and the Motorcycle*. London: H. Hamilton, 1974. p. 116.

_____. *Runaway Ralph*. London: H. Hamilton, 1974. p. 116.

Colbalt, Martin. *Swallows*. London: Heinemann, 1972. p. 30.

Collodi, Carlo. *Pinocchio*. London: Dent, 1976. p. 80.

Colum, Padraic. *Sparrow Alone*. Glasgow: Blackie, 1975. p. 131.

Coombs, Patricia. *Dorrie and the Amazing Magic Elixer*. Tadworth, Surrey: World's Work, 1977. p. 186.

_____. *Dorrie and the Birthday Eggs*. Tadworth, Surrey: World's Work, 1973. p. 186.

_____. *Dorrie and the Blue Witch*. Tadworth, Surrey: World's Work, 1975. p. 186.

_____. *Dorrie and the Fortune Teller*. Tadworth, Surrey: World's Work, 1975. p. 186.

_____. *Dorrie and the Goblin*. Tadworth, Surrey: World's Work, 1974. p. 186.

_____. *Dorrie and the Hallowe'en Plot*. Tadworth, Surrey: World's Work, 1978. p. 186.

_____. *Dorrie and the Haunted House*. Tadworth, Surrey: World's Work, 1973. p. 186.

_____. *Dorrie and the Weather Box*. Tadworth, Surrey: World's Work, 1977. p. 186.

_____. *Dorrie and the Witch Doctor*. Tadworth, Surrey: World's Work, 1977. p. 186.

_____. *Dorrie and the Witch's Imp*. Tadworth, Surrey: World's Work, 1977. p. 186.

_____. *Dorrie and the Wizard's Spell*. Tadworth, Surrey: World's Work, 1974. p. 186.

_____. *Dorrie's Magic*. Tadworth, Surrey: World's Work, 1977. p. 186.

_____. *Dorrie's Play*. Tadworth, Surrey: World's Work, 1977. p. 186.

Cooper, Susan. *The Dark Is Rising*. London: Chatto, 1973. p. 38.

————. *Greenwitch*. London: Chatto, 1974. p. 38.

————. *The Grey King*. London: Chatto, 1975. p. 38.

————. *Over Sea, Under Stone*. London: Chatto, 1974. p. 37.

————. *Silver on the Tree*. London: Chatto, 1977. p. 38.

Coren, Alan. *Arthur the Kid*. London: Robson, 1976. p. 14.

————. *Arthur's Last Stand*. London: Robson, 1977. p. 141.

————. *Buffalo Arthur*. London: Robson, 1976. p. 141.

————. *Klondike Arthur*. London: Robson, 1977. p. 141.

————. *Lone Arthur*. London: Robson, 1976. p. 141.

————. *Railroad Arthur*. London: Robson, 1977. p. 141.

Cresswell, Helen. *The Beachcombers*. London: Faber, 1972. p. 62.

————. *The Bongleweed*. London: Faber, 1973. p. 62.

————. *A Game of Catch*. London: Chatto, 1969. p. 30.

————. *The Nightwatchmen*. London: Faber, 1969. p. 63.

————. *Up the Pier*. London: Faber, 1971. p. 161.

————. *The Winter of the Birds*. London: Faber, 1975. p. 4.

Cunningham, Julia. *Dorp Dead*. London: Heinemann, 1967. p. 4.

Curry, Jane. *Beneath the Hill*. London: Dobson, 1968. p. 173.

————. *The Birdstones*. London: Kestrel, 1978. p. 162.

————. *The Change Child*. London: Dobson, 1970. p. 73.

————. *The Daybreakers*. London: Longman Young Bks, 1970. p. 162.

————. *The Housenapper*. London: Longman Young Bks, 1971. p. 103.

————. *The Lost Farm*. London: Longman Young Bks, 1974. p. 103.

————. *Over the Sea's Edge*. London: Longman Young Bks, 1971. p. 162.

————. *Poor Tom's Ghost*. London: Kestrel, 1977. p. 162.

————. *The Sleepers*. London: Dobson, 1969. p. 187.

————. *The Watchers*. London: Kestrel, 1976. p. 162.

Dahl, Roald. *Charlie and the Chocolate Factory*. London: Allen, 1967. p. 63.

————. *Charlie and the Great Glass Elevator*. London: Allen, 1973. p. 63.

————. *James and the Giant Peach*. London: Allen, 1967. p. 63.

————. *The Magic Finger*. London: Allen, 1968. p. 63.

Dawson, Mary. *Tinker Tales*. Maidenhead, Berks: Parents, 1974. p. 91.

De La Mare, Walter. *Three Royal Monkeys*. London: Faber, 1946. p. 131.

Dickens, Charles. *A Christmas Carol*. London: Dover, 1972. p. 4.

————. *The Magic Fishbone*. London: Chatto, 1969. p. 47.

Dickinson, Peter. *The Blue Hawk*. London: Gollancz, 1976. p. 42.

———. *The Devil's Children*. London: Gollancz, 1970. p. 42.

———. *Heartsease*. London: Gollancz, 1969. p. 42.

———. *The Iron Lion*. London: Allen, 1973. p. 53.

———. *The Weathermonger*. London: Gollancz, 1968. p. 42.

Duggan, Maurice. *Falter Tom and the Water Boy*. London: Kestrel, 1974. p. 102.

Dunlop, Eileen. *Robinsheugh*. London: Oxford, 1975. p. 162.

Eager, Edward. *Half Magic*. London: Macmillan, 1969. p. 64.

———. *Magic or Not?* London: Macmillan, 1959. p. 64.

———. *Time Garden*. Harmondsworth, Middx: Puffin, 1972 (pap.). p. 64.

Eager, Frances. *Time Tangle*. London: H. Hamilton, 1976. p. 171.

Edmondson, Madeleine. *The Witch's Egg*. London: Macmillan, 1975. p. 187.

Eldridge, Roger. *The Shadow of the Gloom-World*. London: Gollancz, 1977. p. 42.

Enright, Elizabeth. *Tatsinda*. London: Heinemann, 1964. p. 47.

———. *Zeee*. London: Heinemann, 1966. p. 92.

Estes, Eleanor. *The Witch Family*. London: Longman Young Bks, 1962. p. 187.

Ezo. *My Son-in-Law the Hippopotamus*. London: Abelard-Schuman, 1973. p. 132.

Farjeon, Eleanor. *The Glass Slipper*. London: Oxford, 1962. p. 54.

———. *Jim at the Corner*. London: Oxford, 1958. p. 25.

———. *The Little Bookroom*. London: Oxford, 1955. p. 25.

———. *The Old Nurse's Stocking Basket*. London: Oxford, 1965. p. 25.

———. *The Silver Curlew*. London: Oxford, 1969. p. 54.

Farmer, Penelope. *A Castle of Bone*. Harmondsworth, Middx: Puffin, 1974 (pap.). p. 5.

———. *Charlotte Sometimes*. London: Chatto, 1969. p. 163.

———. *Emma in Winter*. London: Chatto, 1966. p. 163.

———. *The Summer Birds*. London: Chatto, 1962. p. 163.

———. *William and Mary*. London: Chatto, 1974. p. 175.

Farthing, Alison. *The Mystical Beast*. London: Chatto, 1976. p. 175.

Field, Rachel. *Hitty: Her First Hundred Years*. West Drayton, Middx: Collier-Macmillan, 1969. p. 80.

Fleischman, Sid. *The Ghost in the Noonday Sun*. London: H. Hamilton, 1966. p. 31.

————. *The Ghost on a Saturday Night*. London: Heinemann, 1975. p. 143.

————. *Here Comes McBroom*. London: Chatto, 1976. p. 144.

————. *McBroom's Wonderful One Acre Farm*. London: Chatto, 1972. p. 144.

Fleming, Ian. *Chitty Chitty Bang Bang*. London: Cape, 1971. p. 144.

Foster, Elizabeth. *Lyrico*. London: Macmillan, 1971. p. 101.

Freeman, Barbara. *A Haunting Air*. London: Macmillan, 1976. p. 31.

————. *The Other Face*. London: Macmillan, 1975. p. 163.

————. *A Pocket of Silence*. London: Macmillan, 1977. p. 163.

Gallico, Paul. *Jennie*. London: M. Joseph, 1950. p. 119.

Gannett, Ruth. *My Father's Dragon*. London: Armada, 1976 (pap.). p. 88.

Gard, Joyce. *The Mermaid's Daughter*. London: Gollancz, 1969. p. 193.

Garfield, Leon. *Mister Corbett's Ghost and Other Stories*. London: Longman Young Bks, 1969. p. 31.

Garner, Alan. *Elidor*. London: Collins, 1965. p. 175.

————. *The Moon of Gomrath*. London: Collins, 1963. p. 38.

————. *The Owl Service*. London: Collins, 1967. p. 38.

————. *The Weirdstone of Brisingamen*. London: Collins, 1965. p. 38.

Gathorne-Hardy, Jonathan. *Jane's Adventures in a Balloon*. London: Gollancz, 1975. p. 145.

————. *Jane's Adventures in and out of the Book*. London: Pan, 1972. p. 145.

————. *Jane's Adventures on the Island of Peeg*. London: A. Ross, 1968. p. 144.

Gaunt, Michael. *Brim Sails Out*. London: Cape, 1966 (pap.). p. 132.

Godden, Rumer. *Candy Floss*. London: Macmillan, 1960. p. 83.

————. *Candy Floss and Impunity Jane*. Harmondsworth, Middx: Puffin, 1975 (pap.). p. 83.

————. *The Dolls' House*. London: Macmillan, 1963. p. 83.

————. *The Fairy Doll*. London: Macmillan, 1956. p. 83.

————. *Home Is the Sailor*. London: Macmillan, 1964. p. 84.

————. *Impunity Jane*. London: Macmillan, 1955. p. 84.

————. *Little Plum*. London: Macmillan, 1963. p. 84.

————. *Miss Happiness and Miss Flower*. London: Macmillan, 1961. p. 84.

————. *Mouse House*. London: Macmillan, 1958. p. 119.

————. *The Mousewife*. London: Macmillan, 1951. p. 5.

————. *The Story of Holly and Ivy*. London: Macmillan, 1958. p. 84.

Gordon, John. *The Giant under the Snow*. London: Hutchinson, 1968. p. 65.

Goudge, Elizabeth. *The Little White Horse*. London: Brockhampton, 1946. p. 65.

_____. *Smoky-House*. London: Duckworth, 1940. p. 93.

Grahame, Kenneth. *The Reluctant Dragon*. London: Bodley Head, 1959. p. 88.

_____. *The Wind in the Willows*. London: Methuen, 1971. p. 119.

Gray, Nicholas. *The Apple Stone*. London: Dobson, 1965. p. 65.

Green, Roger. *A Book of Magicians*. Harmondsworth, Middx: Puffin, 1977 (pap.). p. 194.

Grimshaw, Nigel. *Bluntstone and the Wildkeepers*. London: Faber, 1974. p. 104.

_____. *The Wildkeepers' Guest*. London: Faber, 1976. p. 104.

Guillot, René. *The Elephants of Sargabal*. London: Oxford, 1968. p. 48.

_____. *The Great Land of the Elephant*. London: Oxford, 1971. p. 48.

_____. *Master of the Elephants*. London: Oxford, 1969. p. 48.

Hale, Lucretia. *The Last of the Peterkins*. London: Dover, 1966. p. 145.

_____. *The Peterkin Papers*. London: Dover, n.d. p. 145.

Harris, Rosemary. *The Bright and Morning Star*. London: Faber, 1972. p. 42.

_____. *The Lotus and the Grail*. London: Faber, 1974. p. 20.

_____. *The Moon in the Cloud*. London: Faber, 1968. p. 42.

_____. *The Seal Singing*. London: Faber, 1971. p. 108.

_____. *A Shadow on the Sun*. London: Faber, 1970. p. 42.

Hauff, Wilhelm. *The Adventures of Little Mouk*. London: H. Hamilton, 1974. p. 48.

Hayes, Geoffrey. *The Alligator and His Uncle Tooth*. London: Andersen, 1977. p. 47.

_____. *Bear by Himself*. London: Harper, 1977. p. 81.

Hendrich, Paula. *Who Says So?* London: G. K. Hall, 1974. p. 65.

Hilton, James. *Lost Horizon*. London: Macmillan, 1933. p. 176.

Hoban, Russell. *How Tom Beat Captain Najork and His Hired Sportsmen*. London: Cape, 1974. p. 145.

_____. *The Mouse and His Child*. London: Faber, 1969. p. 6.

_____. *A Near Thing for Captain Najork*. London: Cape, 1975. p. 145.

_____. *The Sea-Thing Child*. London: Gollancz, 1972. p. 120.

Hoke, Helen. *Devils, Devils, Devils*. London: Watts, 1975. p. 86.

Holman, Felice. *The Witch on the Corner*. London: Tandem, 1977 (pap.). p. 194.

Housman, Laurence. *Cotton-Wooleena*. London: Kaye, 1968. p. 95.

Hughes, Peter. *The Emperor's Oblong Pancake*. London: Abelard-Schuman, 1975. p. 48.

Hughes, Richard. *The Spider's Palace*. Harmondsworth, Middx: Puffin, 1972 (pap.). p. 26.

Hughes, Ted. *How the Whale Became and Other Stories*. London: Faber, n.d. p. 26.

_____. *The Iron Man: A Story in Five Nights*. London: Faber, 1968. p. 97.

Hunter, Mollie. *The Haunted Mountain*. London: H. Hamilton, 1972. p. 93.

_____. *The Kelpie's Pearls*. Harmondsworth, Middx: Puffin, 1973 (pap.). p. 102.

_____. *A Stranger Came Ashore*. London: H. Hamilton, 1975. p. 108.

Hutchins, Pat. *Follow That Bus!* London: Bodley Head, 1977. p. 146.

_____. *The House That Sailed Away*. London: Bodley Head, 1976. p. 146.

Ibbotson, Eva. *The Great Ghost Rescue*. London: Macmillan, 1975. p. 31.

Ingelow, Jean. *Mopsa the Fairy*. London: Dent, 1964. p. 93.

Ingram, Tom. *The Night Rider*. London: Hutchinson, 1976. p. 163.

Irving, Washington. *Rip Van Winkle*. London: Watts, 1970; London: Heinemann, n.d. p. 66.

Jansson, Tove. *A Comet in Moominland*. London: Benn, 1965. p. 99.

_____. *The Exploits of Moominpappa*. London: Benn, 1952. p. 99.

_____. *Finn Family Moomintroll*. London: Benn, n.d. p. 99.

_____. *Moomin, Mymble and Little My*. London: Benn, 1976. p. 99.

_____. *Moominland in Midwinter*. London: Benn, 1958. p. 99.

_____. *Moominpappa at Sea*. London: Benn, 1966. p. 99.

_____. *Moominsummer Madness*. London: Benn, 1965. p. 99.

_____. *Moominvalley in November*. London: Benn, 1971. p. 99.

_____. *Tales from Moominvalley*. London: Benn, 1963. p. 99.

Jarrell, Randall. *The Animal Family*. London: Kestrel, 1976. p. 6.

_____. *The Bat Poet*. London: Kestrel, 1977. p. 120.

_____. *Fly by Night*. London: Bodley Head, 1977. p. 66.

Johnson, Sally (ed). *The Book of Princesses*. London: H. Hamilton, 1963. p. 48.

Jones, Diana Wynne. *Cart and Cwidder*. London: Macmillan, 1975. p. 43.

_____. *A Charmed Life*. London: Macmillan, 1977. p. 164.

———. *Dogsbody*. London: Macmillan, 1975. p. 120.

———. *The Ogre Downstairs*. London: Macmillan, 1974. p. 66.

———. *The Power of Three*. London: Macmillan, 1976. p. 43.

———. *Wilkin's Tooth*. London: Macmillan, 1973. p. 188.

Juster, Norton. *The Phantom Tollbooth*. London: Collins, 1962. p. 177.

Kastner, Erich. *The Little Man*. London: Cape, 1966. p. 104.

———. *The Little Man and the Little Miss*. London: Cape, 1969. p. 104.

Kellam, Ian. *The First Summer Year*. London: Oxford, 1972. p. 182.

Kingsley, Charles. *The Water Babies*. London: Dent, 1973; London: Constable, 1975. p. 94.

Kipling, Rudyard. *All the Mowgli Stories*. London: Macmillan, 1961. p. 133.

———. *The Jungle Book*. London: Macmillan, 1965. p. 21.

———. *Just So Stories*. London: Macmillan, 1965. p. 21.

———. *Puck of Pook's Hill*. London: Macmillan, 1965. p. 96.

———. *Rewards and Fairies*. London: Macmillan, 1965. p. 96.

———. *The Second Jungle Book*. London: Macmillan, 1965. p. 21.

Kirkegaard, Ole. *Otto Is a Rhino*. London: Pelham, 1975. p. 67.

La Motte Fouqué, Friedrich de. *Undine*. Bath: Brodie, 1928; London: Calder, n.d. p. 7.

Lagerlöf, Selma. *The Wonderful Adventures of Nils*. London: Dent, 1951. p. 105.

Lamorisse, Albert. *The Red Balloon*. London: Allen, 1957. p. 6.

Lancaster, Clay. *Periwinkle Steamboat*. London: Kaye, 1962. p. 75.

Lancaster, Osbert. *The Saracen's Head, or the Reluctant Crusader*. London: J. Murray, 1948. p. 55.

Lanier, Sterling. *The War for the Lot*. London: Sidgwick, 1977. p. 133.

Lawrence, Ann. *The Half-Brothers*. London: Macmillan, 1973. p. 49.

———. *Tom Ass*. London: Macmillan, 1972. p. 75.

Lee, Tanith. *Animal Castle*. London: Macmillan, 1972. p. 55.

———. *Princess Hynchatti and Some Other Surprises*. London: Macmillan, 1972. p. 21.

Le Guin, Ursula. *Earthsea*. London: Gollancz, 1977. p. 39.

———. *The Farthest Shore*. London: Gollancz, 1973. p. 39.

———. *The Tombs of Atuan*. London: Gollancz, 1972. p. 39.

———. *The Wind's Twelve Quarters*. London: Gollancz, 1976. p. 21.

———. *A Wizard of Earthsea*. London: Gollancz, 1971. p. 39.

Levitin, Sonia. *Jason and the Money Tree*. London: Harcourt, 1974. p. 147.

Lewis, C. S. *The Horse and His Boy*. London: Collins, 1974. p. 177.

_____. *The Last Battle*. London: Bodley Head, 1956. p. 177.

_____. *The Lion, the Witch and the Wardrobe*. London: Collins, 1974. p. 177.

_____. *The Magician's Nephew*. London: Bodley Head, 1955. p. 177.

_____. *Prince Caspian*. London: Collins, 1974. p. 177.

_____. *The Silver Chair*. London: Collins, 1974. p. 177.

_____. *The Voyage of the "Dawn Treader."* London: Collins, 1974. p. 177.

Lewis, Hilda. *The Ship That Flew*. London: Oxford, 1965. p. 164.

Linde, Gunnel. *The White Stone*. London: Dent, 1977. p. 76.

Lindgren, Astrid. *The Brothers Lionheart*. London: Brockhampton, 1975. p. 7.

_____. *Karlson Flies Again*. London: Methuen, 1977. p. 104.

_____. *Karlson on the Roof*. London: Methuen, 1977. p. 104.

_____. *Pippi Goes Abroad*. Harmondsworth, Middx: Puffin, 1977 (pap.). p. 147.

_____. *Pippi in the South Seas*. London: Oxford, 1957. p. 147.

_____. *Pippi Longstocking*. London: Oxford, 1954. p. 147.

Lindsay, Norman. *The Magic Pudding*. Brighton: Angus, 1976. p. 134.

Lively, Penelope. *Astercote*. London: Heinemann, 1970. p. 14.

_____. *The Driftway*. London: Heinemann, 1972. p. 165.

_____. *The Ghost of Thomas Kempe*. London: Heinemann, 1973. p. 165.

_____. *The House in Norham Gardens*. London: Heinemann, 1974. p. 165.

_____. *A Stitch in Time*. London: Heinemann, 1976. p. 32.

_____. *The Whispering Knights*. London: Heinemann, 1971. p. 67.

_____. *The Wild Hunt of Hagworthy*. London: Heinemann, 1971. p. 40.

Lockley, Ronald. *The Seal Woman*. London: R. Collings, 1974. p. 108.

Lofting, Hugh. *Doctor Dolittle: A Treasury*. London: Cape, 1968. p. 148.

_____. *Doctor Dolittle and the Green Canary*. London: Cape, 1966. p. 148.

_____. *Doctor Dolittle and the Secret Lake*. London: Cape, 1966. p. 148.

_____. *Doctor Dolittle in the Moon*. London: Cape, 1966. p. 148.

_____. *Doctor Dolittle's Caravan*. London: Cape, 1966. p. 148.

_____. *Doctor Dolittle's Circus*. London: Cape, 1966. p. 148.

_____. *Doctor Dolittle's Garden*. London: Cape, 1966. p. 148.

_____. *Doctor Dolittle's Post Office*. London: Cape, 1924. p. 148.

————. *Doctor Dolittle's Puddleby Adventures*. London: Cape, 1966. p. 148.

————. *Doctor Dolittle's Return*. London: Cape, 1933. p. 148.

————. *Doctor Dolittle's Zoo*. London: Cape, 1966. p. 148.

————. *Gub Gub's Book*. London: Cape, 1974. p. 148.

————. *The Story of Doctor Dolittle*. London: Cape, 1966. p. 148.

————. *Tommy Tilly and Mrs. Tubbs*. London: Cape, 1968 (pap.). p. 148.

————. *The Twilight of Magic*. London: Cape, 1958. p. 148.

————. *The Voyages of Doctor Dolittle*. London: Cape, 1966. p. 148.

McCaffrey, Anne. *Dragonflight*. London: Corgi, 1970 (pap.). p. 89.

————. *Dragonquest*. London: Rapp, 1973. p. 89.

————. *Dragonsinger*. London: Sidgwick, 1977. p. 89.

Macdonald, George. *At the Back of the North Wind*. London: Dent, 1956. p. 7.

————. *The Golden Key*. London: Bodley Head, 1972. p. 7.

————. *The Light Princess*. London: Bodley Head, 1972. p. 7.

————. *The Light Princess and Other Tales of Fantasy*. London: Gollancz, 1972. p. 7.

————. *The Lost Princess*. London: Dent, 1965. p. 49.

————. *The Princess and Curdie*. Glasgow: Blackie, n.d. p. 50.

————. *The Princess and the Goblin*. London: Dent, 1949. p. 50.

Mace, Elizabeth. *The Ghost Diviners*. London: Deutsch, 1977. p. 165.

————. *Ransome Revisited*. London: Deutsch, 1975. p. 43.

McNeill, Janet. *Best Specs*. London: Faber, 1970. p. 76.

Maeterlinck, Maurice. *The Blue Bird*. London: Oxford, 1977. p. 14.

Manning, Rosemary. *Dragon in Danger*. London: Longman Young Bks, 1972. p. 90.

————. *The Dragon's Quest*. Harmondsworth, Middx: Puffin, 1974 (pap.). p. 90.

————. *Green Smoke*. London: Longman Young Bks, 1972. p. 90.

Masefield, John. *The Box of Delights*. London: Heinemann, 1935. p. 76.

————. *The Midnight Folk*. London: Heinemann, 1927. p. 76.

Mayne, William. *Earthfasts*. London: H. Hamilton, 1966. p. 166.

————. *A Game of Dark*. London: H. Hamilton, 1971. p. 166.

————. *The Grass Rope*. London: Oxford, 1972. p. 68.

————. *It*. London: H. Hamilton, 1977. p. 32.

————. *A Year and a Day.* London: H. Hamilton, 1976. p. 94.

Merrill, Jean. *The Pushcart War.* London: H. Hamilton, 1973. p. 48.

Miles, Patricia. *The Gods in Winter.* London: H. Hamilton, 1978. p. 8.

Milne, A. A. *The Christopher Robin Story Book.* London: Methuen, 1927. p. 81.

————. *The House at Pooh Corner.* London: Methuen, 1974. p. 81.

————. *The Hums of Pooh.* London: Methuen, 1972. p. 81.

————. *Once on a Time.* Harmondsworth, Middx: Puffin, 1971 (pap.). p. 56.

————. *The Pooh Story Book.* London: Methuen, 1967. p. 81.

————. *Winnie the Pooh.* London: Methuen, 1973. p. 81.

————. *The World of Christopher Robin.* London: Methuen, 1924. p. 81.

————. *The World of Pooh.* London: Methuen, 1926. p. 81.

Molesworth, Mary L. *The Cuckoo Clock.* London: Dent, 1954. p. 178.

Morgan, Alison. *River Song.* London: Chatto, 1976. p. 134.

Mulock, Dinah. *The Little Lame Prince.* Derby: Pilgrim Press, 1949. p. 50.

Nesbit, Edith. *The Complete Book of Dragons.* London: H. Hamilton, 1972. p. 89.

————. *The Enchanted Castle.* London: Dent, 1977. p. 68.

————. *The Five Children and It.* London: Benn, n.d. p. 68.

————. *Harding's Luck.* London: Benn, n.d. p. 166.

————. *The Magic World.* London: Benn, n.d. p. 21.

————. *The Phoenix and the Carpet.* London: Benn, n.d. p. 68.

————. *The Story of the Amulet.* London: Benn, 1957. p. 68.

Newman, Robert. *Merlin's Mistake.* London: Hutchinson, 1971. p. 195.

————. *The Shattered Stone.* London: Hutchinson, 1976. p. 139.

Nickl, Peter, and Shroeder, Binette. *The Crocodile.* London: Cape, 1976. p. 123.

Norton, André. *The Crystal Gryphon.* London: Gollancz, 1975. p. 44.

————. *The Jargoon Pard.* London: Gollancz, 1975. p. 44.

————. *Knave of Dreams.* London: Kestrel, 1976. p. 178.

————. *Red Hart Magic.* London: H. Hamilton, 1977. p. 167.

————. *Steel Magic.* London: H. Hamilton, 1977. p. 178.

————. *Wraiths of Time.* London: Gollancz, 1977. p. 179.

Norton, Mary. *Are All the Giants Dead?* London: Dent, 1975. p. 179.

————. *Bedknob and Broomstick.* London: Dent, 1957. p. 69.

————. *The Borrowers.* London: Dent, 1975. p. 104.

———. *The Borrowers Afield*. London: Dent, 1975. p. 104.

———. *The Borrowers Afloat*. London: Dent, 1975. p. 104.

———. *The Borrowers Aloft*. London: Dent, 1975. p. 104.

———. *The Borrowers Omnibus*. London: Dent, 1976. p. 104.

———. *Poor Stainless*. London: Dent, 1971. p. 104.

Nostlinger, Christine. *Conrad: The Hilarious Adventures of a Factory-Made Child*. London: Andersen, 1976. p. 149.

O'Brien, Robert C. *Mrs. Frisby and the Rats of NIMH*. London: Gollancz, 1972. p. 123.

———. *The Silver Crown*. London: Gollancz, 1973. p. 179.

Ormondroyd, Edward. *Time at the Top*. London: Heinemann, 1976. p. 167.

Pardoe, M. *Argle's Oracle*. London: Routledge, 1959. p. 179.

Parker, Richard. *The Old Powder Line*. London: Gollancz, 1971. p. 167.

———. *Spell Seven*. London: Longman Young Bks, 1971. p. 69.

Patten, Brian. *Mr. Moon's Last Case*. London: Allen, 1975. p. 100.

Pearce, Philippa. *Mrs. Cockle's Cat*. London: Longman Young Bks, 1961. p. 76.

———. *The Squirrel Wife*. London: Longman Young Bks, 1971. p. 14.

———. *Tom's Midnight Garden*. London: Oxford, 1958. p. 168.

Peck, Richard. *The Ghost Belonged to Me*. London: Collins, 1977. p. 33.

Peet, Bill. *The Whingdingdilly*. London: Deutsch, 1971. p. 123.

Peyton, K. M. *A Pattern of Roses*. London: Oxford, 1972. p. 33.

Phipson, Joan. *The Way Home*. London: Hodder, 1977. p. 168.

Pinkwater, D. Manus. *Blue Moose*. Glasgow: Blackie, 1977. p. 123.

Pomerantz, Charlotte. *Detective Poufy's First Case*. London: Addison-Wesley, 1976. p. 149.

Postgate, Oliver, and Firman, Peter. *The Ice Dragon*. London: Kaye, 1968. p. 57.

———. *King of the Nogs*. London: Kaye, 1974. p. 57.

———. *Nogbad and the Elephant*. London: Kaye, 1972. p. 57.

———. *Noggin and the Moon Mouse*. London: Kaye, 1972. p. 57.

———. *Noggin and the Whale*. London: Kaye, 1965. p. 57.

Potter, Beatrix. *The Fairy Caravan*. London: Warne, 1952. p. 124.

———. *The Tale of the Faithful Dove*. London: Warne, n.d. p. 124.

Preussler, Otfried. *The Final Adventures of the Robber Hotzenplotz*. London: Hodder, 1977 (pap.). p. 156.

———. *Further Adventures of the Robber Hotzenplotz*. London: Abelard-Schuman, n.d. p. 156.

———. *The Little Witch*. London: Abelard-Schuman, 1969. p. 195.

———. *The Robber Hotzenplotz*. London: Brockhampton, 1974 (pap.). p. 156.

———. *The Wise Men of Schilda*. London: Abelard-Schuman, 1974. p. 156.

Price, Susan. *The Devil's Piper*. London: Faber, 1973. p. 40.

Proysen, Alf. *Little Old Mrs. Pepperpot*. London: Hutchinson, 1958. p. 22.

———. *Mrs. Pepperpot Again*. London: Hutchinson, 1960. p. 22.

———. *Mrs. Pepperpot in the Magic Wood*. London: Hutchinson, 1968. p. 22.

———. *Mrs. Pepperpot to the Rescue*. London: Hutchinson, 1963. p. 22.

———. *Mrs. Pepperpot's Busy Day*. London: Hutchinson, 1970. p. 22.

———. *Mrs. Pepperpot's Christmas*. London: Hutchinson, 1972. p. 22.

———. *Mrs. Pepperpot's Omnibus*. London: Hutchinson, 1968. p. 22.

———. *Mrs. Pepperpot's Outing*. London: Hutchinson, 1973. p. 22.

———. *Mrs. Pepperpot's Year*. London: Hutchinson, 1973. p. 22.

Pushkin, Alexander. *The Tale of Tsar Saltan*. London: Methuen, 1974. p. 50.

Pyle, Howard. *King Stork*. Tadworth, Surrey: World's Work, 1975. p. 191.

———. *Pepper and Salt*. London: Dover, n.d. p. 22.

Pyle, Howard and Pyle, Katherine. *The Wonder Clock*. London: Dover, 1966. p. 22.

Raskin, Ellen. *The Tattooed Potato*. London: Macmillan, 1976. p. 157.

Reeves, James. *Sailor Rumbelow and Britannia*. London: Heinemann, 1962. p. 27.

———. *The Strange Light*. London: Heinemann, 1964. p. 183.

Richler, Mordecai. *Jacob Two-Two Meets the Hooded Fang*. London: Deutsch, 1975. p. 150.

Rodgers, Mary. *A Billion for Boris*. London: H. Hamilton, 1975. p. 150.

———. *Freaky Friday*. London: H. Hamilton, 1973. p. 150.

Ruskin, John. *The King of the Golden River*. London: H. Hamilton, 1978. p. 8.

Saint-Exupéry, Antoine de. *The Little Prince*. London: Heinemann, 1945. p. 8.

Sandburg, Carl. *Rootabaga Stories and Rootabaga Pigeons*. London: Garland, 1976. p. 22.

Sauer, Julia. *Fog Magic*. London: Hodder, 1977. p. 168.

Selden, George. *The Cricket in Times Square*. London: Dent, 1977. p. 124.

————. *Harry Cat's Pet Puppy.* London: Dent, 1978. p. 124.

Sendak, Maurice. *Higglety Pigglety Pop! or There Must be More to Life.* London: Bodley Head, 1969. p. 124.

Seuss, Dr. *The Five Hundred Hats of Bartholomew Cubbins.* London: Collins, 1966. p. 51.

Severn, David. *The Girl in the Grove.* London: Allen, 1974. p. 33.

Sharp, Margery. *Bernard the Brave.* London: Collins, 1966. p. 125.

————. *Miss Bianca.* London: Collins, n.d. p. 125.

————. *Miss Bianca and the Bridesmaid.* London: Heinemann, 1972. p. 125.

————. *Miss Bianca in the Antarctic.* London: Heinemann, 1971. p. 125.

————. *Miss Bianca in the Arctic.* London: Armada, 1977 (pap.). p. 125.

————. *Miss Bianca in the Orient.* London: Heinemann, 1970. p. 125.

————. *Miss Bianca in the Salt Mines.* London: Heinemann, 1966. p. 125.

————. *The Rescuers.* London: Armada, 1977 (pap.). p. 125.

Sheehan, Carolyn and Sheehan, Edmund. *Magnifi-Cat.* Aylesbury, Bucks: Milton, 1975. p. 136.

Singer, Isaac Bashevis. *The Fools of Chelm and Their History.* London: Abelard-Schuman, n.d. p. 151.

————. *Naftali the Storyteller and His Horse, Sus, and Other Stories.* London: Oxford, 1974. p. 23.

————. *Zlateh the Goat and Other Stories.* London: Longman Young Bks, 1970. p. 23.

Sleigh, Barbara. *Carbonel.* London: Longman Young Bks, 1973. p. 136.

————. *Jessamy.* London: Hodder, 1976 (pap.). p. 172.

————. *The Kingdom of Carbonel.* London: Longman Young Bks, 1973. p. 136.

Smith, Dodie. *The Hundred and One Dalmatians.* London: Heinemann, 1956. p. 125.

————. *The Starlight Barking.* London: Heinemann, 1967. p. 125.

Smith, Emma. *Emily's Voyage.* Harmondsworth, Middx: Puffin, 1971 (pap.). p. 125.

Steele, Mary Q. *Because of the Sand Witches There.* London: Macmillan, 1976. p. 71.

————. *The First of the Penguins.* London: Macmillan, 1974. p. 169.

Steig, William. *Abel's Island.* London: H. Hamilton, 1977. p. 125.

————. *Dominic.* London: H. Hamilton, 1973. p. 125.

————. *The Real Thief.* London: H. Hamilton, 1975. p. 125.

Stewart, Mary. *The Little Broomstick*. London: Brockhampton, 1971. p. 191.

_____. *Ludo and the Star Horse*. London: Brockhampton, 1974. p. 9.

Stockton, Frank R. *The Bee Man of Orn*. London: Bodley Head, 1975. p. 9.

_____. *The Griffin and the Minor Canon*. London: Bodley Head, 1975. p. 100.

Storr, Catherine. *Clever Polly and the Stupid Wolf*. Harmondsworth, Middx: Puffin, 1967 (pap.). p. 157.

_____. *Polly and the Wolf Again*. Harmondsworth, Middx: Puffin, 1970 (pap.). p. 157.

_____. *Thursday*. London: Faber, 1971. p. 94.

Stranger, Joyce. *The Fox at Drummer's Darkness*. London: Dent, 1976. p. 9.

Swahn, Sven. *The Island through the Gate*. London: Methuen, 1973. p. 179.

Swift, Jonathan. *Gulliver's Travels*. London: Dent, 1952. p. 180.

Sykes, Pamela. *Come Back, Lucy*. London: H. Hamilton, 1973. p. 169.

Tarn, William Woodthorpe. *The Treasure of the Isle of Mist*. London: Oxford, 1959. p. 77.

Terlouw, Jan. *How to Become King*. Glasgow: Blackie, 1976. p. 51.

Thackeray, William M. *The Rose and the Ring*. Glasgow: Blackie, n.d. p. 51.

Thurber, James. *Many Moons*. London: Kaye, 1975. p. 52.

_____. *The Thirteen Clocks and The Wonderful "O"*. London: H Hamilton, 1966. p. 10.

_____. *The White Deer*. Harmondsworth, Middx: Puffin, 1963 (pap.). p. 10.

Titus, Eve and Galdone, Paul. *Basil and the Lost Colony*. London: Brockhampton, 1975. p. 126.

_____. *Basil of Baker Street*. London: Brockhampton, 1975. p. 126.

Tolkien, J. R. R. *Farmer Giles of Ham*. London: Allen, 1976. p. 89.

_____. *The Fellowship of the Ring*. London: Allen, 1974. p. 40.

_____. *The Hobbit*. London: Allen, 1975. p. 40.

_____. *The Lord of the Rings*. London: Allen, 1968. p. 40.

_____. *The Return of the King*. London: Allen, 1974. p. 40.

_____. *Smith of Wootton Major*. London: Allen, 1975. p. 71.

_____. *The Two Towers*. London: Allen, 1974. p. 40.

Townsend, John Rowe. *The Xanadu Manuscript*. London: Oxford, 1977. p. 169.

Travers, P. L. *Mary Poppins*. London: Collins, 1956. p. 71.

———. *Mary Poppins Comes Back*. London: Collins, 1958. p. 71.

———. *Mary Poppins in the Park*. London: Collins, 1956. p. 71.

———. *Mary Poppins Opens the Door*. London: Collins, 1956. p. 71.

Tregarthen, Enys. *The Doll Who Came Alive*. London: Abelard-Schuman, 1972. p. 82.

Turnbull, Ann. *The Frightened Forest*. London: Kestrel, 1974. p. 192.

———. *The Wolf King*. London: Kestrel, 1975. p. 94.

Twain, Mark. *A Connecticut Yankee at the Court of King Arthur*. Harmondsworth, Middx: Penguin, 1971 (pap.). p. 169.

Uttley, Alison. *A Traveller in Time*. London: Faber, 1939. p. 172.

Vildrac, Charles. *The Lion's Eyeglasses*. London: Abelard-Schuman, 1975. p. 137.

Voegeli, M. *The Wonderful Lamp*. London: Oxford, 1955. p. 57.

Wahl, Jan. *How the Children Stopped the Wars*. London: Abelard-Schuman, 1975. p. 10.

———. *Pleasant Fieldmouse*. Harmondsworth, Middx: Puffin, 1976 (pap.). p. 126.

———. *Pleasant Fieldmouse's Halloween Party*. Tadworth, Surrey: World's Work, 1976. p. 127.

Weir, Rosemary. *Albert and the Dragonettes*. London: Abelard-Schuman, 1977. p. 91.

———. *Albert the Dragon*. London: Abelard-Schuman, 1973. p. 91.

———. *Further Adventures of Albert the Dragon*. London: Abelard-Schuman, 1973. p. 91.

———. *Pyewacket*. London: Abelard-Schuman, 1974. p. 137.

Welch, Ronald. *The Gauntlet*. London: Oxford, 1955. p. 172.

Wenning, Elizabeth. *The Christmas Churchmouse*. Tadworth, Surrey: World's Work, 1961. p. 127.

Westall, Robert. *The Wind Eye*. London: Macmillan, 1976. p. 170.

White, E. B. *Charlotte's Web*. London: H. Hamilton, 1952. p. 127.

———. *Stuart Little*. London: H. Hamilton, 1946. p. 127.

White, T. H. *Mistress Masham's Repose*. London: Cape, 1947. p. 106.

———. *The Once and Future King*. London: Collins, 1959. p. 52.

———. *The Sword in the Stone*. London: Collins, 1977. p. 52.

Wilde, Oscar. *The Happy Prince*. London: Kaye, 1977. p. 11.

———. *The Happy Prince and Other Stories*. London: Dent, 1968. p. 23.

Williams, Jay. *The Hawkstone*. London: Gollancz, 1972. p. 71.

Williams, Ursula Moray. *Adventures of the Little Wooden Horse*. London: H. Hamilton, 1969. p. 84.

_____. *Castle Merlin*. London: Allen, 1972. p. 34.

_____. *Johnnie Tigerskin*. London: Harrap, 1964. p. 153.

_____. *Malkin's Mountain*. London: H. Hamilton, 1971. p. 84.

_____. *The Three Toymakers*. London: H. Hamilton, 1970. p. 84.

_____. *The Toymaker's Daughter*. London: H. Hamilton, 1968. p. 84.

Wrightson, Patricia. *The Ice Is Coming*. London: Hutchinson, 1977. p. 40.

_____. *The Nargun and the Stars*. London: Hutchinson, 1973. p. 40.

_____. *An Older Kind of Magic*. London: Hutchinson, 1972. p. 72.

Yolen, Jane. *The Girl Who Loved the Wind*. London: Collins, 1973. p. 12.

_____. *The Moon Ribbon and Other Tales*. London: Dent, 1977. p. 24.

York, Susannah. *Lark's Castle*. London: Hodder, 1976. p. 192.

Zimnik, Reiner. *The Crane*. London: Brockhampton, 1969. p. 15.

Directory of Publishers

This directory provides the full names and addresses for all British and American publishers of books included in the in-print sections of the chapter listings and in the guide to Titles Available in the United Kingdom.

Abelard-Schuman
  450 Edgware Rd.
  London W2 1EG

Addison-Wesley Publishers (U.K.)
  West End House
  11 Hills Place
  London W1R 2LR

Addison-Wesley Publishing Co.
  Jacob Way
  Reading, MA 01867

George Allen & Unwin Publishers
  40 Museum St.
  London WC1A 1LU

Andersen Press
  3 Fitzroy Square
  London W1P 6JD

Angus & Roberston
  16 Ship St.
  Brighton BN1 1AD,
  England

Archway Paperbacks
  (see Pocket Books)

Armada Books
  14 St. James's Place
  London SW1A 1PS

Astor-Honor
  48 E. 43 St.
  New York, NY 10017

Atheneum Publishers
  122 E. 42 St.
  New York, NY 10017

Atlantic/Little
  (see Little, Brown and Co.)

Avon Books
  959 Eighth Ave.
  New York, NY 10019

BBC Publications
  35 Marylebone High St.
  London W1M 4AA

Ernest Benn
25 New Street Square
London EC4A 3JA

Biblio Distribution Centre
81 Adams Dr.
Box 327
Totowa, NJ 07511

Blackie & Son
Bishopbriggs
Glasgow G64 2NZ,
Scotland

Blond & Briggs
44-45 Museum St.
London WC1

Bobbs-Merrill Co.
4300 W. 62 St.
Indianapolis, IN 46206

The Bodley Head
9 Bow St.
London W2CE 7AL

Bookstore Press
Box 191, RFD 1
Freeport, ME 04032

Bradbury Press
2 Overhill Rd.
Scarsdale, NY 10583

British Book Centre
Fairview Park
Elmsford, NY 10523

Brockhampton Press
(see Hodder & Stoughton)

James Brodie
15 Queen Square
Bath BA1 2HW,
England

Buccaneer Books
Box 168
Cutchogue, NY 11935

Calder and Boyars
18 Brewer St.
London W1R 4AS

Jonathan Cape
30 Bedford Square
London WC1B 3EL

Chatto & Windus
40-42 William IV St.
London WC2N 4DF

Childrens Press
1224 W. Van Buren St.
Chicago, IL 60607

Collier Macmillan
Stockley Close, Stockley Rd.
West Drayton, Middlesex UB7 9BE,
England

Rex Collings
69 Marylebone High St.
London W1M 3AQ

William Collins Sons and Co. (U.K.)
14 St. James's Place
London SW1A 1PS

William Collins + World Publishing Co.
2080 W. 117 St.
Cleveland, OH 44111

Constable & Co.
10 Orange St.
Leicester Square
London WC2H 7EG

Contemporary Books
180 N. Michigan Ave.
Chicago, IL 60601

Corgi Books
Century House
61-63 Uxbridge Rd.
Ealing, London W5 5SA

Countryman Press
Taftsville, VT 05073

Coward, McCann & Geoghegan
200 Madison Ave.
New York, NY 10016

Crane, Russak & Co.
347 Madison Ave.
New York, NY 10017

Criterion Books
(see Harper & Row, Publishers)

Thomas Y. Crowell
10 E. 53 St.
New York, NY 10022

Crown Publishers
One Park Ave.
New York, NY 10016

John Day Co.
Dist. by Harper & Row

Delacorte Press
(see Dell Publishing Co.)

Dell Publishing Co.
One Dag Hammarskjold Plaza
245 E. 47 St.
New York, NY 10017

J. M. Dent and Sons
Aldine House
26 Albemarle St.
London W1X 4QY

André Deutsch
105 Great Russell St.
London WC1B 3LJ

Dial Press
One Dag Hammarskjold Plaza
245 E. 47 St.
New York, NY 10017

Dobson Books
80 Kensington Church St.
London W8 4BZ

Dodd, Mead & Co.
79 Madison Ave.
New York, NY 10016

Dolphin Publishing Co.
At the Sign of the Dolphin
Milton Rd.
Aylesbury, Buckinghamshire
HB21 7TH

Doubleday & Co.
245 Park Ave.
New York, NY 10017

Dover Publications (U.K.)
Dist. by Constable & Co.

Gerald Duckworth & Co.
The Old Piano Factory
43 Gloucester Crescent
London NW1 7DY

E. P. Dutton
2 Park Ave.
New York, NY 10016

EMC Corp.
180 E. Sixth St.
St. Paul, MN 55101

Evans Brothers
Montague House
Russell Square
London WC1B 5BX

Faber & Faber
3 Queen Square
London WC1N 3AU

Farrar, Straus & Giroux
19 Union Square, W.
New York, NY 10003

Four Winds Press
(see Scholastic Book Services)

Gambit
27 North Main St.
Meeting House Green
Ipswich, MA 01938

Garland Publishing
545 Madison Ave.
New York, NY 10022

Victor Gollancz
14 Henrietta St.
Covent Garden
London WC2E 8QJ

Granada Publishing
1221 Avenue of the Americas
New York, NY 10020

Granada Publishing (U.K.)
P.O. Box 9, 29 Frogmore
St. Albans, Hertfordshire AL2 2NF,
England

Greenwillow Books
105 Madison Ave.
New York, NY 10016

Grosset & Dunlap
51 Madison Ave.
New York, NY 10010

E. M. Hale & Co.
128 W. River St.
Chippewa Falls, WI 54729

G. K. Hall & Co. (U.K.)
Dist. by George Prior Associated
Publishers

Hamish Hamilton
90 Great Russell St.
London WC1B 3PT

Hamlyn Publishing Group
Astronaut House
Hounslow Rd.
Feltham, Middlesex TW14 9AR,
England

Harcourt Brace Jovanovich
757 Third Ave.
New York, NY 10017

Harcourt Brace Jovanovich (U.K.)
24-28 Oval Rd.
Camden Town
London NW1 7DU

Harper & Row (U.K.)
28 Tavistock St.
London WC2E 7PN

Harper & Row, Publishers
10 E. 53 St.
New York, NY 10022

George G. Harrap and Co.
182-184 High Holborn
London WC1V 7AX

Hart-Davis Educational
(see Granada Publishing, U.K.)

Hastings House, Publishers
10 E. 40 St.
New York, NY 10016

Hawthorn Books
260 Madison Ave.
New York, NY 10016

William Heinemann
15-16 Queen St.
London W1X 8BE

Heritage House Publishers
Box 52298
Jacksonville, FL 32201

Hill & Wang
19 Union Square, W.
New York, NY 10003

Hodder & Stoughton
47 Bedford Square
London WC1B 3DP

Holiday House
18 E. 53 St.
New York, NY 10022

Holt, Rinehart & Winston
383 Madison Ave.
New York, NY 10017

Houghton Mifflin Co.
1 Beacon St.
Boston, MA 02107

Hutchinson Publishing Group
3 Fitzroy Square
London W1P 6JD

Hyperion Press
45 Riverside Ave.
Westport, Conn. 06880

Michael Joseph
52 Bedford Square
London WC1B 3EF

Kaye & Ward
21 New St.
London EC2M 4NT

Kestrel Books
Bath Rd.
Harmondsworth, Middlesex
UB7 0DA,
England

Alfred A. Knopf
201 E. 50 St.
New York, NY 10022

Allen Lane
17 Grosvenor Gardens
London SW1W 0BD

J. B. Lippincott Co.
East Washington Square
Philadelphia, PA 19105

Little, Brown & Co.
34 Beacon St.
Boston, MA 02106

London Magazine Editions
30 Thurloe Place
London SW7

Longman Young Books
(see Kestrel Books)

Lothrop, Lee & Shepard Co.
105 Madison Ave.
New York, NY 10016

McClain Printing Co.
212 Main St.
Parson's, NY 26287

McGraw-Hill Book Co.
1221 Avenue of the Americas
New York, NY 10020

McGraw-Hill Book Co. (U.K.)
McGraw-Hill House
Shoppenhangers Rd.
Maidenhead, Berkshire SL6 2QL,
England

David McKay Co.
750 Third Ave.
New York, NY 10017

Macmillan Publishers (U.K.)
4 Little Essex St.
London WC2R 3LF

Macmillan Publishing Co.
866 Third Ave.
New York, NY 10022

Macrae Smith Co.
Routes 54 and Old 147
Turbotville, PA 17772

Merrimack Book Service
99 Main St.
Salem, NH 03079

Methuen
Dist. by Biblio Distribution Centre

Methuen Children's Books (U.K.)
11 New Fetter Lane
London EC4P 4EE

Milton House Books
(see Dolphin Publishing Co.)

William Morrow & Co.
105 Madison Ave.
New York, NY 10016

John Murray Publishers
50 Albemarle St.
London W1X 4BD

Thomas Nelson
405 Seventh Ave. S.
Nashville, TN 37203

Oxford University Press
200 Madison Ave.
New York, NY 10016

Oxford University Press (U.K.)
Ely House
37 Dover St.
London W1X 4AH

Pan Books
18/21 Cavaye Place
London SW1O 9PG

Pantheon Books
201 E. 50 St.
New York, NY 10022

Parents' Magazine Press
52 Vanderbilt Ave.
New York, NY 10017

Parents' Magazine Press (U.K.)
Dist. by McGraw-Hill Book Co.
(U.K.)

Parnassus Press
4080 Halleck St.
Emeryville, CA 94608

Pelham Books
52 Bedford Square
London WC1B 3EF

Penguin Books
625 Madison Ave.
New York, NY 10022

Penguin Books (U.K.)
Bath Rd.
Harmondsworth, Middlesex
UB7 0DA,
England

S. G. Phillips
305 W. 86 St.
New York, NY 10024

Pierpont Morgan Library
29 E. 36 St.
New York, NY 10016

Pilgrim Press
Lodge Lane
Derby DE1 3HE,
England

Pocket Books
1230 Avenue of the Americas
New York, NY 10020

Prentice-Hall
Englewood Cliffs, NJ 07632

George Prior Associated Publishers
Rugby Chambers
2 Rugby St.
London WC1N 3QU

Puffin Books (U.K.)
(see Penguin Books, U.K.)

G. P. Putnam's Sons
200 Madison Ave.
New York, NY 10016

Random House
201 E. 50 St.
New York, NY 10022

Rapp & Whiting
105 Great Russell St.
London WC1B 3LJ

Reilly & Lee
(see Contemporary Books)

Robson Books
28 Poland St.
London W1V 3DB

Alan Ross
(see London Magazine Editions)

St. Martin's Press
175 Fifth Ave.
New York, NY 10010

Schocken Books
200 Madison Ave.
New York, NY 10016

Scholastic Book Services
50 W. 44 St.
New York, NY 10036

Charles Scribner's Sons
597 Fifth Ave.
New York, NY 10017

Seabury Press
815 Second Ave.
New York, NY 10017

Sidgwick & Jackson
1 Tavistock Chambers
Bloomsbury Way
London WC1A 2SG

Simon & Schuster
1230 Avenue of the Americas
New York, NY 10020

Souvenir Press
43 Great Russell St.
London WC1B 3PA

Stemmer House Publishers
2627 Caves Rd.
Owings Mills, MD 21117

Tandem Publishers
44 Hill St.
London W1X 8LB

Transworld Publishers
Century House
61-63 Uxbridge Rd.
Ealing, London W5 5SA

Tundra Books
Dist. by Charles Scribner's Sons

Frederick Ungar Publishing Co.
250 Park Ave. S.
New York, NY 10003

Vanguard Press
424 Madison Ave.
New York, NY 10017

Viking Press
625 Madison Ave.
New York, NY 10022

Henry Z. Walck
750 Third Ave.
New York, NY 10017

Walker & Co.
720 Fifth Ave.
New York, NY 10019

Frederick Warne & Co.
101 Fifth Ave.
New York, NY 10003

Frederick Warne Publishers (U.K.)
40 Bedford Square
London WC1B 3HE

Warner Books
75 Rockefeller Plaza
New York, NY 10019

Franklin Watts
730 Fifth Ave.
New York, NY 10019

Franklin Watts (U.K.)
Aldine House
26 Albemarle St.
London W1X 4BN

Westminster Press
905 Witherspoon Bldg.
Philadelphia, PA 19107

David White Co.
14 Vanderventer Ave.
Port Washington, NY 11050

Windmill Press
1369 Linwood
Holland, MI 49423

World Publishing Co.
(see William Collins + World
Publishing Co.)

World's Work
The Windmill Press
Kingswood, Tadworth
Surrey

Author and Illustrator Index

This author/illustrator index provides page references to the specific works of all authors and editors of books mentioned in the text, including out-of-print works. Variant titles, such as British or paperback titles, are included in parentheses. An adapter or reteller may be identified by the inclusion of the main author's name in parentheses following the book title. Illustrator entries refer to page numbers only, and do not list specific works.

Title Index

This index provides page references to all titles mentioned in the text and in the author/illustrator index, including variant titles. The author surname appears in parentheses following the book title.